¡VIVA TEQUILA!

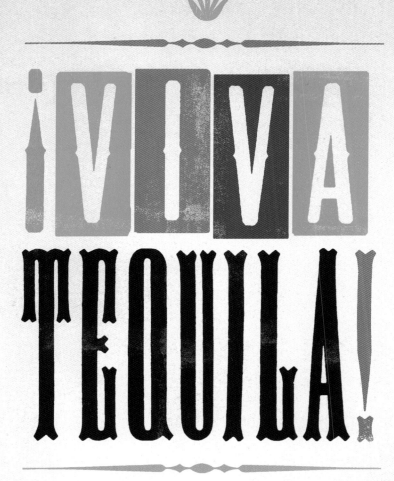

¡VIVA TEQUILA!

Cocktails, Cooking, and Other Agave Adventures

Lucinda Hutson

FOLK ART PHOTOGRAPHY BY JOHN POZDRO

UNIVERSITY OF TEXAS PRESS ❖ AUSTIN

Requests for permission to reproduce material
from this work should be sent to:
   Permissions
   University of Texas Press
   P.O. Box 7819
   Austin, TX 78713-7819
   http://utpress.utexas.edu/about/book-permissions

The paper used in this book meets the minimum
requirements of ANSI/NISO Z39.48-1992 (R1997)
(Permanence of Paper). ∞

Design by Lindsay Starr

LIBRARY OF CONGRESS CATALOGING-IN-PUBLICATION DATA
Hutson, Lucinda, 1950–
    ¡Viva tequila! Cocktails, cooking, and other agave adventures
/ by Lucinda Hutson ; folk art photography by John Pozdro. —
First edition.
        pages   cm
    Includes bibliographical references and indexes.
    ISBN 978-0-292-72294-1 (cloth : alk. paper)
1. Cooking (Tequila) 2. Tequila. 3. Tequila agave. I. Title.
    TX726.H884 2013
    641.2'5—dc23   2012031470

doi:10.7560/722941

The publication of this book was made
possible by the generous support of Ellen
and Ed Randall in honor of Elle, Lucy,
and Landis Middleton and Adrian Rohan.
Salud, pesetas y amor, y tiempo para gustarlos.

ENDSHEETS: Camarena agave estate in Arandas, Jalisco.

FRONTISPIECE: *Trastero* (hutch) with bottles of tequila
and folk art from author's collection.

P. V: Handblown Mexican glass.

Para México—
¡Lindo y querido!

—

For Mexico—
Beautiful and beloved!

¡Salud, dinero y amor,
y bastante tiempo para gozarlo!

—

Health, wealth, and romance,
and enough time to enjoy them all!

CONTENTS

Part 3: Tequila Cocina

Note: Recipes that appear in the text, when referred to elsewhere, are indicated in the color of blue agave. Readers may find these recipes by referring to the Cantina and Comida indexes or by consulting the lists that appear at the part openers.

¡VIVA TEQUILA!

Denomination of Origin of Mexico's Agave Spirits and Primary Pulque-Producing States

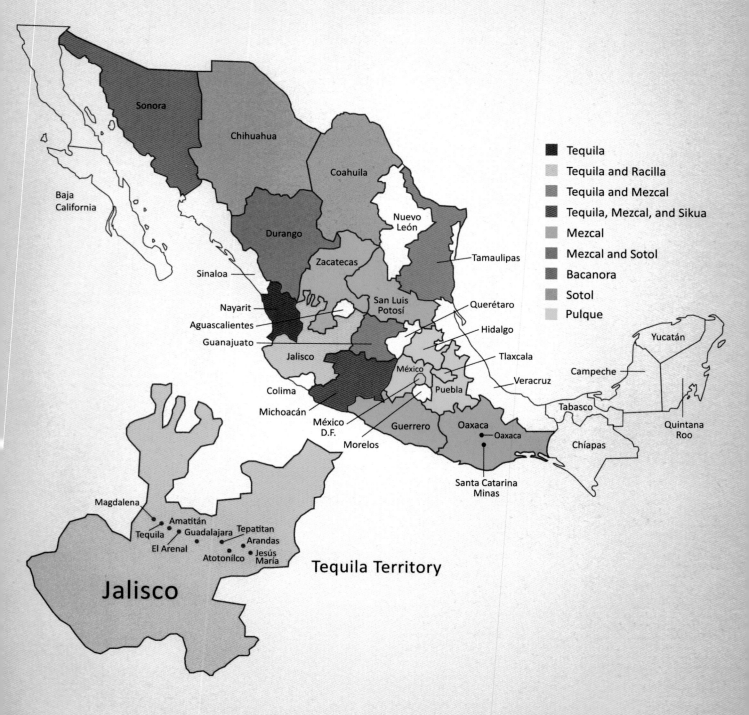

Legend:
- Tequila
- Tequila and Racilla
- Tequila and Mezcal
- Tequila, Mezcal, and Sikua
- Mezcal
- Mezcal and Sotol
- Bacanora
- Sotol
- Pulque

Baja California

Sonora

Chihuahua

Coahuila

Nuevo León

Durango

Zacatecas

Tamaulipas

Sinaloa

Nayarit

Aguascalientes

Guanajuato

San Luis Potosí

Querétaro

Hidalgo

Jalisco

México

Tlaxcala

Colima

Puebla

Veracruz

Campeche

Yucatán

Michoacán

México D.F.

Morelos

Guerrero

Oaxaca

Tabasco

Quintana Roo

Oaxaca

Chíapas

Santa Catarina Minas

Magdalena

Amatitán

Tequila

Tepatitan

Guadalajara

El Arenal

Arandas

Atotonílco

Jesús María

Tequila Territory

Jalisco

Map of Mexico, created by Bill Bishel.

Tequila, mezcal y amor
Hay que tomarlo con sabor.

—

Tequila, mezcal, and the one you adore
Savor them with pleasure for sure.

Introduction

TEQUILA IS MY SOUL MATE. Mexico in a bottle. Its flavor is as melodic to the mouth as a mariachi tune is to the ear—bold, spicy, and full of life! Upon the first taste, it gives a liquid jolt to the senses that makes our tongues trill, trumpets resound in our ears, and throatily bellowed ¡ay, ay, ay! *gritos* fill the air. Tequila makes macho men burst into passionate lyrics of unrequited love and shy women dance on tables.

My affinity for tequila seems to be a natural one, a legacy from my West Texas hometown of El Paso, a border town steeped in three noteworthy events in tequila's history: (1) the first three barrels imported into the United States passed through there in 1873, (2) the first margarita may have been poured in a bar in nearby Juárez in 1942, and (3) it was where I first learned how to drink tequila.

Back then, good food and fun were always found in Juárez, on the Mexican side of the Río Grande. In the late 1960s, our coming-of-age initiations included escapades in rowdy Mexican cantinas on Saturday nights. The most dangerous thing about Juárez then was tipsy Texan teenagers running amok drinking nickel shots of tequila with dime beers. In 2009, Juárez was deemed the most dangerous city in the world, overtaken by battling drug cartels, and it has since remained in the top ten most violent cities in the world. In 2010, more than three thousand people lost their lives to violence in Juárez. Few now brave crossing the border—all the more reason to create our own tequila cantinas at home.

Looking back, we were young and life was an uncomplicated fiesta. While my companions guzzled Singapore Slings and Zombies—cloying concoctions promising speedy inebriation—I would slip into the kitchen of our favorite Juárez cantina. Tío Mauro Orozco, the uncle of my family's housekeeper, was the cook. He would pour me a shot of tequila *reposado*, and with *ranchera* music blaring on the radio to the rhythmic patting of tortillas, I learned how to cook and how to drink tequila. Meanwhile, my amigos eagerly imbibed what they would regret the following morning.

My love for Mexico persisted. Her *comida y canciones* (cuisine and songs) and the generous spirit of her inhabitants filled my heart. Often, I felt more at home in that country than in my own. Speaking Spanish fluently and longing for adventure, I had no fear of riding buses to visit small towns, the only *güera* (fair-skinned female) aboard. Before the age of twenty, I had traveled alone throughout many parts of Mexico.

More often than not, I ended up in simple kitchens, much to the surprise and delight of my humble hosts, who did not expect such enthusiasm for their country from a *gringa*. And many times, that precious bottle of tequila or mezcal was brought down from the shelf for a toast to friendship and to *la vida buena*.

In 1976, I visited La Perseverancia, the Sauza tequila distillery in the town of Tequila, Jalisco, Mexico. There I saw another lone blonde, dancing barefoot to her own tune, her scarlet sheath slipping from her shoulders. An expression of sheer pleasure lit her face. One hand was flung in the air, clutching a bottle of tequila; the other linked her to a circle of dark-haired Mexican maidens frolicking in Bacchanalian delight. This image hung on the thick-plastered walls of the distillery, part of a mural painted by Gabriel Flores, depicting the fateful discovery and production of tequila in the sixteenth century. I was astonished: the blonde in the painting even looked like me! My curiosity was aroused. I knew I wanted to learn more about tequila, the seductive spirit that sang to my soul.

So began another Mexican journey—this time, a tequila quest. I visited fields planted with endless rows of blue agaves, formidable plants with a profusion of sword-like blades exploding from a central core. I learned that these noble agaves take nearly a decade to reach maturity for harvesting. In rustic and modern distilleries alike, I watched the agave's magical transformation into tequila, the spirit of Mexico. I tasted shimmering silver tequilas straight from copper pot stills and amber-hued ones from fine oak casks.

I also sampled memorable meals in the homes of field-workers and in the homes of distillery owners. As a cook, I recognized tequila's potential in the kitchen as well as in the cantina but was surprised to find that Mexicans seldom cooked with it. Tequila's versatile nature—lively, peppery, and robust, with herbaceous and fruity characteristics—complemented my own style of cooking. I eagerly embarked upon a new culinary ad-

Mural painted by Gabriel Flores in Sauza's La Perseverancia distillery, Tequila, Jalisco, depicting the production of tequila:
1. *Cubetero*, *batidor*, and fermentation barrel. 2. *Tahona* grinding wheel. 3. *Horno* for cooking *piñas*. 4. Freshly harvested *piña*.

venture, using recipes to showcase tequila in a festive way in food and in drinks. With an emphasis on garnish and presentation, and inspiration drawn from the libations enjoyed by Mexicans, I created drinks that highlight tequila in fresh and bright ways, far beyond the ubiquitous margarita. In this celebratory fashion, one drink becomes a special event.

About the New Book

The first edition of this book, published in 1995 by Ten Speed Press, was "one of the most trail-blazing books on tequila," according to Wyatt Peabody, a spirits contributor for *LA* (*Los Angeles Times Magazine*), who's written several intriguing articles about mezcal and tequila.

Since then, I have embarked upon other agave expeditions, returning with more stories to tell and recipes to share. I've even added more tales of my earlier adventures. I'll tell you about visiting a remote *palenque* (rustic distillery) in Oaxaca, where mezcal is made just as it was four hundred years ago by the Spanish, and about following an old woman in Michoacán as she tapped the sweet *aguamiel* (honey water) from a giant *maguey* plant to make *pulque*, another agave elixir. We'll visit a distillery that is handcrafting tequila in an old-fashioned manner that makes grape stomping look like child's play.

I've once again traversed the tequila-producing state of Jalisco and will share my adventures with you. In the lowlands, I visited distilleries that have withstood the test of time, those of tequila's founding fathers—Cuervo, Sauza, and Herradura—as well as other innovative, smaller producers. Across the state in the highlands, I've watched once-sleepy villages hosting family-run tequila distilleries transform into bustling towns. Following in the footsteps of much

5. Author in another life. 6. Bacchanalian delight!

of the tequila production in the lowlands, giant multinational spirits corporations have built huge high-volume distilleries, often disregarding tequila traditions in their pursuit of profit. Along the way, I've had the pleasure of visiting Mexican family-run distilleries striving to preserve tequila's character and authenticity.

Tequila's inimitable flavor has seduced drinkers worldwide, and enthusiasts quaff it fashionably and frequently. However, I sometimes fear the soul of tequila will be forgotten amidst the massive commercialization under way today. That's why I've returned to this book after eighteen years. Though it's timely to write about what is happening in tequila today, I also think it's very important to preserve the tequila of yesterday—the proud heritage of Mexico's beloved national spirit and the traditions that are quickly being left behind.

By knowing more about tequila (and mezcal), we can make our own demands for quality and integrity in what we drink. The tequila industry, once dominated by Cuervo, Sauza, and Herradura, now boasts more than twelve hundred brands, with new ones bombarding the market even as I write. Despite its booming popularity, however, tequila remains the

Author with Mariachi Estrella, Austin, Texas. Photo by Bill Records Photography.

most misunderstood of spirits, its reputation tarnished by erroneous information regarding its origin, production, and characteristic effects.

Let's get to know tequila on its own *tierra* and its own terms in this three-in-one book: a cantina (bar) book, a *cocina* cookbook, and a memoir filled with personal anecdotes for active participants and armchair travelers alike. You'll also discover everything you need to know about agave.

I've collected tequila traditions and customs, *dichos* (proverbs) and lore, folk art and photographs, and recipes and songs to share. Sometimes I've added contemporary twists where appropriate, always honoring and celebrating the agave, the spirit of Mexico. As a cook, a gardener, and an aficionada of Mexican culture, I consider this a joyous task!

As I slowly savored a shot of tequila *reposado* in a Mexican cantina, I scribbled this note on a cocktail napkin:

> *Almost everyone has a tequila story they want to forget. Let's change that to a tequila adventure they want to remember!*

Join me in stepping out of that circle of drunken revelry depicted in the distillery painting from long ago. Let's gather together, linking arms, as fellow tequila enthusiasts with a respect and reverence for the oldest distilled spirit in America. Let's raise our glasses in appreciation, a toast to tequila, and, yes, upon the first sip, we hear the mariachis begin to play!

Toma buen tequila,
pero no dejes que el tequila te tome a ti.

———

Please drink your agave spirits
respectfully and responsibly!

One

PLANT

Three

SPIRITS

Understanding *the*

AGAVE

A N UNDERSTANDING OF the agave (commonly called "maguey" in Mexico) will give you a newfound reverence for the plant itself and for its many gifts, including tequila, mezcal, and pulque. Unlike grapes and grain, which are harvested every year to make wine and spirits, an agave must grow for nearly a decade before it can be harvested to make mezcal or tequila. Once in its lifetime, the agave shoots its *quiote*, a gigantic flowering spear, into the sky, then dies. As we will see, the entire agave plant must be harvested before this happens in order to preserve its precious fermentable sugars.

Maguey plants have flourished for thousands of years throughout semiarid regions of Mexico, where other plants wither during ruthless seasons of drought. Born of ashes, a phoenix among plants, the agave appears to have erupted out of molten volcanic earth. Its sword-like arms reach for the heavens, each blade a tapered trough directing precious rainwater to its core, where it is hoarded for times when water is scarce.

The agave most commonly recognized in the Southwestern United States is the century plant (*Agave americana*). Although many people mistakenly assume that it blooms only once in a century, in fact, it blooms once in a decade.

History of *La Milagrosa*, the Miraculous Maguey

Mexico's indigenous peoples cleverly discovered how to use every part of the maguey for their daily survival, selecting the best attributes from many species. They ate her flowers and roasted the *quiote* for sustenance. They quenched their thirst by tapping her central core, savoring the nutritive *aguamiel* (honey water) within. They wrapped meat in her succulent leaves, to keep it moist and flavorful while cooking, and buried it in hot coals. Even the worm that resides in the plant became an edible delicacy. It's no wonder that the maguey had mystical and sacred significance to the early Mexicans.

These native people also roasted the heart of the agave, which converted its starchy core into a sweet and nourishing food source. This sacrificial heart—for indeed the entire plant died upon its removal—offered vital sustenance.

Hand-carved agave with *quiote* stalk in bloom, made in Oaxaca.

But the magical maguey provided more than nourishment. Pre-Hispanics made needles and nails and ornaments and weapons from the spiky tip of the agave's large stiff leaves. When this thorn was pulled off in a swift downward stroke, it came attached to a long, thin, strong fiber—a needle not needing threading! They extracted coarse fiber called *ixtle* from within the leaves, weaving it into fine cloth, mats, woven belts, and baskets. (Today, all-natural bathing scrubbers and netted bags made from this fiber are quite popular.) They also made a parchment-like paper from the protective cuticle within the agave's leaves and baskets, brushes, and brooms from the dried roots.

El árbol de las maravillas—the *quiote* as it shoots into the sky.

For centuries, *campesinos* (rural people) have used agaves in ancestral ways and do so still today. Almost everything they need for a simple lifestyle is contained within one plant. Certain species produce sisal for sandals, henequen for rope, vinegar, agave nectar, medicine, and soap. The dried *pencas* are employed as roofing for houses, cattle food, and precious household fuel for fires. Even their ashes become fertilizer. Planted close together, these sharp-tipped plants serve like barbed wire, forming protective fences around property.

And, of course, the admirable agave produces the three national drinks of Mexico: pulque, mezcal, and tequila. Great confusion surrounds this trio, and they are often mistaken for one and the same. But each is derived from different species of agave, generally grown in different regions of Mexico. Although pulque, mezcal, and tequila derive from plants in the *Agavaceae* family, they are cousins, not siblings, and have very different characteristics.

From the book *El Maguey*, written in Spanish by Jennie Ostrosky for the Consejo Nacional Para la Cultura y las Artes, I learned that when the Spanish arrived in Mexico, they called the maguey *el árbol de las maravillas* because of its rare and marvelous appearance, characteristics, and multiple uses. Imagine a plant whose central stem can shoot more than twenty feet into the sky, where its branches of inflorescence can reach nine feet in width!

Glossary: A Plant with Many Names

Agave (ah GAH veh)—The name of a genus of plants classified by Swedish naturalist Carolus Linnaeus, considered the "Father of Taxonomy." The name "agave" derived from the Greek word for "noble" or "admirable." Agaves were once classified in either the family *Amaryllidaceae* or *Liliaceae*, along with lilies, aloes, and amaryllis. Botanists today give the agave merit of its own, in the family *Agavaceae*. Over 150 species have been recorded in the Americas. Tequila, mezcal, and pulque are alcoholic beverages made from different species of the agave. Only the "blue" agave may be used to make tequila.

Blue agave—In 1902, the German botanist Franz Weber, who classified flora in Mexico, named this agave "*Agave tequilana* Weber, variety *azul*," because of the blue cast to its leaves. Its high sugar content makes it the most favorable for producing tequila.

Maguey (mah GAY)—The common name for the agave plant in Mexico. The Spanish explorers named it after a plant that they first encountered in the Caribbean. The word "maguey" is used interchangeably with agave or mezcal.

Mescal (mes KAHL)—The English spelling for mezcal and the name for the peyote cactus (*Lophophora williamsii*), from which mescaline is produced. Mescal is also the name of the hallucinatory "bean" or seed of the mountain laurel (*Sophara secundiflora*). Neither the cactus nor the laurel is related to the agave.

Metl (MEH tl)—The Náhuatl name given collectively to many species of agave. Early codices (chronicles of pre-Hispanic culture typically written on paper made from agave fiber) cited descriptions and virtues of fourteen species of agave.

Mezcal (mes KAHL)—Derived from the Náhuatl word *mexcalmetl*, meaning "agave species." In Mexico today, the term "mezcal" refers both to the maguey or agave plant and to the powerful distillate made from it.

Pencas (PEN cahs)—Long, sword-like leaves of the agave, growing out from the plant's rosette, or central core. *Pencas* are tipped with a very sharp thorn.

Piña (PEEN yah)—The central rosette of the agave plant, revealed once the *pencas* have been cut away from the central core. It resembles a huge pineapple, hence the name *piña*. It's also sometimes called a *cabeza*, or "head."

Quiote (kee OH teh)—This inflorescence of the agave shoots up into the sky from the plant's core at the end of the agave's life. It simultaneously bursts into flower and sprouts seeds and vegetative offshoots. Once it begins its upward journey, it takes only a few weeks to attain twenty or more feet in height; the plant then perishes.

Three Agave Elixirs

PULQUE

- Pulque (POOL-keh) is a fermented (but never distilled), mildly intoxicating alcoholic beverage. This milky-white, foamy, viscous brew was the revered drink of Aztec nobility, Spanish conquistadors, landed gentry, Independence revolutionaries, bohemian artists, and nursing mothers.

- Pulque is produced from fermenting *aguamiel* (honey water), tapped from within the heart of one of six species of large, succulent agaves (primarily *Agave atrovirens*, *A. salmiana*, and *A. mapisaga*). These agaves grow in the high, cool, semiarid regions of Mexico's Central Plateau, most notably in the states of Hidalgo, Mexico, Puebla, and Tlaxcala.

- Pulque is fermented in *tinacales* (fermentation houses) and is a regional drink because it's highly perishable and does not transport easily. It cannot be palatably canned or bottled, though some have attempted to do so.

- Pulque may be "cured" (flavored) with fruits and vegetables, nuts and grains, herbs and chiles, sugar and spice, and eggs and cream.

- Pulque is rich in nutrients, protein, amino acids, mineral salts, sugars, and vitamins B, C, D, and E. Long known for its nutritive attributes, it is renowned as a medicine, a restorative, and an alleged aphrodisiac.

- Pulque, often regarded as the poor man's drink, has unfortunately been replaced by beer and cheap grain alcohol.

- Pulque, because of its health benefits (when imbibed in moderation) and the reemerging popularity of Mexican traditions, is becoming popular again.

MEZCAL

- Mezcal is a clear, high-proof, fermented, and distilled spirit that can be made from more than twenty-eight varieties of agave.
- Mezcal is often consumed in its place of origin, known by regional names like *sotol*, *bacanora*, *raicilla*, and *sikua*. The best-known mezcal comes from the state of Oaxaca.
- Mezcal is often handcrafted in rustic distilleries called *palenques*. It has a characteristic smoky flavor, derived from cooking the agave hearts in underground-fired ovens as well as from smoke from the wood fires used throughout the distilleries.
- Mezcal made in the handcrafted style appeals to those seeking a more natural, authentic, flavorful, and noncommercialized agave spirit and has become very popular internationally.
- Mezcal has government-regulated standards for certification called NORMA (Norma Oficial Registrada Mexicana), established in 1994 to preserve and protect its quality, establish a denomination of origin, and provide certification for its commercial sales/export. Some laws are even more stringent than those governing tequila.
- COMERCAM (Consejo Mexicano Regulador de la Calidad del Mezcal), a nonprofit regulatory group created in 1997, oversees compliance of regulations with NORMA to protect the integrity of mezcal.

Laws Governing Commercial Mezcal Per NORMA Regulations

- Mezcal can be commercially produced in only eight Mexican states: Oaxaca, Durango, Guerrero, Guanajuato, Michoacán, Zacatecas, Tamaulipas, and San Luis Potosí. Bacanora, from the state of Sonora, and sotol, from Chihuahua, Durango, and Coahuila, have their own denomination of origin with separate considerations, as does sikua from Michoacán.
- Mezcal is made in ten other Mexican states that are not yet protected by laws of denomination of origin.
- Mezcal can be made from any of approximately twenty-eight species of maguey and sometimes a combination of them. The six main maguey from Oaxaca include:

> *Espadín* (*Agave angustifolia Haw.*, blue var.)
> *Del cerro*, *bruto*, or *cenizo* (*Agave asperrima Jacobi*)
> *Mezcalero* or *verde* (*Agave salmiana Otto ex Salm ssp.*)
> *Mezcal* (*Agave weberi Cels.*)
> *Tobalá* (*Agave potatorum Zucc.*)
> *Madrecuishe* (*Agave karwinskii Zucc.*)

- Mezcal comes in two classifications: 100% agave, or 80% agave with 20% added sugars. In the production of tequila, 49% added sugars can be used.
- Mezcal has three aging categories: *abocado* (*joven*, or young) and unaged, with the smokiest and most apparent mezcal flavor; *reposado* (aged two to eleven months in a wooden vat), which softens the flavor; and *añejo* (aged in oak barrels for at least a year).
- Mezcal *cremas* contain natural flavors such as fruits, nuts, chiles, herbs, and dairy products.
- Mezcal only sometimes has a worm in the bottle.
- Mezcal must be bottled at point of origin and not exported in bulk, like *mixto* tequila.

- Tequila is a high-proof agave spirit made from only one variety of agave, the *azul*, or blue, agave.
- Tequila can be made only from agaves grown in a designated territory (Appellation of Origin) and must be produced within that region, just like the French Appellation d'Origine Contrôlée oversees the production of cognac and champagne.
- Tequila may be highly commercialized and produced in state-of-the-art distilleries or it may be made in small family-run distilleries implementing traditional methods.
- Tequila is a very versatile spirit that comes in five distinct categories of aging, ranging from a crystal-clear distillate to one of deep amber color influenced by oak.
- Tequila also comes in two distinct styles, 100% agave tequila and *mixtos*, which contain added sugars.
- Tequila is regulated by NORMA (Norma Oficial Registrada Mexicana), which sets quality standards and a denomination of origin. These laws are continually updated to protect tequila's authenticity and integrity.
- Tequila companies complying with NORMA standards are certified by the CRT (Consejo Regulador del Tequila), also known as the TRC (Tequila Regulatory Council), which ensures that tequila producers comply with rules.

Laws Governing Commercial Tequila Per NORMA Regulations

- Tequila is made from the *Agave tequilana* Weber, variety *azul*. The silvery-blue leaves of this plant and its characteristic high sugar content and flavor distinguish it from other agaves.
- Tequila can be produced only from agaves grown in five Mexican states: the entire state of Jalisco and designated areas in Guanajuato, Michoacán, Nayarit, and Tamaulipas.
- Tequila must contain 51% sugars of "blue" agave; the remaining 49% may come from added sugars.
- Tequila has two categories: 100% agave, also called *Ciento por Ciento Agave*, and *mixto*, made with 49% added sugars, colors, and flavorings.
- Tequila made exclusively of 100% blue agave must say so on the label and be bottled in Mexico. *Mixtos* can be exported in bulk and bottled outside of Mexico.
- Tequila has several aging categories: *blanco* (white), often called *plata,* or silver; *joven abocado* (young), often called "gold"; *reposado* (reposed); *añejo* (aged); and *extra añejo* (extra aged).

Hand-carved *tlachiquero* gathering *aguamiel* from heart of maguey to fill gourds, made in Oaxaca.

¡Qué lindo es el jugo
del verde maguey,
y fresco al beberlo.
Si crudo me ven!

———

How lovely is the sweet nectar
of the green maguey,
so refreshing to sip.
I'll not care if I lose my way!

MANY OF YOU HAVE NEVER tasted pulque. Most of you never will. Nevertheless, I want to pay homage to the original agave inebriant, the forerunner to mezcal and tequila, imbibed for 8,000 years!

Many of today's flavored tequila and mezcal drinks—such as fruity margaritas, tequilas infused with fruits and citrus, and oyster shooters—most likely derived from original pulque drinks.

Let's go on a pulque adventure and learn more about the agave elixir that nourished a country, delighted poets and politicians, and has rich cultural and historical intrigue.

In Search of Pulque

Agave plants meet their demise when workers yank them from the earth to make tequila and mezcal. When making pulque, workers tap the fermentable juices of the plant while it's still alive, a daily wellspring of sweet *aguamiel*. To better understand pulque's virtues, I flew to Mexico City in the late 1970s and drove with a guide two hours northward into the state of Hidalgo. We passed Teotihuacán and the magical pyramids of the sun and moon—now ruins, mere reminders of lost gods.

Spiny nopal (prickly pear) cactus and giant maguey (agave) covered the roadside, patches of green in a sunbaked land. The maguey's huge spiky *pencas* spiraled from their centers, bending gracefully with open arms, some of them tattooed with the carved initials of lovers. As Mexican *ranchera* music idol Vicente Fernández sings in "La Ley del Monte" (composed by José Ángel Espinoza):

Grabé en la penca de un maguey tu nombre
unido al mío, entrelazados.
Como una prueba ante la ley del monte
Que allí estuvimos enamorados.

———

I engraved your name in the flesh of a maguey
entwined with my own.
In the law of the mountain it proved
As lovers we'd be known.

Hand-carved wooden plaque depicting a *tlachiquero* siphoning *aguamiel* with an *acocote* (gourd), circa 1940s.

These agaves of Mexico's Central Plateau are of a much larger species than those that thrive in the hotter and drier tequila-producing regions of Mexico. Many are more than seven feet tall and just as wide; their large, thick, fleshy gray-green leaves bear little resemblance to the narrow, silvery sword-like blades of the tequila-producing agaves.

As we approached Apan, once the heart of Mexico's pulque-producing region, I was surprised to see so few magueys. Instead, a dust bowl of parched, eroded earth and dried corn greeted us. Pulque, I would learn, is not easy to find. Huge haciendas resembling feudal castles loomed on the horizon. Today the locals raise fighting bulls and cattle instead of the pulque-producing magueys for which they were once acclaimed.

My guide and I drove down a desolate dirt road just outside of San Juan Ixtilmaco, sharing it with a herd of rowdy goats. Eventually we arrived at a crudely built cinder-block structure, its windows boarded up with metal scraps to keep out dust.

Mario Gómez Amador, a humble farmer and *pulquero* (one who makes pulque), tipped his straw sombrero to welcome us. We asked for pulque and he went inside, returning with a blue plastic pail filled with a milky white, frothy liquid.

Scooping a *jícara* (a gourd serving as a bowl and ladle) into the pail, he topped it with some creamy white foam and handed it to me. I certainly had second thoughts as I raised the pulque to my lips, gulping it down and nearly gagging on its albuminous consistency. Nevertheless, I found its flavor intriguing: slightly sweet yet acrid, yeasty, earthy, and herbaceous, with a hint of salt.

At once I understood the ancients' reverence for this mystical drink. Just as the hermaphroditic characteristics of the maguey suggest both phallus (stalk) and lactiferous breast (*aguamiel*), pulque is at once reminiscent of semen and mother's milk. The ancients greatly prized this clearly symbolic gift from the gods, one that is nutritive and sustaining.

We shared a desolate dirt road with a herd of rowdy goats as we searched for pulque near San Juan Ixtilmaco, Hidalgo.

ONE PLANT, THREE SPIRITS

Señor Amador took me to a field where a few precious maguey plants grew amid stalks of withered corn. I asked him why there were so few. He replied that pulque had lost its demand. Instead of raising maguey, wealthy landowners now have more profitable interests, cattle, overgrazing the land and not replenishing it with more maguey. As he looked toward the heavens, he said sadly:

> *Por eso no tenemos lluvia.*
> *El maguey llama la lluvia.*
> *Ahora hay poco maguey, poca lluvia.*
>
> ———
>
> *This is the reason we have no rain.*
> *The maguey calls forth the rain.*
> *Now we have few magueys, little rain.*

Still, he waited patiently for his maguey to mature.

He explained the pulque-producing process. When the plant is eight to ten years old, its *corazón* (heart, or center core, from which its new leaves continually unfold) engorges in preparation for its *quiote's* mighty thrust toward the sky. The emerging stalk must be cut off so that the maguey's vital juices will be contained within the heart of the maguey instead of used to feed the flowering stalk.

Within a few months, when the castration scar heals, Señor Amador begins to extract the *aguamiel*. He removes a large stone that he'd placed at the center of the plant to keep out thirsty animals in the night, disclosing a cavity filled with a clear liquid.

> Legend says that a farmer's wife observed a mouse gnawing a hole in the heart of the maguey from which to drink the naturally fermenting aguamiel within. She watched the rodent running about in happy intoxication, and tried some, too!

Still employing the pre-Hispanic techniques of his ancestors, Señor Amador dips the narrow end of a long-necked bottle gourd (reinforced with a cow horn tip), called an *acocote*, into the cavity *para chupar el aguamiel* (to siphon the sweet sap) from within. It tastes fresh,

Top: Cavity of maguey filled with clear, sweet *aguamiel* after scraping with a metal *raspador*. *Bottom*: Señor Amador and his son with a pail of pulque and a tasting gourd.

pure, and soothing—with nuances of herb-scented honey and desert rain. At this stage, the *aguamiel* is highly nutritive, full of minerals, and has medicinal value and purported powers as an aphrodisiac.

Then, just like his fellow *tlachiqueros* (from the Náhuatl word meaning "those who scrape"), Señor Amador scrapes away some of the fibrous pulp within the now-empty cavity from which the *quiote* once sprouted. Using a *raspador*, a short-handled tool with a blade that resembles a large metal fingernail, he enlarges the cavity, which irritates the "wound," encouraging more sap or *aguamiel* to flow (in Mexico, opossum are called *tlacuache* because they use their sharp fingernails to tap the *aguamiel*).

At dawn and dusk, he repeats this ritual of his forefathers, collecting about four liters of the precious honey water daily. This process prevents fermentation from occurring naturally within the plant (to the dis-

may of marauding rodents). The plant perishes usually within three to six months, a vegetal spring run dry.

On a subsequent sojourn to Michoacán, my sister and I came across an almost eighty-year-old woman who trudged twice daily a half mile down a dusty road to gather *aguamiel* from a lone maguey, then carried the heavy pail home. We offered her a ride and had to lift her up into the truck. She had never before ridden in a vehicle!

Producing Pulque

In years past, *tlachiqueros* took the sweet *aguamiel* collected from the fields in large goatskin flasks carried on their backs, or in barrels strapped on burros, to *tinacales* (fermentation houses) to ferment into the milky brew. During the height of pulque production in the mid-nineteenth century, grand haciendas pro-

Señor Amador and his precious maguey. Note the sharp thorns at the tip of each *penca*.

A modern-day Mayahuel in Michoacán getting ready to collect *aguamiel* from her maguey.

Painted tin *ex-voto retablo* (an offering made in fulfillment of a vow), giving thanks to the Virgen de Guadalupe for a maguey that produces *mucho pulquito*. Made by Dionisio Miranda R., Altosombra, state of Mexico.

duced this "white gold" for the "pulque aristocracy." Trainloads of pulque regularly arrived in Mexico City, providing pleasure and great tax revenues for Mexico.

Now, traditional *tinacales* are scarce. Those that do exist welcome neither strangers nor women. The art of the *tinacal* remains secretive and sacred, with knowledge passed down for generations. Like many ancient customs in Mexico, the magic and the mastery, the ritual and the tradition of the *tinacal* is becoming a thing of the past.

There's one such tradition you probably don't want to hear about! *Pulqueros* sometimes wrapped human feces in a small cloth bag called a *muñeca* (little doll), adding it to the pulque to speed the process of fer-mentation. No wonder it's secretive! Sacred? Well, as friend and food editor for *Texas Monthly*, Pat Sharpe, quipped, "Sounds like holy shit to me!"

Blanco bueno
y puro
Solo en el tinacal
lo juro.

—

Pulque white
and pure
only in the tinacal
for sure.

For commercial pulque production today, *aguamiel* is often fermented in oak barrels instead of traditional goatskin or cowhide troughs called *toros*; little else is required. A naturally occurring and very potent bacteria, *Termobacterium mobile* (and hopefully not the *muñeca*), sometimes augmented with oak leaves and herbs, promotes fermentation.

Depending upon the weather, this process takes from seven to twenty-eight days, at which point the *aguamiel* changes from a clear, still liquid to a very frothy, white, and mildly (4–8%) alcoholic beverage. Pulque must then be transported as soon as possible to the point of its consumption. At the turn of the century, men delivered it in a rather peculiar way: they slung over their shoulders huge *cueros de cerdo*,

entire cured pork hide "flasks" with snout and feet intact, comically resembling bloated, porcine balloons.

Because pulque is not distilled, it's highly perishable and sours rapidly as it continues to ferment, changing from pleasant to putrid (with an ammonia-like odor) within days, especially when not stored well. Today, good fresh pulque is often difficult to find. Some companies sell it canned, which seems to defeat the purpose of drinking it! Sadly, many may never sample freshly made pulque, the *cara blanca*, the pure white milk of Mayahuel, ancient goddess of moonlight and maguey.

Pulquerías: Mexico's First Cantinas

Pulquerías (pulque-drinking establishments) flourished during the mid-nineteenth and early twentieth centuries, when this most Mexican of drinks exemplified the national spirit of the country. Some *pulquerías* had brightly painted façades and picturesque names, often with double meanings. Names like La Nana (the nursing breast), La Buena Baba (the tasty slime), Agua Escondida (hidden waters), or La Gran Herida (the great wound) made reference to the maguey. Others suggested the aftereffects of drinking: El Infiernito (hell), El Aviador (flying high), or Viaje a la Luna (trip to the moon). Others featured names suggesting bawdy, tongue-in-cheek, or grim humor.

Some *pulquerías* catered to the wealthy. In these salons, harp music resonated, crystal chandeliers shimmered, and poets shared their newest verses with elegant patrons. Some establishments drew revolutionaries, politicos, and intellectuals. Inside, walls were painted with imaginative murals (which greatly inspired Diego Rivera) along with proverbial *dichos*, like those peppered throughout this book.

Colorful paper banners welcomed those who entered: artists and writers, landed gentry, and many less illustrious folk. Humor and wit flowed as freely as pulque, which was poured into a variety of mugs and pitchers. These vessels had names given according to the amounts they held or the shape of the glass. Some had women's names; others suggested off-color double

---

Happy Hour in the Field

A Mexican man once told me how his grandfather and fellow *campesinos* celebrated the last day of their work week. They carried personal items tied around their waists in *fajillas*, small, netted bags woven of *ixtle* (agave) fiber. Some days this included a few limes and a little jar of mezcal, most likely poured from a precious bottle stashed away at home.

At the end of another long day, these amigos met in a field near a towering maguey. They stripped away a thin sheath from the inside of a penca, rolling pieces of this "parchment" into green cones, glued together by sticky, succulent pulp.

From the oozing core of the maguey, they dipped out clear, sweet *aguamiel* to fill their handmade cups, lacing it with mezcal and a squeeze of lime. Finally, they rested from hours of hard labor, squatting on their haunches, just like their ancestors, *compadres y compañeros*, discussing the events of their lives in their cantina of agave and earth.

entendres, like *cabrón* (bastardly old goat) or *tornillo* (the "screw," because of the effects of drinking and the corkscrew shape of the glass).

José Guadalupe Posada, a turn-of-the-twentieth-century Mexican graphic artist best known for his life-like skeletons depicting the ironies of the day and for his political satires, celebrated pulque as the national spirit of Mexico. He considered it the drink of the common man and often featured it in his illustrations.

Champaña, tinto, y jerez
Escóndanlos avergonzados,
o marchen precipitados
para su tierra otra vez.

———

Claret, sherry, and champagne,
Hide them all with shame,
Or return to your homeland
as fast as you came.

Songs commemorating the illustrious agave—from "El Maguey" or "El Pulque" to "El Borrachito" (the drunkard) or "Lamentos de un Crudo" (sorrows of a hangover) flourished in this pulque-embracing society. Oh, how I wish I could step back in time!

Women known as *las enchiladeras* set up stalls in front of *pulquerías*, luring patrons with their chile-spiced *botanitas* (snacks), just as vendors do today from street and market stalls throughout Mexico. Many of these dishes remain unchanged. Some specialties, like *pan de pulque*, delicious bread flavored with pulque, and spicy, tequila-spiked Salsa Borracha (Drunken Sauce), remain popular today.

Though the pulque aristocracy thrived during the Porfirio Díaz regime (1876–1911), anti-alcohol sentiment and reprimands from Catholic clergy led the Mexican president to regulate *pulquerías*. By the early 1900s, laws limited the operating hours. They also prohibited music and chairs to prevent lingering. Women, men in uniform, and dogs were forbidden entry. The end of the Mexican Revolution and the emergence of a middle class, which preferred beer and stronger liquor, furthered the demise of these pulque-drinking establishments. Pulque became relegated to the lower class.

A cup of pulque balanced on a drunkard's head in a *pulquería*, state of Hidalgo, Mexico.

LECHE DE LA VACA VERDE
Agua de las verdes matas,
tú me tumbas,
tú me matas,
tú me haces andar a gatas.

———

MILK FROM THE GREEN COW
Nectar of the green maguey,
you knock me down,
you knock me out,
you make me reel and sway.

Today, sawdust floors reeking of spilled pulque and the despair of the poor are too often all that remain of a proud national tradition. In 1981, laws were overturned, allowing women to enter *pulquerías*, but dogs and uniformed men are still not allowed! Most women, however, still prefer to obtain their glasses of pulque by stretching their arms through a small window from a cubicle outside the *pulquería*. Not I.

Modern-Day *Pulquerías*

A popular *pulquería* in Mexico City, Pulquería La Pirata, (another humorous double entendre: "the woman pirate" who steals sobriety and robs you blind), was as busy and rowdy as any bar at happy hour, except that it was eleven o'clock in the morning and only men were inside. Many of them appeared to have been drinking all night, though I still don't understand how anyone could consume enough of the mildly alcoholic bloating brew to become intoxicated. Others stepped inside for *chisme* (gossip) and companionship or for a quick morning perk-up. Some of the men played dominoes, others sang along with a tattered trio of mariachis. And some had simply laid their heads down upon the table.

Si tomas para olvidar,
paga antes de tomar.

If you drink to forget,
pay first.

An altar to La Virgen de Guadalupe hung on the wall, as it does in almost every *pulquería*, a reminder of the Aztec goddess Mayahuel, who sprang from the heart of the agave but was later assimilated into the Catholic hierarchy. A gigantic stone *molcajete*, piled high with guacamole, compliments of the house, sat on the counter. Haphazardly garnished with long stems of cilantro and chopped onions, it resembled a vegetative headdress. Although I was forewarned of its fire, I scooped some

Ice-cold fruit-flavored *curados* served from painted vats.

Cantinero Navarrete with a huge *molcajete* brimming with guacamole for a *botanita* in Pulquería La Pirata, Mexico, D.F.

ONE PLANT, THREE SPIRITS

Top: Barrels of white, foamy pulque. *Bottom*: *Pesos* and pulque at Pulquería La Pirata, Mexico, D.F.

of it onto a warm corn tortilla and took a big bite. Immediately, an explosion of serrano peppers assaulted my tongue (a good way to sell more pulque, no doubt), and the room broke out in good-natured laughter.

A motley assortment of glasses and gourds, pitchers and mugs, and a big oak cask of foamy white pulque lined the back of the bar. The barrel-chested bartender, Salvador Navarrete, enthusiastically took my order, humorously scorning any man daring to pay me attention. Many of the men were drinking from liter mugs, but I chose a small glass. The pulque was fresh and smooth . . . and slimy! I couldn't imagine that it had inebriating effects; it seemed surprisingly "healthy" instead.

Señor Navarrete ladled pastel-colored *curados* (flavored pulques resembling smoothies) from large aluminum pots that were painted with cheerful fruits and had a block of ice inside to keep the contents cool. My favorites were those made from tart fruits such as lime (with some of the peel), guava, prickly pear, and pineapple. One flavored with celery and alfalfa tasted as if it had miraculous curative properties, while the one thickened with egg yolk and almonds and dusted with cinnamon tasted like a rich dessert. Another, called *chilacle*, fermented with chile ancho, epazote, salt, and onion, reeked of pure Mexican bravado. I did not, however, brave the unrefrigerated raw oyster plopped in a glass of pulque topped with *salsa picante* and a squeeze of fresh lime. These original "oyster shooters" have fabled powers as an aphrodisiac.

Today, many Mexican *pulquerías* accessible to tourists serve artificially flavored pulques, just as many American bars today serve artificially flavored margaritas. I don't recommend visiting the more traditional *pulquerías* for those unaccustomed to the language and customs of Mexico. They may not welcome strangers, and one must also take caution not to drink pulque that has been tainted with unpurified ice or water.

I FIRST VISITED LA PIRATA more than thirty years ago. Though there's a new mural on the outside walls, not much else has changed. The saloon doors of this sixty-year-old *pulquería* still swing open. It looks like the

Mayahuel: Goddess of Moonlight, Maguey, and Four Hundred Breasts

Aztec legend says that the beautiful goddess Mayahuel, one of the guardians of the cold moon, longed for the warmth of the sun. Her evil grandmother Tzitzimitl, Devourer of Light, kept her sequestered until Quetzalcóatl, god of the winds, fell passionately in love with her, bringing her to earth. To hide from Tzitzimitl, he disguised the lovers as branches of a tree, caressing in the wind. Still, Tzitzimitl and her four hundred demonic granddaughters discovered them and tore Mayahuel into bits. A devastated Quetzalcóatl buried the remains of her torn branches, drenched with his tears. From this sprouted a magnificent maguey, its leaves radiating from their core like the rays of the sun.

The angry gods sent a violent storm, striking the maguey with lightning and fermenting the sweet nectar found within the plant. The forlorn Quetzalcóatl drank it, finding comfort and inebriated bliss, a state that still brings solace to many. Legend says Mayahuel's milk (*aguamiel*), given to sustain life, oozes from the heart of the maguey.

Considered the goddess of fertility, fecundity, and motherhood, Mayahuel had four hundred breasts (emerging from the innumerable sprouts of each *penca*), from which pure white pulque flowed to feed her four hundred children.

A revered deity in the Aztec pantheon, Mayahuel easily assimilated into the Catholic hierarchy as the most cherished Virgen de Guadalupe, the patroness of Mexico. She is depicted with a crescent moon at her feet, held up by an angel.

same hand-painted vats sitting on the shelf (though chipped from years of use) hold flavored *curados*. Today, pulque is making its comeback, especially among young Mexican hipsters. Nicholas Gilman visited La Pirata and wrote about it in an article for the *Los Angeles Times* in November 2011, "Older, distinctly Mexican traditions are now seen as cool."

This resurgence of *pulquerías* in Mexico seems to go hand in hand with a renewed fervor for *el mexicanísmo* and cultural pride. Pulque's newfound popularity also coincides with the current trend of more healthy, nutritional, and traditional fare. I hope to witness new gathering places emerging where music and art flourish, spirited conversations flow, and artists and philosophers, bohemians and scholars, and others come simply to raise a glass and partake of the merriment, as they did in *pulquerías* of long ago.

Catholicized Mayahuel with her maguey brightly painted on a wooden plaque; a contemporary piece.

¡Viva la penca señores,
La penca que es del maguey!
¡Cuando tomo sus sabores
Me siento como un rey!

——

Hoorah for the agave amigos,
The leaves from maguey so green!
When I partake of its sweet nectar
I feel just like a king!

Many Mexicans believe that pulque continues to ferment in the stomach once ingested and that a shot of mezcal is essential *para despanzar* (to ease bloating). Sounds to me like a good excuse to drink more, and a stronger spirit at that! ¡Viva mezcal!

Mayahuel
"PULQUE" COCKTAIL

Because fresh pulque is not available outside of Mexico, I wanted to create a drink in Mayahuel's honor. It's soothing, yet intoxicating—clear and sweet like *aguamiel*, with a milky, white foam. Tequila *blanco*, fresh lime juice, and a pinch of ground red chile give it a decidedly Mexican flair.

- 2 ounces 100% agave tequila *blanco*
- 1 ounce fresh Mexican lime juice
- 1 tablespoon granulated white sugar
- 1 egg white
- freshly ground *pasilla* chile (or *guajillo*, for more spice)

Vigorously shake tequila, lime juice, sugar, and egg white in a mixing tin until it produces a thick foam. Add several large ice cubes to the shaker; continue to shake vigorously until it's thickly coated with frost (45 seconds at least). Strain into a glass. Sprinkle a tiny areola of chile in the center of the drink.

MEZCAL

Para todo mal, mezcal.
Para todo bien, también.

—

For all that ails you, mezcal.
For all that's good, as well.

MEZCAL. SOME CALL IT THE "mother of tequila," the original agave distillate. The Spanish colonists in Mexico quickly came to long for an inebriant more potent and palatable than pulque, one more akin to the beloved brandy from their homeland. These enterprising Spaniards discovered that the ubiquitous maguey held promise beyond that of pulque. Roasting its starchy central core (called a *piña* because it resembles a huge pineapple) yielded fermentable sugars necessary for distillation.

Using copper pot stills brought from the Old World and ancient Moorish distillation methods, the Spanish colonists are credited with producing *vino de mezcal*, long considered the first distilled spirit of the Americas, although new anthropological evidence sug-

gests that distillation occurred prior to the arrival of the Spaniards (p. 70). This "mezcal wine" was named after the mezcal plant that the pre-Hispanics called *mexcalmetl*. Its higher proof made pulque seem like mother's milk in comparison.

Some of the best mezcal came from the lowlands region of Jalisco near the towns of Amatitán and Tequila, where agaves flourished in the volcanic soils surrounding a majestic volcano, also called Tequila. Later, this mezcal was named after the volcano and known thereafter as tequila. This region eventually became home to Cuervo, Sauza, and later, Herradura, the tequila industry's founding fathers. However, the thirst for intoxicating distillates quickly spread to other regions throughout Mexico and led to the use of other agaves for distillation.

Hand-carved skeletons with mezcal for heaven by Inocencio Vásquez, San Martín Tilcajete, Oaxaca.

Regional Variations

Today, mezcal can be made from any of more than twenty species of agave and sometimes combinations of several. These species usually grow in a lower, warmer, more semiarid topography than the pulque-producing magueys, thriving in the southernmost states of Chiapas and Oaxaca, along much of the lower Pacific coast, throughout the lowlands into the highlands of Mexico's central states, and north into the higher Chihuahua desert.

Local mezcals, known by regional names, are made throughout these areas, often in rustic and remote distilleries, instead of in modern factories. Tequila is considered a regional mezcal, simply because it is an agave distillate, but not all mezcal is tequila. Mexican law protects tequila, distinguishing it from other mezcals, to guarantee its flavor and characteristics, just as the French set rules to distinguish cognac from brandy, though both derive from grapes. Mexican law now gives some mezcals their own denomination of origin (protected geographical indication) as well.

At a quaint open-air restaurant on the Pacific, outside of Puerto Vallarta, Jalisco, I first tasted raicilla, a fruity but high-voltage regional mezcal made from *Agave lechuguilla*. It made the stars fall out of the sky! Bacanora, another powerful inebriant from the northwestern state of Sonora, comes from wild agaves grown in the Sierra Madre (*Agave pacifica*, sometimes called *Agave yaquiano* for the Yaqui Indians there). This mezcal, imbued with a distinctive smoky flavor from agaves roasted over mesquite fire, is often flavored with piñon nuts. The Mexican government once outlawed the production of bacanora, considering it a bootlegged brew, but has now granted it a denomination of origin for commercial production. Two brands now imported into the United States are Vitzo and Cielo Rojo, with alluring sweet yet smoky flavors.

A type of mezcal called "sotol," from the rugged Chihuahuan Desert, has lately garnered attention

Uprooting the Entire Agave

To make mezcal, field-workers uproot the entire maguey plant, which has taken nearly a decade to grow. They shave away its sharp, protective leaves to reveal its vulnerable heart (its central core). Imagining this, I've gained reverence for this mystical distillate and a keen understanding of its significance in ceremonial and spiritual ritual for indigenous people even today. Mezcal has retained that mystique from long ago, and many still consider it a holy inebriant. Its dual nature conjures up demon or deity, fire or water, purification or intoxication—depending upon how much is imbibed!

north of the border. Sotol Hacienda de Chihuahua shares some of tequila's attributes: it is double distilled, aged in oak casks, and bottled in *blanco*, *reposado*, and *añejo* expressions. It is steamed in clay ovens instead of roasted underground like most mezcals. Sotol now has its own denomination of origin: Chihuahua, Coahuila, and Durango states. I'm partial to Don Cuco Sotol, proudly made by the Jacquez family in Chihuahua for six generations.

Sotol is made from a plant species called *Dasylirion*, better known as "Desert Spoon" (because of the spoon-shaped base of its leaves). It's not a true *Agavaceae*, but rather a closely related member of the family *Nolinaceae*. This desert plant cascades in a fountain of slender, flexible, saw-toothed leaves, making it a popular landscaping plant in southwestern gardens. However, plants grown in the wild are harvested to make sotol. Sotol's flavor is sweet, with herbaceous and vegetal characteristics and a peppery finish.

Full Moon & Mezcal in Oaxaca, 1980

The best-known and most exported mezcal comes from Oaxaca, Mexico's fifth-largest state, located in the far southern corner of the country. Oaxaca borders the state of Chiapas, next to Guatemala. It's a diverse land of hills and valleys, seven-thousand-foot mountains, Pacific coastline, tropical paradise, and plains. It also hosts Mexico's most diverse indigenous population. Much of the mezcal there is made as it was four centuries ago in remote villages where Zapotec, Mixtec, and other native dialects are still spoken and handcrafted mezcal traditions have not been lost.

Numerous kinds of maguey grow in this varied region. The ones used for mezcal production have names referring to the area in which they are grown or to the plant's characteristics: *espadín* (sword-like), *verde* (green), *cenizo* (rough-leaved), *azul* (blue), *bruto* (tough), *mezcalero* ("for making mezcal"), the prized high-altitude *tobalá* (from the Zapotec word for "maguey grown in the shade"), and the upright *madrecuishe*.

Many mezcals are produced in primitive, isolated distilleries called *palenques*. Hundreds of them lie hidden in the hills of this state, from just outside of Oaxaca City to more remote counties like Miahuatlan, Tlacolula, and Yautepec. Oaxaqueños come to fill their *garrafones* (plastic jugs) on site because these mezcals are not commercially bottled. (One of the best mezcals I ever tasted was handed to me in a bottle previously filled with soda pop.) Some people make annual pilgrimages down rough terrain and nearly impassable rocky roads just to procure their favorite mezcal straight from the still. Back home, they'll drink it for pleasure, but also for its virtue as a cure-all.

Mezcal bendito, sagrada alimento.
¿Qué haces afuera?
¡Métete pa' dentro!

———

Blessed mezcal, holy elixir.
What are you waiting for?
Let me drink you quickly!

It was almost my thirtieth birthday. I chose to share it with the full moon and mezcal in Oaxaca. I said adios to the matador who had stolen my heart in Mexico City, then headed south. The bus broke down for hours along the way. Arriving far past midnight in a crowded station, I felt frightened and very alone. Little did I know that I was about to embark on perhaps the most synchronistic and memorable adventures of my life.

After a good night's sleep, I began to explore the city. On the streets surrounding Oaxaca's bustling Mercado Benito Juárez, small shops sold local specialties: cinnamon-laced chocolate, burnished black pottery, multi-hued textiles handwoven on back-strap looms, and lots of mezcal.

Brightly colored façades (resembling those of the early *pulquerías*) lured potential customers into mezcal dispensaries. Inside, shelves lined with a colorful selection of mezcals tempted souvenir seekers. Hand-painted bottles, black pottery *ollas* (crocks), painted earthenware monkeys in straw hats, and pigskin flasks awaited purchase. Green-glazed shot glasses and whimsical *zapatillos* (painted earthenware shot glasses shaped like a woman's leg in high-heeled shoes), as well as more erotically suggestive containers hidden on bottom shelves, added ambiance to these picturesque *tiendas* (stores).

Si tomas bastante mezcal,
Puedes ver toda la mujer.

———

If you drink enough mezcal,
You'll see all parts of the woman.

Small *jícaras* (gourd bowls) from which to sip mezcal, painted red and gaily adorned with flowers, were for sale along with small bags filled with salt. But this salt is most peculiar! Flavored with dried ground *gusanos* (worms) that feast on the agave plant and *pasilla* chiles, *sal de gusano* ritually accompanies shots of mezcal, just as unflavored salt sometimes accompanies shots of tequila. Stacks of plastic jugs stood ready to be filled with mezcal directly from a large barrel. After all, in many Oaxacan homes, a bottle of mezcal is as much a staple as a bag of *frijoles negros*. Some Oaxaqueños swear by a shot of mezcal at midmorning and another before bed, just for its health benefits.

I sampled many kinds of mezcal, some quite remarkable and complex: characteristically smoky and earthy with spicy undertones, as well as ones with apparent fruity and floral notes. Others tasted exceedingly crude—like imbibing lighter fluid burning off a charcoal grill, searing all the way down my throat!

Mezcal sweetened and flavored with fresh seasonal fruits, herbs, or almonds and cream is temptingly called *crema de mezcal*. Though quite popular, these drinks are usually too sweet for my taste (although I have sampled a few exquisite ones) and sometimes seem to mask an unrefined product. I prefer a cure-all swig from *mezcal poleo*, heady with the strong minty aroma of pennyroyal, guaranteed to heal what ails you.

In 1980, however, the mezcal most familiar to North Americans was *mezcal de gusano*, the one with the worm in the bottle. The unsuspecting worm resides in the maguey plant before being plopped into the bottle as proof of the proof. It is said that if the worm is truly pickled, the alcohol has not been diluted. Some mezcal aficionados regard the *gusano* as a sales gimmick to seduce wannabe machos eager to prove their manhood (and womanhood!) by slurping the worm from the bottom of the bottle.

Mezcal shop advertising various kinds of mezcal in Oaxaca City.

Red *gusanos* ready for plopping into a bottle of mezcal in Oaxaca.

According to Náhuatl legend, the *gusano*, having once lived within the maguey, ingested the magical spirit of that plant. The *gusano* within the bottle gives the mezcal a spirit of its own. He who swallows the worm in the bottle ingests the soul of the maguey.

It is said that the seemingly lowly worm:

+ Adds flavor to mezcal with its inherent proteins and fats and serves as a filter of impurities.
+ Signifies that mezcal is an agave distillate because the gusano lives in the agave plant.
+ Enhances the libido and increases sexual desire.
+ Honors the lucky guest who gets to swallow it. (Biologist and tequila aficionada Donna Howell says, "Considering that the worm isn't offered until the bottle is drained down to its level, one seldom minds being the honoree.")
+ Makes a good sales gimmick: almost everyone has heard about the worm in the bottle. Besides, if you bite into the worm, you will surely need another sip.

Worm or no worm, I wanted to taste authentic mezcal, not those bottled and surely adulterated for tourist consumption. A lively group of Berkeley anthropology students had hired an English-speaking driver and asked me to join them on an adventure to nearby artisan markets. I was tempted, thanked them politely, and flagged down a cab instead, heading out on my own mezcal quest.

A shy Zapotec man drove me to Ocotlán de Morelos, about forty minutes south of Oaxaca City. I'd heard the mezcal there was good. We stopped to ask

A Worm in the Bottle?

Chinicuiles, small red "worms" (actually, larvae of *Comadia redtenbachi*), also known as *gusanos colorados* (*o rojos*), live within the roots and heart of the maguey. They're toasted on a hot *comal* (griddle), giving them a pungent nutty flavor, and eaten as a delicacy. Small packets of *sal de gusano* are sometimes tied around the neck of bottles of mezcal, both for their unique flavor, to stimulate taste, and as a sales gimmick. *Meocoiles* (larvae of *Aegiale hesperarius*), also known as *gusanos blancos*, live inside the leaves and are also considered a tasty tidbit. Either *gusano* may also be found floating around the bottom of a bottle of mezcal.

Painted earthenware clay *gusano* from Santa Cruz de las Huertas, Jalisco.

directions at a home, the front window of which had caught my eye. Other dwellings on the street, linked together with thick adobe walls, had no outside windows. Instead, large wooden gates opened to sunny courtyards within. Up close, the window proved to be a deeply set niche, protected with thick Plexiglas, which seemed quite odd in a Mexican village. Within, an elaborately wrought medieval-looking steel sword glistened. Befuddled, but obsessed with my mezcal mission, I followed the directions of the maid sweeping the street and headed on my way, bidding adios to the driver.

Within the large courtyard of a nearby home to which she'd directed me, a coppersmith pounded hot metal at his forge, where he crafted pot stills for mezcal distilleries. His son Oscar offered to take me to a nearby town famous for its mezcal. With Oscar's toddler by my side, we drove bumpy and sometimes desolate miles toward the mountains and the village of Santa Catarina Minas. Once renowned for its silver

mines, mezcal was now its glimmering treasure. Oscar told me that *minero*, the mezcal produced there, where springwater and mineral-rich soils abound, was some of Oaxaca's finest. On the way, we passed several white pickup trucks loaded with rifle-wielding policemen, or *federales*. Remembering the sword in the window, I thought it must be my day for unexplained weaponry!

Once again in need of directions, we stopped a man walking down the road. His name was Ángel, a fitting name for a guardian angel. Ángel drank too much mezcal. He had spent one too many siestas on the ground in his woven sombrero, its ruptured crown sprouting bits of straw like a haystack gone awry. Still, he tipped it graciously when we met, his coffee-colored eyes shaded beneath its rim. A safety pin held the fly of his trousers together and his rumpled shirt of cotton *manta*, missing buttons, covered skinny ribs.

I moved the toddler to my lap, as Ángel climbed aboard the pickup to guide us. Politely shielding his breath when he talked, he muttered, "Huelo a mezcal"

Ángel holding the elongated *piña* of a *madrecuishe* maguey in a *palenque* in Santa Catarina, Minas, Oaxaca.

ONE PLANT, THREE SPIRITS

(I reek of liquor!), which I took as a good sign. Soon, the road ended at a flowing stream, a welcome sight, as the child had peed on me. We rolled up our pants to cross and walked a half-mile into the *campo* (countryside). What a motley crew indeed: one slightly inebriated Indian, a mestizo carrying his small son on his shoulders, and a camera-toting blonde.

We came upon the *palenque*, a straw and adobe distillery shack, and startled a band of could-be ruffians, sleeping on the dirt floor in the dark. I feared I'd awakened them from a deep, mezcal-induced siesta, and my imagination ran wild. As they jumped up, one particularly disheveled and barrel-chested character reminded me for a moment that no one in the world knew where I was! I implored the dusty photo of the Virgen de Guadalupe that hung crookedly on the adobe wall to ensure that all would be well. It was.

The unlit room was hazy with smoke from wood-fueled fires burning under clay *ollas*, yet sweet and heady aromas of cooked agave prevailed. I felt as if we were stepping back in time, into a mysterious alchemy of vapor and fire. The *palenqueros* graciously led us on a tour, answering my questions and showing us the mezcal-making process, which still followed age-old traditions.

The most popular maguey in Santa Catarina Minas is the *espadín*, which has long, thick, bluish sword-like leaves, bearing strong resemblance to the blue agave used to make tequila. Sometimes *magueyes silvestres* (agaves grown in the wild) are used like the maguey *cirial* (*Agave karwinskii Zucc.*), also called *cuishe*, a tall-growing maguey the central core of which resembles a giant elongated ear of corn. The first step in making mezcal is roasting the hearts (*piñas*) of the maguey.

Making Mezcal in Santa Catarina Minas

Outside the shack, I saw a neat, conical mound. Beneath was an earthen pit lined with hot stones, fueled by a wood fire. Within this "oven," halved *piñas*, covered with more hot stones, moist maguey leaves, and previously cooked agave fiber were blanketed with straw mats and topped with damp earth to "steam" for three to four days. This caramelizes the *piñas*, turning them a deep golden brown, converting their intrinsic starches into fermentable sugar. It also gives mezcal its inherent and inimitable smokiness.

After the *piñas* have cooked and cooled, they're crushed into a fibrous pulp. Ángel demonstrated this by pulverizing roasted *piñas* with a long wooden mallet in a stone pit. In some villages, beasts of burden pull a *tahona*, a heavy volcanic millstone, round and round a circular cobblestone pit to grind the *piñas*. Workers then carry the *bagazo*, or fibrous pulp (which adds to the flavor), along with the sweet juices in heavy buckets to fermentation barrels, where water is added. I was impressed with the ingenious and intricate aqueduct surrounding the *palenque*, transporting springwater in hollow bamboo-like canes.

One of the workers pulled away a *petate*, a woven palm-fiber mat, protecting the alfresco fermentation.

Top: Underground pit in Oaxaca for roasting *piñas*, which are covered in cooked agave fiber and hot stones. *Bottom*: Mezcal pit in Oaxaca covered in a conical pile of earth, as *piñas* steam.

Top left: *Tahona* millstone grinding cooked *piñas* to release their sweet fermentable juice. *Top right*: *Bagazo* (agave fibers) separated from the sweet agave "must" (juice) in Oaxaca. *Bottom*: Alfresco fermentation tanks.

Within the large oak barrel, a thick, murky brown liquid, mixed with coarse golden agave fibers, had finished fermenting, augmented by airborne microbes and naturally occurring yeasts. (I dared not ask about the spent shotgun casing floating within!) Fermentation takes from five to thirty days, depending upon the weather. The low-proof alcohol (about 5%) was ready for transport to the still, to vaporize and condense in that miraculous process of distillation.

We went back inside. The locally crafted twenty-gallon earthenware *ollas* simmered slowly, *para no quemar el mezcal* (to not burn the mezcal). For complexity of flavor, the *palenqueros* also added some of the cooked agave fiber to the first twenty-four-hour distillation, removing it for the second twenty-four-hour distillation. The craft of a skilled *maestro* (master distiller), passed down for generations, is determined by his ability to capture the agave essence in the final distilled spirit.

The burly man I once feared handed me a small clay cup and I filled it with the crystalline distillate, straight from the still. With that first warm draw of fire and smoke, fruit and flowers, I understood why this divine elixir was worthy of sacred repute. At once, I tasted the fruity agave mingling with the earthy taste of the clay of the pot still. We passed the cup, and with *gracias*, I toasted my new amigos before bidding them a heartfelt adios.

Top left: Tending fire in the smoky *palenque*. *Bottom left*: Clay *ollas* used in Santa Catarina Minas as mezcal pot stills. *Right*: A crude copper distillation pot used in some *palenques* in Oaxaca.

Upon reaching the car, Ángel invited us to his home for coffee with his sister. I had seen her from afar, long braids dangling down her colorful, hand-woven *huipil* (woven top embroidered with flowers) as she hung laundry on a wooden fence to dry. Noting Oscar's disdain, I realized this was a border he did not want to cross—that age-old barrier between mestizo and Indian. *Con un abrazo fuerte*, I offered Ángel some crumpled bills, a *propina* he would not accept.

"No fue por eso," he said sadly as he walked away, "fue por amistad." (It was not for money, but for friendship.) I will never forget him. I hope one day to return for coffee in Santa Catarina Minas with Ángel and his sister and to sip mezcal once more from that magical still.

Oscar, the sleeping child, and I returned to his father's home. The dull and dirty copper pot used to collect mezcal straight from the still that I'd seen earlier in a pile of rubble was freshly polished for me

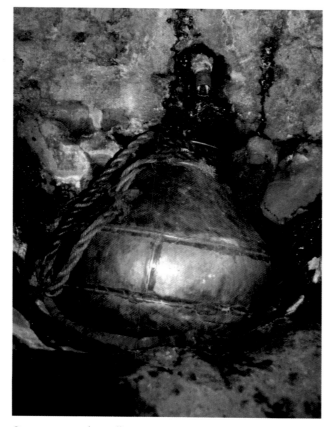

Copper pot used to collect Oaxacan mezcal straight from the still.

to purchase. (I managed to get it home on the plane, and it remains a prized possession in my home.) The coppersmith's wife had transformed his forge into a hot *comal*. She stood flipping quesadillas filled with gooey Oaxacan white cheese and torn bits of *hoja santa*, a large, heart-shaped leaf, fragrant as sassafras, that grew in the courtyard there (and back home in my own garden). I was starving, and the quesadillas tasted delicious! Afterward, Oscar drove me back to Oaxaca.

Panza llena,
Corazón contento.

———

Full stomach,
Happy heart.

That night, the burnished copper pot glowed like a huge pumpkin, guarding my hotel room from its post on my bed. Beneath the light of a Oaxacan full moon, I set out for an evening stroll, clothed in a new cream-colored skirt woven of soft cotton *manta*. I stopped in the town square to buy a gardenia for my hair from a young, dark-skinned Zapotec girl who carried a fragrant basket of them upon her head.

Haunting music lured me into an art gallery. Guests mingled, their shot glasses filled with *mezcal de pechuga almendrado*, flavored with orchard fruit and almonds— the finest in the land, I was told. I'd wandered into a private awards ceremony celebrating local artisans, yet was welcomed kindly. I was astonished to see a collection of hand-forged swords displayed upon a long table, just like the one I had seen in the window in Ocotlán that morning! Judges had just awarded the grand prize to brothers Ángel and Apolinar Aguilar for the intricately carved blades they'd crafted for *Conan the Barbarian*, starring Arnold Schwarzenegger.

I recounted my tale of visiting Ocotlán earlier in the day and peering into the window. When I mentioned Santa Catarina Minas and *federales* with rifles, their eyes widened in astonishment. Apparently, that very day, local land feuds all around me had led to fatal and bloody disputes.

My gracious hosts refilled my *carrizo*, a traditional shot glass fashioned from a hollow bamboo-like reed, and we toasted to a full moon, magic, and mezcal in Oaxaca! The matador? Already forgotten!

Del Maguey Mezcal

It was not until sixteen years later, in 1996, that I met Ron Cooper, a Taos, New Mexico, artist and sculptor who single-handedly changed the image of mezcal in our country and abroad. Each of his Del Maguey mezcals comes from small batches of single-village mezcal (instead of blends) distilled in the traditional, unhurried way. Cooper's motto: "No worm. No salt. No gimmick."

He names his mezcals after the villages in which they're produced: Chichicapa, Santo Domingo Albarradas, San Luis del Río, and my nostalgic favorite, of course, Minero (from Santa Catarina Minas). Del Maguey's Pechuga, like the ethereal one I'd tasted in the Oaxacan art gallery, hints of fresh plums, apples, almonds, and pineapple, which subtly impart their flavors into this beguiling mezcal. In a tradition passed down from the Moors, a raw, skinned chicken breast hangs within the still. The *pechuga de pollo* is thought to "preserve" the sacred spirit of the distillate and balance the flavor of agave and fruit. This limited edition mezcal fetches a price of more than two hundred dollars, but it's worth every cent.

Another of his sought-after rare vintage mezcals, Tobalá, is crafted from a small, wild mountain agave (*Agave potatorum Zucc.*) that thrives in high altitude canyons in the shade of oak trees. I only took my bottle (a precious 2007 vintage) off the shelf to sip and share with special friends. Its *dulce* essence of maguey, hints of orchard fruit, wild mint, and spice is beyond memorable, unlike any spirit most have tasted.

A man with grand reverence for Oaxaca's venerated distillate and its sacred past, Cooper often pours a bit of his precious mezcal on the floor in the form of a cross before taking his first sip. This tradition, an offering of respect to ancestral spirits, is practiced throughout Oaxaca as well as in Mexican *pulquerías*, where a bit of pulque is also purposefully spilled before the first sip.

Mezcal Today

Following in Cooper's footsteps, a handful of others have produced artisanal mezcals. Alluring names add to the mystique: Los Danzantes (ecstatic dancers), smoky Sombra (dark shadow), Los Nahuales (protective animal spirits), Los Amantes (the lovers), and Ilegal. Once mezcal with the worm in the bottle drew attention. Now serious aficionados seek character and the rich, complex essence of maguey captured within the bottle. (Trends come and go. I must say, the worm returns to favor! Some high-end mezcal producers are adding *gusanos* to their mezcals again.)

Alejandro Santa Cruz has a passion for mezcal and his homeland. This native of Mexico City now resides in Austin and has cofounded Wahaka (phonetic pronunciation of "Oaxaca") Mezcal with the Morales family, fifth-generation Zapotec *mezcalilleros*. They produce artisanal, small-batch, award-winning mezcals from the village of San Dionisio Ocotepec in Oaxaca's Central Valley in the municipality of Tlacolula.

Their line includes three traditional unaged *joven* mezcals (with no influence of wood), as well as a blend of all three. Their Espadín is made from estate-grown *espadín* agaves, known for their sweetness and Oaxaca's most popular cultivated agave. Madre Cuishe, with its dry minerality and hints of citrus, is made from the elongated central cores of tall magueys that grow in the wild. Wahaka Tobalá, deliciously floral and herbaceous, derives from small, elusive *tobalá* agaves grown in the rugged, mountainous highlands. Their Wahaka Ensamble, made from 50% Espadín and 25% each of Madre-Cuishe and Tobalá, expresses flavor characteristics of each agave. Interestingly enough, the hearts of these magueys are cooked, fermented, and distilled together, not just blended.

Las Perlas

The pearl-like bubbles remaining on the surface of mezcal after the bottle has been gently shaken are called *las perlas*. Traditionally, the distiller sucks mezcal through a cane straw called a *venencia* and releases some into a *jícara* (gourd). The number of *perlas* formed, their size, and the duration before they pop determines the proof and quality of the mezcal.

Drawing mezcal with a *venencia*, then releasing it to see how many *perlas* (pearl-like bubbles) appear.

I have to admit, Wahaka's Reposado con Gusano, their aged expression, just may change my mind about wood aging mezcal (I want to revel in the smoke and fire, not tame it!) . . . and the worm! They've gently aged this mezcal (only four to six months) in white oak, along with *gusanos*, which the Morales family says enhance the flavor. And yes, there is a worm in each bottle.

Unfortunately, tequila's incredible popularity has encouraged mezcal producers to increase production. By 2008, large spirits companies headed to Oaxaca to build commercial distilleries for high-volume mezcal production, just as they have in Jalisco with tequila. In one day, they can manufacture more mezcal than some *palenques* can produce in years, hastening the process with the same industry shortcuts used in tequila production. Ron Cooper told me that a small *palenque* may produce about ten thousand liters per year, while industrialized mezcal diffusers can produce ninety thousand liters in a day!

In my opinion, commercializing mezcal takes away its integrity. In attempting to imitate the commercial success of tequila, modern production methods have subdued mezcal's unique personality, diminishing its characteristic smoke-and-fire flavor. We're seeing a

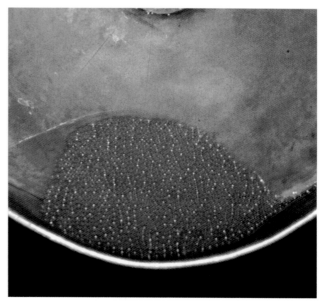

Perlas determine the quality and proof of mezcal.

return to gimmicky, mass-produced inebriants and adulterated, cheap brands that tarnish the reputation of a revered spirit. Aging mezcal and introducing it to barrels used in the repose of other world-renowned spirits seems to be the newest trend—often too long in too much oak. I think that often it extinguishes the fire of mezcal's spirit.

Who knows? Perhaps this gentrified mezcal will appeal to consumers who don't appreciate distinctiveness. But for those agave aficionados seeking a traditional spirit that retains the heart of the maguey and the soul of Mexico, a distillate that sings of earth and fire, artisanal mezcal is particularly satisfying.

REGIONAL VARIATIONS IN ARTISANAL MEZCAL PRODUCTION

+ Species and quality of maguey used and where grown.
+ Design of cooking pit, type of wood used for the fire, and cooking time.
+ Crushing methods (traditional or mechanical).
+ Fermentation methods (natural or commercial yeasts).
+ Clay *ollas* vs. copper pot stills (or crude metal equipment).
+ Single or double distillation for removing impurities.
+ Magic of the *maestro* artisanal distiller.

The New *Mezcalerías*

Today trendsetters revere the magical agave spirit. They gather in American mezcal bars brimming with Mexican ambience and with names like Mayahuel, Las Perlas, Casa Mezcal, and Oyamel. Boutique parlors and cantinas have appeared in cosmopolitan cities across our country, Europe, and Latin America. With *gracias* in part to mezcal visionary Ron Cooper's tireless promotions of Mexico's treasure, patrons now call for single-village mezcals or order signature mezcal drinks.

Surprisingly, mezcal has not until recently been as socially recognized in Mexico as tequila. For many, it was considered Mexican moonshine, the poor man's tipple. Today, with Mexico's flourishing middle class and renewed interest in cultural roots and the spirit of nationalism, mezcal is taking the stage in its motherland, too. Many are drawn to mezcal, finding it reminiscent of disappearing handcrafted tequilas.

Oaxaca City has seen a resurgence of cafés where local intellectuals, artists, and politicos commune while sipping mezcal (often with coffee!), and throughout the country, youthful aficionados celebrating *el mexicanismo* carry personal flasks filled with mezcal from some clandestine distillery.

Mezcalerías, like *pulquerías* of long ago, have become popular. In La Botica Mezcalería in Mexico City, one may order regional mezcals from all around the country. There, as in a *botica* (pharmacy), various kinds of mezcal are dispensed from apothecary bottles holding the "good medicine" within. Mezcal: the alluring intoxicant, restorer of spirits, cure for all ailments (including a broken heart). Mezcal: the gift of the maguey, the treasure of Mexico.

Para el amor
un tequila.
Para el desamor
un buen mezcal.

———

For love
a shot of tequila.
For heartbreak
a lot of mezcal.

Mezcal is on its way to being the next hot spirit! Its authenticity, inimitable flavor, and timeworn traditions have great appeal. The question remains whether artisanal mezcal (and tequila) producers can compete with industrialists. I certainly hope so! And I know which I will choose.

Mezcal in the Kitchen and Cantina

IN THE KITCHEN

Mezcal imparts its smoky, peppery, fruity, complex personality to sauces and other recipes. Guests always love my Negros y Piña a la Criztina, black beans simmered with chiles and chunks of fresh pineapple and mezcal. Add a few shots of mezcal to your favorite chili, stews, soups, sauces, sautés, *salsas picantes*, and meat marinades, too. Splash some in fish and poultry dishes, too.

IN THE CANTINA

I like to savor mezcal from a *caballito* (shot glass) or a traditional small clay cup, given to me by Ron Cooper. For some, the campfire essence of mezcal is an acquired taste—try using half tequila and half mezcal in more delicate drinks.

Substitute mezcal for tequila in many of the drinks in this book—it especially enhances cocktails made with fresh citrus and fruit juices. Use alone, combine with tequila, or use as a "floater" in a traditional margarita or mixed drink. It's delicious in hot punches or in a cup of strong coffee!

Traditional black pottery crock of Crema de Pechuga mezcal from Oaxaca.

Los chapulines:
si los comes,
vuelves a Oaxaca.
Mezcales:
si los tomes,
vuelves a Oaxaca.

———

Grasshoppers:
If you eat them,
You will return to Oaxaca.
Mezcal:
If you drink it,
You will return to Oaxaca.

Grasshoppers and Worms in Oaxaca, Oh My!

Soon after returning from a trip to Oaxaca, we celebrated Día de los Muertos (Day of the Dead) at my home. Friends and I constructed a memorial altar laden with photos and small tokens of remembrance of our deceased loved ones, candlelight, and marigolds.

I'd carried back a bottle of Oaxacan mezcal and *sal de gusano*. Guests drank the mezcal with gusto, many of them bravely accompanying it with a lick of the spicy ground worm salt sprinkled on their palms. A few shots later, I passed around another Oaxacan specialty: small, fried *chapulines* (grasshoppers) spiced with lime and chile. They're tasty, crunchy, salty accompaniments for shots of mezcal, eaten like peanuts. Oaxaqueños sprinkle them on guacamole, scooping it onto warm corn tortillas.

I FIRST TASTED A DONAJÍ COCKTAIL in the early 1980s in Oaxaca. Though I have added my own touches, it remains a favorite of mine today, redolent of mezcal's smokiness, yet tempered with fresh fruit juices. With each sip, I'm transported back to the hills of Oaxaca, to a memorable mezcal quest.

Donají
MEZCAL COCKTAIL

The name "Donají" means "grand spirit" and this drink attests to that. It is the most popular mezcal cocktail in Oaxaca. Like the legend of the princess, many versions exist. I love the rosy color, fresh citrus, and smoky taste of this pretty drink. Sip and savor it, but don't lose your head! Double this recipe, with two lovers in mind.

- Spicy Mexican Seasoned Salt for rim
- 2 ounces freshly squeezed orange juice (blood orange better suits the theme!)
- 1½ ounces pineapple juice
- Juice of 2 small Mexican limes
- 2 ounces best-quality mezcal
- ½–¾ ounces Ruby Pomegranate Syrup
- Garnishes: 1 pineapple leaf (resembles a small agave leaf), a few pomegranate seeds (drops of Donají's blood), or an orange wedge dusted with chile salt

Rub rim of tumbler with a lime half; twirl in seasoned salt. Fill shaker glass with juices and mezcal; add large cubes of ice and shake briefly. Pour into tumbler and add syrup; it sinks to a colorful layer at the bottom of the glass. Place a pineapple leaf vertically in the drink; attach an orange wedge dusted with chile salt to the rim of the glass, and drop in a few pomegranate seeds. Stir into a colorful swirl at the table.

For Donají Shooters: Make a pitcher full of the cocktail; chill, then pour into chile-salt-rimmed shot glasses along with a few pomegranate seeds.

Donají: Zapotec Princess

In Oaxaca, legends abound about the beautiful and beloved Zapotec princess, Donají. My favorite story tells of her love for Nucano, the rival Mixtec prince from Monte Albán, to whom she was given as a peace offering by her father. Concerned for her own people, she sent them a warning, enabling a surprise attack on the Mixtecs. Because of her betrayal, two angry Mixtec warriors kidnapped and beheaded her.

In her memory, the good prince Nucano chose to rule the two tribes peacefully. When a shepherd found Donají's head near the Río Atoyac, he saw that a beautiful water lily grew from her ear, symbolizing immortal love, for that flower never dies.

Dinero, tequila y amor
¡No hay otra cosa mejor!

—

Money, tequila, and the one you adore
Who could ask for anything more?

Blue Agave: The Lily of the Field

ARTISAN MEZCAL producers claim that handcrafted mezcal offers more complexity, character, and pure agave expression than tequila because it comes from various kinds of maguey, often grown in the wild. *Tequileros* have another opinion. They espouse tequila's attributes as a smoother and more sophisticated spirit, carefully regulated by Mexican law to protect its quality and integrity. They believe that agaves grown in different regions may sometimes have harsh, undesirable characteristics.

The blue agave, named for the blue cast of its leaves, is prized for its high sugar content. It is the only agave from which tequila can be made. The blue agave gives tequila its characteristic and inimitable flavor.

To better understand tequila, travel with me through its heartland, through its agave fields. The blue agave flourishes in acidic, volcanic soils, rich in the minerals, ash, and silicate found in five central-western Mexican states (see map, p. 2), most notably Jalisco. Agaves grow everywhere! Iridescent in the sunlight, they shimmer like an unexpected sea, contrasting with the rugged earthiness of the Mexican plains. They cling to hillsides, they're planted in endless rows, or they grow wild in haphazard abundance—even along highways.

Blue agaves ultimately reach about six feet in height and in diameter. Their *pencas*, long, stiff leaves unfolding from a central core, serve as weapons in themselves: each leaf is a formidable blade tipped with a piercing thorn, and leaf margins are lined with tidy rows of small but menacing ridges. They're grown in tight, perilous rows that novices cannot navigate without potential punctures.

I once followed a *mezcalero* (agave field-worker) down a row. He knew to take slight steps sideways to avoid the sharp *espinas*, while I became literally stuck!

Papier-mâché *charro* on horseback from Celaya, Guanajuato, surrounded by shots of *reposado*.

One thorn poked into my shin, another in my ankle, and when I backed up, one jabbed me in the seat of my pants. Timid workers hid their chuckles. One came to my rescue, whacking off the *penca*'s thorns surrounding me with chivalrous machete strokes that came way too close for comfort! Where is the tequila when you need it?

Think of the blue agave as a huge artichoke, its sword-like armor shielding a hidden heart. Buried deep within these protective arms lies a treasure of gold (or silver)—a starchy core that can be converted into fermentable sugars necessary for the distillation of tequila.

Legends abound about how this particular gift of the agave was first discovered. Some say lightning struck an agave in the wild and "cooked" its central core, which then fermented, to the delight of field rodents and farmers who soon reveled in merry intoxication.

More Than a Decade in the Making

Patience is an asset, especially when it comes to growing agaves. These plants take from eight to twelve years to mature! Workers then uproot the whole plant to harvest its central core. Throughout this process, each blue agave demands plenty of personal attention.

Endless rows of agaves, with their plethora of spike-tipped arms, prevent mechanization in the field. Machines cannot maneuver the rows or determine an agave's maturity. Ripened agaves are hand-selected for premium tequilas, just as vine-ripened clusters of grapes are hand-picked for select wines.

However, grapes ripen in three months and their vines continue to produce for many years. The agave, on the other hand, bears its fruit but once in a lifetime. There can be no mistakes! *Mezcaleros* know each agave in a field. Their precise and practiced harvesting techniques have been passed down for generations.

Facing: Blue agave in the red earth, Arandas, Mexico. *Above:* Generations of agave field-workers, Arandas, Jalisco.

Harvesting immature agaves will yield inadequate flavor and sugar content for producing quality tequila. Overripe agaves will rot in the field, representing a decade of waste.

The agave harvest and replanting cycle is continual, and a *mezcalero*'s work is never finished. Year-round care and field maintenance may include: clearing a field; planting agave; controlling insects, fungus, and weeds; fertilizing; pruning to encourage growth of the central core; removing thorny tips; harvesting; transporting the harvested *piñas* (central cores); and then replanting the field. Each grower has his own standards: some use organic methods and sustainable agricultural practices, while others rely upon chemical fertilizers and insecticides. The care given in the field determines the quality of the agave.

Another important field chore is propagation. When the mother agave is about four years old, two to four *hijuelos* or *mecuates* ("children" or genetically iden-

tical offshoots) pop up beneath her protective arms, like aloe vera "pups." They continue to do so yearly for the rest of that agave's life. The midlife offspring are those most prized for propagation, as they are the strongest.

Workers sever these clones from their rhizome roots, choosing the heartiest ones for future planting and discarding weak ones for cattle food. They often plop the small plants into a tall basket attached by a leather strap across a fellow worker's forehead, which allows the burden to rest on his back. (One of these baskets, with its cowhide-enforced bottom, stands inverted as a side table in my home.)

These *hijuelos* are left out of the earth "to get thirsty enough to set roots," a *mezcalero* told me. Then they are replanted in the fields during the rainy season from July through October. Some growers plant the pups in *viveros*, or nurseries, spoiling them for a few years before replanting.

Don Felipe Camarena—always dressed like a gentleman, even in the fields—with a robust *hijuelo* (agave pup) in his hands.

A harvesting basket attached to a worker's forehead with a leather strap.

ONE PLANT, THREE SPIRITS

- The region in which it was grown and the care given to it in the fields. Several producers use organic methods; others attempt to rush growth with chemical fertilizers and pesticides.
- Each producer's own standards. Some use only estate-grown agaves, the cultivation of which is overseen by their own workers. Others purchase agaves from a variety of growers in any of the tequila-producing states.
- How a field is harvested. Some producers harvest an entire field, whether or not all the agaves are ripe; others harvest only ripe agaves. *Piñas* spotted with *sangre* ("blood"-red blotches) indicate ripeness and a good balance of sugar and acidity.
- The skill of the *jimador* (agave harvester). Some use migrant workers instead of experienced hands.
- The *mezcalero*'s keen eye in determining the ripeness of an agave in the field. Now lab testing occurs right in the field, with samples taken from different areas to assure adequate sugar content of agaves.
- Whether or not workers take the time to cut out the spent and bitter *cogollo* from which the *pencas* once sprouted, found at the top of the *piña*.
- The truth of where agaves are grown. Some years ago, during an agave shortage, illegal agaves were shipped from Oaxaca to use in tequila production.

*¡La cosecha de agave
que nunca se acabe!*

—

*May the agave harvest
forever be its best!*

A Necessary Castration

When *mezcaleros* notice an engorging and yellowing of the central core and shriveling of the *pencas*, they know *es tiempo para desquiotar*—time to "castrate" the agave's preemerging *quiote*, or flowering spear. This will concentrate the plant's natural sugars in its core, instead of those sugars being used to nurture the flowering stalk. Within about six months, the agave will be ready for harvest (sometimes *mezcaleros* carve the date in one of the *pencas* as a reminder). Agaves in a particular field usually ripen at the same time because *hijuelos* of the same age were planted there nearly a decade earlier; still, the plants demand a watchful eye, as some may mature earlier or later.

If workers do not sever the *quiote*, it will shoot into the sky, often reaching twenty feet or more in height in a matter of a few weeks. "It looks like a giant asparagus spear on steroids," said friend and *tequilero*

An emerging *quiote* stalk in an agave field (looking like an asparagus spear on steroids); in the background, a truck loaded with *piñas* bound for the oven.

Robert Denton, as we visited a field where one renegade quiote had managed to escape its fate. From a lofty nursery in the sky, enormous branches had simultaneously burst into clusters of yellow flowers, seedpods, and miniature bulbous agaves. In a frenzy of survival of the species, seeds and miniature agaves fell to the ground.

After an agave flowers in the wild, it perishes, leaving its shriveled leaves as fuel for household fires. Sadly, Mexican long-nose bats, *Leptonycteris nivalis*—agave's natural pollinators—have lost their vital food source because cultivated agaves are not allowed to flower. In turn, blue agaves have lost the genetic diversity afforded them from this means of natural reproduction. Instead, agaves now produce the same weaker clones that are less able to adapt to changing environments, making them vulnerable to pests and disease.

In tequila territory, where countless fields full of the same agave clones grow year after year, the effects of monoculture can be devastating. Agaves are particularly susceptible to fungi diseases like *Fusarium oxysporum*, which, when coupled with bacterial infestations, cause the agave to rot, leading to its demise. *Tequileros* fittingly call this syndrome *Tristeza y Muerte*—Sorrow (wilting) and Death.

La Jima (The Harvest)

In the early 1980s, José Fernandez Esparza, a handsome, silver-haired, fifth-generation *jimador* (agave harvester) and field supervisor for Cuervo's vast estates, took me to a field to witness my first agave harvest. (This manner of harvesting remains virtually the same today!) He pointed out the engorged center of an agave, the leaves of which were beginning to yellow and wither slightly. This blue agave had reached its prime: the ceremony of *la jima* could begin.

The tools of the trade are simple: a machete, a shovel, and a *coa* (a half-moon-shaped, sharp-edged tool attached to a long wooden handle), which requires

Sharpening the *coa*.

A beautifully harvested *piña*, Jalisco highlands.

The author's clumsy attempts at "rounding out" a *piña* with a *coa* in Jalisco, while the *jimador* does it with speed and skill.

constant sharpening. Other necessities are tied around the *jimador*'s waist with a rope: a *triángulo* (file), used to sharpen the tools, and a cow's horn filled with lard to keep the hands from blistering.

A *jimador* first whacked away with a machete some of the tough, spiky leaves radiating from the agave's central core. Then he severed its shallow rhizome roots and placed the plant on its side. With a foot on the agave, he rolled it as he swiftly shaved the sword-like leaves from the ripened core, "rounding it out" with accurate strokes from his razor-sharp *coa*.

What remained resembled a gigantic pineapple, about two feet in diameter. Because of its round shape, the *piña* is sometimes also called a *cabeza*, or head. Who ever thought that plucking (or whacking!) away the tough outer leaves of an artichoke or an agave would reveal a delicacy, once cooked?

In fewer than three minutes the agave was harvested. Most *piñas* weigh 70 to 125 pounds, with occasional behemoth surprises. With deft hands and skills passed down for generations, one *jimador* may harvest more than one hundred plants a day, or nearly a ton of *piñas*. If he shaves it too closely, potential sugars may be lost; if not close enough, bitter, waxy residues may prevail. This is no easy task, I guarantee! In my clumsy attempts at *la jima*, the *piña* was mutilated, I nearly lost a foot, and the good-natured *jimador* supervising my efforts almost lost an arm.

In Jalisco, as in many parts of Mexico, more and more workers are emigrating to the United States. As more former *jimadores* and *mezcaleros* have headed *al norte* to work, the art of *la jima* is left to less experienced workers—often from Chiapas and other poor states outside of the blue agave–producing region—who may not have mastered harvesting skills. This loss of experienced workers can affect the quality of the tequila, as *piñas* may be damaged in the field.

Both in fields and in distilleries, workers carry heavy *piñas* balanced upon their heads. Beware of exaggerated claims from some tequila companies that their *piñas* weigh more than two hundred fifty pounds. Imagine hoisting that onto your head! Formerly, workers strapped six *piñas* onto a burro in the field for transport—now piled-high truckloads carry them to the *fábrica* (distillery). Fifteen pounds of *piña* will yield only one liter of tequila. Imagine: after years of constant care, the blue agave yields only about seven liters of tequila per *piña*!

Once a field is harvested, it looks like a ravaged war zone with disturbed earth and amputated *pencas* scattered everywhere, dried and shriveled remains of a decade of growth. Soon it will be time to plant the field again . . . another agave crop to test the mercurial fates.

Before I left the field, I wanted to taste a piece of the *piña*. When sliced, it resembles *jícama* or turnip: crisp and juicy, starchy and white. It has little flavor at this point; in fact, it's quite caustic. Though I had been forewarned that contact with skin causes burning blisters and irritation, I was curious. After a tiny bite, I was in need of a shot of tequila to numb my swollen lip. Fortunately, the distillery was nearby!

Alchemy of an Agave Elixir

Piñas unloaded in the patios of distilleries soon meet their final destiny: the oven! Raw *piñas* must be cooked to convert their inherent starches into fermentable sugars. In artisan mezcal production, *piñas* roast in underground ovens, which impart smoky, earthy characteristics to their flavor. In traditional tequila production, *piñas* cook for several days in *hornos*, large walk-in ovens constructed of adobe brick, masonry, and stone. This slow method of "steaming" helps preserve the natural sugars of the *piñas*.

Join me in a tour of the magical transformation from agave to tequila made in the traditional way—a handcrafted art that is becoming less common. Distilleries today, competing for the burgeoning tequila market, have modernized or built new facilities, taking industrialized shortcuts along the way. Tequila lovers, including myself, believe that a slow, unhurried process produces the best tequila.

Don Felipe Camarena's family had been making Tequila Tapatio for three generations in the agricultural town of Arandas in the Jalisco highlands, a region

Agave Gluts and Shortages

An agave shortage in the 1990s caused a huge increase in the price of tequila. It also led to massive planting of agaves and an ensuing agave glut, which has encouraged all sorts of tequila enterprises. The market became bombarded with brands, too many to count.

By 2011, low agave prices had driven many growers to abandon planted fields (which can lead to disease epidemics) or to destroy their crops. They often replant their fields with annual crops that yield higher, faster returns—such as biofuel corn—instead of agaves that can take a decade to grow. Inevitably, this practice will likely lead to another agave shortage . . . and another increase in the price of a bottle of tequila.

known for growing very large agaves with high sugar content. Mexican tequila aficionados would drive for miles on treacherous roads just to buy this tequila, steeped in heritage and tradition and tasting like what their grandfathers drank.

Tapatio was sold only in Mexico until tequila visionaries Robert Denton and Marilyn Smith (of Robert Denton & Company, Ltd.) discovered it in 1988. They'd been searching for a tequila to export—one with the same fine quality of an artisanal single-malt Scotch or cognac and made of 100% blue agave. At the time, Americans mostly drank "gold" tequilas, *mixtos* blended with non-agave sugars.

They discovered their *tesoro* (treasure) in Tapatío, and they soon exported it as El Tesoro de Don Felipe, named after the titan of tequila of the Mexican highlands. I was delighted when they invited me to visit the distillery at that exciting time, the era of the birth of boutique tequila.

It was a long drive to the town of Arandas from Guadalajara, up steep roads pocked with *baches* (pot-

Upper left: Don Felipe in his beloved red earth. *Upper right*: Headed for the agave fields. *Bottom*: A fine day's work in Arandas, Jalisco.

holes). These remnants from recent torrential rains almost swallowed the car. Don Felipe welcomed us with *caballitos* of El Tesoro Blanco. I tasted a bright, black pepper spiciness that softened to mellow fruit, so unlike the caramel-drenched gold tequila popular at the time. I eagerly raised my glass for more. I could tell this would be a good trip!

Don Felipe was a character. After spending time with him, I understood why *corridos* (narrative ballads sung about heroes and famous personalities) have been written about him. His indefatigable energy, despite his nearly seventy years of age, almost wore me out as we traipsed through his daily inspection of his agave fields and distillery.

At 6:30 the next morning, with Don Felipe behind the wheel of a mud-caked pickup, we bounced down rocky roads, passing fields of corn and agave and little *ranchitos* parceled between stacked stone walls. Don Felipe regaled us with tequila tales, when not stopping to chat and joke with villagers along the way. Everyone knew him!

He followed a truck piled high with *piñas* bound for the distillery, and he stopped frequently to load at least a dozen workers into the back of our truck. Some were shy, with weathered faces shaded by straw sombreros; others, barely teens, had timid smiles. Handfuls of children by the side of the road waved adios.

We pulled into La Alteña distillery, where the truck had just delivered *piñas* into a large packed clay plaza. La Alteña, fittingly called "Our Lady of the Highlands," had hardly changed since Don Felipe's father first built it in 1937. This sprawling adobe brick structure, with a clay tile roof made from the rich, red earth native to the region, blended right in to the landscape. Several covered porches opened to a central courtyard. Immediately, wafts of something sweet baking in the oven lured us inside.

A series of dark, dank rooms with earthen floors awaited us. The rooms were lit only by an occasional lightbulb—fed by a generator because there was no electricity—dangling from the ceiling. All around us, wooden fermentation tanks bubbled, copper pot stills simmered, and *piñas* roasted in adobe brick and stone ovens. The scent permeated the air in a heady stew of damp earth and oak, yeast and steam, and the discernible honeyed aroma of roasted *piñas*.

As Don Felipe led me on a tour, I stepped back in time, envisioning days when Spaniards distilled tequila in a similar ambiance centuries ago. Young workers wearing t-shirts branded with contemporary slogans were the only reminders of a new era.

I watched men carefully stack halved *piñas* onto the slatted wooden floors of an *horno*. This cavernous oven was a room in itself, fortified by packed clay to keep the heat from escaping. Large *calderas* (boilers) produced the steam necessary for leisurely cooking the *piñas* at 140 degrees for thirty-six to forty-eight hours. Afterward, they "steamed" without heat for another twenty-four hours. Nothing was hurried.

A worker handed me a chunk of caramelized *piña* straight from the cooled oven, encouraging me to take a bite. What a remarkable transformation! Who would ever guess that the starchy, white, acidic *piña* that once burned my lips would yield such a sumptuous sweet? Its color and taste reminded me of a baked sweet potato drenched in molasses. Mexicans eat it like candy, nibbling away the sweet pulp from thick, fibrous strands.

From the *horno*, the cooked *piñas* were transported to a large, circular cobblestone pit. There a small tractor (formerly mules) pulled a *tahona*, a gigantic two-thousand-pound volcanic grinding wheel, repetitively around the pit to extract the sweet agave juices from the fibrous pulp.

Once milled, the crushed and soggy brown *bagazo* (agave fiber) and the sweet *aguamiel* (honey water) juices were dumped into five-gallon wooden tubs called *cubetas*. Barefoot and scantily clothed couriers hoisted this heavy cargo upon their heads, balancing it upon a firm nest of worn leather and wrapped rags, then scurried away to empty their load into wooden fermentation tanks. This arduous task had strong-shouldered and seemingly tireless *cubeteros* running to and fro all day long on well-worn clay paths. Some of these *cubeteros* had performed this same duty for more than forty years!

Upper left: Cooked *piñas* spilling from the *horno* (oven). *Upper right*: *Cubetero* carrying bucket of sweet agave juice upon his head to the fermentation tank. *Bottom*: Fermentation tank filled with its golden, bubbly brew.

What I saw next made grape stompers look like sissies. A *batidor* (mixer), clad only in swimming trunks, stepped down a ladder into the fifteen-hundred-liter wooden fermentation tank, to which warm water had been added. Up to his chest in this murky brown bath, he separated the juices from the thick and stringy fibers with his hands and feet! (In days past, naked men did this job because the fermentation corroded their clothes. What about their flesh?) Using a rather primitive instrument called a *pesamiel* (hydrometer), he measured the sugar content of the brew, determining when it was ready for fermentation. It was hard to imagine that the art of distillation would eventually transform this dirty muck into a crystal clear and purified spirit.

Don Felipe explained that a proprietary formula of naturally occurring strains of yeasts and bacteria would be added to promote fermentation. Natural springwater was used as well. The process would take a week or longer, depending upon the weather, as the *mosto* (must) warms to 90 to 100 degrees.

We saw wooden tanks bubbling and churning—dark brown brews capped with rich, golden foam—as live yeasts voraciously feasted upon agave sugars. On the final day of fermentation, the liquid becomes still (*muerto*) and cool. We stopped at a tank filled with *mosto muerto*, where yeast had consumed the sugars, converting them into a mild 4–6% alcohol. I sampled some from the cup of my hand. It tasted rather like warm, flat beer.

Cubeteros carried this *mosto* upon their heads again, emptying it through a wooden funnel into the *alambique*, a long-necked copper alembic pot still glazed with a patina from generations of use. During distillation, the magical alchemy begins. The steam-heated *mosto* vaporizes and then condenses in a cooled coil, separating the alcohols and impurities.

Tequila must be distilled twice, per Mexican law. The first distillation, called *ordinario*, takes about two hours and "separates" the alcohol, producing a 20–30% alcohol distillate composed of three strengths. The *cabeza* (head) and *cola* (tail), at the beginning and end of this distillation, are discarded, removing ethanol and other toxic alcohols, congeners, and impurities.

Only the pure center stream, the *corazón* (heart), is reserved. Distillers originally distinguished the *cabeza y cola* purely by smell (ethanol smells of overripe apples) and viscosity (the tail is heavier in weight), though modern equipment and technicians make this determination today. Don Felipe always left the agave fiber in the still for the first distillation (as do some small-batch mezcal distillers) to intensify the agave flavor. It also adds the extra task of removing the heavy fibers before the next distillation begins.

The second distillation usually takes four hours and "purifies" the alcohol. It is followed by a filtering process, which further removes impurities and elevates the alcohol content to 80–110-proof, ultimately giving tequila its characteristic flavor and crystal-clear color. El Tesoro is bottled at 80-proof to retain more agave flavor. Most other producers distill to more than 100-proof, then add demineralized water to bring it back to the standard 80-proof.

Once tequila leaves the still, it's ready for bottling or for aging in wood into *reposados* or *añejos*. Don Felipe handed me a carved cow horn, the original shot glass, filled with tequila *blanco* straight from the copper still. I raised it to honor him, then brought it to my lips. The essence of agave persevered—the origin of the distillate remained apparent in that unforgettable sip of liquid silver. I remain a great fan of *blanco* (also known as "silver") tequilas for this reason. The quality and flavor of a brand's 100% agave *blanco* tequila determines the profile of that distillery. If you can't taste the agave—if it's harsh or bitter or lacking in flavor—it probably won't get any better with aging.

Don Felipe and I had one more stop: his cellar. As we walked down the stairs, he brought his finger to his mouth with a "shhhh." "Estan dormiendo," he whispered, giggling as he pointed to the "sleeping" barrels—hundreds of them stacked in different stages of aging. Though the distillery seemed primitive, his cellar rivaled those of cognac fame. Unlike many other tequila cellars at that time, his was built underground, with heavy stone walls and a high, arched brick ceiling. His misting system provided cool and constant temperatures and humidity for slowing evaporation from the barrels.

Don Felipe raised his hands to heaven and laughed when he said, "Hay bastante para compartir con los anjeles." (There's plenty still for the angel's share.) The angel's share is that celestial portion of tequila that's lost to evaporation from the barrels during aging.

I visited the distillery again in 2009. Tequilas from this distillery today remain some of the most esteemed tequilas made in the traditional Mexican style. Don Felipe's son, Carlos Camarena, a renowned master distiller, now heads the business. As we stood in the damp cellar amidst those ethereal and almost intoxicating wafts of agave spirits aging in oak, Carlos looked upward and said with a smile, "It's Don Felipe's share." Don Felipe had passed away.

I was touched by a recent note from Carlos that said, "I still remember when you were visiting us and my father would offer you his arm to walk through the agave fields!" (I remember plowing rapidly through treacherous grounds, catapulting over stone walls, and never stopping!)

Production Methods

Tequila production has changed dramatically since my first visits to the land of the blue agave many years ago. Today, even artisan distilleries have converted to mechanized production. Some, like La Alteña, have not lost touch with their traditional roots and still bake *piñas* in *hornos*, use natural yeasts for fermentation, and distill in copper pots.

In most distilleries, conveyor belts now transport materials, and mechanical crushers with big steel blades extract juices, spraying water from rotating metal sprinklers. The *tahona* has mostly become a relic displayed in museums, although a few distilleries still use these grinding mills in small-batch production. *Batidores* no longer submerge themselves in murky fermentation tanks, and stainless steel pipes, instead of men with buckets on their heads, transport liquids.

To meet the increased demand for tequila worldwide, high-volume distilleries implement modern methods to mechanize and hurry the process. They cook *piñas* rapidly (eight to twelve hours) in twenty-

Top: Don Felipe Camarena in the agave fields. *Bottom*: Author and Carlos Camarena raising a traditional cow horn shot glass filled with tequila straight from the still.

to seventy-ton (or larger!) autoclaves, stainless steel steam-fueled pressure cookers. Traditionalists believe such high heat "burns" the flavor of the agave. The slatted wooden floors in traditional *hornos* allow the protective, waxy "bitter honeys" from the outside shell of the *piña* to drip away for discarding. This does not occur with an autoclave and can impair flavor.

An even faster form of processing *piñas* does so without even cooking them. Raw, shredded *piñas* are loaded into diffusers, huge industrial tubular machines. In four to six hours, they extract agave juices by hydrolysis, a process using chemicals, enzymes, and steam to break down the agave's complex carbohydrates (starch) into fermentable sugars. I question what this does to the natural essence of agave. It's like cooking a sumptuous feast in a microwave oven. Brands of tequilas once made in a more traditional manner but now processed in diffusers no longer taste as they once did.

The fermentation process is rushed as well. The fermented *mosto* is piped into 20,000–75,000-liter stainless steel tanks, rather than wooden vats. Commercial yeasts and nitrogen compounds, instead of naturally occurring ones, speed the fermentation process to only two or three days. It is during fermentation that other sugars are added in liquid form to make *mixtos*, those tequilas not made purely from 100% agave.

Distillation also occurs rapidly, in very high volume, and, usually, in giant stainless steel stills or columnar stills (continuous action stills) at very high temperatures. While this distillation process takes much less time than that in alembic stills, it diminishes the pure agave expression and can produce undesirable flavors in the distillate.

Traditional tequila makers use copper alembic stills. Not only does copper conduct heat evenly and efficiently, it also improves flavor by removing sulfurous compounds and other impurities while retaining the character and personality of the distillate. This is why copper stills are used to distill many of the world's other fine spirits. Of course, stainless steel stills are much less expensive to purchase and require less maintenance than copper stills.

Triple (and even quintuple) distillation seems to be the new trend in tequila production, as it has been with vodka. Advocates say it produces a more refined and clean spirit, free of impurities. (Sounds like Mexican vodka to me.) Traditionalists say it diminishes true agave flavor and complexity.

TRADITIONAL VS. HIGH-VOLUME

The elements of handcrafted tequila:

+ Unhurried and artisanal process and limited production
+ Estate-grown agaves
+ *Piñas* cooked slowly in *hornos* (ovens)
+ Cooked *piñas* crushed with *tahona* (grinding wheel)
+ Slow fermentation with wild, naturally occurring yeasts in wooden tanks
+ Double distillation in copper alembic stills, a slow distillation at low heat
+ Preserves flavor, character, and authenticity

The elements of high-volume commercial tequila:

+ Fast and industrialized process and high-volume production
+ Agaves purchased from various sources
+ *Piñas* cooked rapidly at high heat using stainless steel autoclaves, diffusers, and hydrolization
+ Cooked agaves crushed with mechanized grinders and rollers
+ Rapid fermentation with commercial yeasts and accelerators in stainless steel tanks
+ Rapid distillation in huge stainless steel columnar stills at high temperatures
+ Minimizes quality and flavor and maximizes profit

Which manner of production makes the best tequila: those made in small batches in rustic *fábricas* using unhurried, traditional techniques, or those mass-produced in ultramodern distilleries? One method has withstood the test of time; the other reflects the sign of the times. One may argue that immaculate facilities brimming with state-of-the-art equipment and technology, laboratories, and chemists produce a more consistent and regulated product. But is character lost in the more efficient production? I for one think so!

I've wondered how smaller distilleries can compete with industrialists and their slick marketing and advertising. Fortunately, the renewed interest in producing artisanal spirits—those made regionally in limited amounts, like single-malt Scotch and single-barrel whiskey and rum—attracts and delights curious consumers seeking authenticity and tradition along with flavor.

I'll gladly raise a *copita de tequila* to distilleries still producing tequila in the artisanal style!

Tequila Styles, Categories, and Tasting Profiles

Tequila is manufactured in two distinct styles—100% agave and *mixto*, which is blended with other non-agave sugars. It's bottled in five aging categories that range from clear, fresh-from-the-still *blanco* to the ultra-aged *añejo* with its deep mahogany tones. This can be confusing, but tequila is quite versatile, and you'll find a style that suits those who prefer white spirits as well as one for those who favor oak-aged spirits.

Most tequila "houses" (producers) feature the traditional trio portfolio: *blanco*, *reposado*, and *añejo*, and many now offer an *extra añejo* as well. Some offer *mixtos* and 100% agave tequilas within these categories. Imagine the shelf space required!

100% AGAVE TEQUILA (*CIENTO POR CIENTO AGAVE*)

Discerning drinkers demand quality. Paralleling the trend of Scotch connoisseurs switching from blended to single-malt Scotch, tequila aficionados opt to drink 100% agave tequila, sometimes labeled on the bottle as "100% de Agave" or "100% *Puro de Agave*." These tequilas have experienced a record-breaking leap in sales, despite the higher cost.

What Is 100% Agave Tequila?

- Tequila made exclusively from fermented sugars of the blue agave.
- Tequila labeled "100% Agave" on the bottle.
- Tequila bottled in Mexico, under compliance with regulatory laws (a government inspector verifies that no other sugars are added during fermentation).
- Tequila found within the various categories of tequilas: *blanco*, *reposado*, *añejo*, and *extra añejo*.

TEQUILA *MIXTO* (BLENDED)

Mixto tequilas do not say "100% agave" on the label. While some *mixtos* have more integrity than others, many are simply grain alcohol blended with some agave sugars and added flavorings. Some bars and restaurants use these less expensive brands as their "house" or "well" tequilas for margaritas and mixed drinks that have ingredients that camouflage the flavor of tequila. This practice sometimes gives tequila a bad reputation . . . and often gives its imbibers a heck of a hangover!

What Is *Mixto* Tequila?

- Tequila containing at least 51% blue agave, augmented with 49% added non-agave sugars such as cane, *piloncillo* (raw brown sugar), corn syrup, or glucose, added in liquid form during fermentation.
- Tequila with added flavorings and colorings, giving it a "gold" color often mistaken for a result of aging, when usually it is not aged.
- Tequila *blanco* mixed with aged tequila (a few producers actually age their *mixtos* for a better quality product).
- Tequila shipped in bulk at a higher proof for diluting and bottling outside of Mexico.
- Tequila that is not always as strictly governed as other tequilas. Mexican law is striving to control adulteration of product by foreign bottlers who sometimes add other sugars, neutral spirits, and flavorings.
- Tequila that costs much less to make than 100% agave tequilas.

FIVE CATEGORIES OF TEQUILA ESTABLISHED BY MEXICAN LAW

The quality of tequila *blanco* straight from the still determines the profile of the distillery. *Blanco* tequila evolves into these categories: *reposado*, *añejo*, or *extra añejo*.

Aging tequila—the marriage of agave and oak—transforms the youthful spirit into a mature and mellow one with a more complex personality and a rich, golden brown color.

Mixtos and 100% agave tequilas may occur within the categories described below.

Tequila *Blanco*: White or *Plata* (Silver) Tequila

MEXICAN LEGAL DEFINITION:
Tequila fresh from the second distillation, which may be brought to commercial proof with the addition of distilled water.

Blanco tequilas are crystal clear and not influenced by wood or aging, although some producers allow their tequila to "rest" in wood or stainless steel tanks for up to sixty days before bottling.

Quality *blanco* tequilas are spirited and vibrant with vegetal, herbaceous, floral, and citrus notes and a pleasantly peppery bite. I'm a great fan of 100% agave *blanco* tequilas. When pure and untouched, they retain the discernible and innate sweetness and soul of agave, sometimes missing in the aged spirit. Poorly crafted *blancos* may taste fiery and feral. Unfortunately, these throat-searing *blancos* perpetuate tequila's reputation as firewater.

A fine 100% agave *blanco* tequila can be as elegant as an *eau de vie*, as versatile as vodka, and as aromatic as gin, yet it has a unique personality of its own.

Tequila *blanco* is a requisite for classic Mexican margaritas, fruit drinks, punches, and refreshing spritzers. Premium silvers stand alone for sipping. I keep a bottle in the fridge or freezer for hot Texas nights.

Handblown shot glasses adorned with agaves on a *charro*'s sombrero, Jalisco. *Left to right*: Blanco, *reposado*, *añejo*, and *extra añejo*.

Tequila *Joven Abocado*: "Young" Tequila

MEXICAN LEGAL DEFINITION:
Non-aged tequila that acquires its golden color through the use of authorized additives, or that results from a mix of silver and aged tequilas.

Most *joven abocados* are *mixto* tequilas, "mixed" with non-agave sugars. Better known as "gold" tequilas, *mixtos* are made for the North American market, shipped there in bulk for bottling, and not commonly consumed in Mexico. Because of Cuervo and Sauza, nearly everyone's heard about gold tequila. In fact, Cuervo Especial, known as "Cuervo Gold," remains the number one selling tequila in the world.

Because of the rich gold color of *joven abocado*, many assume it's an aged spirit, which gives it a broader appeal. In this category, flavoring and coloring (primarily with caramel, also commonly found in other distilled brown spirits) is left to the discretion of the producer.

"Gold" tequilas remain immensely popular for shooters, margaritas, and mixed drinks because they are less expensive than 100% agave tequilas. I will leave them for those who do not know any better!

Tequila *Reposado*: Reposed (Rested) Tequila

MEXICAN LEGAL DEFINITION:
Tequila "rested" (aged) or softened for a minimum of two months to one year in *roble* or *encino* oak tanks (often holding 20,000 liters) or barrels. Flavorings and coloring agents are permissible, as well as the addition of distilled water to bring it to commercial proof.

There's nothing quite like a good *reposado*! Most Mexicans agree; it's the most popular category of tequila in that country. *Reposados* have a harmonious balance between the natural essence of agave and the subtle influence of oak. The "resting" of *blanco* tequila in wood mellows its youthful and feisty character (but still leaves a discernible peppery bite), while balancing and rounding out any rough edges.

Reposados temper the harshness of unaged tequila, adding hints of oak and subtle spice, yet are not overwhelmed by oak, as are some *añejos*. *Reposados* range in hues from very pale straw color to amber. They're sometimes blended with *añejos* for added color and flavor, yet retain the aging designation of the younger *reposado*.

Reposados are excellent for slow sipping, as well as for mixing in margaritas, mixed drinks, and spritzers.

Añejo: Extra-Aged Tequila

MEXICAN LEGAL DEFINITION:
Tequila aged for at least one year but fewer than three years in government-sealed *roble* or *encino* oak barrels with a maximum capacity of 600 liters. Barrels are sealed with paper stamps, broken only by inspectors who certify the age. Flavorings and coloring agents are permissible, as well as the addition of distilled water to bring it to commercial proof. When tequilas of different ages are blended, the youngest age will be designated.

Añejo tequilas range in color from a subtle amber to a rich brown resulting from longer contact with oak barrels. Some *añejos* are quite luxurious: smooth, elegant, and exquisite. The complex characteristics of oak and agave and the characteristic nuances from barrel aging—depth of aroma, discernible soft tannin, and soft vanilla tones—mingle harmoniously. A fine *añejo* is as memorable as an elegant cognac. At its worst, it's like a bottle of cheap brandy.

The best way to drink *añejo* is from a snifter, which captures the aroma to savor along with the taste. Some pour *añejo* into mixed drinks, lacing them with other liqueurs and added flavorings. But would you pour XO Cognac into limeade? Of course not! If you choose to mix *añejo* into a cocktail, I suggest using it either as a mere floater just to cap the drink or as a splash for depth of flavor.

Extra Añejo: Ultra-Aged Tequila

MEXICAN LEGAL DEFINITION:
This newest category of tequila, established in 2006, labels tequila aged for at least three years as *extra añejo*, though the exact aging time need not be specified on the label. It follows the same aging regulations as other *añejos*, in barrels of maximum 600-liter capacity, and is diluted with distilled water before bottling.

These tequilas can be quite complex and dark in color, due to the characteristics of lingering in the barrel. I find the origin of the spirit—that sweet agave fruitiness—sometimes overshadowed by wood in many of these tequilas. I could almost be drinking another premium brown spirit—cognac, Scotch, bourbon, or whiskey. *Extra añejos* fetch high prices, generally ranging from $100–$200 or more, sometimes because of the quality and time taken for small-batch aging and craft . . . and sometimes just for commercial hype.

TASTING PROFILES

Blanco or *Plata* (White or Silver)

Color: crystal clear and luminous
Aroma of origin intact, with discernible agave fruitiness
Slightly sweet, clean, crisp, mineral
Floral, fruity, vegetal, herbaceous
Tarragon, mint, and anise
Black and white pepper and spice
Citrus peel, orange blossom, lime zest
Tropical fruits
Astringent with a bite, fiery, bright
Dry, medium finish

Joven Abocado

Color: shades of gold
I encourage the consumption of 100% agave tequilas and will leave this flavor profile up to those who choose to compare them.

Reposado

Color: pale straw with pale green or faint rosy hues
Hint of oak, with origin of agave still apparent
Light caramel
Slightly smoky
Cinnamon and spice
Mineral, earthy
Medium to long finish

Añejo

Color: rich amber to mahogany, with copper hues and various intensities
Oak-driven, with richer influence of wood, dependent upon choice of barrels
Aromatic wood and tannins, silky, supple
Cooked agave, spicy, dried fruit
Baking spices, buttery
Smoky, nutty
Vanilla, caramel, cocoa, and spice
Full-bodied, complex, luxurious, round
Long finish

Extra Añejo

Color: dark amber/brown with mahogany hues
Characteristics similar to *añejo*'s
Very oak-driven, heavily wooded
Agave often not as apparent
Buttery, toasty, nutty
Vanilla, toffee, and spice, with sweet tones
Dark leather, wood, earth, tobacco
Velvety, long finish

Fans of vodka, gin, or white rum can substitute tequila *blanco* in cocktails, while those who prefer brown spirits like whiskey, Scotch, and bourbon will delight in the nuances of oak and agave found in *añejo* tequilas. For others who relish a gently reposed tequila, subtly influenced by oak, there is nothing like a good *reposado* to sip and savor.

In the aging of tequila, wood woos agave in a lingering dance. Balance is essential in this harmonious coupling. The sweet and spicy attributes of oak and its rich vanillin (vanilla-like) tones vary from barrel to barrel, depending upon which type of oak is used. The languorous evaporation occurring through the porous wood develops and concentrates flavor. American oak and French oak barrels are most commonly used. Wide-grained American oak barrels offer a sweeter, bolder flavor than the tighter-grained French oak barrels, which allow for a slower integration of fruity, spicy, oaky nuances.

In my opinion, oak often overshadows agave in many exported *añejos*, reminiscent of the early trend of over-oaked California chardonnays. I want an *añejo* to

Don Felipe Camarena's cellar for aging tequila, Arandas, Jalisco.

retain the flavor of the agave that took nearly a decade to grow and to reflect the efforts that went into its production.

Don't always trust that a deep, dark amber-colored tequila, or one that tastes over-oaked, necessarily reflects age and quality. There are many ways to produce color and flavor. The regulated use of colorings and flavorings—such as extracts of natural oak, sherry, vanilla, cocoa, coconut, caramel, chamomile, and citrus—is permissible during finishing stages to intensify and enhance color, aroma, and taste. Upon tasting a popular and pricey *añejo*, I noted the distinct aroma and taste of cocoa and marshmallows. I wanted agave and earth instead!

Some innovative Mexican distillers have introduced novel *añejos*. They've borrowed from the centuries-old art of European barrel aging and blending to craft their own tequilas. They've imported French Limousin oak barrels, once holding cognac, or casks that held Spanish sherry, renowned Bordeaux wines, port, or even Premier Cru sauternes.

As tequila matures in these barrels, it takes on characteristics of those famous foreign elixirs, hopefully retaining the integrity of the agave. The result? A *ménage à trois*! Traditional Mexican tequila crafting, European artistry, and American entrepreneurial marketing have produced some impressive tequilas.

Most tequila aficionados agree that tequila does not age better in the barrel after six or so years. I'd beware of claims of ten-year aging. Tequila does not improve with bottle aging either. So drink that bottle of tequila that you brought back from Mexico or your favorite liquor store—it won't get any better sitting on the shelf!

BARRELS FOR AGING TEQUILA

Barrels previously used for Kentucky bourbon and Tennessee and Canadian whiskey are most commonly used for aging tequila. Since only new white oak barrels can be used in the production of Jim Beam and Jack Daniel's, *tequileros* can recycle barrels at considerably less than the cost of purchasing new ones. Further, the tequila benefits from the flavors these used barrels impart.

Many distilleries have their own cooperage facilities to make or reassemble already-used, wooden-staved barrels. They char the inside of barrels (or purchase them that way), caramelizing the wood, which adds color and flavor as the tequila ages.

New barrels quicken the effect of wood, adding color and intense flavor. However, tequila that ages in new barrels too long can be harsh. They're sometimes first used for *reposados*, which require a shorter aging period.

The quality of the barrels and the conditions of the cellar in which they are stored (controlling humidity and ventilation is vital because of oxidative reactions) will determine the final outcome of the tequila.

Some houses, such as Casa Noble, have garnered acclaim for their single-barrel (limited bottles from one barrel) tequila, a departure from the blending of several similarly aged casks. Other houses offer single- and double-barrel tequilas or select barrel reserves (such as Tequila Leyenda del Milagro). Note that only about two hundred fifty bottles come from one barrel.

THE ART OF BLENDING: A MELDING OF OLD WORLD AND NEW WORLD TRADITIONS

To achieve color, flavor, and complexity, master distillers sometimes blend tequila from different-aged barrels made of different kinds of oak. In doing this, the distiller must also maintain the consistency of the brand. The mastery of the distiller's art is revealed upon that first sip of an *añejo*.

On one of my tequila adventures in the early 2000s, I joined tequila innovators Robert Denton and Marilyn Smith, California winemaker and spirits writer Lance Cutler, and *tequilero* Carlos Camarena in Don Felipe's cellar to taste several separately aged 100% agave *añejos* from distinct barrels. Favorites would be blended into their dream tequila, a concept developed by Smith. Don Felipe and his son Carlos Camarena had also consulted with Alain Royer, producer of the A. de Fussigny line of rare cognacs, for this creation.

Carlos poured us several samples from the barrels. I even had a hand in choosing one for the blend, aged in new French oak, which balanced the sweetness of others aged in bourbon barrels. Once Carlos calculated the proportions needed for blending from the chosen barrels, this mélange aged a few more years in French cognac barrels.

The result? A luxurious five-year aged tequila called Paradiso, at the time one of the most expensive tequilas ever made. It debuted in handblown, cognac-style bottles designed by Smith and Denton. Many other tequila producers followed suit, developing premium *añejos*.

There's Scotch in My Tequila!

For decades, Scotch (called *"Escocés"* in Mexico) has been the preferred tipple for many wealthy Mexicans, who consider drinking it a sign of affluence and sophistication. Perhaps because of this, some distillers want to create that flavor profile in their *añejos*. I am not a great Scotch fan, so I readily detect its aroma and character in some exported *añejos* today.

However, I must admit, a sip from t1 Estelar *añejo* pleasantly surprised me. Master distiller Germán González (of Chinaco fame) ages this tequila in previously used Scotch barrels, producing a memorable *añejo*. It's velvety, with depth and character and an enticing dryness that comes from the barrel, yet it still retains discernible agave fruit.

With the worldwide popularity of premium tequilas, I'm pleased to see many Mexicans who once drank Scotch now realizing the value and flavor of their own national spirit.

Protecting Mexico's National Spirit: Government Regulation of Tequila

Mexicans take great pride in their tequila. To safeguard the authenticity of their beloved national spirit, the government set laws and quality standards in 1978 that are continually updated. These laws distinguish tequila from other mezcals, establishing characteristics necessary for an agave distillate to be called "tequila."

These include designating a controlled territory—an Appellation of Origin—for the cultivation of the blue agave and for the production of tequila (as the French *Appellation Contrôllée* oversees the production of cognac and champagne). The Norma Oficial Registrada Mexicana establishes the legal definition of tequila.

CRT (CONSEJO REGULADOR DEL TEQUILA)

Those tequila companies complying with NORMA standards are certified by the CRT, also known as the Tequila Regulatory Council (TRC), a nonprofit group founded in 1974. It consists of agave growers, tequila producers, bottlers, and marketers, who work together with the Mexican government to enforce regulations regarding tequila production. This includes random, routine inspections of fields and distilleries—which must have on-site laboratories to test all stages of tequila's production—and guarantees that the tequila is aged as stated. Government inspectors apply paper seals to the bungs of barrels, removing them only when the aging is guaranteed. The CRT can shut down distilleries that violate set rules.

Tequila's booming popularity has led to illegal impostors—tequila-like products—especially in China and South Africa. International offices of the CRT in Guadalajara, Madrid, and Washington, DC, continually safeguard tequila's Appellation of Origin around the world.

NOM (NORMA OFICIAL MEXICANA)

The CRT requires an identification number, assigned by the government and printed on the front or back label of each bottle, to trace that tequila to its source. The letters "NOM" and a four-digit number certify that the tequila was made in Mexico and complies with government standards. This NOM identification gives a number for the distillery in which it was produced and the parent company. It does not assure quality; it's simply an identification number. The CRT is striving to enforce regulations on exported bulk tequila not bottled in Mexico.

HOW TO READ A TEQUILA LABEL

Besides the brand name, every tequila label must have a NOM and four numbers designating the distillery from which it was produced, guaranteeing that no other tequila is in the bottle. The front label will also give the size of the bottle (e.g., 750ml), the proof (80-proof or 40% alcohol, or more, by volume), and the category of the tequila (*blanco*, *reposado*, *añejo*, or *extra añejo*). If it is 100% agave tequila, it must say so on the front label and be bottled in Mexico (*Hecho en Mexico*). It may state the name/location of the distillery and the name of the importer.

HAVE SOME FUN WITH NOM!

In 2012, approximately one hundred fifty registered Mexican distilleries produced approximately thirteen hundred or more brands of tequila (with more than two thousand brand names registered). This tells you something! Often, several brands of tequila are made by the same distillery. They will all share the same NOM number.

You can research NOM numbers to learn more about a certain brand of tequila and determine who produces it. I've found the most reliable and updated source is the tequila NOM database found under "Distilleries of Mexico" at www.tequila.net and the accompanying product reviews and photos of bottles. (The CRT also has updated lists to download at www.crt.org.mx.) Enter the NOM number found on the bottle *or* its brand name. Sometimes the NOM only identifies the parent company, instead of the exact location or name of the distillery where that tequila is manufactured. Other times, the name and location of the distillery are cited. Some producers do not have their own distilleries, contracting with established distilleries instead. Also note that NOM numbers may change, as some brands move to other distilleries.

By researching a NOM database, you may find that:

✦ Several tequilas share the same NOM. That one-of-a-kind tequila touted by slick advertising and marketing propaganda may actually be produced in a distillery that makes forty or more brands.

✦ Some distilleries produce tequila only for the domestic (Mexican) market. Some manufacture tequila primarily for export to foreign markets; some produce both.

✦ If you favor/dislike a particular tequila, you may also favor/dislike other tequilas with the same NOM numbers, as they may share "house" similarities in taste.

✦ The origins of a bottle of tequila are identified. It may come from the Jalisco highlands or lowlands, or other tequila-producing regions, like Tamaulipas or Guanajuato.

✦ Tequila companies are owned by multinational corporations such as Brown-Forman, Bacardí, Patrón Spirits, Pernot Ricard, Jim Beam Global Spirits & Wine (Fortune Brands), Diageo, Gallo, and Grupo Campari.

Tequila *Tierra*

I can't begin to review brands of tequila in detail. There are too many of them on the market, with brands coming and going as I write (see Resources at the end of this book for websites and blogs offering reviews, photos of bottles, and NOM numbers). Instead, I'll paint a picture of tequila *tierra*—tequila's heartland—in hopes that it will send you on a journey to discover your own favorite tequilas.

Terroir is the buzzword of the day in tequila circles. Many claim the ability to distinguish the region from which a brand of tequila originates by its taste. I'll replace the French wine term *terroir* (land) with the Mexican word *tierra* because it rolls more gently off my tongue; after all, we *are* talking tequila.

Tierra refers to the land and the merging of natural elements in a particular geographical region: climate, altitude, topography, rainfall, natural water sources, and soil. These give unique flavor characteristics to the tequila produced there. Other factors to consider include: field care, cultivation practices, harvest techniques, and production methods in the distillery. All of these factors can enhance or camouflage the quality and flavor of the tequila's *tierra*.

Agaves grown in regions other than those designated by laws governing tequila production will not have the characteristic flavor of those grown in the acidic, volcanic soil of tequila *tierra*. While there are four other Mexican tequila-producing states—Nayarit, Michoacán, Guanajuato, and Tamaulipas—the state of Jalisco accounts for at least 95% of Mexico's tequila production.

Within that state are the two regions most recognized in the tequila industry: the lowlands and the highlands, each with its own distinct *tierra*. Because of the high altitude there, the term "lowlands" is better recognized as the "tequila valley" by aficionados. Good tequilas come from both areas, with certain profiles unique to each.

The highlands' larger, sweeter *piñas* have been trucked to the lowlands for years for tequila production there. Some distilleries have always used a combination of agaves in their tequilas; they claim this adds complexity and flavor characteristics to their tequila. Therefore, true *terroir* is difficult to ascertain, unless vintage tequila is made from a single estate, like Tequila Ocho (p. 77).

LOWLANDS AND HIGHLANDS TEQUILAS

David Suro Piñera, founder of the Tequila Interchange Project, a nonprofit tequila education organization, and owner of Siembra Azul tequila, explained the significant factors distinguishing these two regions.

Lowlands (El Valle de Tequila)

Tierra: Obsidian, volcanic *tierra negra* (black earth); hilly elevation, ranging from 2,600–4,000 feet above sea level, with temperatures in the average seventies. Fewer agaves (approx. 1,000 per acre) grow in this highly commercialized region than in the highlands.

Piñas: Generally smaller (60–100 pounds), more fibrous, and with lower sugar content than those from the highlands, with an average production of 15-pound yields per liter.

Flavor profile: Bold, dry, spicy, peppery, assertive, herbaceous, earthy, citrus, mineral, astringent, masculine characteristics.

Highlands (Los Altos)

Tierra: Deep, bright red *tierra roja* or *tierra colorada*, rich with iron oxide and minerals; stores moisture for drought. Higher altitude ranges from 6,000–7,300 feet above sea level, with cooler temperatures in the average mid-sixties. The soil here supports approximately 1,600 agaves planted per acre.

Piñas: Generally larger (90–125 pounds) and sweeter agaves than those of the lowlands, with an average production of 12 pounds per liter.

Flavor profile: Round, sweet, fruity, floral, herbaceous, aromatic, citrus notes, and feminine characteristics.

THE LOWLANDS are the home of some of the best-known tequilas: Cuervo, Sauza, Herradura, and Orendain. The mass manufacturing of *mixtos* in this region is evident by the constant procession of stainless steel tankers (down cobblestone streets), loaded with bulk tequila bound *al norte* for bottling in the United States. However, some impressive 100% agave tequilas come from this region, too. In recent years, some distilleries here have been returning to a more artisanal style of production.

The highlands are renowned for handcrafted, small-batch tequilas. However, this Old World style of making tequila is rapidly changing. The surge of interest in artisanal 100% agave tequilas has led to the construction of huge state-of-the-art distilleries by transnational spirits conglomerates. I hope that the time-honored traditions implemented in highlands tequilas will not alter drastically.

As very large distilleries are being built in the highlands, lowland distilleries dependent upon highland agaves may need to look elsewhere for their supply. Generally speaking, distilleries making high-volume tequilas are more apt to outsource their agaves, while smaller distilleries grow their own agaves or purchase them from nearby sources.

To better appreciate tequila and its proud heritage, let's travel through tequila *tierra*. More than 1,200 brands of tequila inundate the market today. I've chosen to mention only a few of the best-known distilleries that first established the industry standards, as well as a few others with innovative (or trendy) production. I trust you'll be inspired to investigate NOMs and discover other brands, tasting them to draw your own conclusions.

JALISCO'S LOWLANDS

I first visited the lowlands with a group of journalists on a tour of La Rojeña, the Cuervo distillery in the town of Tequila, Jalisco, in the early 1980s. We drove from Guadalajara, down the two-lane highway linking Mexico City with the Pacific coast. Fortunately, a profusion of golden sunflowers, green fields of corn, and miles of intriguing hand-stacked stone walls marking parcels of land drew my attention away from the high-speed chase of diesels and dilapidated pickups constantly swerving around our bus. Small roadside stands also distracted me. Vendors sold cowhide flasks, inscribed with drinking *dichos* (proverbs), for filling with tequila; caramelized chunks of oven-roasted agave hearts for sweet snacks; and refreshing *aguas frescas* (nonalcoholic natural fruit punches).

The majestic Sierra Madre loomed on the horizon, and an extinct nearly ten-thousand-foot volcano loomed ahead. The volcano, the town below it, and the potent distillate made from agaves grown all around the valley all share the common name: ¡Tequila! A plethora of colorful, rustic billboards advertising various brands of tequilas promised us that we would soon taste some.

"Tequila" is a derivation of the Náhuatl word *tequitl*, meaning "the place where cutting is done" or the "place where workers toil." Some say it refers to the obsidian once quarried there, though the "cutting" of the agaves seems more relevant today. People still work hard today—arduous days in fields and *fábricas* with little pay, though the tequila industry flourishes.

THE TOWN OF TEQUILA

Within half an hour, we seemed to have stepped back in time. Guadalajara, Mexico's second largest and very cosmopolitan city, seemed far away. The town of Tequila was dusty and rather drab. Near the plaza, the town's charming cathedral and a statue of Mayahuel, the goddess of tequila, each had its own devotees. Lavish haciendas and distilleries were hidden behind thick plaster walls, and townsfolk scurried about the cobblestone streets attending to daily chores.

At that time, distillery tours were unheard of, unless you were an invited guest. Today, the town of Tequila welcomes tourists who come to partake of the magical agave elixir. Tours to distilleries have become a big business; the population of this town has more than doubled since my first trip. Cantinas, curio shops, and liquor stores packed with local tequila brands beckon.

Back then, it was hard to imagine that this lackluster town was home to tequila's founding fathers: José María Cuervo and Don Cenobio Sauza, who remain giants in the industry today. Cuervo first produced *vino de mezcal* in 1795 in the family's La Rojeña distillery, branding it with the image of a black crow (*cuervo*), its namesake. Don Cenobio Sauza later gave the name "tequila" to the local mezcal and claimed to have first exported it to the United States in 1873—and the rest is history!

JOSE CUERVO (NOM 1122): The number one selling tequila worldwide, internationally distributed by Diageo, the British spirits giant. Cuervo lists more than forty tequilas in their lineup, ranging from their signature Jose Cuervo Gold (Especial) to 100% agave tequilas, such as Tradicional Reposado and Reserva de la Familia Extra Añejo, which was released in 1995 to celebrate Cuervo's two hundredth anniversary.

Cuervo also owns (but markets separately) the popular 100% agave brand Tequila 1800, sold in six styles, and the Gran Centenario line, which includes pale pink Rosangel, a *reposado* aged in port casks and infused with jamaica (hibiscus) blossoms. Released in 2008, Maestro Dobel—uniquely blended with three aged tequilas, then filtered to diamond clarity—is the pride of Juan "Dobel" Beckman, the sixth-generation heir to Cuervo tequilas.

SAUZA (NOM 1102): If there's a rooster on the bottle, it's Sauza. Selections include the standard tequila trio, as well as the popular aged Conmemorativo. Sauza has at least twelve brands available, with several aging categories within each brand. Five generations of Sauzas have continued production from La Perseverancia distillery, though Jim Beam Global Spirits purchased the brand in 2005.

Most people have heard about the perennial big seller, Sauza Hornitos. (I'm sorry to disappoint some of you, but the name refers to the *hornos*, or ovens, that cook the *piñas*, not a lusty state of mind.) This *puro de agave* (100% agave) tequila is sometimes considered the workingman's tequila because of its affordability, while Tres Generaciones, a triple-distilled tequila, is their flagship 100% agave super-premium brand.

TEQUILA FORTALEZA (NOM 1493): Called Tequila Los Abuelos in Mexico, pays homage to the Sauzas of long ago. *Cinco generaciones* of distilling in the town of Tequila come to light in this tequila. Guillermo Erikson Sauza turned the family museum distillery into a functioning production once again. In 2002, he produced his first small-batch tequila, using traditional *hornos*, a *tahona*, and copper stills, with plans to use the natural underground caves for his cellars, as they were used in past centuries. I love the Old World style of the bottle that features a replica of a *piña* for its top and a *tahona* on the label. (This tequila is not affiliated with today's Sauza brand.)

ORENDAIN (NOM 1110): One of Mexico's largest commercial producers, Orendain was founded in 1926 by Don Eduardo Orendain. Named in his honor, the ultra-premium brand DON EDUARDO (NOM 1119) was purchased in 2007 by Brown-Forman, the corporation that also owns Tequila Herradura. (Here we see an example of how NOM numbers change.)

ARETTE (NOM 1109): Don Eduardo's successors, brothers Eduardo and Jaime Orendain, produce Arette, a line of highly regarded tequilas, in El Llano distillery in Tequila. Arette reflects Mexican pride, Old World style, and a flavor that celebrates the profile of lowlands tequilas: dry, bold, spicy, yet smooth.

T1 (TEQUILA UNO) (NOM 1146): Germán González, former distiller of the acclaimed Chinaco, created t1, an innovative new line of tequilas, in 2009. The t1 tequilas include: Ultra Fino *blanco*, the 86-proof Selecto *blanco*, Excepcional *reposado*, and Estelar *añejo*, with exciting new editions to come from this true master distiller. González produces his tequilas at La Tequileña, the distillery owned by Don Enrique Fonseca, one of Mexico's largest agave growers, who produces bold tequilas such as PURA SANGRE (NOM 1146).

CASA NOBLE TEQUILA (NOM 1137) charmed Carlos Santana, who became part owner in 2011, paying homage to his Jaliscan forefathers. Casa Noble is produced at La Cofradia distillery, one of the oldest in the lowlands (operating since 1776), which produces over fifty brands. Don Carlos Hernández and cofounder José Hermosillo combine traditional with contemporary methods, such as triple distillation and single-barrel, small-batch editions.

CASA DRAGONES (NOM 1489): Oprah and Martha Stewart love Casa Dragones, created by MTV mogul Robert Pittman and *maestra tequilera* (master tequila *sommelier*) Bertha González Nieves in 2009. Packaged in an exquisite crystal apothecary bottle, with agaves etched in the glass, Casa Dragones comes with a $250.00 price tag. This 100% agave *blanco* is blended with a hint of *añejo*, then pristinely filtered to crystal clear and marketed as a limited edition "sipping tequila."

In an interview with Alexander Perez of Tequila Aficionado.com, Ms. González described the Casa Dragones production process: the juice of *piñas* is extracted *before* cooking, and columnar stills, similar to those used for making vodka, deliver the clean, clear, smooth style of this tequila. Sounds like the new premium agave vodka to me!

REPUBLIC TEQUILA (NOM 1577): Produced in Conquista Agave, a state-of-the-art "green" distillery, Republic Tequila embraces environmental protection policies, using estate-grown agaves and kosher-friendly practices. This tequila, sold in a Texas-shaped bottle (and a taller, Western-inspired bottle), boasts the slogan "Born in Mexico but Raised in Texas."

In fact, it was a Texas cowboy, Tom Nall, product developer for Wick Fowler's 2-Alarm Chili, who partnered with Ken McKenzie, an impassioned California *tequilero* with a Guadalajara bride, to produce Republic Tequila. Republic's three award-winning expressions retain agave fruit, with a bold, peppery kick. And this tequila is organic, certified by the USDA. They also have a line of (refrigerated) all-natural Spirit Blends, made with fresh fruit and sweetened with agave nectar, in Texas flavors like prickly pear and jalapeño lime.

THE TOWN OF AMATITÁN

HERRADURA (NOM 1119) is the tequila with the good luck horseshoe on its label. It was my good luck to taste it, fresh from the still, with Guillermo Romo, whose family had owned the distillery since the 1870s. Its exhilarating burst of flavor—dry and zesty with a bouquet of fresh green herbs, a sparkle of citrus, and authentic agave fruitiness—was indeed a perfect expression of a lowlands tequila.

Bing Crosby thought so, too. He and actor/singer Phil Harris imported the first 100% agave tequila to the United States in the late 1940s: Herradura. Later, Herradura also became the first exported *añejo*.

In 2007, Brown-Forman Corporation, which also owns Jack Daniel's, acquired Herradura for $776 million, an indication of tequila's booming popularity. The company has implemented more industrialized means of production, often to the chagrin of Herradura fans.

Today, Herradura tequilas include the traditional trio, as well their award-winning four-year-aged *extra añejo*, Selección Suprema, one of the first on the market. They've produced 100-proof and more delicate lower-proof expressions, inspiring other distilleries to follow suit with special editions. Their line of Antiguo de Herradura, based upon the original coveted estate tequila served to family and friends, celebrated Herradura's 125th anniversary, while Hacienda de Cristero honors Christian rebels who found refuge at the Herradura hacienda.

EL JIMADOR (NOM 1119): Herradura's sister tequila is a party in a bottle because of its affordability. This 100% agave tequila value brand has reached record sales in both Mexico and the United States. It's a good choice for large batches of fiesta punches and margaritas.

While in Guadalajara, tequila tourists may travel to Amatitán on the Tequila Express train, replete with mariachis and tequila libations, to tour the Herradura distillery. I must say, I'm glad that I got to visit there when it still belonged to the gracious Romo family!

JALISCO'S HIGHLANDS

Los Altos, the highlands plateau of Jalisco, lies directly across the state from the lowlands, stretching nearly eighty-five miles northeast of Guadalajara. When I first visited this area in the late 1980s, our driver had a mission on the treacherous, two-lane winding road: avoiding large trucks zooming down steep inclines. These trucks, piled high with *dulce piñas* grown in the highlands, were bound for distilleries in the lowlands.

As we approached the Los Altos region, we saw the rich, red soil, laden with iron oxide. Ear-popping altitude, crisp, clean air, and massive plantings of blue agaves blending into the sky on the horizon signaled our arrival. Renegade agaves even grew along the roadside.

I was struck by the Old World feeling of Los Altos. This bucolic countryside seemed reminiscent of rural Spain or France. A verdant patchwork quilted the landscape: cornfields and citrus groves, orchards and alfalfa, and rows and rows of blue agave. Picturesque ranchitos with colorful laundry drying on tumbled stonewalls caught my eye, as did stately, historic haciendas, some in sad states of disrepair.

Mexico's Native Firewater?

Mexican tequila historians such as Miguel Claudio Jiménez Vizcarra, author of *Origin and Development of the Agro-Industry of Mezcal Spirits called Tequila*, believe that Amatitán, a town just a few kilometers from the town of Tequila and known for its springwaters, was the birthplace of tequila. Archeological evidence shows that volcanic stone pits carved into the deep volcanic terraces were once used for cooking, crushing, and fermenting agaves. Distillation may have occurred there in clay pots long before the Spanish arrived with their copper stills, making tequila a spirit that's *puro mexicano*. Carl Lumholtz, a Norwegian ethnographer who traveled in Mexico in the 1890s, also found evidence that pre-Hispanic distillation existed, while geographer Henry J. Bruman's research in the 1930s suggested that Filipino seafarers brought stills prior to the Spanish invasion. I look forward to the mystery unfolding as research continues.

Grazing cattle, corralled horses, numerous dairies, and chicken and pig farms indicated that this was Jalisco's ranch and farm belt. Times were slow, cars were old, and many of the *campesinos* were poor. Here, plenty of the locals had fair skin, *ojos claros* (light eyes), and copper-colored hair, a reminder of European colonizers who settled in what once was a remote region. They say that the most beautiful women (*las alteñas*) and the finest tequila in Jalisco are found in Los Altos.

THESE DAYS, traffic seems to be coming from the opposite direction, with sedans filled with international spirits executives and tequila tourists heading for the hills. Four-lane toll roads cut through breathtaking vistas, making forays to tequila country both speedy and scenic. Though the countryside remains pastoral, the towns of Los Altos bustle from the tequila trade. These are the towns that tequila built! Zapotlanejo,

Atotonilco, Arandas, Jesús María, Capilla de Guadalupe, Tepatitlán, and Tototlán—the heartland of highlands tequilas.

Once, distilleries here were small and family-run, known for traditional, handcrafted methods of production. Like those in Oaxaca who travel to far off *palenques* (outdoor distilleries) to find good mezcal, tequila aficionados long braved poor roads in order to purchase the highly regarded Los Altos tequilas—some of which set the stage for the boutique tequilas that emerged in the late 1980s.

Today, some highlands distilleries strive to bridge the gap between traditional methods and modern technology. Their challenge is to do this harmoniously, with a gentle evolution that will ensure steadfast quality. Some will do it with grace and style; others, *sin gracia*, may soon become dust in the wind, not living up to their own promotional hype.

A lovely vista on Carlos Camarena's agave estate outside Arandas, Jalisco.

THE TOWN OF ATOTONILCO EL ALTO

Atotonilco el Alto, an hour drive from Guadalajara, is my favorite of the highlands tequila towns. Its beauty is often commemorated in song.

> *En ese Atotonilco con naranjos en flor,*
> *Parecen las muchachas angelitos de Dios.*
> *Son más lindas que una canción*
> *De esas que son puro amor.*

> ——

> *In Atotonilco where orange trees bloom,*
> *The girls look just like God's angels.*
> *Prettier than any love tune.*

"ATOTONILCO" (TRADITIONAL SONG BY
JUAN JOSÉ ESPINOZA, 1890–1974)

When I first visited this seventeenth-century colonial *pueblo* with its glimmering gold-domed cathedral in the early 1980s, Atotonilco seemed unaccustomed to a lone female tourist—especially one in search of tequila. What I failed to mention in the first edition of this book was that I was the only guest in the only hotel. Only one lightbulb hung from the hallway ceiling. An inebriated doorman, asleep on a hard bench in the tiled lobby, was the only other inhabitant that night. I wish he'd shared some tequila—he snored loudly through what seemed like an all-night tolling of church bells.

Today, this charming town, with rambling, hilly cobblestone streets and a lovely *zócalo* (plaza) with its ornate iron bandstand, has open-air coffee shops (see p. 191) for sampling the local favorite caffeinated brew, good restaurants, and pleasant new hotels. It's abuzz from all of the excitement of the tequila industry and the new distilleries.

Highland's red earth and blue agave, Jalisco.

ONE PLANT, THREE SPIRITS

Real Campestre, the intimate, family-style alfresco restaurant that I'd visited in the 1980s, has today become a destination dining spot, emanating true Jalisciense style, with capacity to seat hundreds of guests. Mexican families and tourists, as well as wheeling and dealing tequila businessmen, linger over afternoon-long meals, rich with traditional fare . . . and plenty of local tequila. Strolling troupes of mariachis serenade, and patrons often sing enthusiastically along.

LET ME TELL YOU ABOUT some of the tequilas from Atotonilco. In 1992, brothers Eduardo and Francisco González commemorated their father with a tequila bearing his name and the year he established his La Primavera distillery. DON JULIO 1942 (NOM 1449) took the United States by storm with its smooth flavor and elegant packaging, becoming one of the top five best-selling tequilas. In addition, TRES MAGUEYES,

After a few shots of tequila, the author joined a mariachi band at Real Campestre in Atotonilco.

the tequila first produced by Don Julio in 1942, remains one of Mexico's best-known brands. Diageo, one of the world's premium spirits distributors, now distributes Don Julio tequilas, along with Cuervo.

I REMEMBER VISITING El Centenario, the distillery founded by Don Ignacio González Vargas (Don Julio's brother), in the 1980s. I watched in awe as TEQUILA 7 [SIETE] LEGUAS (NOM 1120) was made much as it was hundreds of years ago. Soon after my visit, 7 Leguas partnered with Patrón, and the rest is history: the boutique 100% agave business skyrocketed.

Today, although Patrón has its own mammoth facilities nearby, 7 Leguas is once again family-run. Dedicated to preserving quality and tradition, the distillery has reverted to its original formula. The

Copper alembic still, 7 Leguas distillery in Atotonilco.

highly respected Lucretia de Anda de Hernández, one of only a few *tequileras*, and her brother Juan Fernando González de Anda combine their agave-growing and production expertise. They've also built a modern distillery called La Vencedora.

THROUGH PROVOCATIVE advertising, almost everyone knows the name: Patrón. It's the tequila that gave *all* 100% agave tequilas international visibility; in fact, the Patrón Spirits Company created their brand specifically for the export market. PATRÓN (NOM 1492) sells more ultra-premium tequila worldwide than any other producer—more than two million 9-liter cases of tequila in 2010 in the United States alone, excluding additional global sales. Rappers and rockers sing about it. It's the tequila that reflects the sign of the times: contemporary, celebrity-driven, and chic.

On the outskirts of town, the Patrón estate seems to take up most of the Atotonilco Valley. When I visited in the summer of 2010, an armed sentinel greeted us. Agaves and *tequileros* are a precious commodity in these perilous times in Mexico. I have heard of threats, of *tequileros* held for ransom, as well as of truckloads of mature agaves stolen from fields in the night. From the guard post high on a hill, the Hacienda del Patrón far below looked like a grand French chateau, surrounded by countless rows of agaves instead of vineyards.

As we approached, I thought it looked more like a lavish Beverly Hills mansion, a rather surreal image in the midst of rural Mexico. Once inside, I could imagine a dazzling Hollywood beauty descending the spiral staircase to awaiting cameras and lights in this cinematic ambiance. A knowledgeable guide answered questions as she toured us through a demonstration hall where big stone *hornos* and piles of plump and perfect *piñas* sat like props in an elaborate stage setting. In the bottling plant, encased behind glass like a celebrity chef's kitchen, workers in color-coded polo shirts put the finishing touches on the world-famous handblown, individually signed Patrón bottles.

We did not visit the distillery. Instead, we were diverted to a balcony lounge overlooking lush gardens and fountains, where we sampled tequila instead of watching it being made. We sipped liquid gold and silver from snifters: Gran Patrón Burdeos, aged in Bordeaux barrels and retailing for nearly five hundred dollars a bottle, and Gran Patrón Platinum (for about half that price), both bottled in fine crystal. How tequila's image has changed over the years!

In 2009, *Forbes* listed John Paul DeJoria, co-founder of Patrón *and* Paul Mitchell Systems (salon hair care), as one of America's richest men, thanks to those well-quaffed (and/or well-coiffed) consumers.

Along with silver, *reposado*, and *añejo*, Patrón also bottles the famous Atotonilco coffee extract, fortifying it with tequila, under the name "Patron XO Café." They have released a new version, blended with dark cocoa, called "Patrón XO Café Dark Cocoa." Their triple sec, Patrón Citrónge, is widely used in margaritas and mixed drinks.

FOLLOWING IN THE FOOTSTEPS OF PATRÓN, many highlands distilleries now manufacture 100% agave tequilas primarily for distribution to upscale foreign markets, instead of for consumption in Mexico. State-of-the-art distilleries have popped up throughout the highlands region, many owned by big-name international spirits companies: Seagram's (one of the first), Campari, Bacardí, Rémy Martin, Jim Beam Global Spirits & Wine, and Diageo (distributor of Cuervo). Even Gallo joined the tequila troupe!

Small entrepreneurs have joined the bandwagon, partnering with existing distilleries (or building new ones) in the hilly environs of the "golden triangle"— municipalities within Arandas, Atotonilco, and Jesús María. Sprawling modern-day haciendas and ranchos built by *tequileros* dot the countryside in this tequila *tierra*, surrounded by ever-present agave estates.

Tahona grindstone in the 7 Leguas distillery in Atotonilco.

The town of Arandas, the hub of the highlands tequila-producing region, lies about a half hour away from Atotonilco el Alto and eighty-two miles from Guadalajara. It has an even higher altitude than Atotonilco—reaching 7,300 feet in some places. This busy ranching and farming community reminds me of a dusty West Texas town. Farm and ranch supply stores abound. Shops sell *vaquero* attire: boots and handcrafted belts intricately woven *de pita* (of agave fiber) in macho Mexican motifs—*toros y víboras, águilas y nopales* (bulls and snakes, eagles and cacti). Rows of new and used car lots line the road leading into town. Shiny pickups reflect these changing times, suggesting the newfound affluence that tequila's popularity offers.

Arandas boasts the second-highest church steeple in the world, that of a sister cathedral to Lourdes Cathedral. Its bell—the largest in Mexico—was mistakenly crafted too large to fit inside the steeple; instead, it now clangs from an arch that had to be constructed outside the church. Of course, the cathedral is a big tourist destination, but reverence for tequila now brings other worshippers to town.

Some come just to pig out at Jaime's Carnitas, renowned for its regional fare. This roadside restaurant/tequila *cantina* serves platters of melt-in-your-mouth *carnitas* (bites of fried pork), crispy *chicharrones* (pork cracklings), *chamorros* (succulent shanks falling off the bone), and just about any other kind of pork imaginable, with sides of guacamole, quesadillas, and *frijoles charros*. Walls lined with hundreds of bottles of tequila and rousing mariachis keep patrons happy for hours in this festive Jalisciense setting.

Others come just for the tequila. Colorful signs painted on the walls of many shops advertise local brands. *Vinos y licores* (liquor stores) pack their shelves with local tequilas—some in bottles, some in small souvenir barrels—and plenty of tequila memorabilia for tourists. Several new, trendy boutique hotels and restaurants built by tequila families welcome visitors and those in the tequila trade.

DISTILLERIES ABOUND in Arandas. Tequila's founding fathers here were Don Felipe Camarena of Tapatío and El Tesoro de Don Felipe fame and Don Pepe Hernández of Centinela, whose ancestors built the first distillery there in 1904. Strong rivalries developed to see who could maintain the best cellar and produce the *tequila más típico* of the region. Both have been known to produce award-winning *blanco*, *reposado*, and *añejo* tequilas, fine tequilas full of complexity and the fruit-forward agave flavors representative of the highlands.

CENTINELA (NOM 1140): Tres Años, a super premium *añejo* barrel-aged for three years, is full of highlands sweet agave flavor, yet silky and spicy. It is the pride of this family-run distillery. CABRITO (NOM 1140), with the goat on the label, is Centinela's value house brand. It has taken off remarkably in U.S. markets, competing with Cazadores, the tequila with the big buck on the label. (Don't confuse your animal life!)

ALTHOUGH CAZADORES (NOM 1487) implements diffusers and columnar stills to produce volumes of tequila in an efficient manner, they still adhere to a special tradition. From loudspeakers in the fermentation area, they play Mozart, insisting it soothes the yeasts with harmonious vibrations!

Cazadores has become one the largest producers in the area. Founded by the Banuelos family in 1973 and later partnered with Bacardí, Cazadores boasts a new, ultra-modern distillery. Originally producing only *reposados*, Mexico's most popular tequila, they now have a full line, using new oak casks for their aged products to give them characteristic flavor.

Rather than creating a value house brand—like Centinela's Cabrito or Herradura's El Jimador—Cazadores went in another direction. They created a super premium, triple-distilled brand, CORZO (NOM 1487), presented in a very handsome flask that pours from a spout like a waterfall.

EARLIER, YOU READ ABOUT Don Felipe Camarena's distillery, La Alteña, "Our Lady of the Highlands." It remains one of Mexico's revered distilleries. His sons, Carlos and Felipe, keep his innovative traditions alive, always trying something new, while adhering to artisanal production. (Don't confuse them with their cousins, who joined forces with E. & J. Gallo Winery to produce FAMILIA CAMARENA TEQUILA [NOM 1456] with a big, commercialized push in the United States.)

Don Felipe's heirs have made sure that his cellar remains legendary. Carlos, a third-generation master distiller of award-winning tequilas, stands as steward of TEQUILA TAPATIO and EL TESORO (NOM 1139), tequilas made "by hand and with heart," he told me proudly.

Though they sold the brand in 2010 to Jim Beam Global Spirits & Wine, they will continue to make El Tesoro for them. Meanwhile, Carlos always has surprises in store—like collaborative editions with renowned French spirits producer Jean Sebastian Robiquet—and exciting new endeavors with his brother, Felipe.

FELIPE CAMARENA, Don Felipe's namesake, partnered with Tomas Estes, noted European restaurateur and tequila aficionado, to create TEQUILA OCHO (NOM 1474), produced at Tequilera Los Alambiques ("the copper pot stills"), a Camerena family distillery. This impressive line of tequilas comes from agaves grown on single *ranchos* with various microclimates found on Camarena estates. Like vintage wine made from grapes grown in one year, each of these tequilas designates the year and the estate from which it came, in a true testament of *terroir*.

You'll find that each small batch of vintage tequila tastes quite different from those from other *ranchos*. Such diversity makes this tequila special, sought out, and rare, a true gem for tequila aficionados. I suggest sipping Tequila Ocho neat, instead of mixing it, to enjoy its distinctive nuances.

With Felipe, I sampled a 2010 Tequila Ocho Plata from the Los Corrales estate in Arandas and was delighted by its viscosity, bright pepperiness, and agave-fruit forwardness in the true Camarena style. In my opinion, some *añejos* get overshadowed by oak, losing true agave expression. But I'll tell you, the 2007 Rancho El Vergel has me sipping *añejo* with enthusiasm and delight! Its color is rich and golden in comparison to the many dark brown *añejos*, aged in the "whiskey" style of other brown spirits that are popular today. It still sings of agave, sweet and fruity, yet balanced with oak and spice and a discernible earthiness. Yes, I'll gladly have another sip.

DAVID SURO PIÑERA, producer of SIEMBRA AZUL TEQUILA (NOM 1414), crusades continually to educate tequila enthusiasts, bartenders, and mixologists from his base in Philadelphia. He founded the nonprofit Tequila Interchange Project for this purpose. The Project is a network of professionals engaged in promoting and protecting tequila culture in Mexico and abroad. He's also banded with tequila academics in Mexico to

---

Tequila Tapatio Comes to the United States

Two families of artisanal master distillers have joined forces: the Camarenas (Don Felipe's sons, Carlos and Felipe) and the Karakasevics, who operate the distinguished Charbay Winery & Distillery in Napa Valley. As of 2012, Charbay became the U.S. importer of Tequila Tapatio (starting with their *blanco*), the Camarena tequila originally sold only in Mexico. The Karakasevics are the first Americans to distill tequila in Mexico, using their artisanal distilling techniques passed down for thirteen generations. They created CHARBAY BLANCO (NOM 1474), an elegant, herbaceous *blanco*, peppery, yet full of sweet agave flavor, double distilled in copper alembic pots at the Camarena distillery.

research and preserve tequila traditions. This Guadalajara native is also owner of the lovely Tequila's Alta Cocina, an authentic Mexican cuisine/tequila bar and restaurant in Philadelphia, where tastings are often held to celebrate tequilas.

Siembra Azul, a small-batch tequila, has become quite popular among mixologists wanting a 100% agave tequila that is round and smooth, full of highlands agave flavor, affordable, and quite mixable. It's produced by third-generation *tequilero* Feliciano Vivanco in Arandas, who also produces several other tequilas for export.

From the highlands' hotbed of Arandas come other tequilas made primarily for export. Trendy brands include Cabo Wabo, Espolón, Avión (made famous on the MTV show *Entourage*), and Corazón de Agave (the tequila in the long-necked bottle with a heart in an agave on the label). Headquartered in Austin, Texas, Ambhar, with its elegant bottles and 5x distillation, aims toward high-end consumption. Tequila 1921 has become quite popular, too. The Reserva Especial Añejo line now sits longer in American oak for greater depth of character, and 1921 Tequila Cream, full of vanilla cream, caramel, coffee, and cinnamon flavors, will delight after-dinner sippers.

DON PILAR (NOM 1443): Don't miss the *extra añejo* and other expressions from this *tequilero* and highland *caballero* (horseman) from San José.

THE TOWN OF TEPATITLÁN

Tepatitlán, a large, industrialized highlands agricultural town, lies to the northwest of Arandas. Nearby is Casa San Matías, a highly regarded tequila house. Operated by esteemed *tequilera* Doña Carmen López de Villarreal de Román, this distillery, with more than one hundred twenty years of tradition, produces TEQUILA SAN MATÍAS (NOM 1103) and the value brand, Pueblo Viejo, full of true Mexican style and flavor typical of the highlands—lots of agave sweetness and a nice balance of oak and agave in the *reposados* and *añejos*.

Signature very tall cobalt, gold, and orange bottles or clear glass bottles with handblown piñas within showcase the hip MILAGRO (NOM 1559) tequilas. They are especially known for triple-distilled Select Barrel tequilas—*blanco* (mellowed in French white oak for thirty-five days), *reposado*, and *añejo*.

Other Regions in Tequila *Tierra*

Though most tequilas are made in Jalisco state, two other regions produce tequilas of special interest.

TAMAULIPAS

In the early 1980s, spirits consultant Robert Denton tasted a tequila at the Tijuana horse races that sent him trekking to Tamaulipas just to find it. It was a long trip. Unlike most tequilas made in Jalisco and nearby environs, the tequila of his quest was distilled in the state of Tamaulipas, which borders Texas and the Gulf of Mexico.

One can't help but wonder how Mexican law altered its denomination of origin to include this state, as the other tequila-producing states are linked together on the other side of the country. It helped that the founder of this tequila, Guillermo González Díaz Lombardo, was a former head of the Mexican Department of Agriculture and the great-grandson of a president of Mexico, Manuel González (1880–1884). As General González, he had led a cavalry of wealthy landowners and their workers. These rebels, called "Chinacos," defended Mexico in the War of Reform in 1850, riding with kerchiefs wrapped around their foreheads. They say the Chinacos were Mexico's first *charros sin sombreros*.

By 1977, Don Guillermo had already planted agave estates to sell to a tequila producer, who backed out of the contract. With consultation from Guillermo Romo of Herradura, he built La Gonzaleña and turned those agaves into gold. Tamaulipas became a legal tequila-producing state.

At the time, La Gonzaleña produced a brand called "Caliente" (*blanco*) as well as one named "Chinaco" (*añejo*). Denton found CHINACO (NOM 1127) even better than he imagined—lush, spicy, elegant, and full of agave flavor. With his partner, Marilyn Smith, these true tequila pioneers changed the image of tequila and produced the first super-premium tequila *añejo*. They presented this handcrafted 100% agave tequila in signed and numbered handblown bottles, setting the trend for singular tequila containers.

The year was 1983. Denton and Smith introduced the luxurious and elegant Chinaco as they might a fine cognac, to be served in snifters instead of shot glasses. Using their expertise in the single-malt Scotch and fine spirits industry, they launched tequila as a premium spirit. It took America by storm, especially in Hollywood and high-end circles. Other tequila entrepreneurs followed suit, resulting in the proliferation of high-end tequilas today.

Chinaco matched the spirit of its namesake rebels: bold, assertive, sought after, and elusive. Though Chinaco was released in *blanco*, a gorgeous *reposado*, and *añejo* expressions, Don Guillermo and his four sons could not keep up with the demand. The distillery shut down within a few years (with stories about hijacking of precious cargo and counterfeiting of bottles), then opened again, but without one of the sons.

Highly regarded master distiller Germán González, Don Guillermo's son, left Tamaulipas for the Jaliscan lowlands. There he uses the distillery of Don Enrique Fonseca, Mexico's second-largest agave grower (with agaves grown mostly in the Atotonilco area), to produce Tequila t1.

The first "tequila ambassadors" to educate Americans about tequila and change its image, Denton and Smith have since retired. The glory days are over, but the legend survives. The González brothers still produce Chinaco and have unveiled Chinaco Negro Extra Añejo (five-year aged), with each bottle representing an individual cask selection.

A historic hacienda in the town of Penjamo in Guanajuato, a state bordering Jalisco, is home to tequila CORRALEJO (NOM 1368), one of Mexico's oldest tequilas, made since 1775. It's also the birthplace of Miguel Hidalgo, the priest whose "Grito de Dolores" battle cry started the Mexican Revolution and made the sixteenth of September a day famous for tequila revelry on both sides of the border today. Good excuse to drink tequila!

Corralejo's trio of stand-out-on-the-shelf tequilas comes in distinctive, long-necked red (*añejo*), white (*blanco*), or blue (*reposado*) bottles. They also offer a new edition, a triple-distilled *reposado* produced by Don Leonardo Rodríguez Moreno and his family.

Bottles and Brands
Selling the Bottle Instead of the Tequila?

Every time I walk into a liquor store, it seems a new bottle of tequila is making its debut, dressed up in fancy labels and ready to party. Some look classy and elegant, others flamboyant and trendy, and some downright tacky. Others present themselves in an understated fashion, exuding confidence about what lies within.

With so many tequila bottles on the shelf, each brand competes for attention: handblown glass bottles and crystal decanters, handsome flasks bound with leather, voluptuous containers, and sleek, long-necked bottles, all wanting to be the chosen one.

Some stand out in cobalt or other vibrant hues, others hide within painted glazed pottery crocks or artfully designed boxes. Glass *piñas* or agaves sparkle within a few bottles, and family crests etched into the glass adorn others. One comes in a colorfully painted folkloric Day of the Dead *calavera* (skull), and another in a bottle shaped like the state of Texas. You'll find organic tequilas and kosher tequilas, too, and even a tequila sold in a bottle encased in a forged silver armadillo shell fetching $9,000!

Trendsetters for a New Generation: The Birth of Boutique Tequilas

Chinaco's raging popularity sent Robert Denton and Marilyn Smith looking for another artisanal tequila. The pair went on to produce the popular brand El Tesoro de Don Felipe in 1988 with the Camarena family.

I've been fortunate to join them on many early tequila escapades, when roads were rough and distilleries were quite primitive. I watched them tirelessly work to change tequila's image in Mexico and the United States, creating awareness of 100% agave tequila, honoring the true spirit of the agave. Their innovative marketing and distinctive hand-numbered, limited edition bottles set the trend for artisanal, small-batch, boutique tequilas.

In 1987, the year before I first visited La Alteña with them, on a solo adventure I had found another rustic distillery in the highlands town of Atotonilco. It still made tahona-style tequila in the old-fashioned way. Its founder, Don Ignacio González Vargas, whose family had been *tequileros* for three generations, named his tequila 7 Leguas after Pancho Villa's stallion, and it was highly regarded throughout Mexico.

California entrepreneurs Martin Crowley and John Paul DeJoria liked it, too. They bought the brand and changed its name to Patrón, bottling the tequila in a squat, handblown bottle with a big round cork that's become famous. The Patrón partners, with their backers, poured money and ingenuity into marketing. Crowley is now deceased, but Patrón has gone on to build one of the largest commercial tequila empires in the industry, a model for marketing and production that many strive to emulate, especially large spirits conglomerates that have acquired brands once owned by Mexican families.

Though Bing Crosby was the first celebrity to promote tequila, Van Halen's former lead singer Sammy Hagar continued the trend with Cabo Wabo. Vince Neil of Mötley Crue, Billy Gibbons of ZZ Top, Justin Timberlake, Carlos Santana, and George Clooney promote their own tequilas, as do celebrity athletes, from champion surfers to NFL and NBA stars to race car drivers.

Many tequila marketers seem to think their brand needs a gimmick. (And people think the worm in the mezcal grabs attention?) Often, I fear customers are paying more for the bottle than for what's inside. Surely many of these tequila bottles will become collectibles, folk art in themselves, but with so many brands, a lot of space will be needed to house such a collection!

By the time this book is published, many new brands of tequila will have appeared, and some may not have succeeded in this highly competitive industry. I'm sure you'll find plenty of brands to keep you busy tasting, researching, and concocting lively cocktails *y comida.*

¡TEQUILA PURA MEXICANA!

Many popular brands of Mexican tequila are not exported, though some are making their way across the border. Labels on these bottles embody the spirit of tequila: bold, macho, and alluring (as I like my tequila!). Black stallions, *charros* on horseback, fighting cocks, wild bucks, bearded goats, Mexican eagles, and formidable agaves. Depicted in a rustic manner, they contrast with the slick labels found on bottles bound for U.S. markets.

TEQUILA FOR *NORTEAMERICANA* PALATES

Just as "gold" tequila was made for the U.S. market, it seems that many tequilas exported today are also made to suit North American palates. They have a different flavor profile from many tequilas sold in Mexico. In my opinion, some exported tequilas taste sweet, with exaggerated aromas and flavors of butterscotch, vanilla, and caramel, which some mistake for "smooth." Remember, per Mexican law, colorings and flavorings are admissible in the "finishing" of a tequila.

What's most important is what tastes good to you. It's not necessarily the price or the pretty packaging, but quality and taste. What's your preference? Do you want to drink the newest tequila that's all the rage or one that's tried and true? Do you want your tequila to reflect Hollywood . . . or Mexico? Believe me, there's a tequila out there to suit every personality!

Certain brands of tequila are not always easy to find, especially those made by smaller producers. Others are distributed only in large cities, or only in a few states (the border states of California, Texas, and Arizona claim the largest selections). Some tequilas have private brand labels, available only in select stores and cities. Look for specialty tequilas for purchase online.

Tequila Trends

Who would have ever guessed? That agave elixir I sipped from a cow's horn in a rustic distillery more than three decades ago has become one of the world's most popular spirits today. A million cases of tequila sold in 1973; nearly12 million cases sold in 2011. Americans and Canadians love it! Passionate tequila enthusiasts quaff it in Europe and Japan, Australia and South Africa, China and India. Throughout many parts of the United States, the margarita has become the number one mixed drink, eclipsing even the classic-yet-trendy martini. Tequila and mezcal aficionados now call their shots in bars and restaurants, savoring it while paying prices similar to those for fine cognac.

It seems that every few years, tequila reinvents itself. It's almost as if the industry needs to promote the newest agave harvest with a production ploy (though tequila trends seem to be happening more than once in a decade).

TRENDS TO FORGET

For some, the south-of-the-border mystique of tequila still evokes images of dust and bravado, barroom brawls, and the *uno-dos-tres* ritual: a lick of salt, a swig

of a cheap *mixto*, and a bite into a wedge of lime. Some survivors of this sophomoric rite of passage are still trying to get over this stereotypic image and their first experience with tequila. Regrettably, this ceremony seems to continue into successive generations.

TRENDS TO REMEMBER

Fortunately, during the early 1990s, tequila's golden era, 100% agave came into the limelight and started changing people's minds about tequila. Boutique brands proved that finely crafted tequila could compete with other quality world spirits, and their craft was reflected in the cost. Trendsetters blended the best of Mexican and European traditions to create an even more noteworthy New World spirit.

MASS-MARKET TEQUILA TRENDS

Tequila's newfound respectability led to the next ongoing trend: an era of mass commercialization and marketing, often based on more hype than heritage. Too often, the bottle outshines the tequila within. Rock stars and celebrities tout and/or own brands, and growing demand for tequila has prompted a competitive advertising and marketing frenzy. By 2012, an industry once dominated by a few family distilleries now boasts more than one thousand brands bombarding the market and crowding liquor store shelves, with more bottles unveiled monthly. Giant spirits conglomerates have industrialized tequila, and this development is reflected in its quality and flavor.

PRODUCTION TRENDS

Producers just can't seem to let tequila be. They tweak it. They tame it. They try to turn it into something else. They give it names like "cristal" or "platinum," "ultra" or "super-premium." Some producers color it pink to try to appeal to some women or flavor it with fruits and other essences to mirror popular flavored vodkas. Others bottle it at 100–110-proof to pack a wallop! It is now often triple or 5x distilled and/or put through many filtrations. Some popular *añejo/reposado* blends have been filtered back to clarity (like Cuervo's Maestro Dobel Diamond, Don Julio 70 Añejo Claro, and the very expensive Casa Dragones). I'm baffled as to why they would want to remove the color and character that comes from aging *reposados* and *añejos* in oak, only to revert it once again into a clear spirit. They say it's for added smoothness, and I suppose its clarity gives it better mixability or the appearance of a more natural spirit (100% agave *blanco* tequila is on the rise). In any event, it certainly raises the price!

RESURGENCE OF ARTISANAL TEQUILAS

I feel a change in the air. I think we owe *gracias* in part to artisanal mezcal. Its booming popularity today comes from its adherence to rich Mexican heritage, tradition, and craftsmanship. It attracts those wanting a purer and more natural agave spirit. Many mezcals are sold in simple bottles, with more importance given to what's found inside. (We are beginning to see this artisanal trend returning to tequila, too.) However, large spirits conglomerates have headed to Oaxaca. Watch out, mezcal lovers!

I look forward to the resurrection of handcrafted tequila production—for the *tahona* to come out of distillery museums, for tequila to be made in a slow and unhurried way, based upon its artisanal traditions.

I've recently heard of renowned Mexican *tequileros* who sold their distilleries to spirits corporations and are now establishing family-run companies once again, making tequila like it was once made. Once partnered with Patrón, the González family of Tequila 7 Leguas returned to a family-run business. Guillermo Erikson Sauza, a fifth-generation Sauza, restored the original La Fortaleza distillery in 2002 to produce Los Abuelos—sold as Tequila Fortaleza in the United States—in honor of his grandparents.

I've even heard that, because of public demand, some of the large spirits corporations such as Herradura have cut back on the use of diffusers and columnar stills and are returning to more traditional ways of production. And that is the key: public demand! There will always be a market in the United States for *mixtos* and trendy tequilas, but discerning drinkers must be more insistent in purchasing and consuming traditional-tasting tequila and mezcal.

I hope that tequila visionaries today will meld innovative techniques to enhance productivity with timeworn traditions to retain the soul of tequila.

My Demands

- Tequila that retains the essence of agave and the spirit of Mexico.
- Consumers who take the initiative to learn more about the agave spirits they drink, seeking quality, character, and authenticity.
- Producers who implement techno/artisanal production that preserves tequila's integrity.
- Mexicans who protect their national spirit by enforcing and adhering to stricter regulations governing tequila.
- The use of fresh and natural ingredients in cocktails to showcase, not mask, tequila's inimitable flavor.
- Drinkers who imbibe respectfully and responsibly.

My Dismay

- The "vodka-ization" of tequila. Tequila marketers are following vodka trends like triple and 5x distillation, flavored expressions, and multiple filtrations that may diminish tequila's character or disguise its distinctive taste. Tequila is not a neutral spirit!
- The "brown spiriting" of tequila. Some tequila producers tend to over-oak and over-age *añejos* and *extra añejos*, losing the true character of agave and the subtleties of aging. Their products taste more like other aged brown spirits than tequila.
- The "de-Mexicanization" of tequila. Multinational spirits conglomerates have purchased once family-run Mexican distilleries and industrialized tequila production. This seems to be what it takes to stay in this competitive market, where millions of dollars are spent on advertising alone.
- Flavored tequilas and ready-mixed tequila refreshments in a box and cocktails in a can, often adding sweet, artificial flavorings to inexpensive *mixtos*.

◆ Innumerable entries on liquor and bar shelves. Many are overpriced, lacking character and integrity. They often come from the same distillery with different labels, in bottles that are more alluring than what's found inside.

How to Taste Tequila

We've visited Jalisco's tequila towns, traversing tequila *tierra*, and getting to know the homeland of the majestic blue agave. We've seen the wide gamut of tequilas—from classic to contemporary, from lowlands to highlands brands. Now it's time for you to make some choices. What style of tequila best suits your taste? A bright, peppery *blanco*, with its versatility and mixability? The gently rested *reposado*, with its subtle oak influence, ready for sipping or shaking? Or are you a brown-spirits fan desiring a fine *añejo*?

Perhaps your hometown has a restaurant or upscale bar that offers "flights"—a selection of several tequilas in smaller servings—and hosts tequila clubs/tastings. This allows you to sample different brands and cat-egories of tequila, discovering your personal favorites before purchasing a bottle.

While professional tastings, presented by tequila companies, restaurants/bars, and conferences, can be informative, it's fun to have intimate tequila tastings at home. You and your guests can sample several tequilas in a flight, make comparisons, and find which tequila suits your fancy.

I often invite a small group of six to eight guests for a tasting, asking them to bring a pre-determined bottle of tequila, so that we may sample several. Who knows? You just may not go home with the one you brought. At the end of the tasting, bottles sometimes switch hands, as guests find new favorites.

PROVIDE FOR YOUR GUESTS

Map of Mexico showing tequila regions (p. 2)
Tasting profiles (p. 62)
A room with good light
Clear glasses for tasting
Paper and pens for notes
Water to cleanse the palate
No salt and lime!
Plenty to eat afterward

GLASSES

You could need thirty or more tasting glasses—so you'll probably have to mix and match, keeping them similarly sized. Small wine or short-stemmed brandy glasses are ideal. Sometimes I use shot glasses from my collection of *caballitos* brought home from my Mexican travels. You can find "six packs" of inexpensive shot glasses at most discount stores (look for clear ones so you can appreciate the color of the tequila). Avoid paper or plastic cups, as they impair flavor.

Tequila's popularity inspired Riedel, the renowned Austrian wineglass company, to design the "Official Tequila Glass" specifically to capture the essence of the agave—a great gift for aficionados for tasting at home. I'll certainly put them on my wish list!

Tequila's Acclaim

Tequila bars and restaurants across the United States and Europe stock many (sometimes hundreds!) tequilas to sip and savor. Married to Don Felipe Camarena's daughter, Liliana, and dubbed Mexico's "Ambassador of Tequila to the United States" by the state of Jalisco, Julio Bermejo of Tommy's Mexican Restaurant started this trend in San Francisco and has the largest Blue Agave Club in the world. Tomas Estes, cofounder of Tequila Ocho, is the Mexican government's tequila ambassador to the European Union, where he has opened seventeen restaurants and bars, giving tequila great international acclaim.

Always sample 100% agave tequilas for tastings (unless you want to compare them to a *mixto*). I suggest ¾-ounce pours—enough to appreciate aroma. Not all has to be imbibed. Tasters write down their first impressions, being as descriptive as possible in regard to color, body, aroma, taste, and finish. Encourage your guests to rate each tequila; this can lead to spirited discussions. Below are some ideas for tequila tasting flights.

Vertical Flight

Taste one of each of the different categories of tequila from the same brand in this order: *blanco*, *reposado*, *añejo*, and *extra añejo*. Tasters discover the characteristics and differences in the aging categories and become familiarized with the style of that distillery. Try a flight of different categories from one brand from the highlands *and* a flight from one brand from the lowlands to see if you can distinguish characteristics of each.

What Does Cooked Agave Taste Like?

When we taste wine, we're already accustomed to the flavor of grapes. However, how many people have even seen, much less tasted, cooked agave? I only wish you could walk into a distillery and smell *piñas* cooking in the oven, then taste a bite. In a quality 100% agave tequila, especially a *blanco* or *reposado*, the agave flavor should shine through. While notes of black pepper, cinnamon, citrus, and aromatic herbs may be apparent, the agave's earthy and vegetal flavor prevails. It's reminiscent of sweet potatoes and pumpkin baked in a clay pot, floral honey, and molasses.

Horizontal Flight

Include several tequilas from different distilleries within the same category. For instance, taste several brands of *blancos*, or *reposados*, or *añejos* from different distilleries. This helps guests determine their favorite brands. Whenever possible, sip *añejos* from snifters, which, when warmed by the hands, release added aroma and flavor. Though I like to keep a bottle of tequila *blanco* chilled in the refrigerator/freezer, especially during the summer, its nuances are better appreciated at room temperature.

BLIND TASTING

Guests are not told which tequila they are tasting, so there are no preconceived ideas of brand, price, or taste. Surely, there will be some surprises! Make sure glasses stay in order (or are numbered) to avoid confusion when discussion follows. Use your senses. Take sips, not shots!

SIGHT

Hold the glass up to the light (or white paper) and pay attention to the color, determined by the aging category of the tequila and ranging from crystal clear *blancos* to *añejos* of dark mahogany and copper hues. Notice the tequila's viscosity. Swirl the glass gently—the "legs" or "tears" clinging to the sides of the glass indicate the body. They're more opulent with *añejos*, due to natural oils released from the oak barrel.

SMELL

Gently swirl the glass, which releases the bouquet, or nose, of the tequila. Breathe in its bouquet in gentle whiffs, not deep inhalations. Take note of your first impression. Is the agave discernible? Is it fruity and herbaceous, astringent, or harsh? Are you overwhelmed by the scent of vanilla and butterscotch? Remember, flavorings are allowed in tequila production. Is it overpowered by oak or alcohol or does it have a chemical or medicinal scent? What does it evoke for you? Write down your impressions.

Take a small sip and let it rest in your mouth for ten seconds to release flavors, drawing in air with pursed lips. Gently swirl tequila around your mouth with your tongue. What flavors do you taste? What part of the mouth is stimulated? Tip of the tongue or beneath it, back of the mouth, sides? Is it fiery and harsh? Sweet and smooth? Rich and complex? What kind of aftertaste or finish—lingering or short? Mellow or bitter? What appeals to you? Swirling the tequila in the glass and in the mouth oxygenates it, releasing aroma and flavor. Take note of any unsavory characteristics—soapy, petrol, acetone, strong alcohol, musty, chemical, or sulfurous tastes—to consider in tasting discussions.

For a list of potential flavor and aroma descriptors and profiles in the various categories of tequila, see page 62. Have this list available at your tequila tasting, and encourage guests to add descriptors of their own.

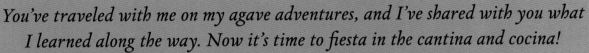

You've traveled with me on my agave adventures, and I've shared with you what I learned along the way. Now it's time to fiesta in the cantina and cocina!

Los compadres en la cantina, carved by Inocencio Vásquez, Oaxaca.

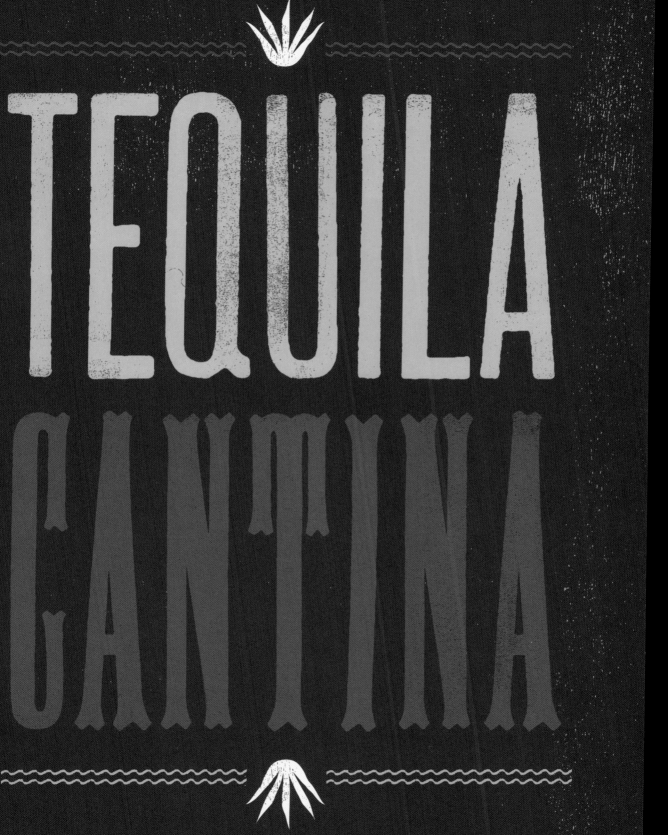

Recipes

IN ORDER OF APPEARANCE

Note: Recipes that appear in the text, when referred to elsewhere, are indicated in the color of blue agave. Readers may find these recipes by referring to the Cantina and Comida indexes or by consulting this list.

Hand-carved animals by Inocencio Vásquez, Oaxaca.

Entra si quieres
Y sal si puedes.

—

Come in when you're stable
Leave if you're able.

FOR SOME, THE WORD "CANTINA" conjures up a dark and dusty saloon with swinging doors that open to boisterous *borrachos* (drunkards) and brawls, a harried *cantinero* (bartender), and sometimes *mujeres de la noche* (ladies of the night). They carouse amidst the wafts of stale smoke and the strains of passionate songs from disheveled mariachis, who stroll from bar to bar, playing for pesos.

While establishments such as these exist throughout Mexico, you'll also find simple, homey cantinas that serve as neighborhood gathering places. Men come for camaraderie, *chisme* (gossip), or *cuentos* (tales) of the day. They eat tasty *botanitas* (snacks), play dominos or Conquian or other card games, and savor a few *copitas* (shots). Until recent years, and often still, women are usually not welcome.

The image of "cantina" that I choose to portray in this book is not just about drinks. It's more about ambiance. (And, of course, in my cantina, women are most welcome!) You may only have a small space, even just a liquor cabinet, in your home to devote to a bar, but it's the hospitality and spirit of entertaining in which you welcome guests that gives them that celebratory and unforgettable cantina experience.

Attention given to garnish and to presentation of distinct cocktails—like homemade *sangrita*, festive party ponches (punches), and other celebratory libations you'll find in Lucinda's Cantina—is sure to please your guests. Serving these drinks with Tequila Cocina recipes will guarantee that you immerse your guests in a truly memorable experience with Mexican flair.

LET LITTLE TOUCHES SET THE MOOD IN YOUR HOME CANTINA

+ Play cantina music! Throughout this book, I've suggested music selections to enhance the cantina spirit—whether it's mariachi or *ranchera*, conjunto or *corridos*, Tejano or the timeless romantic trios, such as Trío Los Panchos, who popularized many of Mexico's favorite love songs.

+ Light plenty of inexpensive Mexican votive saint candles and use colorful textile cocktail napkins and imaginative glassware, even if it's a mix-and-match assortment. Painted four-inch Mexican tiles make fun coasters (glue felt pads on the unpainted side to protect furniture).

+ Celebrate Mexico—while teaching guests some Spanish words—by playing Lotería, a bingo-like card game with fifty-four *puro mexicano* images, each accompanied by a *dicho* or riddle. (Mexicans traditionally use dried *frijoles* for markers.) Find cheap and cheerful Lotería games in Mexican import stores and markets. Make handmade cantina coasters by writing down on individual cardstock squares some of the *dichos* found in this book.

¡SALUD!

Mexican hosts honor their guests with a gracious "¡Salud!"—a *brindis*, or toast, like one of the *dichos* highlighted in the pages of this book. Remember to personally acknowledge each of your guests sometime during their visit by raising a glass to him or her.

Top: Lucinda's Cantina, Austin. *Bottom*: Tequila bottles bordering garden beds beside cantina.

Cantina La Lucinda

MOST OF YOU PROBABLY won't create a Mexican cantina in your yard, so let me tell you about mine. It's secluded and nestled behind the detached garage of my bright purple 1930s "Texican" bungalow in Austin. I've painted the walls bright turquoise, like a *barrio* (neighborhood) cantina south of the border.

A traditional split-cedar *ramada* (porch-like structure) holds a rustic bar table for serving punches and tequila drinks, and a saloon cabinet stores bottles of tequila and mezcal for fiestas. A large rusted metal sculpture of an agave perches atop this *ramada*. Strands of party lights (and sometimes banners strung with *papel picado*) add to the festiveness.

Like cantinas in Mexico, a calendar hangs on the wall to mark off each blessed day, while a small statue of the Virgen de Guadalupe gives protection.

To the side of the cantina, a handcrafted wrought iron bottle tree "grows" empty bottles of tequila from its branches. It sits in a bed mulched with corks and lined with upside-down tequila bottles.

Oak whiskey barrels double as my cocktail tables when upside down or serve as planters filled with small palms or vibrant, cascading bougainvillea. I covered the top of a picnic table and its benches with cheerful Mexican oilcloth—brightly patterned fabric covered in a vinyl laminate—used throughout Mexico as tablecloths. Find it online or in Mexican import stores. (They quickly fade in direct sunlight, so use in covered or shaded areas.)

A trio of *huarache*-shod musicians, each with a distinct personality (one has exchanged his musical instrument for a bottle of tequila), greets patrons of my cantina. Resourceful Mexican craftsmen fashioned them, with incredible attention to detail, from rusty oil drums and found objects.

But perhaps my favorite embellishment is the big copper pot used for distilling mezcal that I brought back with me from Oaxaca, a cherished memento from my mezcal adventure that you'll read about later. Oh, and I have a whimsical outdoor tin shower, just in case a merry reveler gets out of hand! (It's actually for showering after working in my Cantina garden—see page 111—where I grow herbs and edible flowers for flavoring and garnishing my food and libations.)

I've distilled the essence of Mexico into my home cantina—its flavors and character, its spirit and soul. May you be inspired to do the same—to create a warm and inviting atmosphere for the celebration of agave spirits and *amistad* (friendship).

A HEARTWARMING MEXICAN WELCOME

Mi casa es su casa.
I'll add:
Mi cantina es su cantina.

Lady of the Cantina, painted earthenware clay figurine made by Josefina Aguilar, Oaxaca.

Cantina llena
Bebidas buenas.

—

Full bar
Good drinks.

Stocking the Home Cantina

INGREDIENTS YOU'LL NEED ON HAND

Tequila calls forth a fiesta! Stocking the home cantina is part of the fun, especially for curious bon vivants, eager to experiment. Always have ingredients and essentials on hand, whether it's an untried bottle of tequila, a luscious new liqueur, or Cantina Classics found in this book: recipes for homemade, flavored bar syrups and liqueurs; seasoned salts; and tequilas infused with hot chiles, fruits, or fresh herbs.

Today, creative cocktail enterprises abound and their products line shelves: fresh frozen fruit purées, artisanal sodas, exotic fruit juices, liqueurs, flavored syrups, flavored bitters, packaged drink mixes, salts, and seasonings, as well as innovative bar essentials and glassware.

Tequilas

Aficionados collect tequilas in the same spirit of enthusiasm and delight with which wine connoisseurs build their cellars. Each style of tequila has its individual character, from the clear and bright *blancos* to those aged in oak, varying in quality, flavor, and price. Be adventurous!

Tequila is such a versatile spirit. With its lively flavor and personality, it gives vodka, rum, and gin stiff competition for mixability. Keep on hand at least one bottle of each style of tequila for different kinds of cocktails.

Facing: Tequila and mezcal bottles, Inocencio Vásquez, Oaxaca.

WHAT STYLE OF TEQUILA FOR WHICH DRINK?

Why bother with a *mixto?* Instead, invest in premium 100% agave tequilas.

Blanco (Silver or *Plata*)

Shots
Margaritas
Spritzers and frozen drinks
Classic white spirit cocktails
Tropical fruit cocktails and festive punches

Reposado

Shots
Margaritas
Mixed drinks, spritzers, and classic cocktails
Festive punches
After-dinner drinks

Añejo or *Extra Añejo*

Snifters
Classic brown spirit cocktails
After-dinner drinks
Floaters for specialty cocktails

The tequila craze paved the way for other agave spirits like mezcal, sotol, and bacanora. Use them in place of tequila in cocktails (or use ½ of each), sip as shots, or use as floaters to add extra flavor to tequila drinks.

Liqueurs

The skill in making a good tequila drink is in enhancing, not obscuring, tequila's natural essence. Used judiciously, liqueurs balance flavors of citrus, fresh fruits, and aromatics, adding dimension to cocktails, while letting tequila shine. Orange and fruit-flavored liqueurs, and those with aromatic, herbaceous, and nutty flavors, especially complement tequila. (Look for small, 350mg bottles for sampling before investing in larger bottles.) Let the flavor and personality of tequila sparkle!

Classic European aromatic liqueurs such as Chartreuse, Lillet, St. Germain Elderflower, Aperol, Averna, and vermouth are current favorites of mixologists and bartenders. When used in moderation, they can add an unexpected boost to tequila's own peppery, floral, and fruity nuances. However, orange-flavored liqueurs remain tequila's most popular partner.

ORANGE LIQUEURS

Triple sec: a clear, orange-flavored triple-distilled liqueur. Numerous brands exist; remember, the quality of the brand influences the outcome of the drink. Take caution that cognac-based orange liqueurs do not dominate the distinct flavor of tequila.

Cointreau: a premium French triple sec, flavored with bitter and sweet orange. Crystal clear and beautifully balanced, Cointreau has been tequila's favorite partner for years. Cointreau Noir, made with a Remy Martin cognac, is now on the market.

Combier: an all-natural triple-distilled liqueur from the Loire Valley. This distillery claims to use the original recipe for triple sec. Royal Combier is blended with cognac.

Controy: a triple sec made in Mexico and found in a square, green bottle in most Mexican bars, where it is used for making margaritas.

03 Premium Orange Liqueur: DeKuyper & Son's newest and reasonably priced premium 80-proof orange liqueur made from renowned Pera oranges from Brazil.

Grand Marnier: a favorite French liqueur with a cognac base, often used in top-shelf margaritas and other tequila cocktails.

Bauchant: a French Liqueur d'Orange Napoleon made with cognac and orange essence.

Gran Gala: Italy's answer to Grand Marnier, but less expensive. Gran Gala is made of Sicilian oranges with vsop brandy.

Patrón's Citrónge: an 80-proof orange liqueur distilled in Mexico by the producers of Patrón tequila.

Paula's Texas Orange (and Lemon) Liqueurs: a liqueur made in Austin from oranges and lemons, for mixing and for sipping. The label reminds us to "linger over a meal with friends, toasting achievements and dreams."

Stirrings Triple Sec: a 100% natural triple sec using orange peel essence and cane sugar, inspired by the original Caribbean Curaçao recipe.

AROMATIC LIQUEURS

Damiana: a liqueur flavored with a wild Mexican herb from Baja, California del Sur. Damiana stands up to tequila's assertive flavor. It has a lascivious reputation (pp. 146–147) and is sometimes used instead of orange liqueur in margaritas. The most popular brand, Guaycura Liqueur, comes in a bottle shaped like a plump, nude Indian goddess.

Agavero: a tequila-flavored liqueur flavored with Damiana or oranges. Agavero adds sweetness and tequila essence to cocktails.

Domaine de Canton Ginger Liqueur: a cognac-based French liqueur. I like to make my own Cantina Classic Zesty Ginger Syrup and Cantina Classic Ambrosia, an after-dinner liqueur, for spicing up fruit-flavored cocktails, but Canton liqueur, flavored with baby Vietnamese ginger and tropical spice, mingles deliciously with tequila.

PAMA: a pomegranate vodka liqueur laced with tequila. PAMA is very sweet, but adds a pretty ruby color to tequila drinks.

Bauchant XO Pomegranate: an elegant, hard-to-find liqueur, made with XO cognac in France.

Passion fruit: a sensuous tropical fruit that makes a delectable liqueur. The producers of Grand Marnier once made the luscious passion fruit liqueur, La Grande Passion, though it's hard to find and very expensive. I'm eagerly waiting for someone to produce a liqueur made purely from this lush fruit.

For after-dinner and homemade Cantina Classic liqueurs, see pp. 184–187.

Sodas

Effervescence brings sparkle and fizz to tequila spritzers, classic cocktails, and punches. Keep sodas chilled before preparing cocktails, as ice dilutes their flavor. Find glass bottles of Coca-Cola and Fresca exported from Mexico at Latin American markets. Ice down the sodas and a bottle of tequila. Pass ice-filled glasses and plenty of lime wedges, and you'll have the makings for fun and easy party drinks.

Sparkling (seltzer or mineral) water: Mexican brands such as Topo Chico, Peñafiel, and Tehuacan. These brighten up tequila drinks. Find them in Latin American markets, or substitute other top quality brands of sparkling mineral water. Keep plenty of bottles on ice for guests at your tequila fiesta.

Squirt: a grapefruit/citrus soda. Mexicans love this refreshing soda, and so do I. It's a must for my signature punches.

Fresca: another grapefruit soda. Fresca is made with sugar in Latin America, but the U.S. version is calorie-free. Mexican Fresca can now be found in the United States in green glass bottles.

Mexican Coca-Cola: the famous cola, flavored with cane sugar instead of corn fructose syrup. It's now exported in glass bottles to the United States.

Jarritos: a natural tropical fruit-flavored soda made in Mexico and found in Latin American markets. Flavors include *jamaica* (hibiscus), guava, mango, tamarindo, watermelon, and more.

Artisanal sodas: tasty, fizzy soda alternatives made with lower sugar content and natural ingredients in exotic flavors such as such lemongrass, lavender, pomegranate, cranberry lime, Meyer lemon, cucumber, clementine, passion fruit, ruby grapefruit, and mango. Some of the many brands include: Izze, DRY Soda, GuS Grown-up-Soda, Stirrings, R. W. Knudsen, and imported Italian brands.

Reed's Extra Ginger Brew (and their other flavored Ginger Brews): a Jamaican-style ginger soda. This brand gives a spicy kick to tequila drinks.

Tonic: a sweetened, carbonated quinine-based soda. Tonic makes a splash with tequila and other spritzers. Look for new, less sweet, premium brands like Q Tonic, made from Peruvian quinine and Mexican agave, and Fever-Tree Tonic.

Where's the fiesta? A bottle of tequila and sparkling grapefruit soda for making Palomas (p. 117).

Juices/Purées

Freshly squeezed citrus and seasonal ripe fruits produce the best tasting drinks. You'll find freshly squeezed lime juice and citrus juices in store refrigerated aisles. Aliseo (based in Austin), distributor of premium Italian food products, packages fresh blood orange juice and mandarin juices from Sicily. You'll also find refrigerated pure coconut water and other natural fruit blend nectars.

Keep on hand plenty of natural tropical fruit juices and nectars; choose from the many brands in bottles and cartons lining market shelves. Chill before using.

The Perfect Purée from Napa Valley, as well as Boiron and other French companies, offers fresh frozen fruit purées and concentrates, such as pink guava, prickly pear, and passion fruit, as well as mixed fruit blends. Find them online and in specialty stores.

If you must use commercial mixers, look for less sweet and more natural mixes such as Stirrings, Fee Brothers, and ModMix.

Flavorings

SAUCES, BITTERS, AND SYRUPS

Worcestershire or Maggi Seasoning Sauce
Bitters: Peychaud, Angostura, or those flavored with blood orange, grapefruit, orange, and other exotic flavors
Rose water and orange flower water
Authentic Grenadine by Stirrings
Wild Hibiscus Flowers in Syrup (jamaica flowers in syrup)

SPICES

Crushed dried red chiles (red *chile de árbol*, *puya*, cayenne, *pasilla*, *pequín*, *guajillo*, habanero, and chipotle chiles) for the kitchen and the cantina. These can be found in specialty Latin American markets or online.

Whole peppercorns, pink peppercorns, or pepper mélange. Muddle and strain, or add a pinch freshly ground to drinks.
Cinnamon, coriander seeds, nutmeg, vanilla bean, and allspice berries.
Flor de jamaica (*Hibiscus sabdariffa*), often simply called *jamaica*. Dried tropical hibiscus calyces impart tart and tasty flavor and a rich ruby color to punches and syrups. Look for them in Mexican markets, sold in bulk or in packages. Select those that are plump and purplish in color and not too brittle or dry.

HOT SAUCES

People are as picky about their favorite brands of bottled hot sauce as they are about their tequila. My favorites, Valentina and Tamazula, are both made by the same company, Salsa Tamazula, in Guadalajara. These sauces, flavored with Jalisco's *puya* chiles, are Mexico's answer to Tabasco, but they are thicker and less vinegary, with more depth of chile flavor. Find them in extra-hot and mild versions in Latin American groceries and online. These are an indispensable ingredient in my Sangrita, Micheladas, and other spicy cocktails, as well as for dousing on *botanitas* (snacks).

MARMALADES, CHUTNEYS, AND JALAPEÑO JELLY

The British sometimes stir a dollop of tart Seville orange marmalade, ginger preserves, or fruit jams into cocktails to sweeten them and add a burst of flavor. This comes in handy in a pinch, when fresh ingredients are not on hand. See my recipe for Mermelada de Naranja, orange marmalade spiked with tequila, or Drunken Sugarplum Chutney Cocktail. Add jalapeño jelly to your pantry list for a quick fix of *picante* (piquancy) for margaritas and spritzers.

Agave Syrup

Simple Syrup, or "liquid sugar," has always been a bartender's best friend. However, in the 1990s, agave syrup took the market by storm. Sometimes called "agave nectar," it's purported to be organic, unadulterated, and to have a very low glycemic index.

Like tequila, this gift from the agave has quickly become the darling of mixologists, who tout its virtues: it's much sweeter than sugar, soluble in cold drinks, and as easy to pour as simple syrup. It won't crystallize, giving it a remarkable shelf life. Light, amber, and dark versions exist, determined by the amount of cooking and filtering during processing. You'll also find various flavored versions, making it very versatile in hot or cold drinks.

However, too often, too much agave syrup is added to cocktails, masking tequila's flavor and making drinks taste way too sweet, in my opinion. A little goes a long way! In fact, it's best to dilute it in equal parts water or juice before mixing into the drink. About a teaspoon of agave nectar syrup is needed at most, just enough to soften the effect of lime and tequila in a drink.

Many tequila companies have released their own brands of agave nectar, and, as with tequila, private labels abound.

CHOOSE CAREFULLY

Marketers of agave syrup often lead consumers to believe that it is as natural as *aguamiel*, the "honey water" from the agave that has been imbibed for centuries for its nutritive values. To make agave syrup, *piñas* are baked, crushed, and filtered just as they are in the production of tequila. However, some brands are processed at high heat, destroying healthy benefits, resulting in a refined and concentrated hydrolyzed, high-fructose product.

Like a bad bottle of *mixto* tequila, some commercial agave syrups may contain corn syrup and other additives. Because blue agave is precious to the tequila industry, some agave syrups may not be made with 100% blue agave. It's apparent that the U.S. Food and Drug Administration needs to set labeling requirements—just as Mexico has established NORMA for tequila—to set standards and ensure quality.

Sugars
For Sweetening Drinks and Rimming Glasses

Superfine, or castor, sugar: finely ground sugar dissolves more quickly in cocktails than white granulated sugar. Bury a split whole vanilla bean in a jar of granulated sugar for added flavor.

Turbinado or demerara: natural brown sugar made by partially refining sugarcane extract; other brown sugars simply add molasses to refined white sugar.

Piloncillo: Mexican unrefined brown sugar sold in cones.

Sparkling colored sugar crystals (such as those made by India Tree): for light rimming of glasses.

Limes, Ice, and Salt
A Popular Trio

FRESH LIMES

Fresh, fragrant limes are the "key" to good cocktails. Key limes, often called Mexican limes, have the most flavor. The popularity of tequila drinks makes these little limes readily available in many stores, often sold in net bags. Otherwise, use Persian limes or freshly squeezed juice in refrigerated aisles. Don't use bottled sweetened lime juice with artificial flavors! (For more information on limes, see section on margaritas, p. 145.)

ICE

Ice frozen in trays melts slower than smaller cubes found in purchased bagged ice. Use large cubes when shaking drinks or serving on-the-rocks cocktails or spritzers. Look for King Cubes, silicon ice trays for making jumbo ice cubes, which will melt more slowly than standard ice cubes when added to a cocktail, preventing dilution of the drink.

Decorative ice mold trays add a touch of whimsy.

Cubes automatically made in the freezer often taste like yesterday's meal. Make ice cubes ahead and store in plastic bags before a party.

When making frozen drinks, lightly crack large cubes with a mallet, or use purchased bagged ice to save blender blades.

Top spritzers with a big handful of crushed ice.

SALT

Just as salt seasons foods, it really brings out flavor in cocktails, whether used to rim glasses or added by the pinch to enliven drinks. You'll want to experiment with new salts on the market, then enjoy creating your own spicy seasoned salts (see recipes below).

Kosher salt: large, flaky crystals adhere better to glasses, dissolving less easily than granulated table salt. Kosher sea salt is also now available. Use along with lime to rim margarita glasses.

Spicy Mexican Seasoned Salt: spicy salt flavored with chile, lime, and sometimes sugar that Mexicans traditionally sprinkle over fresh fruits, jícama, and cucumbers with a squeeze of fresh lime juice. Look for brands sold in shaker bottles in Latin American markets in the produce aisle. Trechas ("chile powder for fruits and vegetables") and Tajín ("fruit seasoning") are my favorite brands, but it's even better when you make your own (see recipes below). Use these tasty salts to rim glasses and to sprinkle into margaritas and fruit drinks, such as Una Tuna (Prickly Pear Cooler), or El Rey, a refreshing citrus and pomegranate cooler.

Specialty salts: French *fleur de sel*, pink Hawaiian sea salt, or other special coarsely ground and flavored salts.

Sal de gusano: salt flavored with dried, ground agave worms and chile accompanies mezcal in Oaxaca. Some trendy restaurants here use it to rim glasses and flavor drinks. (You may have to travel to Oaxaca to buy it, though!)

*Un tequila sin sal
es como un amor sin besos.*

——

*A tequila without salt
is like love without kisses.*

Cantina Classics

Homemade Seasoned Salts, Flavored Syrups, and Tequila Infusions

Create original cocktails full of freshness and flavor by making homemade Cantina Classics, instead of buying them off the shelf. They make great gifts for tequila and bartending aficionados, too.

CANTINA CLASSIC SEASONED SALTS

Avoid purchasing gimmicky commercial "margarita" salts. Make your own instead; you can create several variations from one master recipe. Add a pinch of these flavorful salts to fruity or savory drinks and spritzers, or use them to rim glasses. Lightly rimming a glass with diluted agave syrup helps homemade salts adhere to the glass, as they have more texture than commercial salts.

Mouth-Puckering, but So Good!

Citric acid, sometimes called "sour salt," is a crystalline, water-soluble compound that looks like sparkling salt. Extracted from citrus and acidic fruits, it's used in tart candies. It also gives a blast of citrusy flavor to homemade seasoning salts—you'll just need a few pinches because it's really sour! Find it in Middle Eastern groceries, online, or anywhere pickling and canning supplies are sold.

Experiment with different kinds of exotic salts, sugars, citrus, spices, dried chiles, and citric acid, which adds a lime-like tartness (see sidebar). Try a combination of dried red chiles for color and flavor, such as *árbol*, cayenne, *ancho*, *puya*, or *guajillo*. Add a pinch of fiery, dried habanero, if you dare. Of course, these seasoned salts are also useful for flavoring foods—I especially like them with homemade chunky salsas frescas.

Seasoned Salts
MASTER RECIPE AND VARIATIONS

From this master recipe, you can make several versions of seasoned salts. Let it inspire your own creations. In small increments, add more sugar, citric acid, chiles, spices, and other ingredients to suit your own taste.

- 4 tablespoons kosher salt
- 1½ teaspoons freshly grated lime zest
- 1½ teaspoons freshly grated orange zest
- 1 tablespoon granulated or turbinado sugar
- ¼ teaspoon citric acid

Gently grind ingredients in a small bowl, using a bar muddler or mortar and pestle. The citrus zest will make the salt rather moist, so spread on a large plate to dry for several hours, stirring occasionally; add other flavorings. Store tightly sealed. *Makes about 8 tablespoons.*

Note: If salt does not dry sufficiently, place in a 200-degree warmed oven; turn off heat and allow to dry, then grind gently again before storing.

Chiles add Mexican flair. Quickly roast (5 seconds per side) dried red chiles on both sides on a hot *comal*, taking caution not to burn them. Remove seeds and stems, then grind chiles (medium grind) in an electric spice grinder. Many spice companies also sell pure ground chile powders; make certain they do not contain salt and other spices.

Spicy Mexican Seasoned Salt with Chile and Lime

Though commercial brands of spicy seasoned salt exist, make your own! While these salts are great with drinks, they are also good on popcorn, fresh fruit, salads, and grilled meats.

Add to 4 tablespoons master recipe:
- 1–2 teaspoons sugar
- ¼ teaspoon citric acid
- 1 teaspoon fine-quality paprika
- ¼ teaspoon freshly ground *chile de árbol, guajillo,* or cayenne
- 1½ teaspoons pure ground *chile ancho*

Follow master recipe instructions.

Sal de Sangrita

This Jalisco-inspired *sal* (salt) is flavored with traditional *puya* chiles used to make *sangrita*, the citrusy and spicy nonalcoholic chaser that accompanies shots of tequila (recipes, p. 134–136). Sprinkle a pinch in *sangrita* or rim glasses of Vampiros or María Sangrita.

Add to 1 tablespoon master recipe:
- ½ teaspoon orange zest
- ⅛ teaspoon citric acid
- ¼ teaspoon sugar
- 1 or more teaspoons ground chile *puya* or *guajillo* chile

Follow master recipe instructions.

Pink Peppercorn Citrus Salt

I love this fragrant salt speckled with pink peppercorns, orange, and lime zests. It is lovely as a rim for Corazón de Melon or Abajito (Kiwi) Margaritas, fruit drinks, and spritzers. Sprinkle it on fresh fruit and salads, or for an unexpected surprise, add a pinch to Margarita Dessert Bars.

Add to 1 tablespoon master recipe:
- 1 teaspoon freshly ground pink peppercorns
- 1 teaspoon sugar
- ¼ teaspoon lime zest
- ¼ teaspoon orange zest

Follow master recipe instructions.

Hibiscus Flower and Orange Zest Salt

This is pretty and exotic—a purple-hued floral salt made with ground hibiscus flowers. It's tart and tangy and delicious with fruity drinks like Piña Fina, Mexican Mermaid, or Flor de Jamaica Hibiscus Flower Cooler.

Add to 1 tablespoon master recipe:
- 1 teaspoon coarsely ground *flor de jamaica* (dried hibiscus flowers)
- ¼ teaspoon sugar
- ½ teaspoon orange zest
- ⅛ teaspoon citric acid

Follow master recipe instructions.

Cantina Classic Seasoned Salts (*clockwise from left*: Spicy Mexican Seasoned Salt, Master Recipe, Pink Peppercorn Citrus Salt).

These flavor-packed syrups add layers of complexity to cocktails and are important ingredients in my recipes. They take the sharp edge off limes and enhance the flavor of tequila and tropical fruits. Some liqueurs, in contrast, can overwhelm these flavors, so consider substituting syrups—adding a splash more tequila to the drink—in recipes that call for liqueurs. Remember, syrups are quite thick and sweet, so use sparingly. For best flavor, make syrups a day or more in advance and keep refrigerated.

Note: For an easy dessert, lightly drizzle syrups over fresh tropical fruits or sorbets along with a splash of tequila.

Simple Syrup

Simple syrup (*jarabe*), an essential ingredient in any cantina, is a convenient remedy for sweetening mixed drinks. Unlike granulated sugar, simple syrup dissolves easily . . . and it's simple to make. For a less sweet version, use a 1:1 or 1½:1 ratio of sugar and water.

- 2 cups granulated sugar
- 1 cup purified water

In a heavy one-quart saucepan, bring sugar and water to a slow boil. Reduce heat and simmer, stirring gently for about 3 minutes, until sugar is dissolved. Remove from heat and cool. Pour into a clean glass bottle. Keep refrigerated for about a month. *Makes approx. 2 cups.*

Citrus Syrup

The aromatic essence of fresh citrus peel enhances this syrup and intensifies the flavors of tequila drinks. Use a splash to sweeten margaritas, spritzers, and other drinks made with fresh fruits and lime.

- 2 cups granulated sugar
- 1 cup purified water
- Peels of 2 lemons, 2 Persian limes, and 1 navel orange or tangelo, cut in continuous spirals or thin, long strips

In a heavy one-quart saucepan, bring sugar and water to a slow boil. Reduce heat; simmer, stirring gently to dissolve sugar. Add citrus peel and simmer for 3 minutes. Remove from heat and allow to stand for several hours, pressing on citrus peels with the back of a wooden spoon to extract flavor. Pour into a glass bottle with some of the citrus peel. "Candy" remaining peels.*

Keep refrigerated for up to two weeks. Substitute tangerine, tangelo, Meyer lemon, blood orange, and other seasonal citrus. *Makes approx. 2 cups.*

*Note: An electric peeler called a "Dazey Stripper" (p. 107) comes in handy when peeling citrus in long strips, especially when syrups are made in quantity. Otherwise, use a canelle knife (p. 106).

To easily candy peel, sprinkle remaining peel with granulated sugar and allow it to dry on a covered plate overnight. Store in an airtight container to use as a garnish for drinks.

Zesty Ginger Syrup

The bright and snappy flavor of fresh ginger and spice accentuates the flavors of tropical fruits and tequila in fruit drinks and spritzers. Try it with a Corazón de Melon Margarita or Fresco (Fresh Cucumber Spritzer).

- 2 cups granulated sugar (preferably vanilla-scented)
- 1 cup purified water
- 6 whole cloves
- 1 teaspoon whole, dried allspice berries
- 4 tablespoons fresh, minced ginger
- Peel of 1 orange and 1 lemon, cut in a continuous spiral or long strips (avoid bitter white pith)

In a heavy one-quart saucepan, bring sugar and water to slow boil along with the spices, ginger, and citrus peel. Reduce heat and let stand for several hours. Remove dried spices; pour into a glass jar with the ginger and citrus peel. Keep refrigerated for up to 2 weeks. *Makes approx. 2 cups.*

Jarabe Tinto RUBY POMEGRANATE SYRUP

Mexicans have long loved pomegranates (*granadas*), a regal gift from Spain. They eat spoonfuls of the ruby jewel-like seeds from paper cones in markets. I add pomegranate juice to Sangrita, the refreshing tequila chaser, or Ponche de Granada, a festive, traditional holiday libation.

I created this crimson syrup using real pomegranate juice to replace the bright red grenadine bar syrup sometimes used to color and flavor drinks. (Most commercial grenadine does not even contain pomegranate juice, but rather is artificially colored and flavored with a high fructose corn syrup.) I've added *flor de jamaica* for color and tartness.

Try this syrup in drinks such as Sonoran Sunrise, Chimayó Cocktail, or Donají Mezcal Cocktail, or to flavor marinades and glazes for wild game, or to drizzle over raspados (snow cones).

- 1 cup granulated sugar
- 1 cup natural 100% pomegranate juice (such as POM brand)
- ⅓ cup *flor de jamaica* (dried hibiscus flowers)

In a heavy one-quart saucepan, bring pomegranate juice and sugar to a slow boil, along with the *jamaica*. Reduce heat to medium and simmer 4–5 minutes, stirring gently. Allow to stand covered overnight. Pour syrup with *jamaica* flowers into a wide-mouthed jar—it gets better with age. Plop whole *jamaica* flowers into drinks like the Mexican Mermaid. Keep syrup refrigerated for about a month. *Makes approx. 1½ cups.*

Note: When I first created this recipe in 1995, I could only find pomegranate juice in Middle Eastern grocery stores. Now it's everywhere, renowned for its nutritious and antioxidant values. Its tart flavor, coupled with its brilliant color, makes pomegranate juice a natural for tequila drinks. Look for the POM brand, a California-based 100% pomegranate juice, in the refrigerated aisle.

Substitute pomegranate seeds for the *jamaica*, pressing down on them with a wooden spoon to release flavor. Strain syrup and bottle.

Jalapeño Syrup

Mexicans squeeze fresh lime and dust spicy, bright-red chile powder on their sliced mangos, cucumbers, and oranges. This spicy syrup gives the same zing to drinks, especially to my favorite Una Tuna (Prickly Pear Cooler), Pepino Picosito (Cucumber-Jalapeño Cooler), and Texican Martini. It also adds zest to marinades and salad dressings. Vary this according to your tolerance of hot chiles.

- 2 cups sugar
- 1 cup purified water
- 2 jalapeños or red Fresnos, halved, seeded, and minced
- 2 serranos, halved, seeded, and minced, optional
- 1 dried red *chile de árbol*, freshly ground in a spice grinder, optional

In a heavy one-quart saucepan, bring sugar and water to a slow boil, stirring gently to dissolve sugar. Add peppers and simmer for 3 minutes. Remove pan from heat and allow to cool. Pour, unstrained, into a bottle. Refrigerate for 2 weeks. *Makes approx. 2 cups.*

Note: Use fewer peppers, if you must, or if peppers are not piquant enough, you can always add more crushed *chile de árbol*. Substitute 1–2 habaneros for the other peppers, if you dare.

Spicy Piloncillo Syrup

Piloncillo is an unrefined sugar that comes in a firm cone shape (it's named after the *pilon*, a conical weight used on scales in Mexico). The discernible flavors of unrefined molasses, Mexican vanilla, cinnamon, and cloves give this rich, dark syrup its distinctive taste. It's an integral ingredient in Ponche de Posada, Ponche Navideño, delicious simmered Christmas holiday punch. *Piloncillo* syrup dissolves easily in coffee drinks and Cantina Classic liqueurs (pp. 184–187), giving them a smooth and luxurious texture.

- 1 8-ounce cone *piloncillo*, crushed with a heavy mallet
- 1 cup purified water
- 4 whole cloves
- 2 3-inch cinnamon sticks
- ¼ teaspoon Mexican vanilla

In a heavy one-quart saucepan, combine *piloncillo*, spices, and water and slowly bring to boil. Reduce heat and simmer until *piloncillo* has dissolved. Allow to cool slightly; add vanilla. Strain spices and pour into a glass bottle. Keeps 4 weeks in the refrigerator. *Makes approx. 1 cup.*

Agria Dulce (Sweet and Sour)

Frozen, powdered, and bottled sweet-and-sour mixes offer a quick fix for home or commercial bartenders. My suggestion? Avoid them! Most are way too sweet, lack the natural essence of fresh lime, and are often filled with artificial additives. Even worse, they mask the flavor of good tequila, enabling bartenders to use cheap well tequilas. A headache in a glass!

However, some find the acidity of limes and the flavor of tequila too strong in character and may prefer a sweeter and milder drink. They may attempt to sweeten it by overcompensating with flavored liqueurs, which then overpower natural fruit flavors. Instead, make your own *agria dulce*. I love it in a Summertime Sandía Watermelon Cooler or a Mango Maravilla, made with frozen mangoes. Use more of this than homemade syrups, as it is not as thick and sweet.

Keep frozen in small containers (adding it frozen to a drink helps keep it colder) to have on hand for flavoring margaritas, mixed drinks, and punches (use instead of frozen concentrated limeade).

- 1½ cups sugar
- 1 cup purified water
- Grated zest of 1 large Persian lime, 1 navel orange or tangelo, and 1 lemon
- 1¼ cups fresh lime juice
- 1 cup fresh lemon juice (or part fresh orange or tangelo juice)
- Agave syrup to taste, optional

In a heavy one-quart saucepan, bring sugar and water to a slow boil. Reduce heat to simmer, stirring gently for 3 minutes to dissolve sugar. Remove from heat and cool for 5 minutes before adding citrus zest. When cool, add fresh citrus juices. Add a small amount of agave syrup if it's too tart for your taste. Cover and refrigerate for a few days, or freeze for future use in 2-ounce containers. Use ½–¾ ounce per margarita or other tequila drink. *Makes approx. 3½ cups.*

Tequila Infused with Chiles, Fresh Herbs,
or Citrus
Chile Pepper–Infused Tequila
Fresh Herb- and Flower-Infused Tequilas
Citrus- and Fruit-Infused Tequilas

Barware

JIGGER

A glass or stainless steel measure with ½-ounce increments is necessary for making consistent drinks. Have
both a 2-ounce and a 4-ounce jigger.

BAR SPOON

A long-handled spoon (about 1 teaspoon) used to
measure ingredients and stir drinks.

LIME SQUEEZER

Handy double-handled metal lime squeezers are used
throughout Mexico. Sometimes these juicers, made
for smaller Mexican limes, are not large enough for
the Persian limes more readily available in the United
States. Most Mexican squeezers are made of aluminum; instead, use nonreactive ones made of stainless
steel or citrus reamers made of wood or glass.

CITRUS PRESS

Long-handled commercial presses quickly extract
juices, separating seeds and peel, and work well for
juicing all citrus and pomegranates. Small electric citrus juicers are great for extracting juice in quantity.

MUDDLER

A long pestle, traditionally made of wood (looks like
a mini baseball bat), a muddler has a rounded end to
bruise or "muddle" ingredients like fresh limes, herbs,
cucumbers, and fruits in the bottom of a glass before
adding liquids. Some contemporary muddlers are made
of plastic or stainless steel, with serrated ends for better
muddling, but a wooden spoon will work in a pinch.

BLENDER

A strong motor, several speeds, and heavy blades are
essential. Stainless steel canisters help keep ice from
melting when making frozen drinks. Those who
entertain often for large groups may consider electric
frozen margarita machines.

SHAKER

A two-piece shaker, known as a "Boston Shaker," consists of a stainless steel mixing "tin" and a pint glass.
It produces an icy drink without diluting flavor. Some
prefer a sixteen-ounce, three-piece shaker, which includes a jigger as a top and a built-in strainer and insulated tin to keep hands from becoming too cold. I have
a set of six brightly colored mini-shakers for guests for
shaking their own cocktails (see Fiesta Margarita and
Texican Martini).

Shake, Shake, Shake!

I've managed to get the shaker's parts stuck
as ice melts within. Try this: fill shaker glass
about ⅔ full with ice and liquid ingredients. Attach inverted mixing tin at a slight angle; give
it a whack on top to push down lightly. Holding
the glass, give the bottom of the tin a firm tap
to create a seal and prevent leakage. Turn upside down and shake for 10–20 seconds (longer for frothier drinks), until the tin becomes
frosty (overshaking dilutes drinks). With the
glass side up and angled toward you and your
hand overlapping the joint where the glass
and the tin meet, open by a firm tap and twist
to break the seal.

STRAINER

A stainless steel, wire mesh bar strainer with a coiled edge (Hawthorne strainer) separates ice from liquid to prevent diluting the drink. A spring-coiled edge prevents spillage. This is needed for the Boston Shaker.

GARNISHING TOOLS

Sharp knives: Paring, serrated, and garnishing knives.
Canelle knife: A sharp curl of metal attached to a handle, used for making a continuous spiral of peel from citrus or cucumber.
Zester: Fine and medium stainless steel graters used for citrus, nutmeg, chocolate, *piloncillo* (brown sugar cone), and ginger.
Electric citrus/fruit peeler: A handy appliance called a Dazey Stripper (doesn't dance on bars!) impales a whole citrus, then quickly removes its peel in a continuous spiral. It's indispensable when making citrus-flavored simple syrup, liqueurs, candied citrus peels, or citrus-infused tequila. Find it online.

MISCELLANEOUS TOOLS

Wooden cutting boards
Bottle openers
Ice bucket, tongs, scoop, wooden mallet for cracking ice
Decorative ice trays
Long stirring spoons (bar spoons)
Electric spice grinder (or coffee mill) for grinding dried chiles and spices

EQUIVALENTS

1 fluid ounce = 2 tablespoons
1 dash = 10 drops
1 jigger = 1½ fluid ounces
1 Mexican lime = approx. ½ fluid ounce
1 Persian lime = approx. ¾ fluid ounce
1 bar spoon = approx. 1 teaspoon

PROPORTIONS

Tequila is sold in 750-milliliter bottles (metric equivalent of a fifth) and in liters.
750 milliliters = 25.4 fluid ounces
25.4 fluid ounces = approx. 16 1½-ounce portions
1 liter = 33.8 fluid ounces
33.8 fluid ounces = approx. 22 1½-ounce portions
1.75 liters = 59.2 fluid ounces
59.2 fluid ounces = 39½ 1½-ounce portions

Glassware

Festive glassware sets the fiesta mood. Like your guests, glasses don't have to match, but they must be interesting. For larger gatherings, I like to mix 1- to 2-ounce shot glasses, small glass *caballitos* (pony glasses), promotional tequila shot glasses, and antique crystal stemmed cordials. Sometimes I serve from miniature earthenware mugs from Mexico.

My favorite margarita glasses from Mexico have bright green glass stems shaped like cacti—perfect compadres for tequila. And I also own shot glasses with handblown agaves found within. Small Mexican glass holders for saint votives make fun containers for drinks (remove any remaining wax from spent glasses with boiling water before use).

Purchase Mexican glassware on your next south-of-the-border sojourn, from online sources, or at discount stores, where gift sets abound.

SHOT GLASSES

Tequila enthusiasts often sip and savor their favorite libation "neat" (straight) instead of mixing it with other flavorings. Clear or etched glasses show off tequila's silver and amber tones. The popularity of tequila makes shot glasses the rage for souvenir shoppers (and logo advertising) in just about every airport, hotel, and cantina/restaurant gift shop, both here and in Mexico. You can often find inexpensive sets in discount stores, too.

I like to welcome guests with my special libations—such as Cinco de Mayo Shooters, Drunken Sugarplum Shooters, Margaritas Picositas, or Cucarracha Shooters—served icy cold in shot glasses. I use larger (about four-ounce) Moroccan tea glasses, which leaves room for festive garnishes.

MARGARITA GLASSES

The margarita's popularity has led to the availability of glasses to suit many styles—from dainty crystal to fishbowl size to poolside plastic. Long-stemmed glasses are best for showing off these refreshing drinks and keeping them chilled, away from warm hands.

PITCHERS AND JARS

Tequila punches and party drinks served in large pitchers or 2½- to 5-gallon glass jars like those used by Mexican street vendors for *aguas frescas* (nonalcoholic natural fruit punches) are my signature libations. Find them in Latin American grocery stores and online.

SNIFTERS

Premium tequila *añejo* is as at home in a snifter as a single-malt Scotch or cognac. The snifter's wide bowl and smaller mouth concentrate tequila's essence so that its bouquet can be savored along with the flavor. Hands also warm the bowl to release aroma. Snifters are nice to use for after-dinner drinks, too.

FINE CRYSTAL

Some aficionados delight in showing off premium tequilas in collectible crystal snifters and shot glasses. For maximum appreciation in tasting tequila, splurge on the "Official Tequila Glass," made by Riedel (p. 83).

CLASSIC BAR GLASSES

Collins: tall, narrow, cylindrical tumbler, great for spritzers; 10–12 ounces.
Highball: shorter and wider than a Collins glass, good for mixed drinks; 8–12 ounces.
Old-fashioned or "on the rocks": Short and rounded tumbler, for drinks with a splash; 6–10 ounces.
Martini: long-stemmed, triangular bowl, for "neat" drinks and margaritas; 4–6 ounces.
Champagne: long-stemmed tulip shape keeps champagne and effervescent cocktails bubbly; 6–10 ounces.
Insulated tumblers: trendy and modern double-walled glass tumblers help keep your cocktails cold.

TO CHILL GLASSES

Rinse glasses and place them stem-side up in a freezer for about fifteen minutes (never place fine crystal in freezer), or fill glasses with ice water, empty, then fill with fresh ice before serving.

Salting rims: Chill long-stemmed margarita glasses. Pour a thin layer of coarse salt on a napkin or saucer. Hold glass upside down and run a quartered lime around the rim, then lightly twirl dampened rim in the salt. Tap off excess salt so that only a delicate crust remains. Rim glasses with salt hours before the fiesta, setting aside on trays to dry. Use homemade Cantina Classic Seasoned Salts for color and pizzazz.

Sugaring rims: Chill long-stemmed glasses. Lightly dip rim in a shallow dish of lime juice, diluted agave syrup, or liqueur, then twirl in a shallow dish of any of the following: sparkling colored sugar crystals in fiesta colors, granulated sugar colored with a few drops of food coloring, granulated sugar flavored with citrus zest, turbinado natural brown sugar, vanilla-scented sugar.

Note: For tropical drinks, rim glass with finely grated coconut and citrus zest. Remove peel from citrus; cut into small pieces. Place in food processor with 4–6 tablespoons grated sweetened coconut. Pulse to desired texture.

Making Festive Ice Cubes

Freeze fresh herbs, chiles, fruits, or flowers into ice cubes. Use ice cube molds in decorative shapes. Let the drinks be your guide in selecting the items frozen in your ice cubes.

Fill ice trays with distilled water to prevent clouding. Use any of these alone or in combination: fresh herb sprigs and edible flowers; small slices of citrus and kumquats; small fresh red and green chile peppers; whole grapes, fresh cranberries, blueberries, and pomegranate seeds. Once cubes are frozen, store in airtight containers to have on hand for special occasions.

Garnishes

The presentation of a drink is the first seduction. No matter how tasty the drink, the special touch of a garnish seems to make it taste even better. Use one or more garnishes, with special attention to contrasting colors, textures, and an element of surprise.

CITRUS

As a garnish, citrus adds a fragrant, color-intense note to margaritas, tropical drinks, punches, and spritzers.

+ Rim edge of a glass with a twist of citrus, then drop it in the drink for added aroma or simply squeeze the twist over the surface of a cocktail so its volatile oils flavor the drink.
+ Flambé orange zest over a classic cocktail; the aromatic oils will leave its essence on the surface of the drink.
+ Score skin of citrus fruit in ¼-inch strips from top to bottom with a canelle knife. When cut into slices, each will have decorative edges.
+ Make a slit in a thick citrus slice to attach it to the rim of a glass.
+ Cut citrus into slices, wedges, thick curls, thin strips, or long twists; using a cocktail pick, twist slices of two citrus varieties together. Skewer kumquats or cut them into thin slices.
+ Freeze slices of citrus on a tray in the freezer; float frozen slices in punch or drinks.

SEASONAL FRUIT

Melons, berries, tropical fruits—use any seasonal fruit to add appeal and boost the flavor of margaritas, fruit drinks, and punches.

+ Use slices or wedges of unpeeled tropical fruits—alone or in combinations such as mango, pineapple, kiwi, prickly pear, or watermelon. Cut triangular wedges of unpeeled watermelon and pineapple.

- Make small slits in fruit to attach to the rim of the glass or spear them with decorative cocktail picks and drop into the drink.
- Use a melon scoop to create colorful balls of honeydew, cantaloupe, and watermelon; spear on cocktail picks.
- Slice unpeeled star fruit (*carambola*) crosswise to form natural star shapes. Float in drinks or attach to rims of glasses. Impale on a skewer for a stir stick.
- Make a small slit in the side of a whole ripe strawberry (hull intact) and hook on edge of glass.
- Sprinkle fresh pomegranate seeds in autumn and winter drinks.
- Use chunks of frozen fruits or cold melon balls to chill the drink.

Making Festive Drink Garnishes

SCALLION SWIZZLE STICKS: Cut end off each scallion (green onion) to remove roots. Trim green ends if necessary. With the tip of a very sharp paring knife make 1½-inch incisions vertically in the white bulb, turning it as you go, until thin strips are incised all the way round. Soak scallions in ice water about 10 minutes until cut strips splay out and curve. Use as swizzle stick with white end above the rim of the glass.

CHILE PEPPER FLOWERS: Use either green or red ripened peppers, such as jalapeños and serranos. With a sharp paring knife, cut chile pepper (one for each glass) lengthwise from the tip to within ¼ inch of the stem to form petals. Remove seeds. Soak in ice water 10 minutes until petals open.

HERBS, AROMATIC LEAVES, AND EDIBLE FLOWERS

For scent, color, and interest, herbs, leaves, and flowers are delightful enhancements. Add one or more of each to margaritas, tropical drinks, spritzers, punches, and infused tequilas.

- Add fresh, fragrant sprigs of herbs to tall drinks and spritzers (see "The Cantina Garden" below).
- Float organic flower blossoms in drinks. Possibilities include hibiscus (miniature varieties), violas (Johnny-jump-ups), violets, pansies, orchids, begonias, rose petals, yucca blossoms, nasturtiums, or borage.
- Place a pineapple leaf vertically in a drink, so that it pokes out of the glass and looks like a pointed *penca* (leaf) of an agave. Use fresh citrus, allspice, or bay leaves in the same way.
- Use sugarcane strips as stir sticks. Fresh stalks are hard to cut; purchase canned ones in Asian markets (Chaokoh brand). Great in Mexican Mojitos.

VEGETABLES AND SAVORIES

Garnish options are limited only by your imagination. In contrast to the many sweet embellishments, savory choices can add a salty, crunchy, or spicy twist to tomato- and vegetable-based drinks.

- Skewer jalapeño-stuffed olives, cocktail onions, or pickled peppers, corn, or okra on picks or bamboo skewers.
- Use fresh scallions as fluted swizzle sticks; cut whole jalapeños and serranos into flowers (see sidebar).
- Cut pieces of nopal cactus and red bell peppers into abstract shapes.
- Skewer cherry tomatoes and small golden, pear-shaped tomatoes on wooden picks.
- Make small notches in whole hot peppers with stems (jalapeños, serranos, and red Fresnos) and attach to rim of glasses.

- Use unpeeled cucumber spears and jícama sticks as stirrers. Add a spiral of cucumber peel to spritzers.
- Stir savory tomato-based drinks with spicy jerky sticks as stirrers.

ADDING FESTIVE TOUCHES

- Wooden, bamboo, or multicolored skewers and picks for garnishes
- Fanciful colored, bendable straws and decorative swizzle sticks
- Cocktail napkins and coasters
- Whimsical drink decorations

The Cantina Garden

Having your own organic garden will help keep your cantina stocked, whether you need the finishing touch of a fresh herb sprig, or an edible flower for garnish, or an exotic ingredient to flavor a cocktail. (You'll find more detailed information on gardening and cooking with herbs in another of my books, *The Herb Garden Cookbook*, University of Texas Press, 2003.) Here are some of my favorite cantina plants to grow:

Fresh chiles: jalapeños, serranos, red Fresno, habanero, *chile pequín*, cayenne.

Fresh mint: many flavorful varieties exist, though varieties of spearmint, called "*hierba buena*" in Mexico, are best in cocktails.

Cilantro: especially good in tropical fruit drinks, savory tomato drinks, and spritzers.

Lemon-scented herbs: lemon balm, lemon verbena, lemon thyme, lemon basil, and lemongrass for muddling and garnish.

Lime-scented herbs: lime balm, lime thyme, lime basil.

Pineapple sage: leaves that smell like pineapple when crushed, with fragrant scarlet flowers—pretty in a bouquet popping out of a party punch.

Edible flowers: sunset-colored, peppery nasturtiums for spicy drinks; organic rose petals, lavender spikes, violets, pansies, Johnny-jump-ups, calendula, and marigold petals and flowers for floating in drinks.

Salad burnet: dainty serrated sprigs with delicate cucumber essence—great in spritzers and tequila and tonic (p. 169).

Borage blossoms: tiny blue star-shaped flowers, lovely in spritzers.

Basil: look for sweet, bush, lemon, dark opal, purple ruffles, or cinnamon-scented varieties for muddling and for garnish.

Mexican mint marigold: anise/tarragon-flavored leaves and bright yellow blossoms.

Bay leaf tree: leaves used for cooking, for garnishing, and for infusing tequila.

Allspice tree: large deliciously pungent leaves, redolent of island spices, fragrant and delicious in punches and tropical fruit drinks.

Key lime tree, Meyer lemon, kumquats, Kaffir lime, and other citrus: use leaves as garnish.

Jamaica hibiscus (*flor de jamaica*): available at some nurseries and by mail order (p. 98). This hibiscus has dark green leaves, red stems, and small yellow flowers with bright red calyces at the base of each flower, which, when dried, make a popular Mexican tea or Flor de Jamaica Cooler.

Dulce tequila
Suave tormento
¿Qué haces aquí?
¡Vamos pa'dentro¡

———

Beloved tequila
Torment without a frown
What are you doing here?
Let me drink you down!

El Arte de la Coctelería

CRAFTING TEQUILA COCKTAILS

Arriba,
Abajo,
Al centro,
Pa' dentro!

—

Up,
Down,
To the heart,
And down the hatch!

Cocktail Mania

THE FINE CRAFT of the cocktail has re-emerged. This has encouraged mixologists, bartenders, and home enthusiasts to conjure up original concoctions, embellish traditional favorites, and prepare and present them with flair.

The greatest gift of this cocktail revival is that it inspires curiosity and creativity. Cocktail enthusiasts delight in making homemade syrups, liqueurs, salts, spice blends (like the Cantina Classics in this book), and other exotic delectables for signature libations. They frequent farmers' markets and specialty purveyors in search of seasonal produce and local fare to enhance their creations.

Forays to local liquor stores, Mexican *mercados* (markets) for south-of-the-border ingredients, and import, kitchen, and homeware stores become part of the adventure. Cocktail mania has also led to the production of countless new commercial liqueurs, spirits, mixers, and flavorings, and a plethora of tequila brands.

Although tequila did not become popular in the United States until the 1940s, its flavor and mixability make it a favorite in this cocktail renaissance. The bright, citrusy, fruity, and peppery notes of tequila *blanco* pair well with fresh, natural ingredients, while oak-aged agave expressions lend color, sophistication, and interest to cocktails.

This return to old-style bartending has led to some imaginative cocktails. Some newfangled libations are brilliant and complex, a seduction at each sip, and retain tequila's integrity. Others, while showcasing tequila's versatile mixability, mask its flavor with the use of too many added flavorings and ingredients. Why risk obscuring the essence of the agave, that magnificent plant that took so long to grow?

Some of these "new" cocktails taste like dessert before dinner, instead of an invigorating drink. They're doused with too many kinds of liqueurs and aromatics and laden with agave syrup, sugar, and/or sweet juices. (My father once told me that if you need a drink full of sugar, then you shouldn't be drinking!)

Cheers to those who have mastered the skill of formulating innovative tequila cocktails (and there are many) . . . ones in which the agave still shimmers and shines through subtle layers of European elixirs, bitters, potions, and purées.

Tequila Drinks *al Estilo Mexicano*

Mexican *cantineros* (bartenders) have always crafted tequila drinks with the simple and natural ingredients they have on hand. They concoct refreshing fruit-flavored drinks, festive holiday punches, and other spirited libations—drinks that are fresh and full of flavor instead of frills.

For the most part, I remain partial to these traditional Mexican libations, some of which have not yet even crossed the border. They celebrate fresh ingredients—ripe tropical fruits, fresh limes, hot chiles, garden-fresh produce and herbs, and even cactus fruit and berries gathered in the wild. They sing of citrus and spice, often with a surprise of unexpected flavorings and garnishes, in the true *estilo mexicano* (Mexican style).

Many of the *bebidas* (drinks) and *cocteles* (cocktails) included in this book have withstood the test of time, tasting as good today as they did years ago in Mexican cantinas and restaurants and at family gatherings.

In chapters to come, I'll introduce you to some beloved Mexican drinks, preserving traditions. I've added contemporary touches to well-known favorites and offered many of my own creations, inspired by Mexican ingredients and ideas. All in hopes of inspiring you to stir it up in the cantina, too.

¡Bienvenidos! Welcome to this gustatory adventure, a quest for discovering the art of crafting unforgettable tequila cocktails. Now it's time for you to choose your favorite brands to take home to your kitchen and cantina and start celebrating the true spirit of Mexico.

First, let me introduce you to the way in which the inhabitants of Jalisco—and Texas!—savor their tequila.

Watercolor rendition of the author's home cantina with metal cut-outs of Jaliscan tapatíos painted by Julie Marshall, from the first edition of this book.

Tequila:
el regalo de Jalisco al mundo.

—

Tequila:
Jalisco's gift to the world.

Charros listos para volar (painted tin *charro* angels flying high with their tequila bottles).

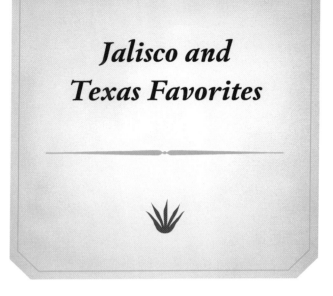

Jalisco and Texas Favorites

How Mexicans Drink Tequila

IN ORDER TO PUT THESE festive libations into a cultural context, let me tell you a bit about Jalisco. The homeland of tequila is steeped in rich traditions: mariachi music, *charros* in silver-studded suits and wide sombreros mounted on horses, and beautiful women dancing the folkloric *jarabe tapatío* (Mexican hat dance) in long, colorful, ruffled skirts and off-the-shoulder blouses. Located in central-western Mexico, Jalisco is the fourth most populated state, bordered by the Pacific Ocean, three other tequila-producing states—Guanajuato, Nayarit, and Michoacán—and the states of Aguascalientes, San Luis Potosí, Zacatecas, and Colima.

Guadalajara, Jalisco's capital and the country's second-largest city is known as "La Perla del Occidente" (the Pearl of the West). It's trendy, sophisticated, and often called the "L.A. of Mexico." Jaliscans are colloquially called "Tapatíos," a word attached to many things that originate in the environs of Guadalajara: tequila, hot sauces, tostadas, and the famous dance, *jarabe tapatío*. Tapatíos are a passionate and proud people who love to have a good time. On weekends, extended families flock to rustic pavilions on the outskirts of town. These open-air restaurants, called *fondas* or *campestres* ("country" clubs), are surrounded by pretty gardens and vistas. Patrons leisurely savor samplings from platters passed around the table: *carnes asadas* (grilled meats), quail and shrimp *a la parrilla* (from a hot griddle), *Quesos Flameados* (melted cheeses), and traditional *antojitos* (tasty tidbits) like taquitos and tostadas Tapatías.

Some places specialize in local favorites like *birria de chivo*, a thick goat stew simmered in a spicy tomato and roasted chile sauce, or pozole, a hearty hominy, pork, and/or chicken stew traditionally flavored with dried red chiles garnished with chopped onions, oregano, and chiles.

Other eateries feature *molcajetes*, a regional specialty named after the volcanic stone mortar in which they are served. (Much smaller versions are used to grind together chiles and spices when making traditional Mexican salsas.) Waiters bring a huge *molcajete*, brimming with a savory fondue bubbling with grilled meats, shrimp, roasted peppers, and lots of gooey, melted cheese for everyone at the table to scoop into warm corn tortillas.

. . . me gusta escuchar los mariachis
cantar con el alma
sus lindas canciones,
Oír como suenan esos guitarrones
y echarme un tequila
con los valetones . . .

———

. . . and I love to hear mariachis
sing beautiful songs with passion,
And listen to their guitars strum
and down a shot of tequila
with proud countrymen . . .

LYRICS FROM "AY JALISCO, NO TE RAJES"

("Oh, Jalisco, Don't Back Down"), composed in 1941 by Manuel Esperón González (1911–2011) and Ernesto E. Cortázar and popularized by Jorge Negrete (1911–1953), "El Charro Cantor," revered musician, actor, and Mexican idol.

Diners hire strolling mariachis by the hour or by the song and burst out singing along with the musicians, an occasional throaty and lovelorn *grito* filling the room . . . "Ay! Ay! Ay!" Sunday meals are called *tardeadas*, because they take up the entire afternoon, or *tarde*. Tapatíos have fun. They laugh. They sing. They revel in merriment. They enjoy good food *and* they love their tequila!

Mariachi at Real Campestre in Atotonilco, Jalisco.

Jalisco is known for its blood-red *sangrita*, a refreshing nonalcoholic chile and citrus chaser for tequila. This lively pair comes to the table in separate shot glasses. Whether tequila is imbibed in this fashion or in pretty fruit-laden concoctions or effervescent spritzers, Tapatíos often sip their favorite tequila drinks, instead of wine, during meals. Once you taste these refreshing drinks, you'll understand why!

. . . quise hallar el olvido
al estilo Jalisco,
pero aquellos mariachis
y aquel tequila
me hicieron llorar . . .

———

. . . I wanted to find oblivion
in the typical Jalisco manner,
but those mariachis
And that tequila
just made me cry . . .

LYRICS FROM "ELLA"

by José Alfredo Jiménez (1926–1973), one of Mexico's foremost and most beloved *ranchero* singer-songwriters

Easy Jaliscan Botanitas

In cantinas throughout Jalisco, tasty *botanitas* (snacks) arrive at the table along with tequila drinks. Crisp and crunchy *chicharrones* (pork cracklings), sprinkled with fiery red Salsa Valentina and a squeeze of fresh lime juice, or red chile–seasoned *cacahuates* (peanuts) are favorites. (Find them packaged in Latin American grocery stores, ready to serve at your next fiesta.) *Encurtidos de verduras*, sometimes called *escabeche*, a savory combination of pickled vegetables—carrots, cauliflower, onions, potatoes, green beans, and jalapeños—and guacamole with homemade tostada chips make tasty tequila accompaniments.

Unlike many cocktails found in American establishments, the drinks favored in Jalisco are neither laden with fancy liqueurs nor over-sweetened. They're fresh and bright! Simple ingredients make them inexpensive to make and light enough to sip throughout a meal. Good tequila, lots of fresh citrus (whenever possible, use small, juicy Mexican limes), and a generous splash of something fizzy bring these cocktails to life. Let the fiesta begin!

Chatazo

Restaurant Real Campestre, an enchanting and popular outdoor eatery in Atotonilco, is surrounded by a vista of hillsides shimmering with rows of silver agave, citrus groves, and a fragrant herb garden. Chatazo is served there in tall glasses. This effervescent cooler might be better named "La Flor de Jalisco" because it's as pretty and pink as a flower. Instead, it's named after Don Chato, a local man who squeezes his own fresh fruit juices to sell from large jugs.

Try it for brunch (instead of a mimosa). Add a splash of Spanish Rosado Cava and garnish with a wedge of unpeeled ruby red grapefruit.

- 5 ounces freshly squeezed ruby red grapefruit juice
- 1½–2 ounces tequila *blanco*
- Splash of Squirt, or your favorite sparkling grapefruit soda, or Spanish Rosado Cava
- Agave syrup to taste, optional
- Garnish: ruby red grapefruit wedge

Fill a tall glass with ice. Stir in grapefruit juice and tequila, then splash with your choice of effervescent. Garnish and serve immediately. Try it with a pinch of Cantina Classic Pink Peppercorn Citrus Salt. *Serves 1.*

Paloma

In the early 1950s, the dashing, pencil-moustached Mexican singer, Pedro Infante, often accompanied by a dozen or more mariachis in traditional attire, helped immortalize the song "Cucurrucucu Paloma" with his crooning voice. It remains one of the most requested mariachi songs today.

Paloma means "dove" in Spanish, and this tequila spritzer will make your spirits soar. More popular than the margarita in Mexico, the *paloma* is the quintessential companion for grilled foods and *antojitos*. It's simple to make and ever so light and refreshing: three ingredients and some salt . . . *nada más*! Some call it the "poor man's margarita."

- Lime and salt for rim of glass
- Salt
- 1½–2 ounces tequila *blanco* or *reposado*
- Juice of 2 Mexican limes
- Squirt, Mexican Fresca, Jarritos Toronja, or your favorite grapefruit soda to taste
- Garnish: lime slice sprinkled with salt

Rim tall glass with lime and salt. Add lots of ice, a pinch of salt, tequila, lime juice, and sparkling grapefruit soda to taste. Stir, garnish, and serve. *Serves 1.*

Hand-painted Talavera *paloma* tile from Dolores Hidalgo.

Jarrito

This lovely libation, made with fresh fruits and citrus, captures the spirit of Jalisco. Mexicans serve it in restaurants and outdoor markets in small clay cups without handles called *jarritos*, which help keep the drink cold. A double portion is served from small clay pitchers called *cantaritos*, and a large earthenware bowl called a *cazuela* holds enough for two to sip through straws. For larger servings, simply increase all ingredients to taste.

Sometimes I serve Jarritos from wide-mouthed and long-stemmed margarita glasses. I've also concocted a party punch called Ponche de Guadalajara, served from a large glass *agua fresca* jar.

- 4 ounces freshly squeezed orange juice
- Generous squeeze of fresh lime juice
- 4 orange wedges
- 3 chunks of unpeeled ruby red grapefruit
- 4 slices of lime
- 4 ounces Squirt or grapefruit Jarritos
- Splash of Topo Chico or mineral water, optional
- 2 ounces tequila *blanco* or *reposado*
- A few pinches of salt

Mix ingredients together with ice in a jumbo margarita glass or clay mug. Squeeze some of the citrus into the drink and eat the citrus from the peel. For larger servings, simply increase all ingredients to taste. *Serves 1.*

Note: Jarritos is also the brand name of a popular soda in Mexico made from natural fruit extracts. To keep your drink cold, freeze thick citrus slices on a tray, then add them right before serving. Take caution not to use glazed earthenware vessels that may contain lead and react with citrus.

Jarritos y Cazuela shot at Robert Denton and Marilyn Smith's lovely *casita* in Ajijic, Jalisco.

Michelada

"¡Compre una michelada. Los mejores están aquí!" cry vendors selling drinks from stalls in the outdoor market of Lake Chapala. Especially welcome on hot, dusty afternoons, *micheladas* are a favorite: a "chela" (cold beer) flavored with chile, spicy seasonings and tart lime juice. *Micheladas* are a tasty chaser to accompany a shot of tequila. Some simply pour the tequila shot into the bubbly brew.

Versions of this popular drink abound in Mexican cantinas, beach resorts, and bars north of the border; it seems every *cantinero* adds a special touch when making one. Budweiser has even put "Chelada" in a can, but like *sangrita*, it's better when you make your own!

When mixing a *michelada*, cold beer is essential (and some ice cubes in the glass, in my opinion), as well as some combination of Worcestershire, soy, and/or Maggi seasoning, and salt and pepper. Some like to add a generous splash of spicy Bloody Mary mix; I prefer adding Sangrita for color and kick. Others add a shot of Clamato, a clam-flavored tomato juice beverage and purported hangover cure.

Refreshment stand in Chapala market, Jalisco.

- Chilled glass rimmed with lime and coarse salt or Cantina Classic Spicy Mexican Seasoned Salt
- 2 or more teaspoons of Salsa Valentina, Tabasco, habanero, or your favorite bottled chile sauce
- Sangrita, spicy Bloody Mary mix, or Clamato to taste, optional
- Juice of 2 Mexican limes
- Generous dash of Worcestershire and/or Maggi seasoning
- Pinch of seasoned salt
- Freshly ground black pepper to taste
- A big shot of tequila *reposado*
- 1 cold Mexican beer, preferably Bohemia or Negra Modelo
- Lime as garnish
- Ice, optional

Rim iced mug with lime and salt. Mix together the chile sauce, lime, Worcestershire, Maggi, salt, and pepper in the mug; add some ice cubes. If you choose to mix in the tequila and the *sangrita* or spicy Bloody Mary mix, do so now. (Otherwise, serve a shot of tequila separately.) Slowly add beer, stirring gently. Garnish and serve.

Note: Stage a *chelada* cantina at your next party. Encourage guests to customize their own concoctions in this "deconstructed" version. Provide iced glasses and cold Mexican beer, a chilled pitcher of Bloody María or Sangrita, chilled Clamato juice, a variety of bottled hot sauces and condiments, Cantina Classics Spicy Mexican Seasoned Salt, tequila *reposado*, and lots of fresh-cut limes.

Charro Negro

As dark and macho as the *paloma* is delicate and light, the *charro negro* celebrates Jalisco's revered *charros*, horsemen renowned for their equine showmanship and graceful twirling lassos. Tequila gives island rum some competition in this Mexican version of the Cuba Libre, making it a favorite in Mexico's largest tequila-producing state.

In Jalisco cantinas, men fill a small glass with tequila and cola (no ice!). They take a bite from a lime wedge and quickly down the *trago* (swig). As my brother Stuart "El Rey" Hutson says, "Why bother with the cola?" Some *mexicanos* drink their *charro negro* "con sombrero," in a glass rimmed with salt; others prefer it "sin sombrero" (without).

- Lime and salt for rim of glass
- 2 ounces tequila *añejo*, *reposado*, or 100-proof *blanco*
- 4 ounces Coca-Cola (preferably from Mexico)
- Juice of 2 Mexican limes
- Garnish: lime wedges

Rim tumbler with lime and salt. Add ice, tequila, Coca-Cola, and a generous squeeze of fresh lime juice, dropping the squeezed lime halves into the drink. *Serves 1.*

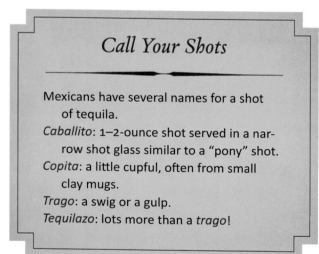

Call Your Shots

Mexicans have several names for a shot of tequila.
Caballito: 1–2-ounce shot served in a narrow shot glass similar to a "pony" shot.
Copita: a little cupful, often from small clay mugs.
Trago: a swig or a gulp.
Tequilazo: lots more than a *trago*!

Vampiro

In crowded open-air Sunday markets near Lake Chapala, Mexico's largest lake located just outside of Guadalajara, families gather for lakeside dining, enjoying the songs of strolling mariachis, or meander through aisles packed with curio vendors. From picturesque stalls, vendors hawk popular drinks—like *vampiros*, *palomas*, and *cantaritos*—to passersby.

The *vampiro*, or vampire—a merry mingling of tequila and *sangrita*, splashed with grapefruit soda—is a favorite drink throughout Mexico. Serve *vampiros* at your next Día de Los Muertos or Halloween fiesta or at a summer barbecue. They're bloody good!

- Lime and salt for rim of glass (try Cantina Classic Sal de Sangrita, or a commercial chile-flavored salt, like Trechas or Tajín)
- 2 ounces tequila *blanco* or *reposado*
- 3 ounces Sangrita
- Juice of 1–2 Mexican limes
- 2–3 ounces Squirt or other grapefruit soda
- Garnish: unpeeled ruby red grapefruit, orange, and/or lime slices

Rim a tall glass with lime and salt. Fill with ice and stir in remaining ingredients. Garnish with fresh citrus. *Serves 1.*

Vicente Fernández

A Bow to the King and a Drink Named in His Honor

Known as "El Rey," the king of *rancheras* ("ranch music"), Vicente Fernández embodies the soul of Jalisco . . . and Mexico! Just ask any mariachis north or south of the border to sing "Volver Volver," one of his greatest hits, and nearly everyone in the restaurant will enthusiastically join in—including the kitchen staff! (This song is so popular that George Strait, a Texan known as the "King of Country," also recorded it in Spanish in 2009.)

Vicente's son, Mexican heartthrob Alejandro Fernández, is a Latin Grammy–winning artist with a wide musical range—from *ranchera* to symphony, from flamenco to pop. Choose from the many albums of both father and son for the soundtrack of your next tequila fiesta.

Vicente appears on stage in lavishly embroidered regalia: huge velvet sombreros and *charro* suits cinched by belts with large, ornate silver buckles. His mariachi band dresses in similar, yet more subtle *ranchero* attire, accompanying him with traditional *guitarrones*, violins, *vihuelas*, trumpets, and harps. Though he packs stadiums around the world, he doesn't forget his heritage,

the Mexican working class, *charros*, and *caballeros*. He sings ballads of love's betrayal and the cherished *ranchera* songs on which he was raised. Vicente loves his homeland—and his tequila, and he has been known to imbibe a bit on stage during his more than three-hour performances. He often plays in Jalisco in crowded outdoor arenas called *palenques* (which sometimes feature cockfights), not to be confused with the name for the *palenque* mezcal distilleries in Oaxaca. Just outside Guadalajara, near his ranch, Vicente's *campestre* restaurant, Los Potrillos (little colts), named in honor of his sons, celebrates tequila and Jaliscan fare.

Painting hanging in Los Potrillos showing Mexico's most beloved mariachis. *Left to right*: Javier Solís, Pedro Infante, Vicente Fernández, and Jorge Negrete.

Great Requests for Any Mariachi Group

"Volver Volver"
"El Rey"
"La Ley del Monte"
"Caminos de Guanajuato"
"Por Tu Maldito Amor"
"Cruz de Olvido"
"De Que Manera Te Olvido"
"Borracho Te Recuerdo"
"Guadalajara"
"México Lindo y Querido"

Look for Alejandro Fernández's beautiful CDs. *Bellas Artes: 100 Años de Música Mexicana* includes many of my favorite songs.

Chente

I wanted to create a very special drink for "Chente," as the adoring fans of Vicente Fernández affectionately call him. Then I realized a bottle of tequila is all he would want!

- 1 bottle of tequila, the true spirit of Chente's "México Lindo y Querido." *Blanco, reposado*, or *añejo*—he drinks whatever his *compadres* offer.

Open the bottle. Raise it into the air and shout "Viva México! Viva El Rey!" Pass the bottle around for all to take a swig and sing along with Chente's passionate *rancheras. Serves an admiring crowd.*

How Texans Drink Tequila

*¡Tequila hoy
tequila mañana
tequila siempre
tequila Tejana!*

—

*Tequila today
tequila tomorrow
tequila forever
tequila Texana!*

LUCINDA HUTSON

Texas and Jalisco share some things in common. They're populated with fun-loving folks who like good food and spirited libations and may even rival each other in gracious hospitality. While Jaliscans gather at outdoor *campestres* and markets to partake of regional grilled foods, Texans travel to destination barbecue establishments (or backyards).

Texans and Jaliscans like tequila with their meals: fresh lime margaritas, refreshing *palomas*, spicy Texican Martinis, signature spritzers, zesty *micheladas*, and *sangrita*. Slow-sipping shots and snifters easily accompany a satisfying Texas meal, just as they do in Jalisco.

Unlike most spirits, tequila can be savored throughout a meal. Tequila's versatility—its bright mélange of herbaceous, fruity, and peppery nuances—brings food to life. It also refreshes the palate in between bites.

Drinking bourbon or Scotch during a meal would annihilate taste buds. Sweet, fruity vodka drinks compete with spicy entrées or subtle sauces. A shot of sweet rum between courses as a refreshing palate cleanser? *¡No, gracias!* But bring on tequila to sip with a combination platter of brisket, sausage, and ribs with tangy Texas barbecue sauce and all the tasty sides, or sizzling fajitas, or anything from the grill.

Texans love Mexican food. Whether it's Tex-Mex enchiladas smothered in cheese, nachos, and melted *quesos*, or authentic interior Mexican cuisine, tequila goes with each mouthful.

Spicy foods just seem to suit the palates of many Texans, so Thai and Vietnamese foods and other full-flavored ethnic cuisines are also very popular in the Lone Star State. Margaritas, spritzers, and tequila cocktails muddled with fresh fruits and cucumbers pair well with these cuisines, too.

AUSTIN-TACIOUS: AUSTIN ORIGINALS

Austin is a young, vibrant, hip-and-happening city. The "Live Music Capital of the World" reverberates with acclaimed music festivals (instead of mariachis), like South by Southwest and Austin City Limits. The city is the state capital and is home to nearly fifty thousand students at the University of Texas at Austin, many high-tech industries, and lots of tequila enthusiasts.

One such enthusiast is the founder of Patrón tequila, John Paul DeJoria, who resides primarily in Austin. Several boutique tequila companies have chosen to headquarter in my hometown—maybe just because so many Texans like tequila so much (and of course, we *are* in close proximity to the border).

Texas Tapas

American bars often serve chips and salsa or nachos, tostada chips layered with refried beans, jalapeños, and other toppings and smothered with broiled cheese. Instead, try Queso Flameado, or, for a lighter snack, and instead of chips, serve Nachos Nopales, which are grilled nopal cactus squares (see p. 216) drizzled with Salsa Borracha (Drunken Sauce) and topped with queso fresco. What could be more *mexicano*— and more fitting for tequila or mezcal drinks?

Any of the chunky salsas, especially Corn Salsa Prontísimo or Fiesta Frijoles, served with chips for dunking, or tostadas, make delicious and filling bar fare.

Five Favorite Tequila and Mezcal Companies Headquartered in Austin, Texas

Ambhar (NOM 1479): Sleek and sophisticated packaging; multi-distilled and filtered expressions in a contemporary and elegant style.

Dulce Vida (1443): The sweet life! Long-necked bottle filled with 100-proof tequila makes it a good choice for Texas cocktails because it preserves tequila's flavor, even when the ice melts!

Pepe Zevada Z Tequila (1464): Founded by Pepe Zevada, former world ambassador for Sauza, who prides himself on this traditional Mexican-style tequila. Bring on the fiesta!

Republic Tequila (NOM 1577): Organic, kosher, and produced in a state-of-the-art "green" distillery, this classic lowlands-style tequila is sold in a Texas-shaped bottle.

Wahaka Mezcal (NOM 0148-x): Premium artisanal mezcal from Oaxaca made from several kinds of estate-grown and wild agaves, using traditional techniques of production.

The following four hometown favorite margaritas help to "Keep Austin Weird" and wonderful! You'll find versions of them at many Austin venues, but I've come up with my own.

Keep all ingredients and glasses chilled before preparing these coolers and use large cubes of ice to avoid diluting drinks. We need our drinks cold in Texas!

Add sweeteners in small increments, using Cantina Classic syrups or Sweet and Sour.

Guacawacky AVOCADO MARGARITA

What will your friends say when you offer them a "Guacawacky"? Mine know to expect the unexpected! But who's ever heard of an avocado margarita? The Garcia brothers of Austin's popular Mexican restaurant Curra's popularized a rich and creamy green "margarita" smoothie years ago.

I've added my own special touches: Cantina Classic Jalapeño Syrup, tart green tomatillo, and a red chile-seasoned salt rim. I muddle and shake ingredients instead of swirling them in a blender with ice so that the drink is not diluted.

Guacawacky is rich and filling, but still refreshing. A fun and unusual addition to any fiesta, it is also a satisfying after-dinner drink.

- 1 ripe (slightly soft) medium tomatillo, husked and cut into eighths
- 2 sprigs of cilantro
- ¼ avocado, peeled (not too ripe)
- ¾ ounce freshly squeezed Mexican lime juice
- ¾ ounce homemade Cantina Classic Jalapeño Syrup *
- 2 ounces tequila *reposado*, chilled
- Cantina Classic Spicy Mexican Seasoned Salt, or commercial brand, for rim
- Garnish: Thick tomatillo slice and/or avocado slices sprinkled with lime and dusted with Spicy Mexican Seasoned Salt, or lime wedge on rim of glass.

Vigorously muddle tomatillo in a pint glass. Add cilantro and avocado and continue to muddle. Add lime juice, Jalapeño Syrup, and tequila. Shake with ice until tin is frosty. Taste, adding more lime or syrup as needed. Pour unstrained into chilled, salt-rimmed, long-stemmed margarita glasses or tumblers with a sprinkle of seasoned salt. Garnish and serve. *Serves 1.*

*Note: Instead of Jalapeño Syrup, you can muddle ½ seeded jalapeño with the tomatillo and add more Sweet and Sour. You may discard the tomatillo peel after muddling, though I like to bite into its tartness in the drink.

Cerveza Loca *Tejas Tea*

In the early 1980s, a fellow Austin tequila enthusiast added some beer to the blender when he made a frozen margarita. I thought him *bien loco* at first, but was pleasantly surprised upon tasting its added fizz and pleasant pungency. Today, versions of this drink abound—mostly ones swirled in the blender with frozen limeade. Try my version instead at your next barbecue, a refreshing cooler served on the rocks.

- Salted rim, optional
- ¾–1 ounce fresh lime juice
- 1½–2 ounces tequila *reposado*
- ¾–1 ounce Cantina Classic Sweet and Sour
- 4–5 ounces ice cold Mexican beer (Bohemia or Negra Modelo) or, for a true Texas touch, Shiner Bock
- Garnish: squeeze of fresh lime with spent lime shells dropped into the drink

Mix ingredients together in a tall glass with ice, stirring in the beer just before serving. *Serves 1.*

Note: Many restaurants today serve a frozen margarita in a jumbo goblet topped with an upside-down bottle of Coronita (a 7-oz. Mexican Corona beer), which drizzles into the margarita.

Texican Martini

I first tasted a Mexican martini in 1975 at Austin's Cedar Door Bar and Grill. Since then, the bar has changed locations four times, but they still serve their famous drink in shakers for patrons to pour at the table. Today, many venues offer a version of this martini on their menu, but often loaded with sweet and sour made from a mix. Here's mine: it's sophisticated, spicy, and sexy! Rim a chilled glass with salt, garnish with skewered jalapeño-stuffed green olives, and start grilling the steaks!

- Cantina Classic Spicy Mexican Seasoned Salt or commercial brand, for rim
- 2 ounces tequila *reposado*
- 1 ounce fresh lime juice
- ¾ ounce orange juice
- ½–¾ ounce Cointreau
- ½–¾ ounce Cantina Classic Sweet and Sour, or agave syrup to taste
- 1 tablespoon chilled brine from best quality jalapeño-stuffed green olives
- Garnish: skewered olives, pinch of Spicy Mexican Seasoned Salt

Rim chilled glass with seasoned salt. Pour ingredients in shaker tin, add ice cubes, and shake until frosty. Strain into prepared glass, with or without ice. It's fun to serve from mini-shakers for guests to shake and pour at the table. *Serves 1.*

Variations: Substitute all/part Chile Pepper–Infused Tequila for the *reposado* or all/part Cantina Classic Jalapeño Syrup for the Cointreau. A version using Austin's own tequila, Ambhar, adds Talk O' Texas Hot Okra Pickle juice (instead of olive) and garnishes the drink with a crisp pickled okra . . . yum!

Güero's Margaritas

Fellow *güeros* (what Mexicans call fair-skinned folks) Rob and Cathy Lippincott have traveled to Mexico for years and love it as much as I do. That love is reflected in their Austin restaurant, Güero's Taco Bar, which has delighted patrons since 1986 with an ambience blending Texan and Mexican cultures.

Güero's offers more than twenty different margaritas, made in the traditional way, with freshly squeezed lime juice and a choice of various tequilas. They also serve *palomas*, *micheladas*, and their version of a *chatazo*, which they call a *mayahuel*.

The Lippincotts and I share the same taste in a margarita: 2 parts tequila, 1 part Cointreau, and 1 part fresh-squeezed Key lime juice. Says Cathy, "They *must* have Key lime juice—a bit sweeter and not so acidic—and they *must* be shaken up a bit so that bits of ice break off into the margarita to dilute the strength just a bit." If you make margaritas in large quantities for parties, this can be accomplished with vigorous whisking with some ice or by adding a bit of ice water to the pitcher. (I like to add a good splash of Topo Chico, Mexican sparking water.)

I've spent many a Sunday *tardeada* sipping hand-shaken margaritas, eating *tacos al pastor*, and dancing to the eclectic music of the Texana Dames. Consider playing their CDs for your next tequila fiesta!

Tequila es para saborear,
no para emborrachar.

—

Tequila is for savoring,
not for inebriating.

Los borrachos (drunkards), carved by Inocencio Vásquez, Oaxaca.

Copitas y Coctelería

SHOTS AND COCKTAILS

Y OU'LL DISCOVER COUNTLESS ways to celebrate tequila and mezcal—from playful shots and *sangrita* to classic cocktails, margaritas, party punches, and after-dinner drinks. Mexicans drink tequila as the French drink wine: as an integral part of a leisurely meal. Mexicans often imbibe tequila straight up in *copitas* (small glasses) or *caballitos* (pony glasses). Extolling its virtues as an aperitif, some sip a shot of tequila *blanco* or *reposado* before eating or savor a shot between the many courses of a large, traditional Mexican meal. After a meal, they may partake in the pleasure of a mellow *añejo*, as richly satisfying as a fine cognac.

Now let me tell you about two meals I'll never forget: one with the original owners of Herradura tequila at their lovely family hacienda and the other with an agave field-worker named Don Aurelio at a humble roadside restaurant. Throughout both meals, the tequila rituals and traditions shared reminded me of the importance of tequila in Mexican culture.

Luncheon at the Herradura Hacienda

I fondly remember a very special luncheon with *tequilero* (tequila producer) Guillermo Romo and his wife, Lupita, at their family hacienda, San José del Refugio, in Amatitán, Jalisco, in 1989. Built by ancestor Feliciano Romo in 1861, this was still a working ranch, as well as home of the distillery for Herradura, one of Mexico's finest tequilas. The distillery, nestled behind thick plastered walls and fed by a pristine underground spring, combined proud family centuries-old traditions with state-of-the-art technology.

Guillermo, famous for his pride and passion, had given me an extensive three-hour tour of all the fields and the distillery, and we were hungry! We sat down at a long dining table looking out on lush terraced gardens. Enticing aromas escaped from the kitchen of Doña Paula, the beloved family cook for more than thirty years. The soft rhythmic sound of clapping hands promised handmade tortillas hot from the *comal*.

Finally, Doña Paula served our meal. Into warm tortillas we scooped steaming *cuitlacoche* (corn fungus), thick and inky as black beans, with a discernible flavor of sweet corn and earthy truffles. A savory salad followed: succulent green strips of *nopalitos* (cactus pads) tossed with chopped tomatoes, serrano peppers, and onions, accompanied by chunky guacamole made with avocados from the orchard outside. The guacamole was prepared in and served from a *molcajete*, a volcanic stone mortar and pestle.

Next, *puntas de filete* (beef tenderloin tips), tenderized in Doña Paula's special marinade of a sweet, mild vinegar that she had made from the fermented *aguamiel* from baked *piñas*, sour oranges, olive oil, and garlic. Frijoles Refritos, drizzled with a fiery red *salsa de chile de árbol* and slices of *queso asadero* (creamy white cheese), certainly left no room for more food! Nevertheless, to complete our Jalisciense meal, Doña Paula delighted us with the family's favorite, flan custard flavored with oranges and sprinkled with cinnamon, served with a small snifter of *añejo*. Such memories and meals inspired the recipes in this book.

Before and during the meal, a server passed a tray of tequilas in handblown shot glasses etched with the Herradura logo: an agave plant within a horseshoe. We sipped Herradura Blanco, and the pronounced essence of the agave was as remarkable as the sublime fruitiness of a French *eau-de-vie*, simultaneously soothing and invigorating.

Later, Guillermo showed me a family heirloom, an intricately carved cow's horn, hollowed out to hold tequila. He held it directly under the spigot of a copper still and filled it with crystal-clear tequila. Raising the horn to my lips, I was transported back in time, conjuring up images of Spanish conquistadores, whose Old World gift of distillation transformed the heart

of the agave into a liquid silver elixir. I imagined them raising that crescent horn in celebration, drinking the fruits of their magical alchemy. The freshly distilled spirit struck me with an exhilarating warmness as I savored its complexities, at once bold and peppery, yet smooth and slightly sweet. Señor Romo raised a toast to me:

> *Al que toma Herradura*
> *su vida más le dura.*
>
> ——
>
> *He who drinks Herradura*
> *will most certainly endure.*

How Don Aurelio Drinks Tequila

Don Aurelio caught my eye and winked. A silver mustache half hid his mischievous grin, and a straw sombrero shaded his twinkling eyes. A bright red poncho with a woven design of white stallions hung over his shoulders to below his knees. Well-worn *huaraches* protected his calloused feet.

Don Aurelio Lozano, renowned *jimador* (agave harvester), had just brought a load of *piñas* down the mountain to the El Viejito distillery in Atotonilco, as he has done for the past forty years. A shiny blue truck now delivers his *piñas* instead of the six mules upon whose backs he used to strap the heavy load. When I asked him how often he harvested and delivered *piñas* to the distillery, he chuckled, "Cuando las piñas necesitan o cuando necesito tequila." (When the *piñas* need harvesting or when I need some tequila.)

A Cow Horn: The First Shot Glass

When raised, its crescent shape represents a universal symbol of drinking.

Besides the art of distillation, Spaniards also brought cattle to Mexico. They used the animals' horns as drinking vessels, unwittingly inventing the first shot glass—and probably the tradition of downing tequila in one big gulp because the horn could not be set down until it had been emptied. In 2010, Sauza tequila cleverly included glass "shooters" shaped like horns in their promotional packaging along with a bottle of their Hornitos.

Cow horn, the original "shot glass" for sipping tequila—because you can't put it down!

Don Aurelio in the agave fields in his red poncho outside of Atotonilco, Jalisco.

I asked to see the fields where he harvested *piñas*, and we drove the twenty miles up to Los Altos. Don Aurelio sang softly in a mysterious Indian dialect as we passed rows of agave, a sea of silver speckled with sunflowers and green corn. The agaves are his amigos. Don Aurelio indeed has the keen insight—an art passed down by generations of *mezcaleros*—to decide exactly when each agave needs harvesting. Its base becomes engorged and spotted with purple patches; waiting just a few days too long could over-ripen the *piña*, which may have taken ten years to mature!

Later, we stopped at a rustic eatery, where I hungrily devoured *birria de chivo*, a regional specialty of steamed goat meat in a thick and spicy chile sauce. Don Aurelio chose chicken and meticulously picked it off the bone, then recited a drinking *dicho* and swallowed some tequila with gusto. He poured a generous shot, extended his arm, bent his elbow to his mouth, and with a wink, chugged it in one long gulp.

> *Estiro el brazo, encojo el codo,*
> *y de un trancazo, me tomo todo.*
>
> ——
>
> *My arm I extend, my elbow I bend,*
> *and without a frown, I drink it all down.*

Then he told me his secrets for longevity and virility. According to Don Aurelio, tequila is essential "para comer y dormir con gusto" (to eat and sleep with pleasure). He awakens every morning at five. At nine, he has two *copitas* of tequila for strength to work. During his main meal at two, he has another two shots. And before bed at nine, he has his last two—perhaps with Coca-Cola and a squeeze of fresh lime. Is tequila the secret to his vibrant good health? Don Aurelio has had two wives (one young enough to be his daughter) and twenty offspring, ranging in age from eight to forty-nine, and he still exudes a lust for life.

After lunch, we went to his home in Arandas, down a dusty street lined with connected adobe houses. From the looks of the street, I would never have guessed what awaited us when Don Aurelio opened the old wooden gate to his home. We walked directly into a central patio bordered by a hay-strewn corral, where a horse, two mules, a cow, a chicken coop, three turkeys, and a rooster greeted us. Surrounding the patio were a few modest rooms with hard-packed clay floors and bright turquoise walls, adorned with hanging birdcages, plastic flowers, and an altar for the Virgen de Guadalupe.

¡Salud!

When Mexicans gather together for meals or drinks, they raise their glasses and toast each other with a hearty "¡Salud!" To health and happiness! Before taking a sip, they clink their glasses, lock eyes, and acknowledge those present and far away with gratitude, nostalgia, and good wishes.

Raising a glass while facing another connects hearts to hearts. A *brindis* (toast) may be an extemporaneous musing or a traditional *dicho* (proverb). I've translated many traditional and well-known drinking *dichos* throughout this book. Some I found inscribed on walls in Mexican cantinas, others came from the mouths of friends, and a few I made up!

Don Aurelio's mother-in-law proudly showed me her pots of sunny nasturtiums, roses, and fragrant herbs on the patio, while his young wife served tequila in colorfully glazed mugs that she had taken down from nails in the plaster walls, where they also served as decorations. We parted with *abrazos* (hugs), and his wife presented me with a bag containing a delicacy: a chunk of baked and caramelized *piña*, reminiscent of candied yam, to eat on the long drive back to Guadalajara.

Often I long for the simplicity of Don Aurelio's life, his mysterious melodies, and his bawdy jokes. To honor him and his reverence for earth and agave, I raise my glass and toast: "To Don Aurelio, to his beloved tequila, and to the twinkle in his eye!"

Tomar tequila, comer bien, montar fuerte,
y esperar la muerte.
El diablo, que no se acerque.
———
Drink tequila, eat well, make lusty love,
and await death's knell.
The devil can stay in hell.

DON AURELIO

Sip and Savor

I like tequila. And I like to drink it *al estilo mexicano* (Mexican style)—simply straight up ("neat") so that I can delight in the nuances and the complexities of the spirit and appreciate its unadulterated flavor.

To me, fine tequila should be sipped and savored. It speaks for itself! It doesn't have to be overpowered in mixed drinks. Instead, sip premium 100% agave tequila *blanco* much as you would fine vodka, delight in the gentle aging of *reposado*, or relish an *añejo* as you would a cognac or a single-malt Scotch. Show off tequila in attractive shot glasses or snifters.

Salt and lime, traditional Mexican favorites, often merely mask the raw flavor of poorly crafted tequilas. I find them unnecessary additions, though sometimes it's fun to follow traditions—if, that is, the tequila is mediocre. However, tasting premium, handcrafted

tequilas with salt and lime is simply a sacrilege. Once a man named Valdo sat down next to me at a bar and ordered a shot of tequila. The bartender asked if he wanted it with salt and lime. He replied, "No training wheels." We became fast friends!

Los Tres Cuates (The Three Chums)

Uno, dos, tres . . . the ritual for drinking tequila: a lick of salt, a shot of tequila, and a bite into a juicy lime wedge. In Mexico, this is known as *los tres cuates.* Perhaps you can master this one-handed ritual: with a swift flick of the wrist, savor the salt, tequila, and lime in one graceful gesture. The first shot is fun to try. Be warned, though: after a few shots of tequila, limes may be flying.

· Salt
· 1 shot (1½ ounces) *blanco* or *reposado* tequila
· 1 lime wedge
· Dexterity

Multiply above ingredients by however many people you're serving. Serve tequila in shot glasses. To drink, squeeze a few drops of lime at the curve between the thumb and index finger (or lick!) and sprinkle with salt. Pick up the shot glass and hold between that thumb and the forefinger; hold the lime wedge between the forefinger and the middle finger. Quickly, lick the salt, swallow the tequila, bite into the lime, and say "¡Salud!" with a smile.

FIESTA TEQUILA FROZEN IN ICE

Surprise and delight your guests with an ice-cold shot served from a bottle of tequila surrounded with "cactus" or flowers frozen in a block of ice. Fiesta tequila makes a memorable (though meltable!) centerpiece. Place the bottle in a *cazuela* to hold the water as the ice melts. Surround the *cazuela* with shot glasses.

To take the salt and lime ritual to a new level of sophistication, serve shots with a platter of inviting embellishments: fresh pineapple chunks, watermelon triangles, cantaloupe and honeydew melon balls, mango and papaya slices, and jícama sticks drizzled with fresh lime juice. Accompany with small dipping bowls of Cantina Classic Spicy Mexican Seasoned Salt and quartered limes. For individual presentations, lightly dip edges of fruit in salt and attach to rim of each glass.

How to Freeze a Bottle of Tequila in a Block of Ice

Place a bottle of tequila *blanco* or *reposado* in a wide-mouthed plastic gallon container, with about a 1½-inch margin around the bottle. Surround the base of the bottle with an assortment of small plastic cacti pressed closely together. They will look surprisingly realistic when frozen in ice. (Find them where florist supplies are sold.) You can also use fresh flowers and/or citrus slices and greenery instead of the cacti. Then, fill with distilled water, leaving the neck of the tequila bottle out of the water.

Make the ice block several days before the fiesta to ensure thorough freezing. Before serving, loosen plastic container by setting it briefly in warm water; let it stand at room temperature for five minutes. Place ice block in a dish to hold the water as it melts.

The bottle will keep for weeks in the freezer, if you want to bring it out, then quickly refreeze it once again. As you pour, hold bottle with a dishtowel to prevent it slipping from your hands.

Fiesta tequila frozen in a block of ice.

Luna de Plata (Silvery Moon)

Sip 100% agave tequila *blanco* from a small, chilled martini glass, as you would premium vodka. Keep the bottle in the freezer prior to serving to make the tequila smooth and syrupy when served.

Luna de Oro (Golden Moon)

I consider it a sacrilege to mix some of the finer premium *añejo* tequilas, camouflaging their rich and complex flavors. Serve them in elegant snifters, as one would a fine cognac, warmed between the palms to release the delicate nuances. Simple yet exquisite!

Marfa Lights

Many have claimed to see a phenomenal spectacle of colorful sparks of lights in the sky above Marfa, a small West Texas town. Once the site for filming the epic *Giant* (1956), Marfa now hosts renowned contemporary modern art galleries and plenty of tequila-sipping artists and eccentrics.

Drink one of these and you just may see the Marfa Lights!

- 1 colorful tissue-wrapped Chinese sparkler
- 2 ounces sotol from the Chihuahuan desert, such as Don Cuco or Hacienda de Chihuahua

Fill a shot glass. Light the sparkler under the stars . . . and pretend that you see the Marfa Lights. *Serves 1.*

Tequila Fría (Tequila on the Rocks)

Ice was once a luxury in Mexico, often not even an option in some parts of the country. Tequila was simply downed in one quick gesture with a lick of salt and a bite of lime.

For sultry Texas nights, premium tequila *blanco* or *reposado* served on the rocks, or with a jumbo ice cube, is the way to go. Add a splash of tonic or sparkling mineral water and a squeeze of fresh lime, if you wish.

Sangrita: Tequila's Spicy Chaser

In Jalisco, a shot glass filled with *sangrita*, a spicy and refreshing nonalcoholic chaser, arrives without request at the table when you order a shot of tequila. A sip of this blood-red chaser simultaneously piques all taste buds in an explosion of sweet, tart, sour, salty, and piquant flavors, making it a natural compadre for tequila. Most *mexicanos* prefer it with a shot of *reposado*, but *blanco* also complements *sangrita*'s fresh flavor.

It's called *sangrita* (the Spanish diminutive for "blood") because of its rich sanguine color. Americans often assume it's made with a Bloody Mary mix. However, authentic *sangrita* gets its color and flavor from fiery red chiles, not from tomatoes. Just as the margarita was first made to please gringo palates, the *sangrita* often served now in Mexico unfortunately reflects North American influences—most notably, the addition of tomato juice. Today even many Mexicans think it is a traditional ingredient.

In authentic *sangrita*, fresh citrus and pomegranate juices offer brightness and balance. (Often, grenadine syrup is substituted instead.) Since fresh pomegranates (or their bottled juice) now are readily available, there's no excuse not to make it in the traditional manner. Bottled Jaliscan red chile salsa, made from fiery *puya* chiles, gives *sangrita* kick and color.

Commercially bottled brands of *sangrita* exist in Mexico and can now be found in some markets in the United States. They don't keep well once opened, are artificially flavored and sweetened, and lack the sassy bite of the *puya*. Although others boast of being the creator of *sangrita*, Guadalupe Sanchez purportedly created the well-known Mexican brand, Viuda de Sánchez, in the 1930s at Lake Chapala, near Guadalajara. American-made brands of *sangrita* are hitting the market, too, though the ones I've seen are made with tomato juice.

My advice? You simply cannot bottle freshness, so make your own!

The best *sangrita* is made from scratch in cantinas and *cocinas*, and the recipes are usually well-guarded secrets. I first created my version in 1990, before *sangrita* became widely known on this side of the border. Because of tequila's popularity today, *sangrita* contests (like hot sauce contests) are the rage. Contestants often add nontraditional ingredients—charred tomatoes, pomegranate molasses, and even garlicky Thai sriracha sauce or horseradish—to their recipes, which, in my opinion, counteract the purpose of this tequila chaser: to highlight, not overwhelm, tequila's flavor.

Following are a few of my favorite *sangritas* and a recipe for homemade Salsa Puya.

Salsa Puya

Salsa Puya is as ubiquitous in Jalisco as Tabasco is in Louisiana. This fiery brick-red hot sauce, bottled in Jalisco, gives this region's *sangrita* its unique flavor. It's also sprinkled on meats and tostadas and all sorts of *botanitas* (snacks). The *puya* chile, related to the *guajillo*, is a dried, blood-red chile about four inches long, tapering to a curved tip. Its flavor is decidedly tart, almost limey, with a piquancy that assaults the back of the tongue.

Look for *puya* chiles in specialty Mexican markets, or substitute combinations of other dried red chiles, such as *chile de árbol, guajillo,* New Mexico, or cayenne. When you can't make your own, use commercially bottled table sauces such as Valentina or Tamazula, imported from Mexico and readily found in Latin American markets.

- 2 ounces *puya* chiles (approx. 30)
- 1½ cups very hot water, to cover
- ¼ cup mild fruity cider vinegar or part rice wine vinegar
- 2 tablespoons chopped red onion
- ½ teaspoon dried Mexican oregano, optional
- ½ teaspoon salt

Briefly toast chiles on a hot *comal*, or griddle, turning continually; take caution not to burn them! Remove stems, seeds, and veins. Place chiles in a small bowl, cover with water, and let soak about 30 minutes. After soaking, place chiles in a blender with just enough soaking water (about ½ cup) to make a thick sauce. Add vinegar, onion, oregano, and salt, and purée. Strain through a sieve and keep refrigerated. (Tightly covered, it will keep in the refrigerator for more than a week and can be thinned with a few tablespoons of water, as necessary.) *Makes 1 cup.*

Devil with his agave spirits, Inocencio Vásquez, Oaxaca.

Sangrita La Lucinda

I have quite a collection of shot glasses just for the *sangrita*/tequila ritual. I store homemade *sangritas* in the fridge in bottles that once held tequila. I must admit, my *sangrita* is always the hit of a party, leaving guests begging for the recipe and attempting to discern the ingredients. It's simple to make!

- 4 cups freshly squeezed orange juice
- 1½ cups 100% natural pomegranate juice
- ½ cup freshly squeezed lime juice, preferably from Mexican limes
- 8–12 ounces commercially bottled Salsa Valentina, Salsa Tamazula, or homemade Salsa Puya
- Salt or Cantina Classic Sal de Sangrita, to taste

Mix ingredients together and chill overnight or longer (it just gets better). Adjust flavorings *al gusto* (to taste) for the perfect balance. Serve chilled in shot glasses to accompany shots of tequila *blanco* or *reposado*. *Sangrita* keeps for more than a week refrigerated. *Makes approx. 7 cups (24 shots).*

Note: I love a glass of this nonalcoholic wake-me-up for breakfast or a midday pick-me-up. Use less salsa for less incendiary *sangrita*.

FOR A FIESTA PRESENTATION, chill bottles of red Sangrita La Lucinda, yellow Sangrita Amarilla, and a green version, Sangrita Verdecita, in an ice bucket, along with a bottle of tequila *blanco* or *reposado*. Let guests choose their favorite sangrita to sip with a shot of tequila.

> *Hacemos un Hidalgo*
> *Pagarás la cuenta*
> *El que deje algo.*
> ———
> *Let's entwine our arms and chug a shot*
> *You'll pay the bill*
> *If I empty it and you do not.*

Bandera Mexicana (Mexican Flag)

Mexicans are patriotic: they immortalize the red, white, and green of their flag even while drinking tequila! Serve this at your next Cinco de Mayo fiesta.

- 1 shot tequila *blanco* or *reposado*, or mezcal
- 1 shot Sangrita La Lucinda
- 1 shot fresh tart limeade or Squirt with a squeeze of lime

Serve each of your guests all three in separate shot glasses. Drink in rapid succession, shouting, "¡Viva Mexico!" or, better yet, sip and savor. *Serves 1.*

María Sangrita
MEXICAN BLOODY MARY

This is much more revitalizing than a Bloody Mary, morning, noon, or night. It's a feisty drink to imbibe at Guadalajara's El Patio Tapatío, while listening to mariachis bellow lusty *rancheras* (ranch songs). Patrons enthusiastically sing along, after spending a day bargaining for pottery, silver jewelry, curios, and crafts in Tlaquepaque. Or serve it at your next Sunday brunch . . . and wish you were in Jalisco.

- 5 ounces Sangrita La Lucinda
- 1¾ ounces silver or *reposado* tequila
- Juice of ½ lime
- Salt and freshly ground pepper to taste
- ½ teaspoon grated onion
- Garnishes: fluted scallion or chile pepper flower (p. 110), orange slice dusted with chile powder, lime wedge

Fill a tall glass with ice and mix in the ingredients. Use a fluted scallion as a swizzle stick, or hook an orange slice dusted with chile powder, a chile pepper flower, or a lime wedge on the rim of the glass. *Serves 1.*

Facing: Painted tin frame saying, "sabor picante" (spicy flavor), with an accompanying shot glass of tequila *reposado*; the other frame says, "el amor es picosito" (love is "hot"), with a shot of sangrita.

Sangrita Amarilla

In this book, you'll find a trio of sangrita "chasers"—red, yellow, and green versions with distinct flavors—to accompany shots of tequila. This fruity *amarilla* ("yellow") version sings of mango, citrus, ginger and pineapple, with a blast of fiery habanero to ignite taste buds ... and make a sip of tequila taste especially good!

- 1 heaping tablespoon fresh, peeled ginger, loosely chopped
- 1 fresh habanero chile, seeded and stemmed, or a few shakes of bottled habanero salsa
- 2 mangos (¾ pound each), not overly ripe, peeled, and loosely chopped
- ⅓ cup loosely chopped red onion
- 1 teaspoon coriander seeds, freshly ground
- 1½ teaspoons spicy Mexican Seasoning Salt
- 1 cup pineapple juice
- 2 cups orange juice with pulp
- ½ cup freshly squeezed lime juice
- Agave syrup to taste, if needed

Grind ginger and habanero in a blender. Add mango, red onion, ground coriander, and spicy salt; coarsely purée. Blend in juices; adjust flavors and chill overnight. Thin with more citrus juices as needed. Serve ice cold to accompany shots of tequila. *Makes approx. 5 cups.*

Sangrita Verdecita

Here's another spicy tequila chaser. Felipe Camarena, founder of Tequila Ocho, a stand-out, single-estate tequila from the Arandas area, described to me a refreshing chaser that he had tasted in London, where tequila has become very popular. I made up my own recipe and call it "Sangrita Verdecita," or "something spicy and green." When served chilled in shot glasses as a chaser for tequila *blanco* or *reposado*, it's quite bright and refreshing and *picosa*.

- 1 pound tomatillos, husked and quartered (10–12)
- 3 or more serranos, seeded, chopped
- 4 green onions, chopped with some of their green tops
- ¾ cup cilantro, chopped
- 4 tablespoons fresh mint, chopped
- ½ cup freshly squeezed lime juice
- 3 cups pineapple juice
- 1 teaspoon Cantina Classic Sal de Sangrita
- ½ teaspoon crushed, dried *chile de árbol* to taste, optional
- agave syrup to sweeten, optional

With slow pulses, grind together tomatillos, serranos, onions, cilantro, and mint in a blender. Add lime and pineapple juices and salt and blend lightly; do not over-blend. Chill several hours or overnight. Adjust flavors, adding more lime juice, *chile de árbol*, or agave syrup, if needed. Keep refrigerated for several days. *Makes 5 cups.*

Tequilas *Picosas*

Mexicans add hot chiles to many of their favorite tequila drinks. They're natural partners. Here are some more fun recipes!

Tequila Macho

In 1990, I was invited to attend the Festival Gastronómico in Cancún, Mexico. The Círculo Culinario Mexicano, a distinguished group of Mexican women chefs, coordinated this culinary and cultural exchange.

One luncheon, served on an open patio overlooking the Caribbean, was especially memorable. I noticed Carmen Martí, a stunning Mexican model with black bobbed hair and an engaging smile. She was dressed in summer whites, and the salt-rimmed martini glass she held in her hand sparkled in the sun. As she raised the glass to her lips, I noticed what looked like an emerald reflected from within—a green serrano pepper! When I asked her what she was drinking, she replied, "Tequila Macho" and demurely took another sip.

You may want to keep a bottle of your favorite tequila *blanco* in the freezer just for this drink.

- Coarse salt
- 1½ ounces chilled 100% agave tequila *blanco*
- 1 green serrano or jalapeño pepper, with stem

Chill a small martini glass and lightly salt its rim. Fill with chilled tequila. Make a small slit in the side of the fiery pepper and "hook" it over the edge of the glass so that it's submerged in the tequila. *¡Cuidado: Picoso! Serves 1.*

Note: For a special presentation, cut the serrano into a flower (p. 110).

Diego Rivera

I have been told that Diego Rivera, the passionate Mexican artist who captured the soul of Mexico in his murals, liked peppers in his tequila. Supposedly, he filled a *copita* with *salsa fresca*—a chunky uncooked table sauce brimming with chopped fresh tomatoes, onions, cilantro, and serrano peppers, as colorful as his palette—and topped it with a shot of tequila and a squeeze of lime and downed it in one big gulp. Indeed, here's a drink guaranteed to connect your eyebrows!

- 1 lime wedge
- Salt or Cantina Classic Spicy Mexican Seasoned Salt
- 1 tablespoon *salsa fresca**
- 2 ounces tequila *blanco* or *reposado*
- Cilantro sprig for garnish

Rim a wide-mouthed shot glass with the lime wedge and salt. Put the *salsa fresca* in the glass, top with tequila, and garnish with a cilantro sprig. Quickly gulp it down, and bite into the lime wedge, shouting, "¡Viva Frida!" *Serves 1.*

* Note: Purchase fresh *salsa fresca* (often called "pico de gallo") in the refrigerated section of your local supermarket or make your own: freshly chopped tomatoes, onions, serranos, garlic, cilantro, and lots of fresh lime juice.

Cantina Classics: Tequilas *Curados* (Cured Tequilas)

CHILE PEPPER—INFUSED TEQUILAS
THE REAL FIREWATER

Experimenting with various types of chile peppers to infuse tequila is part of the fun, as each one offers its unique characteristics. Tiny round balls of *chile pequíns*, feisty green serranos, ripened red jalapeños, anatomically accurate "peter" peppers, and the ferocious bright-orange habaneros have distinctive aromas and flavors. I have even skewered dried, smoky chipotle peppers for a smoke-and-fire-flavored tequila, which is especially good in *frijoles* and marinades.

Sampling from a selection of peppered tequilas will enliven a fiesta. In the summer, serve peppered tequila straight from the freezer followed by a bite from a lime wedge. Or down a shot to take the chill off a winter's night.

Use these firewater infusions instead of vodka in Bloody Marys or as a surprise spark in a margarita. Whether enjoyed straight from the bottle in all its incendiary glory or as a spicy addition to marinades, sauces, stews, and even desserts, Chile Pepper—Infused Tequila is a bottle of fun and makes an imaginative gift.

Hot Shots

One sip from these "hot shots" may pluck the heart out of an unsuspecting neophyte, but chile pepper aficionados will be dancing with the devil. Hot Shots bring out the macho in any crowd.

- 1½ ounces Chile Pepper—Infused Tequila, preferably chilled
- Salt, optional
- 1 lime wedge, optional

Pour your favorite Chile Pepper—Infused Tequila into a shot glass and sip—or shoot, and you may want to jump into the nearest pool to cool off. Salt and lime are optional, but perhaps necessary to quell the fire. *Serves 1.*

Lucinda's La Bamba

This is my signature drink for the wild of spirit and of heart: a ferocious *chile pequín* floats in a shot of tequila. Biting into this may be as much of an adventure as biting into the worm in a shot of mezcal.

- 1 lime wedge
- Cantina Classic Spicy Mexican Seasoned Salt for rim
- 1½ ounces tequila or Chile Pepper–Infused Tequila
- 1 lime slice
- 1 fresh *chile pequín*

Rim a shot glass with a lime wedge, lightly swirl in the seasoned salt. Pour in the tequila and pop in the *chile pequín*. Garnish the rim with a slice of lime. Guzzle it down *muy pronto*, bite into chile, and soon you will be singing all of the verses to "La Bamba"! *Serves 1.*

Margarita Picosita

When acclaimed Texas restaurateur Stephan Pyles asked me to include a drink recipe in his first cookbook, *The New Texas Cuisine*, this was my choice. It's pure Texas bravado in a bold and lusty margarita. It's fun to serve ice cold in shots, too, and will certainly get the party started! Chill all ingredients before mixing.

- Cracked ice
- 5 ounces Chile Pepper–Infused Tequila
- 3 ounces freshly squeezed lime juice
- 3 ounces triple sec (or part Grand Marnier)
- Splash agave syrup, if needed
- Garnishes: salt-rimmed glasses, lime slices, whole chile peppers

Fill a shaker with cracked ice; add ingredients and shake vigorously. Strain into chilled, salt-rimmed margarita glasses. Garnish with lime slices. *Makes 3 margaritas or about 5 shots.*

The *diablo* made me drink it! Painted wooden articulated toy from Oaxaca.

Making Chile Pepper–Infused Tequila

Look for attractive glass bottles, with cork stoppers; don't use metal lids. Sterilize bottles and fill with desired amount of tequila *blanco*, *reposado*, or mezcal. Use 100% agave tequila in the moderate price range. Skewer 2–4 chiles (or more) per bottle on long bamboo picks. (The most difficult part is determining the desired piquancy. Remember: you can always add more chiles if necessary.) Remove chiles within a week, but leave one for identification.

Bloody María
PEPPERED TEQUILA BLOODY MARY

Let Willie serenade you with "Bloody Mary Morning" as you leisurely sip this. Peppered tequila, fresh herbs, and Valentina-spiked tomato juice make spirited partners. Here's a festive garnish: skewer any combination of baby pickled corn, okra, peppers, cherry tomatoes, cocktail onions, and boiled or grilled shrimp—and place the skewer horizontally across the rim of the glass. Before serving, plop in a sprig of basil.

- Cantina Classic Spicy Mexican Seasoned Salt and lime rim
- 2 ounces Chile Pepper–Infused Tequila
- 5 ounces chilled tomato juice (part Clamato, optional)
- Lots of fresh lime juice
- Freshly ground lemon pepper
- 2 teaspoons Worcestershire sauce
- Garnishes: lime wedge, scallion swizzle stick (p. 110), or festive skewers.

Fill a tall glass with ice; stir in other ingredients and garnish. *Serves 1.*

Note: If you don't have Chile Pepper–Infused Tequila on hand, add a few shakes of Salsa Valentina.

Qué bonito es no hacer nada,
y después de no hacer nada, descansar.

—

How beautiful it is to do nothing,
and after doing nothing, to take a siesta.

Pique
SPICY ORANGE AND TEQUILA PERK

I fondly remember once listening to a group of twenty talented young mariachis on stage, in full *charro* regalia, in Guadalajara—many of them following in the footsteps of their fathers, locally revered mariachis. I'm pleased to see many young men and women today following this tradition and mariachi music gaining worldwide acclaim. Every September, Guadalajara hosts the International Mariachi Festival, and I hope to attend it one day soon.

The bartender at the concert, Mario Quiroz, introduced me to Pique, a popular Jaliscan drink that is as colorful and lively as the music itself. Pique owes its piquancy to a good splash of Jalisco's favorite hot sauce, Salsa Valentina, which spikes fresh orange juice and grenadine.

Show off this pretty coral-colored drink in tall glasses or serve it by the pitcher. Like a Torito, it makes a refreshing brunch drink that many have never before tasted.

- 1½ ounces tequila *reposado* (I love it with mezcal)
- 4 ounces chilled fresh orange juice (or part pineapple juice)
- Good splash of Salsa Valentina
- Juice of 2 Mexican limes
- ½–¾ ounce Cantina Classic Ruby Pomegranate Syrup or natural grenadine
- Garnishes: finely chopped red onion, whole green or red chile-pepper flower (p. 110) hooked on side of glass, or scallion swizzle stick (p. 110)

Mix all ingredients together in a tall glass with lots of ice and garnish. *Serves 1.*

Note: Omit the Salsa Valentina and use Chile Pepper–Infused Tequila instead. Freeze slices of fresh red and green chile peppers in ice cubes to embellish this drink.

Fresh Herb- and Flower-Infused Tequila

After all those spicy drinks, you just may need to cool down a bit with something fresh from the garden. When I first visited there, exquisite gardens enclosed within protective adobe walls graced the Herradura estate. The sweet scent of roses, aromatic herbs, and fragrant citrus and avocado trees perfumed the air. Agaves were everywhere: planted in the ground and poking out of rusted gallon tins, waiting to be transplanted in the fields.

On a patio overlooking the gardens, Guillermo Romo's mother and esteemed *tequilera*, Doña Gabriela de la Peña, often served a special libation—tequila *blanco* laced with fresh herbs—from crystal decanters. The aroma and flavor of each herb remained intact, complemented by the spiciness of the tequila. She served them as apéritifs or digestifs in sherry glasses, each sip encapsulating the fragrance of her garden: basil, bay leaf, anise, mint, and rose petals.

Infused tequilas add lots of flavor to classic cocktails—for example, tequila and tonics, fruit drinks, and spritzers—but you may want to simply serve them chilled in sherry glasses, garnished with a fresh herb sprig. The intense herbal flavor and aroma will especially appeal to those who appreciate the flavor of aromatic bitters. Fresh sprigs of herbs and flower blossoms infused in bottles of tequila also make lovely gifts.

Dark opal basil tints the tequila pale lavender with a lingering clove-like spiciness, while nasturtium flowers offer a snappy bite and peachy hues. Oregano lends its bright and peppery flavor, sage its earthy pungency, bay leaf—one of my favorites—and rosemary leave their distinct essences intact, accentuated by the sweet and spicy flavor of the agave. Lemon verbena has a fresh citrusy aroma, whereas Mexican mint marigold is redolent of anise. Or add slightly crushed coriander seeds or pink peppercorns.

Note: You can incorporate these flavored tequilas into marinades and sauces as well as into drinks.

MAKING FRESH HERB- AND FLOWER-INFUSED TEQUILAS

These infused tequilas burst with fresh and aromatic flavors compatible with the peppery and herbaceous essence of the agave. I make them in small corked bottles (6 to 10 ounces) to experiment with different flavorings in small batches; making smaller quantities also ensures freshness. Gather fresh herbs from the garden in the morning or buy them at the market; rinse and pat dry. Place several 4-inch herb sprigs (or a combination of herbs) in each bottle. Cover with premium tequila *blanco*, which will absorb the volatile oils—the natural essence of the herbs.

Let steep in a dark place for several days before tasting. Add more herbs if desired, or remove them if the flavor becomes too strong. Keep refrigerated for fresher flavor. You can always add more tequila (or herbs) as you use the bottle's contents.

¡Salud! (To Your Health!)

Sipping this herbal-infused concoction is at once soothing and restorative of spirit. Think: Lillet or Chartreuse, centuries-old, herb-infused liqueurs. I generally prefer this elixir unsweetened, though some may prefer to add a bit of agave syrup.

- 1¾ ounces herb- or flower-infused tequila
- Twist of citrus peel
- Agave syrup, optional
- Splash of sparkling mineral water or your favorite fizzy soda, optional
- Garnish: 1 fresh sprig of the featured herb

Drink neat, or fill an on-the-rocks glass with ice and pour the infused tequila and over it. Rub citrus twist around the rim of the glass, then drop it into the drink. Add a splash of fizzy soda and garnish with a fresh herb sprig. *Serves 1.*

Citrus- and Fruit-Infused Tequila

Long swirls of aromatic citrus peels (lemon, orange, tangerine, and grapefruit) and acidic fruits (fresh pineapple, strawberries, guavas, and prickly pear) complement tequila and mezcal and enhance cocktails. Use them to flavor margaritas and mixed drinks, for homemade liqueurs, or to serve as ice-cold shots. Be creative in your combinations. Try them in marinades and sauces as well as in drinks. For optimum freshness and flavor, keep these flavored tequilas refrigerated.

MAKING CITRUS PEEL–INFUSED TEQUILAS

Experiment with different types of citrus—tangerine is my favorite. Try tangerine-infused tequila and fresh tangerine juice in a Sonoran Sunrise and you'll see why. Remove peel from citrus in a continuous spiral, making certain to avoid any white pith, which will make the infusion bitter. Use the peel from 1–2 fruits per bottle of tequila (or combine citrus). After 3–4 days, remove most of the peel so that the infusion won't become bitter, but leave a strip for identification. Keep refrigerated for best flavor.

MAKING FRUIT-INFUSED TEQUILAS

Pineapple-Infused Tequila

Peel and cut a ripe, fresh pineapple into chunks and macerate (soften by soaking) in a bottle of tequila or mezcal in a wide-mouthed glass jar. Keep covered and refrigerated for up to 2 weeks, then use in blended drinks, like Carmen Miranda's Downfall or Piña Fina (Pineapple Margarita), or strain and drink in icy shots. A long spiral of lemon peel and/or a split vanilla bean, or chopped fresh ginger, hot green chiles, or fresh mint or basil are optional additions. Try grilling the pineapple first for a special treat. Pineapple tequila is also delicious in marinades.

Strawberry-Infused Tequila

Cut ripe fresh strawberries in half (make small incisions in each half to absorb the tequila) and macerate (as with the pineapple). Place in a wide-mouthed jar with tequila *blanco*. Cover and refrigerate. Keeps for at least a week. To serve, strain and drink in icy cold shots or in an Esa Fresa (Strawberry Margarita). Substitute other berries, or add some quartered fresh guavas along with the strawberries.

Prickly Pear–Infused Tequila

Cut peeled magenta prickly pear cactus fruit in half (make small incisions in each half to absorb the tequila) and place in a large wide-mouthed glass jar (10 prickly pear fruit per 750-ml tequila *blanco*). The cactus fruit vividly tints tequila and flavors it with a ripe watermelon-like aroma and color. Use in Una Tuna (Prickly Pear Cooler) or add to other citrus- or fruit-flavored cocktails. Commercial frozen prickly pear purée is also available for making this infusion.

Mango Django

Mexicans love fresh mangos sprinkled with dried red chile. They also eat dried mangos heavily sprinkled with chile (and often salt) like candy, which inspired this infusion. This mango tequila will add jazz to spritzers, muddled drinks, margaritas, and tropical fruit drinks, or as chilled picante shooters.

- 2 cups tequila *reposado* or Chile Pepper–Infused Tequila
- 4 ounces dried mangos sprinkled with chile*
- 2 teaspoons coriander seeds
- Peel of 1 navel orange cut into a spiral
- 3–4 *chiles pequines*, crushed

Infuse ingredients for a few days. Remove orange peel so it won't get bitter. Store refrigerated. Muddle a bit of the infused mango pieces in cocktails.

*Note: Find dried-chile mangos in Latin American markets, but make sure they are still plump and not too dried out. You may also find them, without chile, in dried fruit bins at grocery stores; add more *pequines* to the infusion.

*Toma lo que puedas
mientras puedas.*

—

*Drink what you can
while you can.*

La Margarita

THE MEXICAN DAISY

History

Life Before Margarita

When bon vivant Charles H. Baker Jr. traveled through Mexico in the late 1930s, he discovered that it was almost impossible to find tequila mixed in a drink because locals all downed it in one big gulp, preceded by a suck of lime and a lick of salt. Baker found imbibing tequila in this manner to be "a definite menace to the gullet and possible fire risk through lighted matches," and he longed for a way to mix it. Of course, the Mexicans thought he was mad. "It was about the same situation which would parallel snooping around Paris for ways to dilute fine champagne, or aged brandy," said Baker.

He also mentioned a drink he tasted in February 1937 at Bertita's Bar, across from the cathedral in picturesque Taxco, a town renowned for silver jewelry. "Take two ponies of good tequila, the juice of 1 lime, 1 teaspoon sugar, and 2 dashes of orange bitters. Stir in a Collins glass with lots of small ice, then fill with club soda. No garnish except crushed halves of the lime."

It seems indeed that Bertita's drink and Armillita Chico were both precursors of the margarita.

Armillita Chico

This was Baker's version of a tequila drink, a formidable one for sure—perhaps even a menace to the gullet! The recipe comes from *The Gentleman's Companion, Volume II: Being an Exotic Drinking Book Or, Around the World with Jigger, Beaker and Flask*, published in 1946. Chico was the foremost matador, the idol of Mexico, at the time Baker's book was published.

- 3 jiggers tequila
- Juice of 2 limes, strained
- 2 dashes orange flower water
- Dash of grenadine

Fill electric shaker with all the finely shaved ice this amount will cover, frappé well, and serve through a sieve, shaking to make the frappé stand up in a brief, rosy, temporary cone. When this subsides, drink to Armillita Chico. *Serves 2.*

TEQUILA'S MOST FAMOUS DRINK

Margaritas: Mexico in a glass. Each sip conjures salty beaches, dusty border town cantinas, and moonlight mariachis. This is a not-so-subtle seduction of the taste buds: the tart and sour flavor of freshly squeezed limes, the bittersweetness of orange liqueur, the complex essence of agave, and a slightly salty edge. Margarita creation myths abound, most of them born in border bars, where a number of proud *cantineros* have boasted that they originated the concoction. One thing is certain: lime juice, orange liqueur, and tequila capture the romance of Mexico.

Of course, I like to credit a *cantinero* in my almost-hometown of Juárez (¡*Ay Chihuahua!*) for the original margarita. According to Brad Cooper's 1974 *Texas Monthly* story, "The Man Who Invented the Margarita," Juárez is the home of this celebrated drink.

As the story goes, in 1942, rowdy soldiers from Fort Bliss and, according to Cooper, "Hemingway-style drinkers who played hard" frequented Tommy's Mexican Restaurant on Juárez Avenue. (No doubt my great-uncle Robert McAlmon often sat at that bar. An expatriate writer and publisher, he drank and caroused with Hemingway and the Lost Generation in Paris in the 1920s, later resuming his drinking in Juárez bars.)

Francisco "Pancho" Morales, the bartender, was mixing drinks for a lively Fourth of July crowd. On this most American of holidays, he created the margarita, the most American of Mexican drinks. A beautiful woman had ordered a "magnolia," a smooth and naughty combination of gin, lemon juice, and grenadine. Pancho improvised by mixing ingredients on hand: the ubiquitous tequila, lime, and Cointreau, a French orange-flavored liqueur. Fortunately, she liked it! Confusing his flowers, Pancho christened his creation with the name "margarita," which means "daisy" in Spanish, certainly suitable for the bright and refreshing drink.

In his time, Pancho was the best bartender in Juárez. He even taught at the Juárez bartenders' school. His margarita quickly became the toast of the town. He later moved, married a woman named Margarita (no kidding), and became the best-known milkman in El Paso, but his margarita lived on.

Cooper's article includes the story of Carlos "Danny" Herrera, who also claims to have invented this all-time favorite drink. In 1948, Herrera and his wife ran a private hotel and restaurant, Rancho La Gloria, located on the road to Rosarito Beach just south of Tijuana. They catered to an illustrious Hollywood crowd, including actor-comedian Phil Harris (who later, with Bing Crosby, became the first importer of Herradura tequila in the United States) and Alice Faye, a blonde sweetheart of the silver screen.

A movie starlet named Marjorie King also frequented Rancho La Gloria to partake of Baja's sunshine and spirits. Marjorie—or Margarita, as she was called in Mexico—fared badly with any liquor except tequila, but she did not want to join the men in their macho shots. So Herrera concocted a more ladylike libation especially for her, softening the impact of the tequila with fresh lime juice and Cointreau. Of course, he named his smooth and icy creation after her. Before long, bartender Al Hernandez was mixing it at La Plaza in La Jolla, California, and by 1950, margarita's fame had spread north and it was a hit in trendy Tinseltown bars. Herrera died in San Diego, California, in May 1992, at the age of ninety, and to many, he will be remembered as the first margarita man.

Or we may raise our glass to San Antonio socialite Margaret (Mrs. William) Sames. Helen Thompson, in the July 1991 *Texas Monthly*, credits Mrs. Sames with mixing the first margarita. I knew I would like her version when Thompson quoted her as saying, "I don't like weak drinks or weak men."

According to Thompson, Mrs. Sames and her husband idled away the hours in the glorious 1940s at their hacienda in Acapulco, where they "gathered about them a close-knit group of eccentric characters and became the center of an intoxicating social swirl." One Christmas, Margaret Sames concocted "the drink" for Nicky Hilton, heir to the hotel fortune, and Shelton A. McHenry, owner of Tail o' the Cock, a famous restaurant in Los Angeles. Her husband later named the drink after her and had a set of glasses made especially for her, etched with her Spanish name, Margarita.

Another claim came from Enrique Bastate Gutierrez, a Tijuana *cantinero* who says he first created the margarita for the lovely and seductive Margarita Cansino—better known by her screen name, Rita Hayworth—while she danced at the Foreign Club there in the 1930s.

In yet another version of the margarita's creation myth, publicists for Jose Cuervo tequila recount the story of Vernon O. Underwood. In 1945, Underwood was granted exclusive rights to distribute Cuervo in the United States, but he wanted to change tequila's coarse image—salt, lime, and shot—to market the spirit to slick Southern California bars. About this time, Johnny Durlesser, the bartender at the aforementioned Tail o' the Cock, duplicated for a woman a drink that she had once tasted in Mexico. Supposedly, her name was Margaret. (Perhaps she had attended a Sames soirée in Acapulco?) Soon after that, Underwood used that concoction to promote tequila in the United States with this advertising slogan: "Margarita. It's more than a girl's name" . . . and the rest is history.

You may take these stories with a grain of salt—or a shot of tequila—but one thing is certain: Pancho, Carlos, Johnny, Enrique, and Mrs. Sames would cringe upon tasting the concoctions served in many bars today. Those iridescent green swirls of artificial flavors, masking the raw flavor of cheap well tequila, in no way resemble their versions of the margarita.

Ingredients

TEQUILA

Traditional margaritas are made with *blanco* (silver) tequila, which complements the flavor of fresh lime juice and orange-flavored liqueur. Cuervo and Sauza tequilas once reigned alone, but now, countless brands crowd the market. Whatever the brand, I always recommend using 100% agave tequila in any drink.

In years past, North Americans have seemed to "go for the gold," thinking gold tequila equaled the best tequila. Actually, these caramel-colored *mixtos* have added flavorings and colors, competing with the clarity and brightness of a classic margarita. Instead, try the mellow flavor of *reposado* tequila. In my opinion, the best place for tequila *añejo* is in a snifter, not in a margarita. Why hide the flavor of aging?

FRESH LIMES

The key to a good margarita is the quality of the ingredients. Small, yellowish-green Mexican *limones*, or Key limes, give Mexican margaritas their inimitable flair. They are often commonly called "Mexican limes" and, because of the margarita's popularity, they are now more easily found in North American markets, often sold in netted bags containing more than thirty limes. Key lime trees are sold at nurseries, so that you may grow your own (they will need winter protection). You won't believe the scent when you pick a small lime right from the tree and its aromatic oils rub off on your hands. Pure heaven!

Because the flavor and acidity of limes vary seasonally and according to which variety is used, it is imperative that you taste the margarita and adjust its flavors before serving. Add more lime juice if needed or mellow the tartness with homemade Cantina Classic sweeteners like Simple Syrup, Citrus Syrup, or Sweet and Sour, which all far outshine anything you could buy in a bottle or a mix.

To rim the glass with salt or not is the ultimate decision. Use freshly ground, coarse-grain sea salt or kosher salt to rim glasses. Or use commercial chile-flavored salts like Tajín or Trechas, or mix your own Classic Cantina Spicy Mexican Seasoned Salts.

ORANGE LIQUEURS

Cointreau, a French triple sec liqueur with a harmonious blend of sweet and bitter orange flavors, was traditionally used to make margaritas, though other triple secs have also become popular. In Mexico, Controy, a less expensive and sweeter version, is popular (first exported by Pura Vida Tequila in 2012). Use cognac-based, orange-flavored liqueurs sparingly so as not to overwhelm the flavor of the tequila (see orange liqueurs, p. 96).

Some people attempt to sweeten margaritas by overcompensating with orange-flavored liqueurs, sweet and sour, or agave syrup, which obscures the flavor of tequila and lime juice. Remember, there should be a balance of flavors: neither the lime nor the triple sec should overpower or distract from the flavor of the tequila, but should instead simply round out the drink.

Para el amor,
No hay como el tequila.

———

For love,
There is nothing like tequila.

SWEET AND SOUR (*AGRIA DULCE*)

For those who like sweeter and less acidic margaritas, make your own Cantina Classic Sweet and Sour. Unlike cloying and artificially flavored commercial mixes, this one, made with only fresh ingredients, is naturally sweet and sour. Use more of this in cocktails than the Cantina Classic flavored syrups found in this book, which are thicker and sweeter.

DAMIANA: *PARA SUBIR AL CIELO* (TO REACH HEAVEN)

Many consider a margarita to be romance in a glass. *Cantineros* in Baja, California del Sur, Mexico, like to make sure of that. They often add a reputed aphrodisiac—Damiana, a sweet, herbaceous yellow liqueur (p. 96)—to their margaritas. Distinctively flavored by a wild herb of the same name, Damiana, with its chamomile and minty undertones, reminds me somewhat of yellow chartreuse, an herbaceous liqueur made by monks in the mountains of France. Use Damiana instead of, or in combination with, Cointreau (or your favorite orange liqueur) . . . or substitute yellow chartreuse and hope the monks don't find out!

The Flavor of Limes

The flavor of a *limón* is a long sigh, a memory of a margarita tasted on a Mexican vacation. Perfumed from the essential oil in its thin skin, the *limón* has an enticing floral bouquet and a pronounced depth of character. It is at once tart, fruity, and quite juicy. Its flavor is best when the peel is somewhat soft and slightly yellow. These limes do not have a long shelf life.

The larger bright-green Persian lime, in contrast, is a mere whimper, a lemon of a lime with an acidic flavor that lacks the complexity and the juiciness of the *limón*. Persian limes are usually readily available and have a long shelf life. Their thicker rinds are best for zesting.

To release more flavor from limes, roll whole limes back and forth on a table before cutting. For the best flavor, squeeze limes just prior to using. If you must, refrigerate juice for no more than 1–2 days ahead of using; freeze extra juice in ice cube trays.

1 ripe Mexican *limón* = about ½ ounce juice
1 ripened medium Persian lime = about ¾–1 ounce juice

Damiana (*Turnera difusa*), a shrubby bush with bright yellow blossoms, thrives in the desert hills of Baja during the rainy season. Mexicans, embracing its reputed powers, drink it before bedtime in hot tea, sometimes dusted with cinnamon, or on the rocks with a twist of lime. The liqueur is now exported to the United States. You can't miss the bottle: it's shaped like the torso of a large-breasted nude goddess. José Pantoja Reyes, manager for more than thirty years of Guadalajara's renowned restaurant, Copa de Leche, told me that Damiana was used in their margaritas until 1975, when it was replaced by Controy.

Margarita Pancho Morales

Many bartenders today over-salt the rim of margarita glasses by dunking the glasses in a saucer of salt, but Pancho Morales, one of the many credited with inventing the margarita (see above), had a more delicate touch. He rubbed the outside rim of the glass with a quartered lime, then sprinkled on salt from a shaker so that it did not overwhelm the drink.

- Salt and quartered lime to rim glass
- 2 parts tequila *blanco*
- Juice of 1 Mexican lime
- 1 part Cointreau

Follow sidebar directions for making this and the following Mexican margaritas. *Serves 1.*

Margarita Carlos Herrera

Carlos "Danny" Herrera said he experimented with various liqueurs before settling on Cointreau to balance the acidity of the lime and the potency of the tequila.

- salt and quartered lime to rim glass
- 3 parts tequila *blanco*
- 2 parts Cointreau
- 1 part Mexican lime juice

Follow sidebar directions for making Mexican margaritas. It's as easy as one, two, three! *Serves 1.*

Making Mexican Margaritas

Chill long-stemmed cocktail glasses prior to serving. Pour coarse salt on a napkin or in a saucer. Hold glass upside down, run a quartered lime around the rim, then lightly twirl it in the salt. Shake off excess so only a delicate crust of salt rims the glass. Or omit salt.

Add tequila, fresh lime juice, and triple sec to a stainless steel shaker cup and fill ⅔ full of ice. Shake briefly until cup is frosty; strain into salt-rimmed cocktail glasses or pour over fresh ice. Dose yourself as you would a martini.

Taste before serving because the acidity of limes varies greatly. Add more lime or sweeten with a splash of simple, diluted agave syrup, Cantina Classic syrups, or Sweet and Sour.

Margarita Mrs. Sames

Still making margaritas as an octogenarian, Margaret Sames's margaritas were not for the timid. I guess that is why I like her version. She served them in chilled glasses etched with her name, and only lightly dusted with salt. Finding other triple secs too sweet, Mrs. Sames only used Cointreau in what she called "the drink."

- Salt and quartered limes to rim glasses
- Ice cubes
- 3 parts tequila *blanco* (she used Sauza)
- 1 part Cointreau
- 1 part Mexican lime juice

Instead of using a shaker, Mrs. Sames mixed her margaritas in a glass pitcher (never a blender!) with a long-handled spoon, lemonade-style, then poured it into glasses over a few ice cubes. *Serves 1.*

Margarita al Aficionado

My friend Germán González, former distiller of Chinaco tequila and now of t1 (Tequila Uno), shared this margarita with me . . . a drink for those who want pure agave expression, without the influence of triple sec. It's made with *reposado*, which many Mexicans favor.

- 2 ounces t1 Excepcional *reposado*
- ¾ ounce fresh Mexican lime juice
- ½ ounce agave syrup

Follow sidebar instructions. *Serves 1.*

Top-Shelf or Skinny

Fashionable bars and restaurants offer "top-shelf" margaritas. They make upscale margaritas using premium tequilas instead of well brands, often lacing them with trendy liqueurs, or an *añejo* or a mezcal floater. Discerning drinkers who splurge on quality especially appreciate the nuances of these margaritas, as do tequila aficionados who delight in requesting their favorite brands (or trying new ones). Top-shelf margaritas fetch much higher prices than the standards. Just make sure these lux libations are not loaded with sweet and sour mix and agave syrup.

If you want to cut out calories, but not sacrifice the fun and flavor of a margarita, order a "Skinny Margarita," found on many bar menus today. You won't find sweet and sour mix in these drinks, though sometimes diet sodas are added. Some bartenders use sugar substitute; others omit sweeteners and use fresh orange juice instead of triple sec. A splash of sparkling water and lots of ice help make these drinks refreshing.

My advice: sip and savor a glorious shot of 100% agave tequila instead!

Margarita Mexicana

Made with Mexican *limones*, this version reminds me of margaritas sipped in the sun on Mexican vacations, a far cry from the artificial sweet-and-sour versions commonly served north of the border.

- Salt and quartered lime to rim glass, optional
- 1½ ounces tequila *blanco* (or *reposado*)
- ¾ ounce fresh lime juice, preferably from Mexican *limones*
- ¾ ounce Cointreau

Follow sidebar directions. If you prefer a more potent margarita, use a 2:1:1 ratio. *Serves 1.*

Note: For those who prefer a sweeter and less astringent margarita, add Cantina Classic Sweet and Sour or agave syrup to taste.

Baja Margarita

Damiana, the bright yellow liqueur made from a wild Baja desert herb, gives this margarita its distinctive flavor and color. It's known as Baja's love potion. When it's combined with tequila, watch out!

- 1½ ounces tequila *blanco* or *reposado*
- ¾ ounce fresh Mexican lime juice
- ¾ ounce Damiana liqueur
- Lime twist

Follow sidebar instructions for making Mexican margaritas; strain over fresh ice, adding lime twist. *Serves 1.*

Sirena's (Mermaid's) Splash

Bartender Jesus "Chuy" Verduzco Miranda was *cantinero* for more than thirty-five years at a Baja fishing resort called Rancho Las Cruces. I often visited there with my father. After a long, hot day at sea, often returning without a catch (I'd asked Neptune to invite his marlin and mermaids to happy hour at the bottom of the sea while we fished), nothing tasted better than this refreshing margarita spritzer. Chuy served it in a tall glass with lots of ice, its cobalt rim encrusted lightly with salt. The effervescence of sparkling soda gives a cooling splash to this mermaid's delight. It remains one of my favorite summer coolers . . . but don't let the ice melt!

- Lime wedge
- Coarse salt, optional
- 2 ounces tequila *blanco*
- Juice of 3 Mexican limes (reserve spent shells)
- 1 ounce Damiana or Cointreau (I like it half and half)
- Long splash of Topo Chico or other sparkling water
- Garnish: spent shells of 3 lime halves

Rim tall Collins glass with a wedge of lime and lightly twirl it in coarse salt, shaking off excess. Fill glass with ice. Add tequila, lime juice, spent lime shells, and Damiana and/or Cointreau. Top it with sparkling mineral water and stir vigorously. *Serves 1.*

Note: In Baja, ice melts in the glass after the first few sips, just as it does during most of the year in the Texas heat. Use large ice cubes (not bagged ice), or better yet, a jumbo ice cube (p. 99) to prevent ice from diluting the drink, as you must with all spritzers.

It's not the drinking that causes the hangover,
It's the stopping.

CHEF ROBERT DEL GRANDE,
CAFE ANNIE, HOUSTON

Fiesta Margarita PARTY PITCHER MARGARITA

Here's my recipe for traditional margaritas made for a crowd. Tart, refreshing, and potent, this cocktail is meant for slow sipping, on the rocks or shaken with ice. Mix up Fiesta Margaritas before your party and guests can serve themselves from a pitcher. You can even salt margarita glasses ahead of time and set them out on a tray. I have a set of six mini-shakers on hand and plenty of ice for those who want to shake and strain their margaritas instead of pouring them from the pitcher.

Personalize this recipe, varying it to suit your whims and creativity. Make it with a flavorful infused tequila (pp. 140–141). Use a combination of fresh lime, lemon, grapefruit, and/or orange juice, or try one of your favorite liqueurs or fresh-frozen fruit purées for color and flavor. For those who prefer sweeter drinks, add Cantina Classic syrups, diluted agave syrup, or Sweet and Sour. Rim glasses with one of the Spicy Mexican Seasoned Salts.

- 1 bottle (750 ml) 100% agave tequila *blanco* or *reposado* (or your favorite infused tequila)
- 1¾–2 cups Cointreau
- 1–1¼ cups freshly squeezed lime juice
- Salt for rims of glasses, optional
- Garnish: slices of limes or fresh fruits

Mix ingredients together in a glass pitcher and chill. Before serving, add lots of frozen slices of lemons and limes. Whisk in some ice to dilute, if you wish. Pour over ice into margarita glasses, shake and strain, or serve as icy shots. *Makes 6–7 cups (approx. 18 margaritas or 24 2-ounce shots).*

Variation: Three Flavors of Margarita from One Pitcher

Divide recipe into 3 small pitchers. Reserve 2 cups of the original recipe, for guests wanting an authentic margarita. To 2 cups, add 4–6 ounces fresh frozen prickly pear, mango, guava, or other frozen fruit purée. To 2 cups, add 3–4 ounces Cantina Classic Sweet and Sour, Cantina Classic syrup of your choice to taste, or diluted agave syrup.

Frescas y Frías

REFRESHING
ICY DRINKS

El primero con agua
El segundo sin agua
El tercero como agua.

—

The first drink with water
The second without
The third one's so mellow,
you'd better watch out!

The Daiquiri Debate

A CUBAN CONCOCTION MADE with lots of island rum, fresh lime juice, sugar, and shaved ice, daiquiris taste so refreshing. Papa Hemingway frequently quaffed them as an after-fishing drink from a "reserved" stool at El Floridita, a bar he helped make famous in Havana.

Daiquiris sailed on to Mexico, like so many popular Cuban *boleros*, *sones*, and romantic songs. Bartenders there substituted tequila and tropical fruits, and sometimes blended it into an icy frappé. In Mexico today, frozen fruit tequila drinks are sometimes called "daiquiris," instead of margaritas, and served either frozen or on the rocks.

For more than twenty-five years, I spent a few weeks each May fishing with my father in Baja, Mexico. We stayed at Rancho Las Cruces, a secluded paradise resort overlooking the Sea of Cortez. When we arrived each year, after a sweltering ninety-minute drive on the steep and narrow dusty dirt road from La Paz, the daiquiris made by Rodolfo "Chacho" Osuna, *el cantinero*, were most welcome!

Five homes surround the private resort, one belonging to Bing Crosby's family. A favorite treasure of mine is a bottle of Herradura Reposado that my father found hidden away in his fishing locker, left by Crosby, the first distributor of Herradura tequila in the United States.

Another nearby home (replete with a guitar-shaped swimming pool) belonged to Desi Arnaz (and now to his son, Desi Jr.). Desi, it is said, liked his daiquiris, and Chacho often made them for him, patiently listening to Desi's tales about the big blue marlin that got away.

*Los niños y los borrachos
dicen la verdad.*

—

*Drunkards and children
can't tell a lie.*

Chacho Borracho TEQUILA DAIQUIRI

Baja sunsets are indescribably beautiful. The dusk explodes into volcanic splendor, outshone in beauty perhaps only by the brilliance of the evening's stars. I have fond memories of sipping Chacho's daiquiris in the midst of such wonder. Coming to shore, sunburned and tired, after fishing since dawn, I wanted nothing more than one of those frozen daiquiris made with chunks of fresh *piña* (pineapple).

- ½ cup fresh fruit such as pineapple, mango, strawberries, or half a banana
- 2 ounces tequila *blanco*
- ¾ ounce freshly squeezed lime juice, preferably from juicy Mexican (Key) limes
- ½ ounce or more Cantina Classic Simple Syrup or Citrus Syrup or Sweet and Sour
- Handful of ice

Mix ingredients together in a blender. Pour into chilled cocktail glass and garnish with a slice of lime or a slice of unpeeled fruit. *Serves 1.*

Note: To make lime daiquiris, without additional fruit, shake ingredients briefly with ice, and pour into a cocktail glass over fresh ice. For a frozen version, blend ingredients with ice.

Raspados Viva GROWN-UP SNOW CONES

Street vendors in Mexico sell snow cones flavored with fiesta-colored fruit syrups. They use a simple metal blade called a *raspador* to shave the ice from a big block. My friend Viva Silverstein had a great idea: snow cones for grown-ups, perfect for slurping by the pool.

- Shaved ice
- Paper cones, sherbet glasses, or wide champagne glasses
- Tequila (preferably citrus- or fruit-infused, pp. 140–141)
- Cantina Classic syrups in citrus, ginger, jalapeño, or pomegranate flavors (pp. 103–105) or Cantina Classic liqueurs (pp. 184–187)

Drizzle tequila mixed with syrup or liqueurs to taste over shaved ice.

Frozen Margaritas

Mariano Martinez Sr. owned El Charro, a Mexican restaurant in Dallas, and his margaritas were famous. It is said that in 1971, his son, Mariano Jr., revolutionized the tequila industry when he invented frozen margaritas, using a soft-serve ice cream machine. Adults took to them like kids to double dips. They were cool, slushy, and sweet, so customers could easily drink more than one.

Today, automated machines in many bars crank out frozen margaritas by the dozens. They're the stuff that gives tequila a bad rap: neon-colored concoctions brimming with cheap well (*mixto*) tequila and artificial flavorings. Those who partake in these overly sweet and seemingly innocuous margaritas just may awaken with the hangover from hell (see hangover helpers, pp. 253–256). Fortunately, some bars use natural fruit purées and pride themselves in creating signature and seasonal creations.

Today, home-style, commercial-quality margarita machines seem to be the rage. Without one, the slushy texture of restaurant margaritas is hard to replicate, but here's a simplified fiesta version.

Quick Frozen Fruit Flavor

Purchase exotic/natural/tropical fruit juices and nectars such as passion fruit, guava, guanabana, mango, and pineapple guava. Freeze juice, drizzled with some added fresh lime juice, in ice cube trays. A quart of nectar fills two standard-sized trays. Once cubes are frozen, store them in freezer bags. Swirl cubes in blender with tequila and other ingredients, adding chunks of fresh frozen fruit when available.

Prontísimo
FROZEN MARGARITA IN A MINUTE

Make this frozen margarita *prontísimo* (quickly) for parties. It's pleasingly sweet and slushy, so imbibe with caution, or Jimmy Buffett's lament, "wasting away again in Margaritaville," could take on new meaning for you. Serve it to friends on February 22, designated as official National Margarita Day.

To achieve the icy texture without diluting, divide the recipe into two batches, freezing one as you swirl the other in the blender with ice. Adding a few thick slices of lime (including the rind) to the mix adds flavor and texture.

- 12 ounces Cantina Classic Sweet and Sour
- 12 ounces tequila *blanco* or *reposado*
- 6 ounces triple sec
- 6–8 ounces fresh lime juice with a few pieces of peel (or part orange juice/peel)
- Garnish: salted rims and lime wedges

Working in two batches, place ingredients in a blender and cover with twice the amount of crushed ice and blend until slushy. Pour into a container and freeze. Repeat with second batch. (You can freeze this a few days in advance.) *Serves 6.*

Variation: Substitute frozen tropical fruit purées or concentrates, such as strawberry guava or orange passion fruit. Or use frozen limeade concentrate (with some added fresh lime juice and zest) when Sweet and Sour is not on hand, or Cantina Classics syrups to taste.

Frozen Tropical Nectar Margarita

The Perfect Purée Company from Napa, California, and other companies, sell delectable frozen fruit purées. My favorites are prickly pear, pink guava, mandarin tangerine, and a mélange of passion fruit, blood orange, and pomegranate. Find them at specialty grocery stores or online for overnight shipping. Or, see the sidebar for an easy way to produce icy drinks with lots of flavor.

Guava Margarita

Sitting in the plush patio of Austin's Fonda San Miguel restaurant, amidst tropical plants, parrots, and an impressive collection of contemporary Mexican art, you would swear that you are in Mexico. But when the waiter brings a guava margarita, you'll think you're in heaven! Pale pink and sensuous, it whispers of grapefruit, pear, and a bouquet of tropical flowers. Because the restaurant's recipe cannot be easily duplicated in home kitchens, I have adapted a recipe using accessible ingredients. Keep all ingredients and glasses chilled before blending.

- 1 ice cube tray of frozen natural guava nectar (2 cups frozen juice)
- 6–8 ounces tequila *blanco*
- 4 ounces freshly squeezed ruby grapefruit juice
- 1 ounce fresh lime juice
- 2 or more ounces frozen Cantina Classic Sweet and Sour
- Small handful of ice
- Garnishes: sparkling sugar crystals or turbinado sugar for rims of glasses, grapefruit wedges, sliced unpeeled guava, or edible flowers

Swirl ingredients together in a blender. Place filled blender jar in freezer for 15 minutes before serving, then blend again. Pour into chilled 5-ounce long-stemmed glasses, garnish, and serve. *Serves 4–6.*

Note: Guavas (guayabas) are small, round, yellow-skinned fruits. Their fleshy pink, highly aromatic fruit is floral and fruity in taste. Scoop it from its skin and separate the pulp from the numerous hard seeds. Guavas also flavor traditional Mexican punches. They're often available, both fresh and frozen, in Latin American markets in the United States. Commercial frozen guava purée is available online.

Variation: Substitute other tropical fruit nectars for the guava nectar and other citrus for the grapefruit. Sweeten with Cantina Classic syrups, if needed.

Too *mucho* tequila! Earthenware painted clay hungover skeleton.

Gilding the Lily
Fancy Fruit Margaritas

Like some of the most interesting people, tequila has a dual nature. Its unparalleled flavor comes from the blue agave, the "lily of the field." Fine tequilas exhibit the inherent sweetness of the agave and need no frills—only a shot glass or snifter—to show them off. At the same time, though, the versatile and seductive character of tequila lends itself to embellishment.

In Mexico, a margarita is a margarita, pure and simple: tequila laced with Cointreau (or Controy) and fresh lime juice in a salt-rimmed glass. But north of the border, the margarita has been dressed up in vivid, tropical colors and laced with fancy liqueurs. Here are a few fun recipes: flaunt them in chilled long-stemmed margarita glasses rimmed with Cantina Classic Spicy Mexican Seasoned Salt or with sparkling colored sugar and festive garnishes (p. 109).

Mango Maravilla
MANGO MARGARITA

This frozen mango drink evokes memories of my child-hood in El Paso. When mangos were in season, we'd peel then freeze them on a fork to eat like a Popsicle.

- 1 cup fresh ripe mango chunks, peeled and flash frozen
- 3 ounces tequila *blanco* or *reposado*
- 1 ounce triple sec of choice
- ½–1 ounce Cantina Classic flavored syrups or Sweet and Sour to taste
- 1 ounce fresh lime juice
- Small handful of ice
- Garnishes: sparkling sugar crystals or Spicy Mexican Seasoned Salt to frost rims; lime slices and/or slices of unpeeled mango

Swirl mango, tequila, triple sec, syrup, and lime juice with ice in a blender until slushy. Add more lime juice or a splash of flavored syrup if needed. Freeze filled blender canister for 15 minutes, then swirl again in blender. Pour into a long-stemmed margarita glass rimmed with Spicy Mexican Seasoned Salt or spar-kling colored sugar crystals and garnish. *Serves 2.*

Variations: Substitute other tropical fruits (like pineapple, banana, or guava), or ripe peaches, instead of or in combination with the mango. For added bite, use Cantina Classic Zesty Ginger Syrup or Domaine de Canton ginger liqueur instead of triple sec, and gar-nish glasses with crystallized candied ginger or flavor with some Cantina Classic Jalapeño Syrup instead of triple sec. Experiment with Cantina Classic infused tequilas like Mango Django.

Esa Fresa
STRAWBERRY MARGARITA

Street vendors in Mexico tempt passersby with plump and juicy strawberries mounded in woven baskets. This vibrant strawberry margarita will similarly tantalize your guests. Try it with Texas sweet Poteet strawberries laced with bright tequila *blanco* and Grand Marnier.

- 1 cup flash-frozen fresh, ripe strawberries
- 3 ounces premium tequila *blanco* or Strawberry-Infused Tequila
- 1 ounce fresh lemon juice
- 1 ounce Grand Marnier
- ½–1 ounce Cantina Classic Simple or Citrus Syrup or homemade Sweet and Sour to taste
- Small handful ice
- Garnishes: sparkling sugar crystals to frost rims; a plump strawberry "hooked" on each glass or impaled on a pick

Swirl ingredients with small amount of ice in blender until thick and slushy. Add more lemon juice or syrup as needed. Freeze filled blender canister for 15 minutes, then swirl again in blender. Pour into long-stemmed chilled glasses, garnish, and serve immediately. *Serves 2.*

Variation: Substitute raspberries for strawberries and St. Germaine for Grand Marnier.

Piña Fina
PINEAPPLE MARGARITA

It's amazing how the heart of the agave resembles a giant pineapple, once its leaves have been shaved away from its core; Mexicans in fact call it a *piña*. The sweet, tart flavor of pineapple and tequila are naturals in this lovely and refreshing drink, made more attractive with a sprinkling of exotic, purple-tinged Cantina Classic Hibiscus Flower and Orange Zest Salt.

- Cantina Classic Hibiscus Flower and Orange Zest Salt, or sparkling sugar to rim glass, optional
- 4 ounces chilled Cantina Classic Pineapple-Infused Tequila or tequila *reposado*
- 1 ounce fresh lime juice
- 1½ cups fresh, flash-frozen pineapple chunks
- 1–2 ounces Sweet and Sour
- 1 ounce Domaine de Canton ginger liqueur, or triple sec
- Small handful of ice
- Garnishes: Cantina Classic Hibiscus Flower and Orange Zest Salt or grated coconut/lime zest for rims (p. 109), unpeeled pineapple wedge, lime zest strips, sprig of red-blossomed pineapple sage.

Rim glass with seasoned salt or sugar. Swirl ingredients together in blender with ice until slushy, adding more lime juice or Sweet and Sour if needed. Freeze filled blender canister for 15–30 minutes, then swirl again in blender before serving. Pour into chilled long-stemmed glasses and garnish to suit your whims. *Serves 2.*

Variations: Sweeten with Cantina Classic syrups, such as jalapeño, citrus, or zesty ginger, instead of Sweet and Sour. Add a dollop of frozen prickly pear purée right before serving—gorgeous!

Corazón de Melon (Heart-of-Melon) Margarita

I named this summery drink after a mambo song made popular by the great Cuban/Mexican orchestra leader Pérez Prado in the 1950s and sung by Rosemary Clooney. Ripe melon stars in this luscious drink, perked up by rimming the glass with Cantina Classic Pink Peppercorn Citrus Salt. It'll make you want to turn up the music and dance!

- 2 cups flash-frozen ripe honeydew melon chunks
- 4 ounces chilled tequila *blanco*
- 1½ ounces fresh lime juice
- 1½ ounces Domaine de Canton ginger liqueur or Cantina Classic Ambrosia liqueur
- 1 ounce Sweet and Sour
- ¼ teaspoon whole pink peppercorns, freshly ground
- Handful ice
- Garnishes: Cantina Classic Pink Peppercorn Citrus Salt for rim, floating; nasturtium blossoms, whole pink peppercorns, and/or colorful melon balls speared on a wooden pick

Swirl ingredients together in a blender until slushy. Freeze filled blender canister for 15–30 minutes, then swirl again in blender before serving. Pour into long-stemmed glasses and garnish. Drizzle each drink with fresh lime juice and sprinkle with a pinch of seasoned salt. Garnish and serve. *Serves 2.*

Variations: Make this instead with fresh cantaloupe or mixture of melons; use an orange Citrus Peel–Infused Tequila, and add Cantina Classic Citrus or Zesty Ginger Syrup to taste. Sweeten drink with Cantina Classic Simple Syrup or diluted agave syrup instead of Sweet and Sour.

Abajito

KIWI MARGARITA

~~~~~~~~~~

Made with kiwi fruit, this creamy, pale-green margarita is speckled with tiny, crunchy brown seeds. I created this drink for my friend Martin Button, a Kiwi from New Zealand and an adventurous cook. (I'd thought that New Zealanders were called "Kiwis" because of the fruit native to their country, but Martin explained that a kiwi is a much-beloved flightless, fuzzy bird that is indigenous to New Zealand.)

- 3 not-too-ripe kiwi fruits, peeled, quartered, and flash frozen
- 4 ounces chilled tequila *blanco* or *reposado*
- 2 ounces guava nectar or pineapple juice
- 1½ ounces fresh lime juice
- 1 ounce Cantina Classic Zesty Ginger Syrup
- Handful of cracked ice
- Garnishes: slice of unpeeled kiwi and a spiral of candied orange peel

Whirl all ingredients in a blender; do not over-blend. Add more syrup or lime if needed. Freeze filled blender canister for 15–30 minutes, then swirl again in blender. Pour into long-stemmed margarita glasses and garnish. *Serves 2.*

Variation: Decrease syrup, and add a splash of triple sec, Domaine de Canton ginger liqueur, or Cantina Classic Ambrosia liqueur.

Rosita

FRESH POMEGRANATE MARGARITA

~~~~~~~~~~

I love serving these margaritas in the fall when *granadas* (pomegranates) are ripe, popping the tart, plump, ruby seeds into my mouth as I separate them from the peel. Save some of the seeds to garnish the drink. Cantina Classic Ruby Pomegranate Syrup gives this drink even more color and flavor.

- 3 tablespoons ripe pomegranate seeds
- 1½ ounces fresh lime juice
- ½ ounce Cointreau
- 3 ounces premium tequila *blanco* or Rosangel
- 1 ounce Cantina Classic Ruby Pomegranate Syrup or PAMA liqueur (p. 104)
- Cracked ice
- Garnishes: sugar crystals for frosted rims, pomegranate seeds, thin strips of lime zest

In a blender, whirl pomegranate seeds with the lime, Cointreau, and tequila until seeds are well blended. Strain, pressing down to release all liquid. Add syrup or liqueur and shake with ice, adding more syrup or liqueur if desired. Strain into chilled long-stemmed glasses, or pour over ice. Garnish and serve. *Serves 2.*

Note: For a frozen version, increase ingredients by ½; return pomegranate mixture to blender after straining; swirl with ice. Let filled canister stand in freezer for 15 minutes, swirl again in blender, and serve.

Want to avoid the hassle of seeding pomegranates? Purchase ready-to-eat pomegranate seeds, called "arils," which are seasonally available in refrigerated sections of grocery stores. Or, you can remove seeds from pomegranates and freeze for future use.

Tequila entra suave,
Pero pega duro.

—

Tequila goes down smoothly,
But packs a wallop.

Sabor a Mí

FRESH FRUIT DRINKS WITH TEQUILA

E YDIE GORME AND Trío Los Panchos popularized "Sabor a mí," one of my favorite Mexican songs, composed by the beloved Oaxacan musician Álvaro Carrillo in 1959. In 2012, Alejandro Escovedo, Austin's acclaimed singer-songwriter, immortalized this song for a new generation on his CD *Big Station*. It captures the essence of love: "en tu boca llevarás sabor a mí" (my kisses will linger on your lips). Artfully prepared libations should leave the lingering and refreshing flavor of fresh fruit and tequila in your mouth . . . and make you want more!

The following drinks are some of my favorites. They celebrate tequila and brim with fresh fruit flavors and vivid colors. Substitute premium mezcal for tequila in any of these fresh fruit drinks, or use ½ of each, if you wish.

Be imaginative in creating, naming, and garnishing signature drinks. Experiment with different fruits, flavorings, and garnishes each time (see sidebar on p. 158 for inspiration) Make it as simple as mixing tequila with freshly squeezed orange juice, like an old-fashioned screwdriver, or conjure up your own favorite blend.

What's mine? In the summertime, I love a combination of chilled pineapple, mango, and passion fruit nectars, with lots of fresh lime juice. In the winter, it's Ruby Fruit Juice Blend.

Sol y Luna (Sun and Moon)

This drink makes me think of Marilyn Smith, cofounder of tequila El Tesoro, who taught me so much about tequila and with whom I shared many *soles y lunas* on our tequila adventures.

- 4 ounces fruit juice, nectar, or combination of several
- 2 ounces El Tesoro tequila *blanco* or *reposado*
- ½–1 ounce favorite liqueur
- ½–1 ounce fresh lime juice
- Garnish *al gusto* (to taste) with chunks of unpeeled fruits

Fill a chilled highball glass with ice, stir in the ingredients, and garnish festively. *Serves 1.*

Note: Experiment with natural frozen fruit purées.

Hints for Making Fresh Fruit Tequila Drinks

+ Use tequila *blanco* or *reposado* to highlight tropical fruit flavors, or tequila infused with citrus peel, fresh fruit, or chiles and spice (recipes, pp. 140–141).
+ Use flavorful Mexican *limones* (Key limes) whenever possible.
+ Add fruit liqueurs sparingly to enhance, not overwhelm, natural fruit flavors.
+ Use Cantina Classic Syrups—such as homemade CITRUS, GINGER, OR POMEGRANATE SYRUPS—or SWEET AND SOUR to sweeten and add extra color and flavor. Use them alone or in combination with liqueurs, adding small increments at a time. Syrups are sweeter than homemade Sweet and Sour, so add accordingly.
+ Use agave syrup/nectar sparingly as a sweetener—it's a quick fix if the drink is too tart. Dilute it first in equal parts water or other liquid in the drink, as it is very sweet.
+ Use chunks of frozen fruits or citrus slices instead of ice cubes. (Flash-freeze fresh fruit and citrus slices on a tray in the freezer.)
+ Squeeze juice from seasonal citrus such as Valencia, Seville, navel, and blood oranges; tangerines and tangelos; Meyer lemons; ruby grapefruit; and Key or Persian limes to use alone or in combination. Extract juice from fresh pomegranates.
+ Use fresh, ripe seasonal fruit. Peel and cut into chunks, drizzle with fresh lime juice, and freeze for future use.
+ Purchase natural fruit juice nectars and blends in tempting tropical flavors. These can be found bottled, frozen, or in refrigerated cartons. Always enhance these juices with freshly squeezed lime.
+ Use natural cranberry, pomegranate, and *flor de jamaica* (hibiscus-flavored) juices for their naturally tart, acidic flavor and ruby color.
+ Purchase frozen fruit purées and concentrates in exotic flavors like prickly pear, guava, passion fruit, or pomegranate. Use 1–2 ounces per drink, or to taste.

El Rey
CITRUS AND POMEGRANATE COOLER

This is my brother Stuart "El Rey" Hutson's signature winter libation, when fresh pomegranates, grapefruits, and oranges are in their glory. (He received a long-handled commercial-style juicer as a Christmas gift just for this purpose.) Serve this cooler in tall, clear glasses to show off the ruby color of the freshly squeezed juices. Spiked with tequila and garnished with pomegranate seeds and a green cucumber spear, it pays tribute to the colors of the holiday season, but brings good cheer at any time during the year.

· 4 ounces freshly squeezed juices (see recipe below for Ruby Fruit Juice Blend)
· 2 ounces tequila *blanco* or *reposado* or mezcal
· ¾ ounce Cointreau
· Squeeze of fresh lime
· Garnishes: lime slice, pomegranate seeds, unpeeled pickling cucumber spear

Squeeze/extract fresh juices and chill. Pour into tall, ice-filled glass and stir with remaining ingredients. Garnish festively. *Serves 1.*

Ruby Fruit Juice Blend

· 1 cup fresh pomegranate juice (2–3 pomegranates), or POM 100% Natural Pomegranate Juice
· 3 cups fresh Texas Rio Star ruby red grapefruit juice (3 grapefruit)
· 1 cup orange juice (4 large navel oranges)

Mix all ingredients together in a pitcher and chill before using.

Note: Sometimes I substitute tangerine for the orange juice or purchase refrigerated Aliseo Blood Orange or Mandarin Juice. To juice pomegranates: cut in half, gently extract juice with a nonelectric juicer. Avoid oversqueezing, as central white pith is bitter. One pomegranate yields ½–¾ cup juice.

Madrugada
TEQUILA SUNRISE

Freshly squeezed orange juice and tequila *reposado*, swirling with Cantina Classic Ruby Pomegranate Syrup, capture the glowing colors of a Mexican sunrise in this updated Tequila Sunrise.

- 4 ounces freshly squeezed orange
- ½ ounce fresh lime juice
- 2 ounces tequila *reposado* (or Cantina Classic Citrus- or Prickly Pear–Infused tequilas)
- Splash of best quality triple sec
- ½–¾ ounce Cantina Classic Ruby Pomegranate Syrup
- Garnishes: citrus slices or spent lime shells

Fill a Collins glass with ice. Add citrus juices, tequila, and triple sec, stirring well. Place a bar spoon in the glass and let the ruby syrup run down the back of the spoon, sink, then rise in a sunrise swirl. *Serves 1.*

Note: My friend Mark Haugen, chef director of the National Football League and chef/owner at Tejas in Minneapolis, calls his version "Sonoran Sunrise." He uses tangerine juice, tequila *añejo*, and Grand Marnier and drizzles it with prickly pear purée (available frozen, or simply purée peeled cactus fruit in a blender; strain out the seeds).

Substitute PAMA (pomegranate liqueur) or Stirrings' Authentic Grenadine for the Cantina Classic Ruby Pomegranate Syrup.

Buenos sabores: fresh fruit in a Mexican market stand in Jalisco.

Chimayó Cocktail

NEW MEXICO APPLE CIDER SPIKED WITH TEQUILA

You can make this drink at home, but you cannot duplicate New Mexico's crisp fall air, the pungent aroma of dried chile clusters hanging in *ristras* to dry, or the enchanting vista from the patio of Rancho Chimayó, the popular restaurant forty miles north of Santa Fe founded by the Jaramillo family. There they serve a specialty drink made from locally pressed apple cider laced with gold tequila, lemon juice, and crème de cassis. In my version, a splash of Ruby Pomegranate Syrup replaces the cassis and I use *reposado*.

- 3 ounces tequila *reposado*
- 2 ounces unfiltered apple cider
- ½ ounce Cantina Classic Ruby Pomegranate Syrup, crème de cassis, or PAMA (pomegranate liqueur)
- ½ ounce fresh lemon juice
- Garnishes: apple slices and sprigs of mint

Combine ingredients in a tumbler filled with ice and stir to blend. Some prefer to shake it with ice, then strain into a small, chilled margarita glass. Garnish!

Una Tuna

PRICKLY PEAR COOLER

You should see the expression on friends' faces when I offer them a "*tuna* margarita." I quickly explain that in Mexico, *tuna* is the name for prickly pear, the ripened fruit of a species of cactus (*Opuntia sp.*). The fleshy, paddle-shaped leaves of this cactus are called "nopal" in Mexico. We ate these as children in El Paso, frozen on a fork and spitting out the BB-like seeds.

My friends' astonishment quickly changes to sheer delight when they see the striking bougainvillea-colored drink and taste its viscous, floral, and intense sun-ripened watermelon/berry essence. This libation celebrates the flavors and colors of Mexico and the way in which *tunas* are consumed there—sprinkled with lime and chile and salt. I like making it with mezcal, or ½ mezcal and ½ tequila, in this ¡Pura Mexicana! libation.

- Cantina Classic Spicy Mexican Seasoned Salt or commercial brand
- 2 large, fresh, ripe prickly pears, peeled*
- 6–8 ounces tequila *blanco* or *reposado* or Prickly Pear–Infused Tequila
- 3–4 ounces fresh Mexican Key lime juice
- 3 ounces Cantina Classic Jalapeño Syrup or Sweet and Sour, to taste
- Garnishes: slice of unpeeled prickly pear or lime wedge

Purée prickly pear in blender. Add tequila, then strain through a fine sieve to remove hard seeds, using a wooden spoon to press out all of the nectar. Stir in lime juice and syrup to taste. (May be frozen at this point.) Shake briefly with ice and strain (or not) into a glass rimmed with Spicy Mexican Seasoned Salt. Garnish and serve. *Serves 4.*

Note: Use frozen purées when fresh *tunas* are not available, decreasing syrup.

Cinco de Mayo Shooters

Make up a batch and keep in the freezer, thaw slightly, then pour as shots. ¡Viva Mexico!

- 15 ounces Perfect Purée Prickly Pear
- 6 ounces fresh juice from Mexican (Key) limes
- 4 ounces Cantina Classic Jalapeño Syrup
- Cantina Classic Spicy Mexican Seasoning Salt to taste

Mix ingredient together and chill or freeze. Mix tall shot glasses with equal parts (about 1½ ounces each) tequila and/or mezcal and prickly pear blend—or serve in separate shots. Sprinkle with Spicy Mexican Seasoning Salt.

Jorge Negrete immortalized the prickly pear fruit in one of my favorite songs, "Me he de comer esa tuna," reminding us of a valuable life lesson: no pain, no gain!

Me he de comer esa tuna
aunque me espine
la mano.

———

I must eat the tuna fruit
even though it pricks
my hand.

COMPOSED BY MANUEL ESPERÓN GONZÁLEZ
AND ERNESTO E. CORTÁZAR

When Tuna *Is Not a Fish*

Throughout late summer and fall, prickly pear fruit, called *"tunas,"* poke out of spiny, paddle-shaped nopal cacti that flourish throughout Mexico and the Texas Hill Country. A tough skin, studded with tiny, almost invisible spines that painfully nestle in your skin, protects the juicy fruit within. This kind of *tuna* fruit, about the size of a kiwi, comes in wild shades ranging from green to screaming magenta, with a sweet-and-tart flavor. They're available seasonally in specialty markets throughout the Southwest, where chefs purée them for tasty sauces, sorbets, and margaritas. The vivid color of the magenta ones makes them popular in commercial frozen purées and drink mixes.

If you opt to pick *tunas* yourself, be sure to wear gloves to protect your fingers from the bothersome spines. Rub their skin with a crumpled newspaper or remove spines with a sharp knife. Cut both ends off the *tuna*. Make a lengthwise slit just through the skin so that you can peel away and discard the fleshy skin, revealing the fruit. You may freeze them whole and unpeeled in airtight bags for future use; peel before using. Cut *tunas* in half and macerate them in a wide-mouthed jar in tequila *blanco* for an exquisitely colored Prickly Pear–Infused Tequila.

Agarita Margarita

Agarita bushes (*Berberis trifoliolata*), with their bright-red, mouth-puckering berries, ripen throughout the Texas Hill Country in early summer. My friend Bruce Auden, chef/owner of BIGA on the Banks on the River Walk in San Antonio, has used them to make a ruby-colored sweet-and-sour sauce for antelope, which inspired my Agarita Margarita. You must literally beat the bush to gather the berries. Place a large tablecloth or a sheet under the bush to collect them. Wear gloves to avoid the prickly, holly-like leaves.

Rinse the berries. Barely cover them with water and bring to a low boil. Immediately lower heat, simmering for about 8 minutes. Allow to cool, then strain through cheesecloth for several hours. Freeze juice to use as needed. Pour agarita juice with tequila on the rocks with a squeeze of lime and diluted agave syrup or Sweet and Sour to taste.

Carmen Miranda's Downfall
TEQUILA PIÑA COLADA

I have a confession. I own a Carmen Miranda headdress bursting with tropical fruit and flowers that I sometimes wear to parties. I *had* to name a drink in Carmen Miranda's honor. Sip it with someone you love from fanciful *popotes* (straws) in a hollowed-out fresh pineapple. Tequila brightens fruity flavors and is not as sweet as rum, which is traditionally used in piña coladas.

- 1 fresh pineapple
- 4 ounces tequila *blanco* or Pineapple-Infused Tequila
- 1 ounce tequila *añejo*
- 4 ounces chilled pineapple juice
- 3 ounces cream of coconut (sweetened coconut milk), optional*
- ¼ teaspoon Mexican vanilla
- ½ cup fresh pineapple pulp, frozen
- 2 ounces fresh lime juice
- Cantina Classic Citrus Syrup or Zesty Ginger Syrup to taste (for sweetening), optional
- cracked ice

Cut the top off the pineapple (and reserve for drink's headdress), leaving its leaves intact. Scoop out the pulp, leaving a ¾-inch shell. Chill the pineapple shell and top. Freeze the pineapple pulp until ready to use. Whirl ingredients in a blender with cracked ice until thick and slushy; sweeten if needed. Pour into chilled pineapple shell and top it with its sombrero (pineapple headdress) before serving. If imbibed from glasses (instead of the pineapple shell), garnish each with a few pineapple leaves and a chunk of unpeeled pineapple. *Serves 2.*

Note: If you prefer a lighter drink, omit the cream of coconut, and sweeten lightly with your favorite Cantina Classic sweetener like Zesty Ginger Syrup or Sweet and Sour.

Flor de Jamaica (Hibiscus Flower) Cooler

A crimson-colored *agua fresca* (nonalcoholic cooler), served by street vendors in Mexico from large glass jars, inspired this lovely drink. Made from *flor de jamaica* (dried hibiscus), it has a decidedly tart and fruity flavor reminiscent of sour cherries and cranberries with floral undertones, making it a natural for tequila. Although commercially bottled brands of hibiscus punch are available, they are generally too sweet and sometimes artificially flavored.

I grow this tropical hibiscus in my garden (see Cantina Garden, p. 111); its calyces are a deep ruby color when dried and called *flor de jamaica*. Purchase them in Mexican markets and health food stores. You may also find them preserved in syrup.

- 4 ounces Flor de Jamaica Punch (recipe follows)
- 2 ounces Rosangel tequila (p. 68) or tequila *blanco*
- Squeeze of fresh lime
- *Jamaica* flowers
- Splash of mineral water, optional
- Sweeten as needed
- Garnishes: lime wedge or orange slice and fresh mint

Mix ingredients together and serve in a tall glass with lots of ice and some *jamaica* blossoms reserved from the punch. Garnish and serve. *Serves 1.*

Note: This is delicious sweetened with Cantina Classic Ruby Pomegranate Syrup. Sometimes I substitute a strong, chilled brew of Celestial Seasonings Red Zinger Herbal Tea or Austin's own Nile Valley Pure Hibiscus Tea for the homemade punch.

Blue Weber

Tiki meets tequila in this dazzling blue retro cooler: tart limeade made with fresh coconut water sweetened with agave syrup and spiked with tequila *blanco*. Whimsical garnishes of *piñas y pencas* pay homage to the "blue" *Agave tequilana* Weber, the species from which tequila is made. Sipping one of these always sends me back to the azure rows of agave shimmering in the Jalisco sunshine.

- 14 ounces 100% natural coconut water (not coconut milk!)
- 8 ounces fresh lime juice, preferably juiced from Mexican (Key) limes
- 3 ounces agave syrup, first diluted in some of the above liquid
- 2 ounces blue Curaçao
- 12–14 ounces tequila *blanco*
- Lime wedges
- Garnishes: 1 pineapple leaf, 3 fresh pineapple chunks impaled on a swizzle stick skewer, and lime wedge

Mix ingredients together in a container and freeze for several hours. Add ice to a Collins glass or a 10-ounce tumbler. Pour 5 ounces spiked limeade into each glass; squeeze some lime juice in each. Poke a pineapple leaf vertically out of each glass as well as skewered pineapple chunks. *Serves 8.*

Note: Fresh coconut water from within young, green coconuts, brimming with electrolytes and potassium, is a trendy health drink today and popular for rehydration. It also pairs well with tequila. Find it in refrigerated aisles.

Painted papier-mâché *Lady of the Cantina*, with articulated joined (sometimes called "Lupitas," because each doll bears a name; this one is named Eloísa), from Celaya, Guanajuato.

Ponche Flor de Jamaica (Hibiscus Flower Punch)

In a 2-quart stainless steel or enamel pan, combine 2 cups dried *jamaica* blossoms with 6 cups boiling water and ¾ cup sugar; simmer for 3 minutes; let steep for several hours. Pour into a glass pitcher; chill several hours or overnight. Reserve the blossoms for garnish. Keeps for several days refrigerated. *Makes 1 quart.*

*Una mujer sin tequila
es como el cielo sin luna.*

———

*A woman without tequila
is like the sky without a moon.*

LUCINDA HUTSON

Muddle, Splash, Spritz

A boca de borracho
Oídos de cantinero.

—

From the drunkard's mouth
Into the bartender's ears.

Muddle It Up!

MUDDLING, OR GENTLY BRUISING fresh citrus, herbs, and spices with a long-handled muddler or pestle, extracts the essential oils and releases the inherent flavors of fresh fruits and vegetables. Muddle ingredients in the bottom of a heavy pint glass (thin glass may chip or break) or tin with gentle twists of the muddler. There's no need to overly mash ingredients—in fact, that may cause bitterness. Sugar acts as an abrasive to help in the process, so add a few teaspoonsful, if you wish.

Once ingredients are muddled, add tequila *blanco* or *reposado*, or mezcal, and flavor and sweeten *al gusto* (to taste) with citrus juice, syrups, or liqueurs. Stir or shake with ice. Some choose to strain shaken muddled drinks (or even double strain with a fine mesh strainer *and* a bar strainer) to remove particles, then serve chilled in margarita/martini glasses.

Although I sometimes suggest straining shaken drinks over fresh ice, I like the added flavor, texture, and color of muddled ingredients, and often do not strain. I have a collection of small spoons (that double as stirrers) for eating the muddled ingredients from the glass.

TIPS ON MUDDLING LIMES

Roll limes on counter to release aromatic oils. Cut ends off and cut in half vertically. Remove the center bitter white pith, then cut limes into quarters for muddling. If you muddle too intensely, the limes will taste bitter.

CHOOSE INGREDIENTS FOR MUDDLING

Fruits (choose one or more)

1 or more quartered fresh limes
1 thick slice of orange, lemon, tangerine, clementine, or blood orange
3 large chunks of fresh pineapple, mango, watermelon, or other melons
2–3 large ripe strawberries
Small handful raspberries or blueberries
½ fresh peeled peach, plum, or nectarine
2 tablespoons pomegranate seeds

Herbs and Spices (use sprigs of the following, alone or in combination)

Mint (spearmint varieties are best)
Basil (many aromatic varieties from which to choose)
Lemon-scented herbs
Thyme

Cilantro (tasty with tropical fruits)

Lemongrass, 1-inch piece of stalk

Fresh ginger, about 3 quarter slices

¼ teaspoon whole peppercorns, allspice, pink peppercorns, or coriander seeds

Vegetables

4–5 slices of hothouse or pickling cucumbers, unpeeled

1 jalapeño or other chiles, seeded and stemmed

½ small, ripe peeled tomato

Sweeteners

Cantina Classic Syrups or Sweet and Sour Sugars (p. 99)

Liqueurs

Your favorite Cantina Classic liqueurs or commercial liqueurs

Effervescent Sodas

Here are some of my favorite tequila drinks that require some muddling. Each one is colorful, flavorful, refreshing, and high-spirited!

Mexican Mojito

I wish I could have sipped mojitos in Havana at La Bodeguita del Medio in the 1940s with Ernest Hemingway and Pablo Neruda, who both frequented the bar where this rummy limeade spritzer originated. This popular Cuban cooler, made by muddling fresh mint with lime juice, now competes with the margarita in bars worldwide. Using tequila instead of the traditional rum makes this drink less sweet and more refreshing—more *charro* than *cha cha cha*.

- 10–12 fresh spearmint leaves, without stems, torn in half
- 2–4 teaspoons granulated or turbinado sugar
- 2 ounces fresh lime juice, preferably Mexican (Key) limes
- Crushed ice

- 2 ounces tequila *blanco* or *reposado*
- Splash of sparkling water
- Garnishes: fresh mint sprig, lime wedge, and/or a sugarcane stir stick (p. 110)

In a tall, sturdy glass, gently bruise mint with sugar using a muddler. Mix in lime juice and fill glass with crushed ice. Pour tequila over the ice and stir in a splash of sparkling water. Rub mint around the rim of the glass. Add a sugarcane stir stick and garnish with a sprig of fresh mint. *Serves 1, but you'll want another!*

Note: Traditional Cuban mojitos are made with freshly squeezed lime juice, instead of muddled limes. If you prefer a very limey drink, muddle a few lime quarters in your mojito. You can also muddle 2–3 large sprigs of mint with stems, but the stems may impart bitterness.

Variation: I am an avid herb enthusiast—see my book *The Herb Garden Cookbook* (University of Texas Press)—and I sometimes substitute other aromatic herbs and flowers for *hierba buena*, that tasty herb we know as spearmint. Create your own versions of these drinks using one or more varieties of herbs and flowers. Dark opal basil colors the drink a pale purple. Lemon verbena, lemon balm, and lemongrass add citrus notes, while lavender and rose petals add floral tones. Add some fizz and a pretty garnish and sit back and admire your own cantina garden.

CAIPIRINHAS, BRAZILIAN limeade coolers, have also become very popular in bars today. They are made without mint but have a great limey flavor that comes from muddling a lime cut into quarters with sugar. Caipirinhas are flavored with cachaça, a sugarcane juice distillate, instead of rum. Try one with tequila *blanco* or *reposado* instead! Serve shaken or stirred, without the sparkling water. I've seen them presented with an upside-down frozen fruit bar as the stir stick, which adds flavor of its own and keeps the drink chilled (use natural fruit-flavored bars).

Today you can also find mojitos and caipirinhas muddled with fresh fruit like mango, pineapple, strawberries, passion fruit, and watermelon.

Muddled Mango Cooler

Speckles of golden mango swirl about in this fiesta cocktail. You'll have fun coming up with your own versions using Cantina Classic sweeteners and liqueurs to suit your taste. I like to serve it in a tall glass with a Spicy Mexican Seasoned Salt rim and lots of ice.

- Cantina Classic Spicy Mexican Seasoned Salt rim, optional
- ¼ large, ripe, peeled mango (or ½ peeled peach)
- 1–2 teaspoons sugar, optional or Sweet and Sour
- Lime wedges, optional
- 2 ounces tequila *blanco* or *reposado*
- ¾ ounce Domaine de Canton ginger liqueur (or triple sec)
- ¾ ounce fresh lime juice
- Reed's Extra Ginger Brew or other sparkling soda
- Garnishes: fresh lime wedges, unpeeled mango slice, dried mango slice sprinkled with chile, mint sprig

Muddle mango with sugar in mixing glass (add a few lime wedges, if you wish). Fill glass with ice and stir in remaining ingredients, topping it off with sparkling soda. Garnish, stir, and serve. *Serves 1.*

Variations:

- Use Cantina Classic Jalapeño Syrup instead of the Domaine de Canton, with an extra splash of *reposado*.
- Muddle ½–1 seeded jalapeño along with the mango.
- Use Cantina Classic Zesty Ginger Syrup with a splash of *reposado*, instead of the Domaine de Canton, and a splash of triple sec.
- Make it with ripe Texas Hill Country peaches instead of mangoes and use lemon juice instead of lime juice.

Pepino Picosito
CUCUMBER-JALAPEÑO COOLER

This perky cucumber and jalapeño cocktail tastes so refreshing in the summertime, but it's a favorite year-round, too. Make it with hothouse cucumbers or small pickling cucumbers to prevent bitterness. Shake and strain it, or better yet, don't strain, and eat the cold, crunchy cucumber/pepper bites with a spoon.

- Cantina Classic Spicy Mexican Seasoned Salt or commercial spicy seasoned salt, optional
- 5 slices unpeeled hothouse cucumber slices or small pickling cucumber slices
- ½–¾ ounce Cantina Classic Jalapeño Syrup
- 2 ounces tequila *blanco* or *reposado*
- 1 ounce freshly squeezed lime juice
- Splash of Topo Chico or your favorite fizz, optional
- Garnishes: seasoned salt rim, fresh lime slice, unpeeled cucumber spear or slice, salad burnet (an herb with a cucumber essence) sprig (p. 111)

Rim chilled glass with Spicy Mexican Seasoned Salt. Muddle cucumbers in the bottom of a shaker glass. Add syrup, tequila, and lime juice. Shake briefly with ice (strain only if you wish) and pour into glass. Add a splash of fizz and a sprinkling of Spicy Mexican Seasoned Salt and serve. *Serves 1.*

Variations:

- Omit Jalapeño Syrup and use Cantina Classic Chile Pepper–Infused Tequila; sweeten with Sweet and Sour.
- Replace Jalapeño Syrup with Cantina Classic Citrus Syrup and muddle 1 seeded jalapeño (cut into slices) with the cucumber and add a splash of triple sec.
- Substitute Cantina Classic Zesty Ginger Syrup for the Jalapeño Syrup and add a splash of Reed's Extra Ginger Brew.

La tarde está tequilera.

—

It's a tequila afternoon.

Summertime Sandía
WATERMELON COOLER

This drink reminds me of summers long ago when we injected an ice-cold, whole watermelon with vodka for a beach party in Laguna. And now we know that tequila has more flavor! My nephew, Whit Hutson, adds a splash of St. Germaine Elderflower liqueur to his icy watermelon drinks and a good splash of mezcal; others add triple sec, but I like the simple flavors of a tequila-spiked watermelon!

Use a melon baller to make watermelon balls to freeze as ice, so you don't dilute flavor. I like to rim the chilled glass with homemade Cantina Classic Pink Peppercorn Citrus Salt or Spicy Mexican Seasoned Salt.

It's 106 degrees in Texas: I think I'll make another!

- Chilled glasses, essential!
- Frozen watermelon balls for ice
- Salted rims, optional
- ⅓ cup seeded and peeled frozen watermelon chunks
- ¾–1 ounce Cantina Classic Sweet and Sour or your favorite syrup or other sweeteners
- ¾ ounce fresh lime juice
- 2 ounces tequila *blanco*, chilled

In a shaker tin, muddle watermelon into a thick purée (more muddling than I usually recommend). Add Sweet and Sour, lime juice, and tequila. Shake with a handful of ice. Pour into chilled glass along with the muddled watermelon, for added flavor and texture, or strain into chilled glasses. (I like to freeze it for 10 minutes before serving.) Serve with 4 or 5 frozen watermelon balls as ice. *Serves 1.*

Note: My nephew has another good idea. He intensely purées ripe watermelon in a blender, then freezes it in jumbo ice trays, which he later transfers to resealable bags, for future use. He then shakes 2 frozen jumbo cubes with other ingredients until it melts enough to make a frosty drink.

Tejana Bluebonnet

I live in a Texican *casita* (cottage) painted bright purple, reminiscent of the gaily colored homes south of the border. It's surrounded by whimsical gardens filled with fresh herbs and flowers . . . and bluebonnets in the spring. How could I not include a purple drink? I love making a Tejana Bluebonnet in the spring, when I can garnish it with purple pansies, but it's mighty good during the summertime Texas blueberry season, too.

I splurge on three of the world's finest spirits for this special occasion drink: 100% blue agave tequila *blanco*, champagne, and Crème Yvette, a purple-hued French liqueur, flavored with violet petals and ripe berries.

Make sure all ingredients are chilled, even the glasses! Share this with someone special.

RECIPE CONTINUED ON NEXT PAGE

Painted earthenware "La Sandía" (watermelon) tile inspired by Mexican *lotería* game.

- ½ cup ripe, chilled Texas blueberries
- 1 ounce fresh lemon juice
- ½–¾ ounce Cantina Classic Citrus Syrup or Simple Syrup
- 3 ounces tequila *blanco*
- 1½ ounces Crème Yvette*
- Brut champagne or your favorite sparkling wine
- Garnishes: frozen blueberries, a purple pansy, several sprigs of fresh lemon verbena and/or lemon thyme or lemon peel curl

Muddle blueberries in the bottom of a chilled shaker glass. Add remaining ingredients and a small handful of ice and shake quickly. Pour into chilled champagne flutes (I don't strain) and add a splash of champagne. Garnish from the garden. *Serves 2.*

Note: Substitute Texas blackberries or dewberries. It's delicious with strawberries or raspberries, too. Made by the producers of St. Germaine Elderflower liqueur, Crème Yvette first became popular in the 1890s. For a variation, substitute St. Germaine Elderflower or fine Italian limoncello or Paula's Texas Lemon Premium Liqueur.

How to Make Cocktails

◆ Stir with ice: Chill drink by mixing ingredients with a bar spoon. Use a gentle circular motion (you don't have to hear the ice clink!) in a glass filled with ice. Strain cocktail into serving glass with fresh ice.

◆ Build over ice: Create drink in the glass in which it is served by pouring ingredients over ice and stirring.

◆ Shake and strain: Shake ingredients with ice in a cocktail shaker. Strain and pour straight up or over fresh ice. (For ice advice, p. 95.)

Drunken Sugarplum Cocktail
TEQUILA MARMALADE OR CHUTNEY COOLER

When fresh ingredients aren't on hand, make a quick-fix cocktail flavored with homemade or farmers' market fruit preserves, chutney, or orange marmalade (p. 98), as the Brits do. I use a dollop of my homemade Drunken Sugarplum Chutney, which gives the drink a gorgeous rosy glow and makes it a special libation for Christmas or Valentine's Day—and all year round.

- 1 generous tablespoon Drunken Sugarplum Chutney or your favorite fruit chutney or preserves
- 1¾ ounces tequila *blanco* or *reposado*
- ¾ ounce fresh lime juice
- ½ ounce of your favorite ginger or orange liqueur
- Garnishes: orange slice or skewered cranberries and/or kumquats, and a pinch of cinnamon or cayenne

In a pint glass, muddle chutney. Add tequila, lime juice, and liqueur. Shake with ice and pour into a tumbler. I like the muddled fruit for color and texture, and I serve the drink with a small spoon; strain if you wish. *Serves 1.*

Note: For a Naranja Dulce Cocktail, substitute orange marmalade for the chutney. Make a spicier version by using red jalapeño jelly.

For Drunken Sugarplum Shooters (great for the Christmas holidays), shake and strain into ice-cold shot glasses straight out of the freezer. A double recipe will make 3 large shots (I use Moroccan tea glasses) or 4 standard shots.

Make a Splash!

M. F. K. Fisher wrote passionately about the celebration of life with food and friends. No wonder she was a tequila aficionada! She ranked it with vodka as "the two most appetizing firewaters in the world" (from *The Art of Eating*).

While tequila speaks for itself in a shot glass or a snifter, its complex and intriguing flavor also mixes well. It outshines vodka, in my opinion. (If you could distill a potato or a lily, like the agave, which would you choose?) Though it shares vodka's versatility, tequila has much more personality, making it a natural for spritzers and classic cocktails. With its bright

A festive spritzer with cucumbers and salad burnet sprigs.

herbaceous and vegetal notes and agave essence, tequila rivals gin in flavor and is less sweet than rum. Today the margarita may be the most popular cocktail, but tequila shows off in classic cocktails too.

I hope you'll agree that 100% blue agave tequila makes classic cocktails taste even better because it doesn't need other aromatics and added flavorings just to liven it up! If you like martinis, or fizzy, citrusy cocktails—like Tom Collinses, Ramos Gin Fizzes, or gimlets—make them with 100% tequila *blanco* instead of gin and use fresh lime instead of lemon juice.

Exchange vodka for tequila *blanco* or *reposado*, when making Sea Breezes, Screwdrivers, Salty Dogs, Bloody Marys, or martinis. Some bartenders serve vermouth-laced Manhattans made with *añejo* instead of whiskey—but then you already know I prefer my *añejo* unadulterated and sipped from a snifter.

TNT TEQUILA AND TONIC

Tequila is an explosion of flavor in this classic, more so than gin or vodka. TNT is the favorite cocktail of Guillermo Romo, the original producer of Herradura Tequila.

- Ice
- 1½ ounces tequila Herradura *blanco* or *reposado*, chilled
- tonic water, preferably Fever-Tree or Q Tonic, chilled
- Two Mexican limes
- Dash of bitters, optional (I like Peychaud, which makes the drink pink)
- Garnishes: lime wedges, unpeeled cucumber or jícama spear, salad burnet sprigs, blue borage flowers (see Cantina Garden, p. 111)

Rim a chilled highball glass with lime and fill with ice, or better yet, with one jumbo ice cube (p. 99). Add tequila and tonic to taste. Squeeze limes into drink. Stir. Garnish and serve. *Serves 1.*

Note: For an aromatic burst, use an herb- or citrus-infused tequila (pp. 140–141).

Tequini
TEQUILA MARTINI

Premium 100% agave tequila *blanco* gives vodka or gin competition in this upscale Mexican Martini. Forget the dry vermouth and use your favorite aromatic homemade herb-infused tequila instead (see Note). Keep tequila and glass chilled before making this elegant drink.

- 2 ounces premium tequila *blanco*, chilled
- ½ ounce Cantina Classic Herb-infused Tequila or ¼ ounce dry vermouth, chilled
- Large cubes of ice
- Dash aromatic bitters, optional
- Lemon or lime peel

Pour tequila and herb-infused tequila (or vermouth) over ice in a mixing glass. Stir gently until chilled, 20–30 seconds. (For a milder drink, shake gently with ice in a chilled shaker.) Strain immediately into a chilled martini glass. Cut away a piece of lime peel, twist it over the drink to release its volatile oils, then run peel lightly around the rim of the glass. Drop it in and serve immediately. *Serves 1.*

   Note: Create your signature herbal infusion for this drink—bay leaf, rosemary lemon verbena, coriander, black peppercorns? (pp. 140–141)

Blue Agave Mist

This cool and shimmery drink shows off 100% "blue" agave tequila just as a Scotch mist highlights single-malt Scotch. It's perfect for sipping while watching a southwestern sunset—that is, when you can't see the shimmering agave fields of Jalisco.

- Lime twist
- Crushed ice
- 1½–2 ounces 100% tequila *reposado* or *añejo*

Rim edge of a chilled old-fashion glass with lime twist. Fill glass with crushed ice. Add tequila and a lime twist. *Serves 1.*

Mexican Mermaid
ROSE-COLORED CHAMPAGNE COCKTAIL

In Mexico, *sirenas* (mermaids) represent temptation, desire, and carnal sin. I had to create a drink worthy of such allure, a combination inspired by three of my favorite things: tequila, bubbly, and mermaids. It's colored by Rosangel, a hibiscus-flavored tequila, and a *flor de jamaica* that is soaked in crimson syrup and opens up like a rare sea flower when submerged in the drink. This shimmering and seductive cocktail is certain to make a splash at any party.

- 1½ ounces Gran Centenario Rosangel tequila or *reposado*, chilled
- Dry and fruity champagne or Spanish cava, chilled
- A *flor de jamaica* (hibiscus) flower soaked in Cantina Classic Ruby Pomegranate Syrup
- Spiraled twist of lime peel "seaweed"

Add tequila to a champagne flute. Top with champagne. Submerge the flower and serve immediately. *Serves 1.*

   Note: The Wild Hibiscus Flower Company (Australia) sells Wild Hibiscus (Flowers in Syrup) when you cannot make your own syrup.

Give It Some Spritz!

Poolside, seaside, or in the middle of the desert, refreshing tequila spritzers delight anywhere, anytime. They'll prompt you to put your feet up and relax—or kick up your heels and dance! Spritzers are easy to prepare and make a quick welcome for unexpected guests. Set up a spritzer cantina at your next fiesta with ingredients on hand for guests to create their own cocktails.

Tequila Spritzer

This tall drink is as simple to make as a Tom Collins—"that gin and sparkling lemonade" cocktail that's been popular since 1876, when purportedly created by Jerry Thomas, the "father of mixology." Create signature "spritzers" by experimenting with different brands of tequila, effervescent mixers, sweeteners, and a variety of garnishes. Use the following recipe as an example; see next page for extra tips. Remember, balance of ingredients is the key to a good cocktail. Use large cubes of ice (or a jumbo cube, p. 99) to keep the flavors from diluting.

- 1¾–2 ounces tequila *blanco* or *reposado*
- 1 ounce fresh lime or lemon juice (or combination thereof)
- ½–1 ounce sweetener
- 2 ounces sparkling water or your favorite fizzy soda to taste
- Garnishes: see next page

Rim Collins glass with lime. Fill glass with ice and stir in ingredients *al gusto* (to your taste), finishing with a long splash of your favorite fizz. Stir and garnish festively. *Serves 1.*

Fresco FRESH CUCUMBER SPRITZER

It's hot as firecrackers on the Fourth of July in Texas! I created this drink to beat the heat, using ingredients from an ice chest on hand while camping on the Llano River. The spicy flavor of Jamaican-style ginger ale complements tequila.

- Twist of lime peel
- 4 thick slices hothouse cucumber, unpeeled
- 1½ ounces tequila *reposado*
- Lots of freshly squeezed lime juice to taste
- Generous splash of Reed's Extra Ginger Brew or imported ginger beer

Rub twist of lime peel along rim of tall glass. Layer ice and cucumbers in glass. Add remaining ingredients to taste. Stir and serve. Finish the drink, eat the cold, crunchy cucumbers, then make another one! *Serves 1.*

Torito (Little Bull)

Mexican lager (like Dos Equis) gives the sparkle to this drink. During fiestas in his hometown of Luvianos, Mexico, my friend Javier Aviles and his amigos make this lively tequila spritzer. They squeeze the juice from oranges and the *limones* growing nearby, spike it with *bastante* (lots of!) tequila, season it with finely chopped chile serrano peppers and red onions, and add a good splash of beer to give it some fizz. Sounds like this may cure a hangover before it happens.

Move over, *micheladas*, mimosas, and Bloody Marys! Toritos make a sparkling and cool brunch drink. Serve them by the glass or pitcher. Chill all the ingredients before making the drink.

- 6 cups freshly squeezed orange juice
- 1 cup freshly squeezed lime juice
- 2 cups tequila *blanco* or Chile Pepper–Infused Tequila
- 1 teaspoon salt
- 3 or more serrano peppers or red Fresnos, finely chopped
- 1 Mexican beer (12 ounces)
- ⅓ cup red onion, finely chopped

In a glass pitcher, mix together citrus juices, tequila, salt, and peppers; chill for several hours. Before serving, add beer and sprinkle with chopped onions. Serve in tall glasses over ice. Try festive ice cubes with chile peppers, or chile pepper flowers hooked over the rim of the glass (p. 110). *Serves 6–8.*

Making Spritzers
Keeping It Cool

Keep all ingredients and glasses chilled in the fridge or freezer before mixing. Top drinks with big handful of crushed ice. Enjoy before the ice melts and dilutes the fresh and lively flavor of the drink.

Choose your fizzy soda

Sparkling water
Squirt and other citrus sodas
Natural and low-sugar artisanal mixers and sodas
Reed's Extra Ginger Brew (or Reed's Light, for fewer calories) or ginger beer
Champagne, Spanish cava, or prosecco
Beer

Pick your citrus

Mexican (Key) limes or Persian limes
Lemons and Meyer lemons
Oranges, blood oranges, mandarins, and tangerines
Ruby red grapefruit

Sweeten to taste

Cantina Classics syrups
Sweet and Sour
Agave Syrup diluted with liquid (p. 99)

Add if you wish (but don't overwhelm tequila's bright flavor)

Aromatic bitters
Orange or rose flower waters

Garnish

Fresh, unpeeled citrus slices, wedges, curls, or zest
Jícama sticks
Whole kumquats on spear
Cucumber spears or slices with peel
Fresh herb sprigs and edible flowers from your cantina garden (p. 111)

Punches for Parties

THROUGHOUT MEXICO, street stall vendors enticingly display and sell fresh fruit punches called *aguas frescas*. They ladle the drinks from large, clear glass *jarros* (jars with lids) into cups for passersby. These nonalcoholic punches glisten in the sun, candy-colored and filled with chunks of tropical fruits: *sandía* (watermelon), *melón* (cantaloupe), *coco* (coconut), *jamaica* (hibiscus flowers), mango, *tamarindo* (tamarind pod), and *pepino* (cucumber).

Aguas frescas inspired my tequila *ponches* (punches), signature libations for festive occasions. Tequila is my magic ingredient, brightening and balancing the flavors of tropical fruits, citrus, herbs, and spices reflected in jewel-like splendor within the jar. Find glass *jarros* or *agua fresca* jars that resemble old-fashioned pickle barrels at Mexican specialty markets, import stores, or online, as well as other clear glass vessels.

Tequila *ponches* make perfect party drinks because guests serve themselves, allowing the host to mingle and have a good time. They also serve as spectacular table centerpieces.

Festive Centerpiece for the Table or Cantina

For your fiesta, wreath the base of a punch jar (or punch bowl) with clusters of whole fruits—lemons, oranges, kumquats, limes, and strawberries with green hulls. Fill in with sprays of greenery and fresh flowers. Embellish with seasonal ornaments, folk art, colorful garlands, or strings of lights. If you wish, surround the jar with long-stemmed margarita glasses piled high with sliced lemons, oranges, limes, and strawberries, and guests can choose their own garnishes for their drinks.

Those cloying, concentrated fruit juice and soda pop concoctions that revelers dread (devised to stretch and mask flavors of inexpensive brands of liquor) won't be found in your punch jar! Instead, fresh, flavorful fruits and juices, herbs and aromatics—and always an element of surprise—will delight guests.

Serve punches from simmering pots from the stovetop or chilled, depending upon the season.

The author serving *ponches* from traditional *agua fresca* punch jars.

- 46 ounces unsweetened pineapple juice
- 4 oranges, cut into bite-sized wedges
- ½ medium watermelon, cut into bite-sized chunks or triangles with peel
- 3 lemons, sliced
- 6 limes, quartered
- 3 small ruby grapefruit, cut in bite-sized wedges
- 2 star fruit sliced into star shapes
- 4 cans (12 ounces each) Squirt

Place pineapple chunks in a wide-mouthed glass jar. Add tequilas, juices, and sliced oranges. Chill overnight. Add watermelon, lemons, limes, grapefruit, and star fruit and chill several more hours, stirring occasionally. Add Squirt immediately before serving. *Serves approx. 20.*

Note: The flavor of this punch improves with age. It keeps for several days in the refrigerator; watermelon will lose its texture, and should be stored separately (if there's any punch left!). Lemons, limes, and grapefruit become bitter when left in the punch too long.

Ponche de Guadalajara (Guadalajara Punch)

Throughout Jalisco, this refreshing drink is served in large, wide-mouthed clay bowls called *cazuelas*. Citrus wedges are eaten or squeezed into the drink. Partakers pop chunks of watermelon and fresh pineapple into their mouths and sip the tequila-laced libation through a straw.

Cazuelas inspired this party punch. Present it in an *agua fresca* jar to show off the colorful fruits, and ladle it into long-stemmed jumbo margarita glasses (alternatives for clay bowls) with some ice. A guest once called this drink "the quintessential finger bowl"; I call it the "the ultimate fruit cocktail"! Make sure that guests get plenty of the spiked watermelon and pineapple.

- 1 fresh pineapple, cut into bite-sized chunks
- 1-liter bottle tequila *blanco*
- 2 cups tequila *reposado*
- ½ cup fresh lime juice
- 6 cups fresh orange juice

Verano Tropical TROPICAL SUMMER PUNCH

Serve this exotic and exceptionally refreshing punch on a sultry summer evening. Fresh pineapple chunks absorb the flavor of the tequila, while fragrant stalks of lemongrass, mint sprigs, and citrus lend Asian mystique. Jamaican-style ginger ale, added just prior to serving, adds sparkle to this intriguing drink. Even after the punch is gone, guests enthusiastically munch on the spiked fruit and fragrant lemongrass.

- 2 large ripe pineapples, cut into chunks
- 2 cans (46 ounces each) pineapple juice (or part other tropical juice)
- 1.5 liters of tequila *reposado*
- 4–6 fresh stalks of lemongrass with rough outer leaves removed, cut in half lengthwise, then cut into 2-inch segments and slightly mashed to release flavor
- 2–4 large bunches fresh mint, lemon verbena, lemon balm, or a combination

- ½ cup freshly squeezed lemon juice
- ½ cup freshly squeezed lime juice
- Sweeten to taste (see note for optional ingredients)
- 2 lemons, sliced
- 6 limes, sliced
- 3 (12-ounce) bottles Reed's Extra Ginger Brew or your favorite sparkling soda
- Garnishes: Fresh mint sprigs and peeled sugarcane stalks
- Long, unpeeled sugarcane stalk for stirring punch

Place pineapple chunks and juice in a 2-gallon glass jar and cover with tequila. Add lemongrass segments, fresh herbs, and lemon and lime juices, and chill overnight. Sweeten to taste with optional ingredients. A few hours prior to serving, remove herbs, wringing them to release flavor (replace with fresh ones, if possible.) Add lemon and lime slices. Before serving, splash with Ginger Brew.

Ladle into tall glasses with plenty of fruit and ice; garnish and serve. *Serves approx. 20.*

Note: Other optional flavorings and sweeteners include Cantina Classic syrups like Zesty Ginger or Citrus, Ambrosia or Domaine de Canton liqueurs, and Sweet and Sour.

Ponche Guadalajara served in the author's garden.

Ponche de Manzana
SPICY APPLE PUNCH WITH POMEGRANATE SEEDS

The aroma of hot mulled cider simmering on the stove reminds me that it's autumn. Often, however, the mild southwestern climate does not cooperate, and an iced drink is more inviting, so I offer two versions. This punch is a good alternative to hot mulled cider (see note for hot version), paying tribute to the season's glory—tart green apples, fresh mint, crimson pomegranate seeds, cinnamon, and spice. Spiking it with tequila (or mezcal!) instead of the more traditional rum makes it especially tasty.

- 1 gallon unsweetened apple juice or cider
- 3 tablespoons mulled spice mix (see Note)
- 6 3-inch cinnamon sticks
- 1½ cups golden raisins
- 4 lemons, sliced
- 2–4 large bunches fresh mint (or part Mexican mint marigold or other sweet herbs)
- 3 Granny Smith apples, cut into small chunks, sprinkled with lemon juice
- 3 small crisp red apples, cut into small chunks, sprinkled with lemon juice
- Juice of 3 lemons
- 1.5 liters tequila *reposado* (or part mezcal)
- 2–3 bottles (12 ounces each) Reed's Extra Ginger Brew, ginger ale, sparkling apple cider, or Sidral (Mexican apple soda)
- 1 pomegranate, seeded, optional
- Garnishes: cinnamon sugar to rim glasses; large bouquet of fresh mint sprigs or mint marigold, with its bright yellow autumn blossoms; long cinnamon sticks; whole crabapples
- Optional sweeteners: Cantina Classic Zesty Ginger, Citrus, or Ruby Syrups to taste

Pour 8 cups of the apple juice into a small saucepan. Add mulled spice, cinnamon sticks, raisins, and slices of 1 lemon; bring to boil. Reduce heat and simmer for 10 minutes. Allow to cool and set for several hours. Strain, reserving cinnamon sticks and raisins.

Day of the Dead Ponche de Manzana surrounded by sugar skulls.

Pour into a large glass jar with remaining apple juice, cinnamon sticks, raisins, sliced lemons, fresh mint sprigs, and apples, along with the tequila and lemon juice. Chill overnight. Sweeten as needed.

Before serving, wring mint to release flavor, then discard, replacing with a fresh bunch and a long stick of cinnamon. For effervescence, splash with ginger ale or apple cider just before serving. Ladle into wide-mouthed goblets with plenty of the spiked apples, and sprinkle pomegranate seeds in each glass. Garnish and serve. *Serves approx. 20.*

Note: For mulled spice mixture, combine 1 tablespoon each whole allspice and whole coriander, 1 teaspoon whole cloves, 2 teaspoons anise seeds, freshly grated nutmeg, a few sprigs of fresh mint and/or Mexican mint marigold, and 4 bay or allspice leaves.

To serve punch hot:

Use unfiltered apple juice for the recipe and omit Ginger Brew. Bring punch ingredients, except tequila, to a boil; reduce heat and simmer for 30 minutes. Pour into mugs and spike each cup with a shot of tequila *reposado* or mezcal. Serve with a cinnamon stick stirrer.

*Las penas
con ponche de granada son menos.*

——

*Woes
with pomegranate punch go.*

En Salón Tenampa

In 1992, I visited one of Mexico City's most famous and historic cantinas, Salón Tenampa, a veritable shrine to the most famous mariachis. Upon entering the swinging doors of this boisterous cantina, famous Mexican musicians greeted me—Jorge Negrete, José Alfredo Jiménez, and Lola Beltrán, the "queen of *ranchera*," among others, depicted in colorful murals on the walls, along with lyrics to their songs. At either end of the room, dueling mariachi bands vied to outshine each other. Some passionate customers stood up to accompany them in song.

Juan Hernández from Cocula, Jalisco, the reputed birthplace of mariachi music, founded Salón Tenampa in 1925. He brought with him the music from his hometown, while his wife, Amalia, brought the punch. She heated her sweet and spicy pomegranate brew on coal burners, serving it from steaming clay *jarros* to mariachis and patrons alike to assuage the bitter chill of a winter night. *¡Dulzón pero fuerte!* (Sweet, but strong!)

Outside this popular cantina today, in the rowdy, crowded Garibaldi Plaza, dozens of rival mariachi bands and romantic trios from all over Mexico stroll about, seeking requests for songs for hire. A cacophony of trumpets and violins, guitarrones and harps, and an occasional marimba from southern Mexico fills the air along with tantalizing aromas wafting from the many *puestocitos* (small stalls) selling regional specialties like *birria* (meat and chile stew), pozole, quesadillas, taquitos, and plenty of *menudo para los crudos* (a spicy hangover stew).

The dangers of this *barrio*—known for drug trafficking, bordellos, bawdiness, and gunslinging taxi drivers—seem not to deter the hundreds who flock there nightly until the wee hours of the morn to eat, drink tequila, and lose their inhibitions. Some come for sheer pleasure, others to drown their sorrows or to woo a woman with serenades of love (or love lost!), and many—displaced laborers and lonely hearts in a massive, crowded metropolis—come simply to return to their rural roots and their *rancheras* for one night . . . at least in song.

Sadly, traditions vanish, and that is why I am preserving in this book as many as I can. Salón Tenampa still offers Ponche de Granada, though now served chilled from plastic cups, and *narcocorridos* (drug-smuggling ballads) are more familiar to youths than the romantic classics. Still, in Garibaldi Plaza, a veritable melting pot of food and song, traditions of mariachi and tequila prevail.

The Mexican government is revitalizing the environs of this popular, though rather seedy, nightspot, making it safer to revel in the joyful spirit of Mexico and mariachis and for tourists to learn more about the culture. An agave garden, the Museo de Tequila y Mezcal (MUTEM), and the School of Mariachi opened to the public in 2010 to preserve *el mexicanismo.*

Ponche de Granada (Pomegranate Punch)

For generations, women in Jalisco have made a tasty simmered punch in the fall using the juice from fresh, newly ripened pomegranates, a recipe undoubtedly brought from Spain. Sipped from small clay *jarros*, this punch is traditionally imbibed at the many fiestas and street fairs occurring in the month before Christmas. Party hosts fill a *garrafón* (large plastic jug) with tequila right from the local still to have on hand for those who choose to add some punch to their punch!

Numerous versions of Ponche de Granada exist, some laced with tequila, others with mezcal. Some people ferment the fresh juice of pomegranates, serving it like a fortified wine. Others grind the seeds, then simmer the juice in cinnamon syrup. Any way it's served, the rich, ruby color of pomegranate and its dense, sweet, and tart flavor is a natural for agave spirits.

Delight your holiday guests with this traditional Mexican favorite that many from our side of the

RECIPE CONTINUED ON NEXT PAGE

border have not tasted. It fills the room with alluring scents of fruit and spice as it simmers. Spike it with your favorite agave spirit for a memorable hot toddy.

Ponche de Granada lends itself to unexpected garnishes. I usually serve this regal punch steaming hot from mugs in the true Mexican style—each cup sprinkled with chopped peanuts or pecans, pickled jalapeños and pomegranate seeds, all adding crunch to the punch. Depending upon the weather, however, I may serve it chilled, garnished with chopped fresh cucumbers and jalapeños. Stirred with an unpeeled cucumber spear and sprinkled with pomegranate seeds, it makes a refreshing autumn spritzer. (On a hot autumn eve, I offer guests a chilled version served from slow-sipping shot glasses.)

This punch is easy to make because fresh pomegranates are now readily seasonally available in most markets, and bottled pomegranate juice has become a popular and healthy drink option. The only things missing are the mariachis at Salón Tenampa!

Ponche de Granada Shooter garnished with allspice leaf and pomegranate seeds within a frame decorated with Mexican *milagros*.

- 1 8-ounce cone *piloncillo* (unrefined brown sugar, p. 99)
- 1 cup water
- 3 small sticks cinnamon plus one long stick
- 2 large pomegranates, seeded, with any juice reserved
- 2 quarts natural 100% pomegranate juice
- 3–4 Valencia oranges, sliced
- 1 handful dried *jamaica*, optional (p. 98)
- 1 bottle tequila or mezcal (I especially like mezcal with this)
- Garnishes: fresh pomegranate seeds, cinnamon sticks, pickled jalapeños, chopped pecans, peanuts, chopped cucumbers, orange slices, lime wedge

In a small, heavy saucepan, bring *piloncillo*, water, and small cinnamon sticks to a slow boil, heating until sugar dissolves into amber syrup. Set aside. In a 4-quart saucepan, mash pomegranate seeds slightly. Add pomegranate juice, orange slices, ¾ of the *piloncillo* syrup, the long cinnamon stick, and *jamaica* and bring to a slow boil. Reduce heat and simmer 20 minutes. Turn off heat and allow to sit for several hours for added flavor. Sweeten with remaining *piloncillo* syrup, if necessary. Reheat and serve steaming cups spiked with mezcal or tequila in each mug. Or strain and chill overnight, if serving cold. *Serves 10, or more as shots.*

Note: 1 medium pomegranate yields about ¾ cup seeds.

VERSATILE PRESENTATIONS FOR PONCHE DE GRANADA

- Ponche de Granada mugs: Fill mugs with hot punch and add suggested garnishes. Spike punch with an agave spirit and stir with a cinnamon stick.
- Ponche de Granada Shooter: Strain punch and chill overnight. Fill a large, clear shot glass (4-ounce Moroccan tea glasses are great for this) halfway with the chilled punch, top with chilled silver tequila or mezcal and a squeeze of fresh Key lime juice, and stir. Place an allspice or citrus leaf vertically in the glass, then sprinkle with pomegranate seeds.

- Ponche de Granada Spritzer: Fill Collins glass with ice. Add 4–5 ounces chilled and strained punch, 2 ounces tequila *blanco* or *reposado*, or mezcal (or a combination) and a good squeeze of fresh lime juice. Sprinkle with pomegranate seeds, finely minced pickled or fresh jalapeños, and cucumbers. Stir with an unpeeled cucumber spear.
- Ponche de Granada Ice Pop: Freeze strained punch in ice-pop molds. Bite into the frozen-pop-on-a-stick and follow with a shot of *blanco* tequila.

Memories of Holiday Punch in Atotonilco

A boisterous street party takes place every night from November 30 to December 8 in the tequila-producing town of Atotonilco, Jalisco. One would never expect such merriment after the sacred events of the early dawn. Each morning at 5:30 during this time, villagers carry a carved wooden virgin, La Imaculada Concepción de María Purísima, through the streets on their shoulders so that she will bless their homes. I joined the procession from the *iglesia* (church) in the plaza down a long cobblestone street packed with devoted followers, who sang and prayed to their patron saint.

That night, the solemnity of the chilly dawn was magically transformed into fiesta and revelry. The streets that had been blessed by the Virgin that morning became the scene of the evening's *posada*, a festivity that welcomes people door to door. Neighbors had worked for months on decorations to make their street the most impressive. They had strung intricate paper cutouts, banners, flags, and colorful crepe paper flowers across the streets and gaily adorned the doorways and streetlamps. Firecrackers exploded in the sky, church bells clanged, and the thump thump of *tambores* (drums) from small bands resonated in the night. Troupes of animated dancers—dressed in costumes of *muertos* (skeletons), *diablos* (devils), and wild animals—performed in the streets.

On each corner, vendors sold crispy *buñuelos* (crispy, sweet, fried tortilla-shaped fritters), drizzled with *piloncillo* syrup; *churros* (twisted crullers sprinkled with cinnamon sugar); and *cajeta* candies made from sweetened goat's milk. Children sucked nectar from sugarcane segments and munched on roasted *cacahuates* and *palomitas* (peanuts and popcorn). Others ate steamed garbanzos tucked into small brown paper sacks and sprinkled with fresh lime juice, salt, and chile powder.

Dense crowds paraded through the streets. Merrymakers knocked on the doors of houses, welcomed by women offering trays full of cups of simmering *ponche*, thick and flavorful punches brimming with exotic stewed fruits—*guayaba* (guavas), *tamarindo*, *jamaica*, *tejocotes* (fruits from the Mexican hawthorn tree), and *granadas*—spiced with *canela* (cinnamon) and sprinkled with crushed pecans. Each *ponche* was a specialty of the house, some of great renown, as the lines forming outside that home attested. Some revelers spiked the punches, using tequila from the gallon jugs filled from one of the town's distilleries.

I saw a group of mariachis in obsidian-colored suits studded with shiny silver buttons and bearing the words "Tequila El Viejito" embroidered across their backs. Introducing myself as an amiga of the owner of the distillery, I found myself with attentive chaperones, although some of the town's matrons looked with disdain at a *gringa* following the mariachis. One man hired the mariachis for hours to serenade his family and neighbors while they sipped tequila-laden *ponche*, singing along from their chairs parked in the street in front of the house. But at the stroke of midnight, the lead mariachi banished me to my hotel because, he said, "nice girls must be in at that hour." I admit that I longed for the freedom to sing and dance and drink tequila in the streets until dawn. *¡Gringa en México con corazón mexicano!*

> *Y que le sirvan ponche caliente*
> *a las viejitas*
> *que no tienen dientes.*
>
> ———
>
> *And let them serve punch that's steaming*
> *to little old ladies*
> *whose teeth are leaving.*

Posadas Navideñas

In villages throughout Mexico, locals partake of celebrations called *posadas* during the nine days before Christmas. They reenact Mary and Joseph's pilgrimage, seeking shelter in Bethlehem. Candlelight processions go door to door, singing and praying, and are turned away until they reach the "inn," a home predestined for the fiesta. There, the pilgrims gather around an ornate nativity scene. Like most Mexican religious observances, the sacred nature of the *posadas* soon gives way to merriment—tasty food, *piñatas*, and steaming cups of *ponche* for the travelers, sipped from earthenware mugs called *jarritos* and often spiked with tequila or mezcal.

Many North Americans—especially in the Southwest—also embrace the *posada* tradition. *Luminarias* (small paper bags, partially filled with sand, holding a glowing candle) light the way to the door. Whether part of the procession of a *posada* or simply served in a small gathering, *ponche* is part of a tradition that most Mexican families look forward to during the holidays. Sharing this drink is a way to assure a "Feliz Navidad, Prospero Año y Felicidad."

On Christmas morning, I simmer a big pot of *ponche* on my stove. Wafts of enticing and comforting aromas fill my house, bringing back memories of my beloved Mexico. Sometimes this punch is hard to duplicate in the United States because of the unavailability of the exotic fruits. However, Latin American markets and *pulgas* (flea markets) north of the border stock *ponche* ingredients during the Christmas season just for this revered tradition.

I love visiting these venues at this time of the year, joining others who come to hand-select fruits and spices, long stalks of sugarcane, crimson *jamaica* flowers, and cones of brown *piloncillo* sugar for this annual ritual. I often ask them to share their *ponche* recipes with me, though it's usually simply *una cuchara*, *un poquito*, or *una copita* of ingredients ("a spoonful of this," "a little of that," or "a little cupful").

Once, in my best Spanish, I told a *viejita* (old Mexican woman) as she frugally picked a handful of fruit for her Christmas punch, "Voy a hechar tecolotes en mi ponche." The little woman jumped back, wide-eyed and terrified! The other women around us broke out in merry laughter. I had told her I was going to put *owls* in my punch! She must have thought I'd been sipping tequila before even making the punch . . . or was planning to conjure up a dark *brujas* (witches) brew.

I meant to say *tejocotes*, the name for the small, hard, black-speckled orangish fruits that are a favorite seasonal ingredient for *ponche*. These fruits come from various species of Mexican hawthorn trees and taste rather like crabapples, although *tejocotes* are usually about half the size, with several big, hard seeds. Tart and mealy until cooked, *tejocotes* produce a pectin that naturally thickens the *ponche* and are a highly sought-after and expensive ingredient during the holidays.

Though traditional *ponche* calls for many ingredients, it's easy to make. I have allowed for a choice of substitutions in my version. You'll find that tropical fruit nectars add flavor when the more unusual fresh fruits are not available. Dried apricots, prunes, cherries, and apples may be substituted as needed, and a handful of fresh cranberries adds pleasing tartness (see note following recipe).

Ponche Navideño
TRADITIONAL CHRISTMAS PUNCH

Serve Mexico's beloved Christmas punch from clay *jarritos* or small mugs and spike with your favorite tequila or mezcal—or a splash of both! Provide a spoon for eating the stewed fruit. It's delicious for a holiday gathering that might include Mexican Wedding Cookies, crispy *buñuelos*, *polvorones* (cinnamon-sprinkled sugar cookies), or *pan dulce* pastries from your favorite Mexican bakery.

- 1 sugarcane stalk, about 3 feet long, cut into segments with a sharp knife (discard tough or stringy segments; see note)
- 3 quarts water
- 2 8-ounce cones of *piloncillo* or equivalent brown sugar
- 6 sticks Mexican *canela* (cinnamon), 3 inches long
- 2 teaspoons whole allspice berries
- 1 teaspoon whole cloves
- 2 teaspoons anise seeds
- 6 stalks lemongrass, rough outer leaves removed, cut into 3-inch pieces, slightly mashed, optional
- 10 large *tamarindo* pods, brittle shell peeled away and fibrous veins removed
- ½–¾ pound *tejocote* (see Note)
- 2 crisp red apples, cut into bite-sized chunks
- 1–2 *membrillos* (quince), or 2 crisp Asian pears, cut into bite-sized chunks
- 1 pound *guayaba* (guavas) or assorted dried fruits (see Note)
- 1 cup golden raisins
- 12 plump prunes
- ¾ cup dried *jamaica* flowers
- 4 fresh allspice or bay leaves, optional
- Split vanilla pod or splash of Mexican vanilla, optional
- 3 oranges, sliced
- 1–2 quarts fruit nectar (such as guava, *tamarindo*, or unfiltered apple juice)
- Agave syrup to taste
- 1 bottle or more tequila *reposado* or *añejo* and/or mezcal

With a sharp, sturdy knife (and caution!), trim away the tough peel of the sugarcane segments; cut each segment into lengthwise pieces about the size of celery sticks and set aside (approx. 25 pieces).

Bring water to boil in a large, heavy stockpot. Add *piloncillo*, cinnamon sticks, and spices; lower heat slightly. Stir occasionally until *piloncillo* has melted, about 10 minutes.

Add sugarcane, lemongrass, *tamarindo*, *tejocote*, remaining fresh or dried fruits, and 1½ quarts fruit nectar and simmer for nearly an hour, until aromatic and slightly thickened, adding oranges toward the end of cooking. Add more nectar or water as needed.

Turn off heat and preferably let *ponche* sit for several hours (or overnight). Reheat at a gentle simmer. Ladle piping hot punch into mugs, along with some of the fruit and a piece of sugarcane, and let guests add tequila or mezcal to taste. Guests can chew on the sugarcane segments, discarding the fibrous remains along with seeds, spices, and *jamaica* flowers in small bowls on the table. *Serves approx. 25.*

Note: Mexicans usually drop *tejocotes* whole into the punch and spit out the seeds. Substitute other tart fruits like crabapples when *tejocotes* aren't available. You may also find canned *tejocotes en miel* or *almíbar* (syrup), but use fresh whenever possible. Often, frozen whole guavas are available during this season.

If you are lucky, you'll find sugarcane already cut into sections. You'll also find canned sugarcane segments and lemongrass in Asian markets, as well as *tamarindo* (tamarind pods), the tart, sticky pulp of which adds rich flavor and color to the punch.

How about some nontraditional ingredients? Add fresh or dried cranberries, dried cherries or apricots, kumquats, or crabapples. Sometimes I'll add some crushed, dried red cayenne to liven it up!

Holiday Piñata Ponche filled with surprises.

Piñata Ponche
FESTIVE PIÑATA PUNCH

The colorful surprises found within this enticing libation remind me of the candy treasures within a Mexican piñata. Fresh cranberries, blueberries, and crabapples; chunks of apples and pears; and slices of citrus sparkle in this ruby-red punch. The tart, acidic contrast of cranberry juice with tequila *blanco* is a natural, while cinnamon sticks, *jamaica* (dried hibiscus flowers), and spicy ginger brew enhance the flavor of each cup of good cheer.

This punch has become a favorite at large holiday parties, where guests can serve themselves. Festively served from an *agua fresca* jar, it makes everyone merry.

- 12-ounce package fresh cranberries
- 1 gallon natural cranberry juice (or cranberry-pomegranate juice)
- 1.75-liter bottle of tequila *blanco*
- 2 cups of your favorite triple sec
- 3 navel oranges, sliced
- 3 Granny Smith apples, cut in bite-sized chunks
- 12 or more crabapples
- 15 kumquats, optional
- ¾ cup *jamaica* (dried hibiscus flowers)
- 3 10-inch cinnamon sticks
- 12-ounce can undiluted frozen limeade concentrate or Sweet and Sour
- 2 lemons, sliced
- 2 limes, sliced
- 1 12-ounce package frozen blueberries
- 1 12-ounce package frozen peaches
- 2–3 star fruit (*carambola*), sliced
- 2 or 3 12-ounce bottles Reed's Extra Ginger Brew
- Long stalk of sugarcane as a stirrer, optional

Rinse cranberries and drain in a colander. Freeze half of them in decorative ice cubes, along with a strip of orange peel, and freeze the rest on a tray, then store in a freezer bag.

Pour cranberry juice, tequila, and triple sec into a 2½-gallon glass container. Add fruit, *jamaica* flowers, and cinnamon sticks. Add 6 ounces of the limeade or Sweet and Sour; chill overnight or longer.

A few hours before serving, add more limeade or Sweet and Sour, if needed, and the lemon and lime slices. Just prior to serving, add some of the remaining frozen cranberries, blueberries, and peaches, (replenishing them as needed to keep punch cold), and the star fruit. Splash generously with Ginger Brew and serve in wide-mouthed glasses filled with the decorative cranberry ice cubes and pieces of fruit. *Serves approx. 25.*

After-Dinner Drinks

*Con barriga llena,
el corazón contento.
La tequila buena, las penas ya no siento.*

—

*With a full belly,
a happy heart.
A good tequila makes my troubles depart.*

F ROM SNIFTERS TO SHOOTERS, icy frappés to hot coffee drinks, tequila is always good for the last sip of the day. It cuts the heaviness of sweet liqueurs, offering nuances of its own and making drinks more complex and interesting.

Edward Weston, whose memories of Mexico in the early 1920s are as sensitive and beautiful as his photographs, said of the magical powers of tequila, "Strange how one can understand a foreign tongue with tequila in one's belly." After imbibing these luscious after-dinner drinks, you may be speaking Spanish, too!

Cantina Classic Liqueurs

The market is inundated with liqueurs to mix with tequila, but I've concocted my own Cantina Classic elixirs, some based on traditional recipes. Create signature cocktails with them or simply savor them in shots or snifters—with or without ice. They also make wonderful gifts for tequila aficionados. (To create a presentation as enticing as the contents, use decorative bottles with corks, not metal lids . . . or fill up empty tequila bottles.)

Almendrado
ALMOND-FLAVORED TEQUILA LIQUEUR

In Mexico, Casa Orendain's popular Crema de Almendrado liqueur is served in snifters, over ice with a twist of lemon, or with coffee. The flavor of tequila remains intact, making Crema de Almendrado less sweet than other almond-flavored liqueurs. It's hard to find, unless you travel south of the border. I've recently seen some other brands on the market, but why not make your own?

Almond/tequila mixture:
- 8 ounces whole, unpeeled, toasted almonds (see Note)
- ½ vanilla bean, split, scraped of seeds, or ½ teaspoon Mexican vanilla
- 2 3-inch cinnamon sticks
- ½ teaspoon pure almond extract
- 1 bottle (750 ml) tequila *reposado* or *añejo* (or a combination)

For the syrup:
- 3 or more tablespoons Spicy Piloncillo Syrup

Coarsely chop almonds. Place them in a jar, along with the vanilla bean, cinnamon sticks, and almond extract. Cover with tequila and steep for 2 weeks in a cool, dark place, occasionally shaking gently (murky sediment is natural). Strain several times through paper coffee filters. Add syrup a tablespoon at a time, tasting after each addition, until satisfied with flavor. Add a bit more almond extract, if necessary. Pour into sterilized dark-colored jars; allow to set for 2 weeks, adding more syrup if needed. *Makes about 3½ cups.*

Note: To toast almonds, place on baking sheet in a preheated 350-degree oven and toast for about 10 minutes, until golden brown, turning occasionally. Alternatively, place almonds in an ungreased cast-iron skillet and stir over medium heat until golden brown.

Rompope
MEXICAN EGGNOG

Early Christmas morning, friends and neighbors gather at my house to sing carols accompanied by guitar and plenty of eggnog. There's a special twist to this tradition: guests arrive wearing pajamas, and the eggnog is spiked with tequila.

Nuns in Mexican convents first made *rompope*, a rich thick eggnog with ingredients introduced to the New World from Spain: sugar, nutmeg, brandy, and cream. Most eggnogs are too dense and cloying for my taste; my version, doused with tequila, is rich and luscious but not as sweet as those made with rum or brandy. It's flavored with spirals of citrus peel and dusted with freshly grated nutmeg. (Many swear that it's the best eggnog they've ever tasted.) Serve in small pottery mugs or elegant crystal sherry glasses.

In Jalisco's tequila-producing town of Atotonilco, Mexicans layer an almond-flavored eggnog called "Atotonilli" in a snifter with the rich, dark coffee tequila liqueur that's famous there and now bottled as Patrón XO Café.

- 12 eggs, yolks separated
- 1 pound confectioners' sugar
- 1 bottle (750 ml) tequila *añejo*
- ½ teaspoon Mexican vanilla extract or ½ split vanilla pod
- Continuous spiral of 1 orange peel and 1 lemon without bitter white pith
- 2 quarts half-and-half
- Garnish: freshly grated nutmeg

In a large bowl, beat egg yolks with a whisk until thick and pale yellow in color. Slowly add sugar and half the tequila, mixing well. Let stand for an hour, then whisk in the remaining tequila, vanilla, citrus peel, and half-and-half. Pour into a large pitcher and chill overnight. Fill each glass with Rompope, adding a piece of twisted orange peel and dust with a pinch of freshly grated nutmeg. *Serves 16.*

Note: For those leery of raw eggs, adapt recipe using a cooked egg custard process. For an even lighter version, some may choose to beat the egg whites to a soft peak, then fold them into the Rompope.

Painted clay skeleton taking a siesta with his tequila bottle.

Para Mi Amante (For My Lover)

In Provence, the season's ripest fruits are layered with sugar and spice and Armagnac brandy. At my house, I use tequila *añejo* instead. Para Mi Amante is very versatile: serve it in snifters or with a bit of fruit, or use it to flavor other cocktails. Drizzle it over flan, sorbets, ice cream, or Spanish Almond Cake. Make this concoction a month in advance to allow the tequila, fruit, and spices to mellow. The colorful array, presented in a pretty French wide-mouthed canning jar, makes a charming Christmas and Valentine's Day gift.

- 2 navel or blood oranges, sliced into rounds with peel
- 1 lemon, sliced into rounds with peel
- 2 tangerines, sliced into rounds with peel
- 1 pint blueberries
- ½ pint raspberries
- 1 pound slightly firm mangos, peeled and cut in wedges
- 12 ounces pitted sour cherries, drained of their syrup, optional
- 2 star fruit (*carambola*), sliced to form star shapes
- Seeds of 1 pomegranate, optional
- 1 bottle premium tequila *añejo* (750 ml)
- 3 cinnamon sticks
- 1 vanilla bean, split
- Peel of 1 orange cut in continuous spiral or long strips
- ¼–½ cup citrus, ginger, or pomegranate Cantina Classic Syrup of your choice, or agave syrup to taste

In a 2-quart wide-mouthed jar, layer fruits (and pomegranate seeds, if using), placing the more fragile fruits on the top layers. Cover with tequila, and insert cinnamon sticks, vanilla bean, and orange peel spiral in the jar. Sweeten with flavored syrup (or a combination of several).

Gently shake jar occasionally, keeping fruit covered in tequila. Simply add more layers of fruit as they come into season and more tequila and syrup to taste as the level diminishes. For freshest flavor, keep refrigerated.

Note: Cantina Classic Ruby Pomegranate Syrup lends pretty color to this concoction, while Citrus Syrup and Zesty Ginger Syrup add some snap.

Ambrosia
GOLDEN NECTAR OF THE GODS

Tropical fruits and tequila *reposado* shine in this amber liqueur, laced with candied ginger, cardamom, cinnamon, allspice, coriander, and cloves. Spoon Ambrosia over ice cream, orange segments sprinkled with toasted coconut, or pound cake. Serve in elegant cordial glasses or add to your signature tequila cocktail.

- 1 orange, sliced
- 2½ ounces Australian crystalized ginger (candied), chopped (about ½ cup)
- 1 tablespoon freshly grated ginger
- 1 cup golden raisins
- 3 ounces dried mango or pineapple, coarsely chopped
- 2 teaspoons whole allspice
- 2 teaspoons whole coriander seeds
- ¼ teaspoon whole cloves
- ½ teaspoon cardamom pods, slightly crushed
- 2 cinnamon sticks
- 2 dried red cayenne peppers, optional
- 1 bottle (750 ml) tequila *reposado*
- 3 tablespoons Cantina Classic Zesty Ginger Syrup or Citrus Syrup, or amber agave syrup

In a 1½-quart jar, layer the candied ginger, grated ginger, raisins, mango (or pineapple), and spices between the orange slices. Cover with tequila and allow to steep for 2 weeks. Sweeten with syrup to taste. Keep refrigerated for freshest flavor, adding more fruit and tequila mixture as needed.

Note: Use for a glaze or sauce for ham or pork.

Orange-flavored: Grand Marnier, Cointreau, or Cointreau Noir, made with Rémy Martin cognac.

Tequila-flavored: Agavero, a blend of *reposado* and *añejo* with Damiana essence. (Agavero Orange is a new version.)

Coffee-flavored: Patrón XO Café, 70-proof, less sweet than some coffee liqueurs and brimming with flavors of roasted coffee beans and Patrón tequila. Their newest edition, Patrón XO Café Dark Cocoa, melds Mexican Criollo cocoa with the coffee liqueur. Also try Kahlúa, the ever-popular Mexican liqueur, and Kahlúa Especial, the 70-proof version, for real coffee lovers.

Cream-flavored: Rompope, Mexico's beloved eggnog, is available in U.S. markets, but I like to make my own. Also, 1921 Crema con Tequila, with café latte caramel and wildflower honey (keep refrigerated after opening), and Hacienda de Chihuahua Crema de Sotol, a blend of wild-harvested sotol blended with Mexican cream and pecans.

Nut-flavored: Mexican Almendrado (almond), with a discernible tequila taste. From Italy: Amaretto (almond) or Frangelico (hazelnut).

Aromatic: Damiana, flavored with the wild herb of the same name from Baja, Mexico. Licor 43 Cuarenta y Tres from Spain, brandy-based with orange, vanilla, and many other ingredients—in total, 43—and Tuaca, from Italy, with similar flavorings. Navan, from the house of Grand Marnier, blending Madagascar vanilla with French cognac. Xtabentún, a floral honey-anisette liqueur, from Mexico's Yucatán.

Serving After-Dinner Drinks

◆ Glasses and mugs: Snifters, shot glasses, long-stemmed glassware with handles, small margarita (or martini) glasses, earthenware mugs.

◆ For rims: Lightly dip rim in a shallow bowl of beaten egg whites, tequila, diluted agave syrup, or liqueur. Twirl moistened rim in any of these: cinnamon sugar, sparkling sugar crystals, grated Mexican chocolate, orange zest, toasted coconut flakes.

◆ For garnishes: Chocolate-covered espresso or coffee beans, shaved chocolate, toasted and ground nuts, twist or spiral of orange or lemon peel, fresh herb sprigs, edible flowers, pinch of cinnamon, nutmeg, or cayenne.

◆ For stirrers: cinnamon or chocolate sticks.

NEW WORLD GIFTS: TEQUILA, CHOCOLATE, AND VANILLA

Like tequila, chocolate and vanilla originated in the New World. These three ingredients complement one another in after-dinner drinks.

Mexican chocolate: Ground almonds and cinnamon traditionally flavor Mexican chocolate. Ibarra and Abuelita are popular commercial brands available in the United States, though I love to bring back freshly ground chocolate when I visit Oaxaca.

Mexican vanilla: From the dried pod of a tropical orchid (*Vanilla planifolia*) grown in Veracruz. The unripened pods first ferment and dry before producing the exquisite vanilla bean essence. Look for bottled pure Mexican vanilla extract and whole beans in Latin American markets or online.

Kakawa cocoa beans: Whole cocoa beans, fresh roasted and covered in layers of chocolate (white, milk, and dark) and velvety cocoa powder, available online through Cocoa Puro in Austin. Savor these scrumptious bite-sized morsels with a cup of coffee and a snifter of *añejo*.

Tequila Nightcaps

Tequila *añejo* swirled in a snifter makes a perfect nightcap, but sometimes I enjoy tequila mixed with a compatible Cantina Classic or commercial liqueur and perhaps a splash of rich cream.

BASIC RECIPE

- 1½ ounces tequila *añejo* or *reposado* (or combination of two)
- ¾ ounce liqueur
- ¾ ounce cream or half-and-half, optional
- Garnishes

NIGHTCAP THREE WAYS

1. Snifter: Swirl and sip, simple and elegant. Garnish with citrus zest or coffee beans. Cream optional.
2. Shooter: Combine ingredients (or shake with ice) and pour in a tall shot glass (I like to freeze it for 10 minutes); garnish and stir with a cinnamon stick.
3. Shaken: Shake with ice, strain, and pour into a small chilled margarita (martini) glass and garnish.

(I have a set of small, double-insulated clear espresso glasses that are ideal for after-dinner drinks.)

La Cucaracha Shooters

This drink is named after a *corrido* (ballad) that dates back to the Mexican Revolution. "Ya no puede caminar" is taken from one the song's verses about a *cucaracha* that can no longer walk . . . which could happen to you, if you like this drink too much!

- 1½ ounces tequila *añejo*
- ¾ ounce Kahlúa Especial or your favorite coffee liqueur
- ¾ ounce organic heavy whipping cream, or half-and-half, optional

- Garnishes: coffee beans, chocolate-covered espresso beans, pinch of cinnamon, grated dark chile-flavored Mexican chocolate, cinnamon stir stick

Mix ingredients together in a 4-ounce shot glass. Freeze for 10 minutes before serving. (Sometimes I let it freeze longer and eat it with a spoon.) Garnish festively!

Make it more decadent by adding ¼ ounce of another favorite liqueur like Almendrado or Navan, or replace the coffee liqueur with any of your other favorite liqueurs. Try a cream-based liqueur, like Rompope or 1921 Crema con Tequila, instead of half-and-half or cream. *Serves 1.*

Amoroso   LUSTY NIGHTCAP

Game fish mounted on the walls seem to be swimming amid sunburned gringo fishermen at Playa de Cortez fishing hotel in Baja, California del Sur, Mexico. Some say it's the best fishing in Baja. Bartender Héctor Castro Ruiz first told me about Damiana, Baja's renowned liqueur, in the 1970s. It's reputed to have powers of an aphrodisiac. *¡Cuidado!* (Watch out!)

- Twist of lime peel
- 1¾ ounces tequila *reposado*
- ¾ ounce Damiana
- Cracked ice, optional
- Squeeze of fresh lime juice
- Garnishes: pinch of freshly grated nutmeg, lime or orange curl

Rim highball glass (or snifter) with twist of lime peel. Pour the tequila and Damiana over ice, drop in the citrus curl and a squeeze of lime juice, and sprinkle lightly with the nutmeg. *Serves 1.*

No hay mal
Que por bien no venga.

———

Nothing bad happens
That good will not follow.

Coffee and Tequila: Always *Compadres*

After dinner, it's time for tequila and coffee. These soul mates—strong in character, earthy, and robust—are easily paired in drinks. Add a flavorful liqueur and you have a happy trio.

Whether served hot or on the rocks, laced with exotic liqueurs or with a cap of sweet cream, coffee tequila drinks are the perfect finales for a special dinner. Serve them instead of dessert, topped with freshly whipped cream and stirred with a cinnamon stick.

Experiment and you'll discover your preferred proportion of tequila to liqueur. In keeping with the theme, purchase organic Mexican coffee. Warm mugs before serving.

After special dinners, set up a tray of tequilas, liqueurs, a pot of freshly brewed coffee or espresso, and bowls filled with assorted toppings and whipped cream. Let guests create their own concoctions. (And don't forget the Mexican Wedding Cookies, shortbread delights that are good with hot chocolate, too.)

The following recipes are per cup of coffee. Serve with Mexican Whipped Cream.

Naranja Noir (Dark Orange)

- 1½ ounces tequila *añejo*
- ¾ ounce Grand Marnier
- Garnishes: grated Mexican chocolate to rim glass and sprinkle on top, spiral of orange peel and chocolate stick stirrer

Piel Canela (Cinnamon Skin)

- 1½ ounces tequila *añejo*
- ¾ ounce Cantina Classic Almendrado or Amaretto
- Garnishes: cinnamon sugar to rim glass, cinnamon stick for stirring

Sugar and Cream with Your Coffee?

MEXICAN WHIPPED CREAM

- ½ pint organic heavy whipping cream
- Confectioners' sugar to taste (2–3 tablespoons)
- ¼ teaspoon pure Mexican vanilla extract
- 2 teaspoons tequila *añejo*
- Pinch of ground cinnamon (or cayenne!)

In a chilled stainless steel mixing bowl with chilled beaters, whip cream until it thickens slightly. Slowly add confectioners' sugar, vanilla, tequila, and cinnamon and beat until it forms stiff mounds.

AZÚCAR (SUGAR) AND OTHER SWEETENERS

- Cinnamon sugar: granulated sugar mixed with powdered cinnamon
- Vanilla sugar: add 2 cups sugar per 1 split bean
- Grated *piloncillo*: unrefined Mexican cane sugar
- Cantina Classic Spicy Piloncillo Syrup
- Turbinado sugar: unrefined, coarse sugar
- *Cajeta*: thick and creamy goat's milk caramel sold in jars in Latin American markets

Bésame Mucho (Kiss Me Often)

- 1½ ounces tequila *añejo*
- ¾ ounce Damiana liqueur
- Garnishes: sparkling sugar rim, orange spiral, and freshly grated nutmeg

Café Olé

- 1 double shot freshly brewed cappuccino
- 1½ ounces tequila *añejo*
- 1 ounce Kahlúa or your favorite liqueur
- Garnishes: finely ground coffee beans/sugar to rim glass, 1 Kakawa bean, cinnamon stick for stirring

Note: Use *extra añejo* in place of *añejo*, if you wish.

Café de Cajeta
COFFEE FLAVORED WITH MEXICAN CARAMEL

Cajeta is a rich caramel sauce made from goat's milk. Its consistency is similar to that of a thick butterscotch sauce. It was originally packaged in small wooden *cajas* (boxes) in Mexico, but now you'll find it in jars in Latin American markets. It's hard not to eat by the spoonful!

I first tasted this coffee drink many years ago at the Konditori, a popular restaurant founded by a Danish family in Mexico City's Zona Rosa.

- 1 double shot freshly brewed cappuccino
- 1½ ounces tequila *añejo* or *reposado*
- Big dollop of Mexican *cajeta*
- Cinnamon

Place a dollop of *cajeta* in a warm mug. Add tequila and fill with steaming cappuccino, dust with cinnamon, and serve. *Serves 1.*

Café Caramba
FROSTY MEXICAN CAPPUCCINO

Dessert in a glass! This drink is frothy, fabulous, and deliciously decadent.

- 2 cups strong coffee, preferably made from Toddy cold-water process (see Note, next page)
- 6 ounces chilled tequila *añejo*
- 2 ounces coffee liqueur

- 2 ounces Cantina Classic Almendrado or Amaretto
- ½ teaspoon ground cinnamon
- ¼ teaspoon Mexican vanilla extract
- 1 pint vanilla bean or coffee ice cream
- Cinnamon sticks for stirring

Combine all ingredients except ice cream in a blender jar and refrigerate. Just prior to serving, add ice cream and whirl in the blender. Pour into long-stemmed glasses or champagne flutes. Dust lightly with cinnamon, stir with a cinnamon stick, and serve immediately. *Serves 6.*

Café del Diablo (Devil's Coffee)

The renowned Café Brûlot in New Orleans travels south of the border in my version—a devilishly good drink, made with tequila *añejo* (or *extra añejo*) instead of brandy. Turn off the lights and enjoy the spectacle of this flambéed elixir.

- 2 tablespoons brown sugar
- Peel of 1 orange, cut in a continuous spiral
- Peel of 1 lemon, cut in a continuous spiral
- 12 whole cloves
- 2 sticks of cinnamon, broken into bits
- 3 cardamom pods, slightly bruised with the back of a knife
- ¾ cup tequila *añejo* (part *extra añejo*)
- 2 tablespoons Grand Marnier
- 4 cups hot strong coffee

In a chafing dish or a fireproof dish over an open flame, combine sugar, citrus peels, spices, tequila, and Grand Marnier. Heat, stirring gently with a ladle, but do not boil. Place some tequila in a tablespoon with some brown sugar and light it. Ceremoniously (but cautiously), use it to ignite the simmering contents. Stir gently for a minute and allow the flambéing liquid to cascade from the ladle. Gradually pour in the hot coffee from the side of the dish, so as not to extinguish the flames, stirring for another minute. Immediately ladle into demitasse cups and serve. *Serves 6.*

Café Atotonilco

When I first visited Atotonilco, Jalisco, in the early 1980s, its narrow cobblestone streets and colonial churches reminded me more of Spain than Mexico. Three companies in this agrarian town produced tequila to sell only in Mexico. Their primitive distilleries, using mule-drawn *tahonas* and simple copper pot stills, made wonderful tequila from the renowned sweet *piñas* grown there.

The townspeople also boasted of their coffee drink made from locally grown coffee beans. Sipping it during the siesta hours (apparently, they didn't nap!) was a daily ritual for some residents.

The open-air shop famous for its *café estilo Atotonilco* hosted daily domino games, where men (and men alone) nursed small glasses filled with the strong dark libation and shots of tequila and contemplated their next move. I braved the curious stares of the patrons in order to sample that much-touted brew.

The sullen coffeemaster seemed none too eager to welcome a woman, much less to offer me a glass, but I boldly persisted. I learned that he makes a potent coffee extract, using a slow-drip, cold-water process. He steeps his proprietary dark-roast blend of ground beans overnight. The blend slowly drips through tiny holes in a metal filter. Each morning, he bottles this extract to sell and to serve in his shop. Locals often sip it after meals in snifters layered with a locally made eggnog.

He handed me my coffee, along with a bowl of unrefined sugar. I added the sugar sparingly, although many *mexicanos* seem to add it by spoonfuls. It was indeed delicious—rich and strong and dark. Immediately, I imagined it as a luscious liqueur, laced with tequila *añejo* and sweetened with a splash of Almendrado. And on that hot and dusty day, I also longed to taste it over ice. Patrón Tequila had the same idea, eventually packaging the renowned coffee extract in a fancy bottle, spiking it with their Añejo XO in a 70-proof elixir.

I hope the sullen barista now has a smile on his face!

Note: Coffee brewed using the cold-water ("Toddy") drip system (a glass beaker with filter attachment) retains rich coffee flavor without bitterness or acidity. In this concentrated form, you can mix coffee with cold or boiling water to desired strength (approx. 1 part coffee to 2 or 3 parts water). Store in the refrigerator.

Chocolate and Tequila: An Ancient Love Potion

Amor de Montezuma (Emperor's Love)

The Aztec emperor Montezuma voraciously consumed a chilled chocolate beverage laced with fragrant flowers, chile peppers, and spice and served by beautiful maidens. The only ingredient missing was tequila. My warm version just may spice up your life!

- 1 cup Mexican hot chocolate, prepared with milk according to directions on package, with a pinch of ground, dried cayenne, if you wish
- Pinch of ground cinnamon
- ¼ teaspoon pure Mexican vanilla extract
- 1½ ounces tequila *añejo*
- 1 ounce liqueur (Damiana, Almendrado, Cointreau, Licor 43, or your favorite combination)
- Garnishes: cinnamon stir stick, pinch of cinnamon, thin strips of orange zest, shaved dark chocolate (try chile-flavored)

Prepare hot chocolate according to directions of chosen brand (Ibarra and Abuelita are readily available in U.S. markets), adding cayenne and cinnamon. Remove from heat, adding vanilla extract. Pour hot chocolate in a mug with the tequila and liqueur, stirring gently. Add garnish. *Serves 1.*

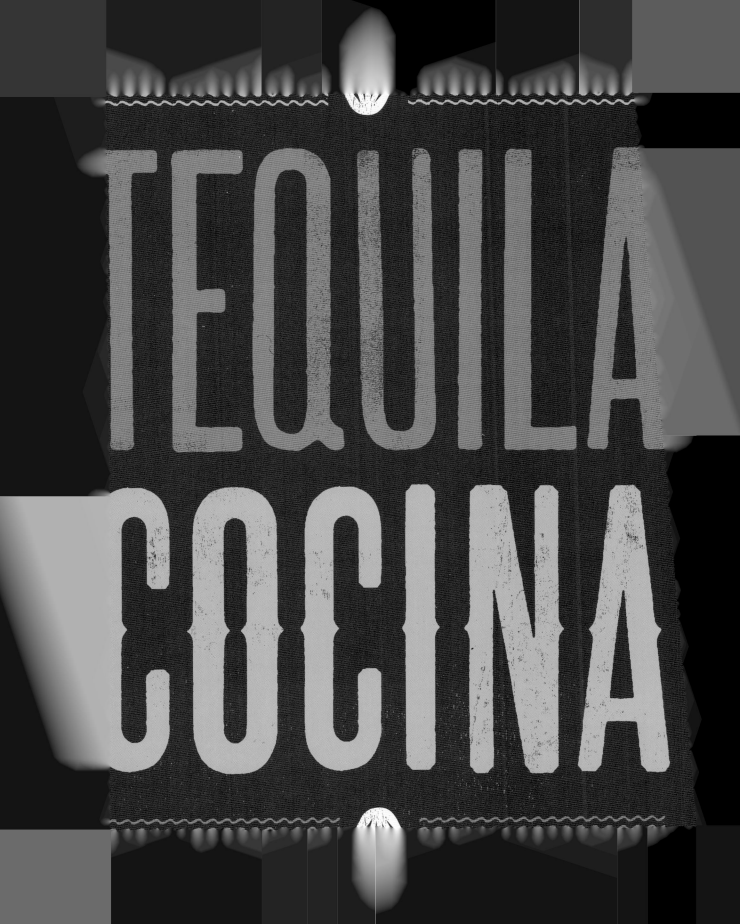

Recipes

IN ORDER OF APPEARANCE

Talavera plate with lilies from Dolores Hidalgo, Guanajuato.

Fiesta sin comida
no es fiesta cumplida.

—

A party without a feast
is a party incomplete.

T EQUILA AFICIONADOS are likely as passionate about chiles, spices, and other lusty flavors as I am. My recipes reflect this fervor—spirited and lively food for spirited and lively people. To match tequila's spirit, I've created fiesta recipes full of character, color, and surprise. Unexpected ingredients and eye-catching presentations promise festivity and fun.

I've gathered New World ingredients and techniques from Mexico's kitchen; fresh produce, fragrant herbs, and *chiles picantes* from her verdant garden; and agave spirits from her cantina. You'll find original recipes and traditional ones, some of which I've altered with contemporary touches.

You'll also discover versatile ways to prepare and present recipes. Recipes that appear in the text, when referred to elsewhere, are indicated in the color of blue agave. Readers may find these recipes by referring to the Cantina and Comida indexes or by consulting the lists that appear at the part openers. Menu suggestions help plan meals that you won't find at other gatherings. From lavish buffets to last-minute happy hours, leisurely afternoon *tardeadas*, morning *meriendas* (brunches), or dessert socials, these festive foods are sure to please.

In my recipes, I combine numerous ingredients to enhance flavor: aromatic herbs and freshly ground spices, seasonal produce, and special flavorings. However, they are not difficult to make. Many may be prepared in advance, simplifying the art of entertaining. Join me in this culinary adventure, *por favor*.

"Mermaid's Last Supper" made by the author's godson's father, Esteban Basilio Nolasco, from Ocumichu, Michoacán.

Tomas tequila—quema la gallina.

—

Too many shots burn the chicken in the pot.

Cantina and Cocina

COOKING WITH TEQUILA

Y OU COOK WITH TEQUILA?" people ask me, rather astonished. They assume that tequila's robust and assertive flavor belongs in a rowdy cantina instead of the *cocina* (kitchen). Tequila's not just for drinking! Its inimitable flavor lends new dimensions to cooking.

- Balances and brings out natural flavors.
- Has great versatility—add to a searing chile salsa or to an elegant flan.
- Offers unique flavors—*blanco*, *reposado*, or *añejo*, each with its own attributes.
- Brightens uncooked foods—salsas, marinades, gazpachos, and salads—as well as cooked dishes.
- Highlights fresh vegetables, herbs, and tropical fruits with its inherent vegetal, fruity, and complex flavor.
- Imparts the sweet, mellow fruitiness of agave as the alcohol burns off flambéed or sautéed sauces.
- Offers an earthy, herbaceous, and robust pairing for *frijoles* and dried red chiles, garlic, and spices.
- Tempers the acidity of fresh lime juice and other citrus.
- Gives added flavor to many dishes when infused with fresh herbs, chile peppers, or fruits.

Ingredients to Stock

DRIED SPICES AND HERBS

Freshly ground spices make all the difference in a dish and are important ingredients in many of my recipes. Purchase whole spices in small quantities to grind as needed in a small electric coffee/spice grinder or volcanic stone *molcajete*. The flavor far surpasses that of bottled ground spices and chiles. Don't cook with dried herbs, chiles, and spices that have been in bottles on shelves for more than a year and have lost their flavor. Replenish them! Keep on hand whole spices such as peppercorns (black, white, pink, and a colorful mélange), coriander seeds, cumin seeds, allspice, and cloves for grinding, as well as nutmeg for grating, *canela* (cinnamon sticks), and vanilla pods.

FRESH HERBS AND EDIBLE FLOWERS

You'll learn which herbs and flowers to grow in the cantina garden (p. 111) for flavoring and garnishing recipes, but if you don't have a garden, most grocery stores now sell fresh bunches of aromatic herbs and flowers.

Facing: Mexican *trastero* (kitchen hutch child's toy) for *trastes* (dishes).

FOUR FAVORITE MEXICAN SEASONINGS

Cilantro (*Coriandrum sativum*): Its bright green, pungent leaves enliven salsas, tortilla dishes, and soups and provide ubiquitous edible garnishes for all kinds of foods. Coriander seeds, the dried seeds of cilantro, have a lovely citrusy perfume—use whole in soups and stocks or freshly ground in many recipes.

Mexican oregano (*Lippia graveolens*): This highly aromatic wild oregano has both a peppery bite and fruity sweetness. Used dried, it's the oregano found in Mexican markets and favored by Mexican cooks. It's readily available in packages in Latin American markets.

Comino or cumin (*Cuminum cyminum*): Toasting the seeds of this aromatic herb brings out its pungent, earthy spiciness. It's vital for flavoring Mexican soups, stews, red chile salsas, beans, and meats.

Epazote (*Chenopodium ambrosioides*): The pungent, serrated leaves, with their potent resinous/camphor flavor, season beans—reputedly preventing the embarrassing consequences of eating them—chile-based soups and stews, and quesadillas.

CHILES

Dried and fresh chiles are essential to many of my dishes. These recipes call for chiles that are readily available in North American markets or by mail order.

Dried Chiles

Chile colorado: New Mexico red chiles traditionally hung in *ristras* (clusters) to dry in the sun; popular in northern Mexican and southwestern cuisines; 5–7 inches long with a bright, earthy flavor ranging from mild to *picoso* (hot).

Chile de árbol: 2–3 inches long; shiny, bright red, thin skin, pointed tip, and lots of seeds; searing hot; adds instant flavor when freshly ground and sprinkled on a dish or toasted and ground into a sauce; cayenne or *japón* may be substituted.

Chipotle: Dried, ripened, smoked jalapeño; toasty brown and wrinkly; smoke- and fire-flavored; often canned in *adobo*, a thick sauce flavored with tomatoes, vinegar, and spices.

Pequín (*chilpiquín*): Tiny, oval-shaped, and fiery hot; used interchangeably with the small, round *tepín* (*chiltepín*).

Ancho: Dried poblano 4–5 inches long; thick-fleshed and wrinkly with piquant, raisiny flavor and dark, reddish-brown color. *Pasilla* chiles, the dried form of the *chilaca* pepper, can be substituted for anchos.

Guajillo: 4–6 inches long; shiny and thin-skinned; sweet-hot flavor; may be used interchangeably with the *puya* or *chile colorado*.

Puya: 3–4 inches long, with a curved tip; thin-fleshed and slightly acidic with a fiery finish; *guajillo* may be substituted.

Fresh Chiles

New Mexico or Anaheim (green or red-ripened): 6–8 inches long; thin-skinned with flavor ranging from mild to *picoso*; to use, roast and peel.

Poblano: 4–5 inches long; dark green, thick-fleshed, triangular, and wrinkly; flavor that ranges from sweet and mild to fiery; to use, roast and peel.

Jalapeño: 2–3 inches long; bright green ripening to red; thick-fleshed and shiny; heat ranges from mild to hot.

Fresno: Resembles a ripened red jalapeño—with broad shoulders and sweeter—but usually hotter in flavor.

Serrano: 1–2 inches long; dark green ripening to red; usually very hot with a fresh, bright flavor.

Habanero: 1½–2 inches long; wrinkly, bright orange ripening to red; fruity but ferociously hot.

Manufactured Chile Products

Keep on hand small cans of *chipotle chiles en adobo*, pickled jalapeños, Salsa Valentina (Mexico's spicier, and less vinegary, version of Tabasco) or your favorite salsa, as well as refrigerated, locally prepared hot sauces. When you don't have time to roast and peel fresh red bell peppers, use good quality, fire-roasted bottled brands (I like roasted *piquillo* red peppers); rinse and pat dry before using. Freshly roasted New Mexico green chiles are often seasonally available; freeze them for future use.

QUESOS

Mexican-style cheeses have become more available in North American markets but sometimes lack the flavor and texture of those produced in Mexico. However, with the increased demand, quality is improving.

Asadero: A specialty of northern Mexico, this soft, white cheese melts perfectly for *chile con queso* and *queso flameado*, with a flavor reminiscent of mozzarella. (Any combination of Monterey Jack, Muenster, or mozzarella may be substituted.)

Queso fresco: This "fresh" cheese has an acidic flavor and is delicious crumbled over salads, refried beans, and tostadas. (Substitute rinsed feta.)

Queso blanco: Like *asadero* and *queso fresco*, *queso blanco* is now often found in North American markets. It's a creamy, mild, unaged cheese especially used for melting. Some cheeses labeled *queso blanco* are virtually tasteless, however, and some are rubbery in texture. Insist on sampling before purchasing, or substitute Monterey Jack or Muenster.

Queso Cotija: This is a firm, but moist, salty, crumbly cow's milk cheese for sprinkling over tostadas, salsas, and salads.

Queso añejo: A firm, aged, skimmed milk cheese for grating or shredding, like Parmesan.

Queso Chihuahua: Creamy, white cheese originally made by Mennonite communities in the northern Mexican state of Chihuahua and once sold in wooden boxes. It's delicious in Queso Flameado or authentic *chile con queso* made with freshly roasted green chiles. Mennonites have dispersed, and good Chihuahua cheese is hard to find. A combination of Monterey Jack, Muenster, and mozzarella may be substituted.

See "Stocking the Home Cantina" (pp. 95–111) for other basic ingredients and Cantina Classics (such as homemade flavored salts and syrups). You'll also find flavorful *tequilas curados* (herb-, citrus-, fruit-, or chile-infused tequilas) for using in marinades, sauces, and salads. Of course, always keep in stock extra virgin olive oil and a good selection of vinegars: red and white wine, balsamic, rice, and cider.

Create Fiesta Tablescapes

◆ Decorate the table with colorful Mexican textile runners and napkins, Mexican votive saint candles, and folk art.

◆ Place small pots planted with succulents that resemble miniature agaves on the table.

◆ Fill assorted vases with brightly colored flowers and fragrant herbs.

◆ Mix and match pottery serving bowls, platters, and small baskets, as well as dishes and glasses.

◆ Find sets of small forks, knives, and spoons at import stores for appetizer portions.

◆ Set out several small bowls filled with crushed dried chiles, oregano, and salt, and larger bowls with condiments such as chopped cilantro, fresh hot chiles, onions, and salsas. It's fun to have an assortment of bottled hot sauces, too.

◆ Find ways to lift serving platters to varied levels on the table or buffet; for instance, cover sturdy boxes of different heights with festive linens.

◆ Present a festive party punch as the centerpiece of your table.

Fiesta Food

Tostadas *Compuestas*

A TOSTADA *COMPUESTA* (layered tostada) fiesta is a fun, buffet-style way to entertain, easily pleasing vegetarians and those who have diet restrictions, as well as those who do not. Tostadas are crispy, fried whole tortillas that serve as edible "plates." Place bowls filled with tasty toppings on the table so guests may choose to suit their whims: refried beans, guacamole, chunky salsas, grated and crumbled cheese, marinated and grilled meats and fish, and crunchy, colorful chopped or shredded vegetables. Don't forget bowls of homemade or bottled red *and* green *salsas picantes* (hot sauces) and condiments: chopped onions, jalapeño or serrano peppers, cilantro, and quartered limes to squeeze for the finishing touch. Tequila drinks are essential!

Drink Suggestions

Shots: Sangrita, Sangrita Verdecita, Donají shooters
Glass: Micheladas, Palomas, Tejas Tea
Pitcher: Fiesta Margaritas, Vampiros, Toritos
Punch jar: Ponche de Guadalajara, Fiesta Margarita, Güero's Margarita

Jalisco's traditional *tostadas tapatías* are spread liberally with refried beans, then layered with chunks of spicy pork called *puerco al pastor*, shredded lettuce, onions, avocado slices, and crumbled *queso fresco* or *Cotija*, then doused with *salsa picante*.

I've come up with some other fun and easy ways to serve tostadas. In fact, the possibilities are endless. How about black beans with pickled jalapeños, crumbled *queso fresco*, and sliced radishes? Add avocado slices or Pancho Villa's Nopalitos. Everyone loves chunky guacamole spread on tostadas, with or without refried beans. If you want a more substantial meal, add sizzling fajita meat served with Corn Salsa Prontísimo. For a refreshing light meal, make tostadas layered with grilled fish or shrimp and shredded purple cabbage and topped with Mango and Pineapple Salsa Tropicana.

Perhaps my favorite tostadas are those layered with Salpicón—a spicy, chipotle-marinated, shredded chilled beef dish from Northern Mexico—and garnished with chunks of avocado and cubes of Monterey Jack cheese.

Tostadas smothered in *chile con queso*—that creamy melted *queso blanco*, flavored with *rajas* (strips of freshly roasted green chiles)—is a far cry from that gloppy processed cheese spread served in many Tex-Mex restaurants. For a special treat, try my version, Queso Flameado, flambéed at the table with tequila.

If you don't have time to make Pollo Borrachito, shred a rotisserie-style chicken atop a layer of refried beans on tostadas, and liberally spoon tequila-spiked Salsa Borracha over it.

Think of tostadas as Mexican open-faced sandwiches.

SOMBREROS: TOSTADA TOPPINGS

Be creative! Choose ingredients from the following lists, so that you and your guests can create your perfect combo.

Frijoles

Refritos (refried beans, black or pinto)
Frijoles Negros (black beans)
Negros y Piña a la Criztina (Black Beans and Pineapple Spiked with Mezcal)
Black bean dip
Muy Bueno Bean Dip
Fiesta Frijoles (chunky bean salsa)

Platos Fuertes (Main Dishes)

Salpicón Norteño (Spicy Shredded Marinated Beef in Chipotle Marinade)
Pollo Borrachito (Roasted Chicken in Drunkard's Chile Sauce)
Camarones a la Diabla (Chile-Seared Shrimp)
Camarones Cantineros (Bartender's Shrimp Sautéed with Summer Tomatoes and Basil)
Tacos al Pastor or Carne Adobada (Spicy Pork in Red Chile–Spiced Marinade Jalisco Style)
Pescado Margarita (Grilled Fish with Sassy Citrus Tequila Vinaigrette)
Shredded rotisserie chicken

Quesos

Queso Flameado (Melted Cheese Flambéed in Tequila)
Queso Sabroso (Snookered Goat Cheese)
Crumbled Mexican queso fresco (or rinsed feta and farmer's cheese)
Cotija (or freshly grated Parmesan)
Grated cheddar and Jack cheese

Chunky Salsas Frescas

Barco de Oro (Mango and Pineapple Salsa Tropicana)
Fiesta Frijoles
Corn Salsa Prontísimo
Vuelve a la Vida (Seafood Cocktail)
Pancho Villa's Nopalitos (Cactus Salad)
Chunky guacamole

Other Salsas and Drizzles

Javier's Salsa de Aguacate (Creamy Avocado Sauce)
Salsa Borracha (Tequila-Spiked Chile Sauce)
Chimichurri Rojo (Salsa de Chile de Árbol)
Chipotles en Adobo
Sweet and Spicy Tomato Salsa
Salsa Valentina or Tamazula
Your favorite salsa picante (red or green)

Condiments

Red or white onions, sliced or chopped
Avocado wedges sprinkled with fresh lime juice
Rajas (strips of roasted chile peppers)
Sliced or grated radishes
Grated carrots
Pickled beets
Shredded iceberg and romaine lettuce
Escabeche (spicy pickled vegetables)
Quartered limes
Crema Mexicana or sour cream

Crispy Tortilla Cups

With a 3-inch scalloped cookie cutter, cut circles out of 6 corn tortillas. In a deep-fat fryer or heavy saucepan, heat enough vegetable oil to 375 degrees for frying. Hold tortilla down in hot oil with a small ladle, and fry it until it's golden brown and its edges curl up to form a cup shape around the ladle. (Specially designed devices are also available for this purpose.) Remove from hot oil, sprinkle with salt, and invert to drain on brown paper bags. Store in an airtight container at room temperature 2 days. Heat in a 325-degree oven for a few minutes to re-crisp. Fill just prior to serving with refried beans, guacamole, Salpicón, or Puerco al Pastor.

To Warm Corn Tortillas

Sprinkle tortillas with water and wrap in foil. Heat in 300-degree oven for 15 minutes, or warm individually on a hot *comal,* or griddle. Keep warm in a cloth-lined basket.

DIRECTIONS FOR MAKING HOMEMADE TOSTADAS

Fried whole corn tortillas provide a crisp, flat surface for layering fiesta foods. Homemade tostadas usually taste fresher and crisper than most commercially available ones, but the El Milagro Tostadas Calidad Caseras (home-style) brand is hard to beat. This Austin-based company now distributes their crunchy tostadas in other major cities.

In Northern Mexico and the American Southwest, cooks also fry homemade flour tortillas in hot oil to make tostadas, which puff up and become flaky and crispy.

To fry: Place tortilla in ½ inch of *hot* vegetable oil and fry until crisp, turning once with tongs. Drain on brown paper bags and sprinkle lightly with salt.

Note: To assure crispness of tostadas, place corn tortillas on a tray and allow to dry for several hours or overnight before frying.

DIRECTIONS FOR MAKING TOSTADA CHIPS

Tortilla wedges fried until crisp in hot oil are also called "tostadas," and sometimes *totopos*. Like edible "spoons," they scoop up salsas and dips. When mounded with toppings and melted cheese, they're called "nachos." Good tostada chips are sometimes hard to find, so why not make your own?

To fry: Stack 4 corn tortillas at a time. (See note under "Directions for Making Homemade Tostadas.") With a sharp knife, cut tortillas in half; cut each half into 3 triangular wedges. Heat ½ inch of vegetable oil in a heavy skillet. Add tortilla wedges, a few at a time. Fry, turning occasionally with tongs, until crisp and golden (about 3 minutes). Remove with a slotted spoon, drain on brown paper grocery bags, and sprinkle with salt.

To bake: Lightly brush whole tortillas on one side with seasoned oil (omit oil, if you wish). Cut into wedges as described above and place on an oiled baking sheet. Bake in 350-degree oven for 20 minutes, until crisp and golden, turning occasionally with tongs. Sprinkle with salt as desired.

For seasoned oil: Combine ¼ cup vegetable oil, 2–3 teaspoons pure hot chile powder, and salt to taste.

To store/reheat tostadas: Place in an airtight container for up to 3 days. Briefly heat in a preheated 325-degree oven before serving.

Flautas

Flautas are corn tortillas spread with savory fillings and rolled up in the shape of "flutes." Flavorful finger food, they're fried until crispy and easy to pick up to dunk into hot sauce (or Javier's Salsa de Aguacate). Spicy shredded chicken or beef make tasty fillings, especially with the addition of a few roasted chiles *rajas* (p. 208) and cheese. Try a combination of sauteed fresh squash, corn, mushroom, *rajas*, and cheese. Guacamole, shredded lettuce, chopped tomatoes, Crema Mexicana (sour cream), and hot sauce usually accompany flautas. Be inventive! Use any of the tostada toppings listed earlier to create and garnish your signature flautas. Then, bring on the margaritas, Micheladas, and Vampiros! Allow 3–4 flautas per serving.

To make flautas: In a heavy skillet, heat ½ inch of vegetable oil over medium-high heat. Soften corn tortillas by quickly "wilting" them in the hot oil for just a few seconds. Blot tortillas on paper towels to absorb excess oil. Put a generous tablespoon of filling in the center of the tortilla and place a few *raja* strips vertically. Sprinkle with grated or crumbled cheese of your choice. Roll into the shape of a flute (secure with a toothpick, if you wish). Add more oil to the skillet, if necessary, and bring to medium-high heat. When hot, place 4 flautas, seam-side down, into the hot oil. Heat until crisp and golden (about 40 seconds per side). Keep warm before serving.

Note: Flautas may be also be baked, seam-side down, in a preheated 400-degree oven for about 18 minutes, but the rolled tortilla will not be as crispy.

Crema Mexicana (Homemade Sour Cream)

Crema Mexicana is rich, tart, and deliciously creamy. It's more flavorful and not as thick as store-bought sour cream, making it scrumptious for dipping and drizzling. Serve it with tostadas and flautas, atop spicy enchiladas and black beans, or, with chipotle pesto, as a dip for roasted potatoes.

My friend and fellow cookbook author Jim Peyton, who has written four books about Mexican/Southwestern cuisine, shares his quick recipe for Crema Mexicana: Heat 1 cup whipping cream to 85 degrees, stir in 2 tablespoons buttermilk. Leave at room temperature overnight, then refrigerate for a day.

¡Tequila y Queso, Por Favor!

DELIGHT GUESTS WITH something other than wine and cheese, or chips and salsa, at your next gathering. Jalisco restaurants serve sizzling melted cheese with *rajas de poblano* (strips of roasted poblano peppers) from shallow earthenware dishes. Diners scoop the *queso* into hot tortillas, accompanied by grilled meats and shots of tequila and *sangrita*.

In Mexican restaurants in the United States, people dunk tostada chips into *chile con queso* between sips from icy margaritas. Few, however, think of teaming tequila and cheese together in a dish, even though they are natural companions.

Drink Suggestions

Pitcher: Fiesta Margaritas, Bloody Marías
Shots: Sangrita and tequila, Margaritas Picositas, Los Tres Cuates
Tequila frozen in a block of ice
Glass: margaritas, María Sangrita, Tequila Macho, spritzers,
Texican Martini

Queso Flameado
MELTED CHEESE FLAMBÉED IN TEQUILA

Jalisco's famed melted cheese dish, *queso fundido*, is better known as *"queso flameado"* in the northern state of Chihuahua. For a spectacular presentation, dim the lights and flambé it at the table. Serve with warm tortillas or crispy tostada chips or as an accompaniment to grilled meats for a heartier meal.

- ½ large white onion, cut into thin slices
- 2 cloves garlic
- 1 tablespoon vegetable oil
- 2 teaspoons butter
- 4–6 New Mexico or Anaheim green chiles or *poblanos*, roasted, peeled, seeded, and cut into *rajas* (see sidebar, p. 208)
- 2 jalapeños or serranos, stemmed and seeded, chopped, optional
- 2 tablespoons tequila *reposado* plus 2 more tablespoons to flambé
- Salt and pepper to taste
- 12 ounces creamy white cheese, such as *queso Chihuahua, queso asadero, queso blanco* (p. 201), Monterey Jack, Muenster (or any combination), grated

- Condiments: chopped tomatoes, avocado wedges drizzled with fresh lime juice, chopped green onions, chopped fresh cilantro, and your favorite salsa
- To serve: 12 warm flour or corn tortillas, tostada chips, or red bell pepper wedges and other vegetable crudités

Briefly sauté onion and garlic in the oil and butter; add chile *rajas* and jalapeños or serranos, 2 tablespoons tequila, salt and pepper to taste, stirring until the tequila is absorbed. Do not overcook.

Place grated cheese in a shallow 9 × 9-inch earthenware dish or in 6 individual flameproof ramekins. Top with the pepper/onion mixture. Place 6 inches under a pre-heated broiler and heat until bubbly, melted, and lightly browned (about 4–5 minutes). *Serves 6.*

To serve: Dim lights. Remove cheese from oven. Briefly heat remaining 2 tablespoons tequila in a small, heavy saucepan; do not boil! Bring to the table, carefully igniting warmed tequila as you pour it from the saucepan over the sizzling cheese. Accompany with small bowls of condiments, a basket of hot tortillas, crispy tostadas, or crudités.

Variation: Sauté a handful of sliced mushrooms or squash blossoms with the pepper/onion mixture. Or substitute about ½ pound of crumbled fried *chorizo* (spicy Mexican pork sausage) for the *rajas*.

Chile con queso in vintage painted clay *cazuela*.

Roasting Chiles and Making Rajas

Roasting fresh Hatch (New Mexico), Anaheim (California), or poblano chile peppers removes their tough skin, leaving a pleasant charred flavor. Stuff whole, roasted chile peppers with fillings or cut into strips called *rajas*. Roast red, green, or yellow bell peppers in this same manner. Marinate with minced garlic, olive oil, and salt for more flavor.

To roast chiles: Poke whole chiles with a fork to keep them from bursting. Place chiles on a baking sheet and roast 4–6 inches from the flame of a preheated broiler, char over the open flame of a grill or on a hot *comal*, or hold chiles individually directly into the flame of a gas burner. Using tongs, turn occasionally for even blistering.

Place charred chiles in a damp dishtowel or plastic bag after roasting; steam for 10 minutes. Peel away charred skin. (Don't rinse chiles under running water or you'll lose flavor!) Make a slit in each chile, but not all the way through. Remove seeds; leave stem intact. Chiles are ready for stuffing.

To make *rajas* (green chile strips): Remove seeds and stems from the roasted chiles. Cut them into 3-inch × ⅜-inch strips.

Smoky Chipotle Torta con Pepitas

CHILLED CHEESE TERRINE WITH SMOKY CHIPOTLE PESTO AND ROASTED PUMPKIN SEEDS

The Italian-inspired basil torta, a rich and creamy chilled cheese terrine layered with roasted red bell peppers, pine nuts, and basil pesto found in my first book, *The Herb Garden Cookbook* (University of Texas Press), was so popular that it has remained on the menu of three Austin restaurants for more than a decade.

Hopefully, my Mexican version, featuring chipotle pesto, spiked with tequila, and roasted pumpkin seeds will be as popular. It's feisty and flavorful and makes delicious party fare, especially when accompanied with bowls of sassy, chunky, colorful salsas like Fiesta Frijoles, Corn Salsa Prontísimo, or Pancho Villa's Nopalitos . . . and of course, requisite icy tequila drinks to quell the fire.

It's delicious on Austin's own Doctor Kracker Pumpkin Seed Cheddar Crispbreads (sold nationally), but it's also tasty on tostada chips, crostini, or red bell pepper and other crudités.

Part of the fun of this recipe is arranging the top layer of the torta artistically with a combination of any of the garnishes.

- ¾ pound sharp provolone, sliced just thick enough not to tear (15 slices; see Note)
- 1 cup Sí, Pica (Smoky Chipotle and Toasted Pepita Pesto), plus about ¼ cup for garnish
- 1 recipe Queso Sabroso, room temperature (p. 210)
- ⅓ cup shredded Parmesan cheese
- 4 green onions, chopped with some tops
- 2 medium red bell peppers, roasted, peeled, and cut into *rajas* (see sidebar)
- ½ cup roasted, salted pumpkin seeds (*pepitas*), for roasting (p. 213)
- Additional garnishes: roasted red bell pepper strips or *piquillo* ("little beak") peppers, sun-dried tomatoes, canned chipotles in *adobo* (cut into strips), chopped green onions, Parmesan, and sprigs of cilantro *al gusto*.

Line a 5-cup loaf pan with plastic wrap, leaving a 1-inch overhang on all sides. Cover the bottom of the terrine with overlapping slices of provolone; lightly press more slices along the sides to form a shell (you'll use 10 provolone slices to make the shell).

In a medium-sized bowl, with an electric mixer, combine Sí, Pica and Queso Sabroso. Evenly spread ½ of it as the first layer in the provolone shell, making sure to fill in corners of the terrine. Sprinkle with ½ of the Parmesan, 2 chopped green onions, and ½ of the red pepper strips. Cover with 2 slices of provolone and press down firmly, before spreading the remaining cheese/pesto mixture. Repeat with a layer of Parmesan, green onions, and red bell pepper strips. Top with 3 slices of provolone, pressing down firmly. Fold the shell's edges over, forming a tight packet. Cover tightly and chill overnight. Serve within 4 days.

To serve: Lift torta from the mold and carefully peel away plastic wrap. Invert onto a platter. Spread a wide band of the reserved Sí, Pica pesto across the smooth top of the torta. Press red pepper strips along with any other chosen garnishes onto the torta in a decorative design. Sprinkle generously with roasted, salted *pepitas*. Torta will slice best when chilled, but tastes better at room temperature. *Serves 15 or more.*

Note: Have your deli slice provolone into ⅛-inch thickness, placing waxed paper between slices to prevent sticking.

Variations: Substitute mozzarella slices for provolone. Use pistachios or unsalted toasted sunflower seeds instead of *pepitas*. Use red roasted *piquillo* peppers (found bottled) instead of the roasted red bell peppers. Should you have any leftover torta, spread some on Doctor Kracker Crispbreads and heat in a hot oven until cheese melts. Garnish this easy flatbread pizza as you please. Yummm!

Drink Suggestions

Pitcher: Fiesta or Güero's Margaritas
Shots: Fiesta Tequila, ice-cold shots of *reposado*
Glasses: Texican Martini, spritzers, Tequini

Smoky Chipotle Torta con Pepitas.

Quick Quesadillas

Quesadillas, the Mexican version of grilled cheese sandwiches, make quick and tasty snacks morning, noon, or night. Simply enfold cheese and other tasty fillings in corn or flour tortillas and heat on a griddle until the cheese has melted. Choose your cheese—any white Mexican cheese, Pepper Jack, sharp cheddar, cream cheese, ricotta, or even Brie. Add extra fillings of your choice and serve with chunky salsas (p. 219). For a treat, add a spoonful of chutney or orange marmalade to the quesadilla for breakfast . . . or dessert!

For fillers, add *rajas* (p. 208), mushrooms and/or squash blossoms sautéed in onions, Camarones a la Diabla (chile-seared shrimp), grilled or roasted vegetables or meats, or rotisserie barbecue chicken. In Oaxaca, a pungent leaf of epazote is found tucked inside quesadillas.

To make: Rub *comal* or griddle lightly with oil (or butter). Once the surface is hot, heat tortilla briefly on one side. Place several tablespoons of grated cheese (less of creamy cheeses) and other fillings on half of the tortilla, not too close to the edge. Fold over the other half, pressing to seal. Heat until cheese melts and tortilla has browned lightly, turning once. Keep warm until serving with your favorite hot sauce.

Tequila-Spiked Jalapeño Jelly Glaze or Dipping Sauce

Jalapeño jelly was popular in our household in El Paso. The jelly was made from jalapeños picked on my brother's chile farm. We ate it instead of fruit jellies and preserves, even on peanut butter or cream cheese sandwiches.

Use this spicy glaze to embellish a cheese ball or use as a dipping sauce for grilled meats (especially lamb) and fish or Spicy Bison Meatballs. It reminds me of a sweet and spicy Asian dipping sauce, but spicier and not so sweet!

To make: Empty an 8-ounce jar of red jalapeño jelly into a small saucepan. Add 1–2 fresh green chopped jalapeños, 2 tablespoons tequila *reposado*, and a pinch of salt. Heat until melted and tequila has absorbed. Let cool and then stir in fresh lime juice to taste.

Variations: Substitute your favorite chunky fruit preserves or chutney (cranberry, pear, apricot, or apple) or orange marmalade. Add some cayenne, orange zest, chopped cilantro, and green onions. Add 3 chopped *chipotles en adobo* for added kick.

Queso Sabroso
SNOOKERED GOAT CHEESE

The assertive flavors of goat cheese and tequila partner well in this versatile recipe. Form into one large cheese ball and top with one of the colorful salsas like Fiesta Frijoles. For a variation, glaze cheese ball with Tequila-Spiked Jalapeño Jelly Glaze (see sidebar) or top with Drunken Sugarplum Chutney. Serve with tostada chips or crackers.

You may also form cheese into *quesitos*, bite-sized round balls. Roll each in a variety of freshly minced herbs, chiles, spices, or coarsely ground tostada chips for crunch, or sprinkle lightly with Cantina Classic Seasoned Salts. When arranged on a platter, *quesitos*, with their confetti of colors, look so inviting.

- 8 ounces cream cheese, softened
- 4 ounces goat cheese
- 2 tablespoons butter, softened
- 2 teaspoons olive oil
- 2–3 cloves garlic, minced
- 2 teaspoons tequila *reposado* or Chile Pepper–Infused Tequila
- Salt
- ¼–½ teaspoon crushed dried cayenne or *chile de árbol*

- To garnish cheese ball, or for rolling *quesitos*: minced fresh herbs such as rosemary, basil, oregano, sage, Mexican mint marigold; crushed and dried red chiles; toasted *comino* (cumin) seeds; finely ground tostada chips; Cantina Classic Spicy Mexican Seasoned Salt.

Blend cheeses, butter, olive oil, garlic, tequila, salt, and chile in food processor or with mixer. Turn out onto plastic wrap and form into a loose ball; cover and refrigerate overnight. Form into one round cheese ball or into individual *quesitos*. Chill for several hours. Once firm, roll in garnishes of choice and chill until ready to serve. Serve at room temperature. *Makes approx. 25 quesitos, or one large cheese ball, or enough filling for one Smoky Chipotle Torta.*

Note: Slightly flatten *quesitos*, coat both sides with coarsely ground tostada chips; broil for 1 minute. Serve in soup, on crostini, or atop salads.

Baja Bravo

MARINATED CHEESE WITH TEQUILA, ANCHOVIES, AND JALAPEÑO-STUFFED GREEN OLIVES

Many moons ago, my amigo Guillermo and I drove a pickup truck across a deserted mountain road in Baja, California del Norte, to the Pacific Ocean. We had packed some ripe tomatoes, a slab of creamy cheese, tinned sardines, and some crusty *bolillos* (Mexican rolls) for what we thought would be an afternoon picnic. It took many more hours than we expected to reach the sea as we drove up and down a winding desert dirt road. When we finally had our picnic, it was on a desolate strand at sunset. Thankfully, we had a bottle of tequila in the truck (but no blankets). Warming sips and the full moon were our only company. Not daring the drive back, we spent the night in the back of the truck.

This recipe recreates for me a magical evening, and though I have embellished the ingredients and made it for a crowd, I offer it for kindred souls with a passion for bold flavors and adventures.

Serve this marinated cheese on crostini garnished with fresh basil or cilantro, or, better yet, stuff it into hollowed-out *bolillos* or baguettes with some tinned sardines. It still makes delicious picnic fare, even if it's in the backyard! Don't forget the shots of tequila!

Marinade:
- 3 cloves garlic, minced
- 1 tablespoon concentrated Italian tomato paste
- 2–3 tablespoons tequila *reposado* (part Chile Pepper–Infused Tequila, if on hand)
- 3 tablespoons capers, drained
- 1 tablespoon balsamic vinegar
- 1 tablespoon fresh lime juice
- ½ teaspoon crushed dried red chile pepper
- 2 teaspoons fresh rosemary, minced
- 4–6 flat fillets of anchovies, chopped
- 4 tablespoons olive oil

Tomato-Olive-Cheese Mixture:
- 2 cups ripe Roma tomatoes, chopped, lightly salted, and drained in a colander
- 6 green onions, chopped
- 15 large green jalapeño-stuffed olives, each cut in half
- 1 red bell pepper, roasted and cut into *rajas* (see sidebar, p. 208)
- ¾ cup chopped basil and cilantro *al gusto*
- 8–10 ounces *queso blanco* or Monterey or Pepper Jack, cut into small cubes
- Fresh lemon or lime juice to taste
- Salt and freshly ground pepper to taste
- Garnishes: shredded Parmesan, whole anchovy fillets, fresh basil or cilantro sprigs, or minced rosemary, tinned sardines packed in olive oil

Prepare the marinade by combining the ingredients in a small bowl, whisking in the olive oil last. Set aside.

In a medium-sized bowl, combine tomatoes, green onions, olives, red pepper, fresh herbs, and cheese. Toss with marinade. Add lemon or lime juice and salt and pepper to taste. Cover (or refrigerate for several hours) and allow to sit at room temperature for an hour before serving. *Makes 4 cups.*

RECIPE CONTINUED ON NEXT PAGE

Note: Baja Bravo makes a delicious uncooked sauce for pasta in the summertime. The hot pasta will melt the cheese and bring out tequila's flavor. Try it as well on grilled fish or chicken. Mound Baja Bravo into a roasted whole poblano for a special presentation (p. 220).

Variations: New Mexico green chiles, cut into *rajas* (p. 208), instead of red bell pepper. Italian *tonnino* (yellowfish tuna) in olive oil, instead of sardines. Feta cheese, instead of *queso blanco.* Red cherry and yellow pear tomatoes, instead of Roma.

¡Ay Caramba!
GINGERED CURRY CHEESE BALL

Curry and crystallized ginger in a tequila-spiked cheese ball? *¡Ay Caramba!* (Yowee!) It's good! Friends love it as a gift during the Christmas holidays, along with a jar of Drunken Sugarplum Chutney, though it's good any time of the year.

For a festive presentation, roll cheese ball in chopped cilantro, and stud with ruby pomegranate seeds. Or top it with chutney and chopped green onions. Surround it with crisp pear and apple slices and sesame crackers, as an appetizer or dessert. It's delicious spread on roast turkey or pork sandwiches, too, or in a quesadilla with some chutney.

- 16 ounces extra-sharp cheddar cheese, grated
- 8 ounces cream cheese, softened
- 3 tablespoons butter, softened
- 4 tablespoons chopped Australian crystallized ginger
- 2 bunches green onions, chopped with some green tops
- 2–3 teaspoons hot curry powder
- ½ teaspoon crushed cayenne
- 2 teaspoons paprika
- 2 tablespoons tequila *reposado*
- 1 tablespoon Cointreau
- Garnishes: finely chopped cilantro, green onions, pomegranate seeds, chutney

Blend ingredients in a food processor or mixer. Turn out onto plastic wrap and form into a loose ball. Cover and chill overnight for flavors to intermingle—it just gets better with age.

To serve: Form into desired shape and chill again. Garnish festively before serving.

Note: Make sure your jar of curry has not sat on the shelf for months! Use fresh, hot, and spicy curry for color and flavor.

Drink Suggestions

Pitcher: Fiesta Margaritas
Punch Jar: Ponche de Granada, Ponche de Manzana
Glass: Chimayó Cocktail, Rosita (**Fresh Pomegranate Margarita**), Drunken Sugarplum Shooters, **spritzers**

Sazonando: Spicing It Up!

PESTOS, MARINADES, SAUCES, CHUTNEYS, SALAD DRESSINGS, AND SALSAS PICANTES

TEQUILA BRINGS OUT FLAVOR in recipes, just as it often brings out the spark in shy personalities. I've added tequila to many of my favorite condiments, some of which are not Mexican in origin, like honey mustard, aioli, ketchup, sriracha (Thai hot sauce), jams, jellies, chutneys, and preserves. They sure taste better with the added jolt!

Sí, Pica
SMOKY CHIPOTLE AND TOASTED PEPITA PESTO

This pesto is *muy picoso*—full of fire and flavor. Smoky chipotle peppers, toasted *comino*, crunchy *pepitas*, and tequila ignite the taste buds. It's delicious with grilled meats or shrimp, soups or *frijoles*, or spread on home-made pizza crust. Toss it with pasta or potato salad. Forget the butter—I love to mash a big spoonful of this spicy pesto on a baked sweet potato instead.

Just wait until you mix some of this pesto into softened butter, with a good splash of mezcal, and spread it over squash, corn on the cob, tortillas, and just about anything else. Sí, Pica is an integral ingredient for Smoky Chipotle Torta, a layered, chilled cheese terrine that is always a fiesta favorite.

RECIPE CONTINUED ON NEXT PAGE

Toasting Nuts and Seeds

Place pecans, pine nuts, pumpkin *(pepitas)* or sunflower seeds on a baking sheet in a pre-heated 325-degree oven. Toast until golden brown, turning occasionally, *or* toast them on a hot *comal* on the stove. Once browned, remove from pan to prevent overcooking.

For whole *comino* and other seeds: toast briefly in a dry (no oil), hot pan or on a *comal* to bring out flavor.

To Roast Tomatillos

Place green tomatillos in their husks on a preheated *comal*. Roast them, turning often, until husks lightly brown and tomatillo becomes soft (about 8 minutes). Remove husks, and use roasted tomatillos in sauces.

For a delicious accompaniment for Texican Margaritas or shots, serve a bowl of roasted new or fingerling potatoes to dunk into bowls of Sí, Pica and Crema Mexicana (Mexican sour cream found in most Latin American markets).

This recipe may be halved, or freeze some of it in jars for future use.

- 4 cloves garlic
- 1¼ cups fresh cilantro, tightly packed
- 1 teaspoon toasted *comino* (cumin)
- ½ teaspoon dried Mexican oregano
- ¾ cup *pepitas* (pumpkin seeds), toasted (p. 213)
- ¾ cup roasted red bell pepper strips (p. 208)
- 2 tablespoons sun-dried tomatoes packed in olive oil, drained, and finely chopped
- 3 tablespoons red onion, finely chopped
- 1 7-ounce can whole *chipotles en adobo* sauce
- 2 tablespoons tequila *reposado* (or part mezcal, if you wish)
- 1 cup Parmesan cheese, grated
- 2 tablespoons Romano cheese, grated
- ¾ cup olive oil (or slightly more)

In a food processor, grind garlic and cilantro. Add *comino*, oregano, *pepitas*, roasted peppers, sun-dried tomatoes, and onion. Mix in chipotles, tequila, and cheeses. Slowly pour in enough olive oil to form a pesto-like consistency; do not over process. Best made a day in advance in order to repose before serving. Keeps for more than a week refrigerated. *Makes approx. 3½ cups.*

Note: For a less piquant version, use less chipotle in the recipe. You may use bottled fire-roasted red peppers (I like *piquillos*), rinsed, drained, and chopped. Find *pepitas* in specialty and health food stores; taste before using, as they become rancid easily. Unsalted, roasted sunflower seeds or pistachios may be substituted.

Smoky Chipotle Tequila Marinade

This smoke-and-fire salsa adds spark to grilled pork chops, steaks, shrimp, or fish. Rub on quail and poultry (and under the skin) before roasting. Mix together: 3 tablespoons Sí, Pica, 1 tablespoon mezcal or tequila *reposado*, and 1 tablespoon fresh lime juice. Whisk in 2 teaspoons olive oil, salt, and freshly ground pepper to taste. Let it rest several hours before using. Makes about ⅓ cup. If you prefer a sweeter flavor, lightly add brown sugar, agave syrup, or orange marmalade to taste, and use as a dipping sauce for Spicy Bison Meatballs.

Mantequilla Mezcalito
SÍ, PICA CHIPOTLE BUTTER SPIKED WITH MEZCAL

With its rich orange color and spicy flavor, Mantequilla Mezcalito is a perfect addition to corn on the cob, potatoes, acorn and other squash, pumpkin, or sweet potatoes. Add a pat to steak or grilled fish, or rub on poultry before roasting.

To make: In a small bowl, blend: 1 stick softened unsalted butter, 2 tablespoons Sí, Pica, 2 teaspoons smoky mezcal or tequila *reposado*, a squeeze of lime, and salt to taste. Let it mellow several hours before serving. It won't last long!

Chimichurri Rojo
SALSA DE CHILE DE ÁRBOL

It's no wonder the Restaurant Campestre Real, on the outskirts of Atotonilco, is a favorite of nearby tequila producers and families who flock there for weekend *tardeadas*. The gaily painted patio and open-air bar overlook hillsides shimmering with rows of blue agave. After a long day of trekking through tequila terroir, my friends and I sipped Ponche de Guadalajara through straws from glazed earthenware bowls laden with fresh chunks of citrus or pretty pink grapefruit Chatazos laced with tequila. Aromas of sizzling garlic and meats on the grill made us ravenous.

Owners Lulu and Luis Navarro combine traditional ingredients with contemporary presentations. They lovingly prepare their dishes, using garnishes in the same vivid colors as those found in the handwoven tablecloths. Unpeeled pink shrimp or beef tenderloin tips *a la parrilla* (from a hot griddle) arrived on platters adorned with crimson beets and carrots, grilled plantains, purple onion rings, and shredded cabbage. Bowls of *frijoles refritos*, freshly made tostada chips, *queso fresco*, and plenty of hot tortillas followed, along with shots of tequila and their homemade *sangrita* (for my Sangrita recipe, see p. 135).

Luis brought a bowl of his *chimichurri*, a salsa fashioned after a garlicky green herb and vinegar table sauce that accompanies grilled meats in Argentina. He seasoned his version with fiery red *chiles de árbol*. To everyone's surprise, I added a good splash of tequila to it, and the other ingredients began to dance in the bowl! We dunked shrimp in it, drizzled it over steaks hot from the grill, and spooned it on garlicky crostini made from crusty *bolillos* that Lulu brought to the table in a basket.

Chimichurri Rojo keeps for a few weeks in the refrigerator. Keep it on hand to perk up any tortilla-based recipe, roasted chicken, or even chunky mashed potatoes with chopped cilantro. Add it to marinades, sauces, aioli or mayonnaise, and salad dressings. Use it as you do sriracha (nearly everyone's favorite Thai hot sauce) to spice up foods in a pinch. What's my favorite quick fix? Chimichurri Rojo drizzled on goat cheese and field greens wrapped in a warm tortilla. Try it on crunchy peanut butter, or on a cracker with cream cheese. Remember though, a little goes a long way . . . it's *picoso*! (Use fewer chiles in the recipe, if you wish.)

- 25 dried *chiles de árbol* or *japón*
- 5 cloves garlic
- 4 tablespoons fresh cilantro
- 4 tablespoons mild cider or rice vinegar
- 1 tablespoon red wine vinegar
- 2 tablespoons tequila *reposado* (or part mezcal)
- ½ teaspoon dried Mexican oregano
- ½ teaspoon salt
- ⅓ cup olive oil, or more

On a hot griddle, toast chiles for a few seconds on each side—do not burn! Discard stems and most seeds. Grind chiles in a blender with the garlic and cilantro. Scrape down sides and add vinegar, tequila, oregano, and salt; pulse to blend (flecks of red chile and cilantro will be apparent). Slowly drizzle in the olive oil to form a thickened drizzling sauce, adding more oil if needed. Chill and allow to season for several hours or overnight before adjusting flavors. *Makes ¾ cup.*

*Cuando andes a medios chiles,
búscate medias cebollas.*

—

*When you are half-pickled,
look for the barrel.*

Salsa Borracha (Drunken Sauce)

Traditionally, Mexicans make *salsa borracha* with dark, mild *chile pasillas* and flavor it with pulque. Instead, my version features the more piquant flavor of dried red New Mexico, or *guajillo*, chiles and tequila or mezcal. Serve as a table sauce or as a dip for homemade tostada chips. Rub it on chicken (and under the skin) before roasting for color and flavor (see Pollo Borracho). Offer it as a condiment for hamburgers, grilled meats, shrimp, Muy Bueno Bean Dip, or cactus nachos.

- 5 tablespoons tequila *reposado* or mezcal
- 10 plump tomatillos in husks
- 8 New Mexico dried, hot red *chiles colorados* or *guajillos*
- 4 cloves garlic
- ½ teaspoon salt
- 1–2 dried, ground *chile de árbol*, optional
- ½ white onion, finely chopped
- 3 tablespoons cilantro, finely chopped

In a small, heavy saucepan, heat tequila (don't boil) briefly to burn off some alcohol; remove from heat. Roast tomatillos (p. 213) on a hot griddle; set aside. Toast chiles on griddle for 10 seconds each side; don't burn, or they'll taste bitter. Remove and discard the seeds, stems, and fibrous veins of the chiles.

Tear chiles into small pieces and soak for about 10 minutes in a bowl in which you've poured a cup of boiling water. Drain chiles, reserving soaking water. In a blender, grind garlic and tomatillos along with the soaked chiles and just enough of the soaking water to make a thickened sauce. Mix in the tequila or mezcal and salt. Allow sauce to mellow for several hours, or preferably overnight. If it is not piquant enough, flavor with crushed *chile de árbol*. Before serving, sprinkle with chopped onion and cilantro. This sauce keeps well for a week in the refrigerator. *Makes 2 cups.*

Note: Guajillos, with their fruity, sometimes fiery, flavor are more readily available than Jalisco's favored *chiles puyas*, which have more authority (p. 200). Sometimes, I'll use a few *puyas* for extra flavor.

Nachos Nopales

For a healthy alternative, make nachos with grilled nopal cactus squares instead of fried tostada chips. Cactus nachos are an appetizer you won't find at every party.

To make: Purchase whole fresh nopal cactus paddles trimmed of spines. Scrape both sides lightly with the tines of a fork. Rub both sides lightly with olive oil and sprinkle with salt and pepper. Heat for about 4 minutes on a hot grill or *comal*. Flip and grill other side, and cook until lightly charred. Cut each nopal paddle into 2–3 inch "chips." Drizzle with Salsa Borracha or Chimichurri Rojo and top with crumbled *queso fresco* or feta. Garnish each with a cilantro sprig and chopped green onions, and pass on a platter.

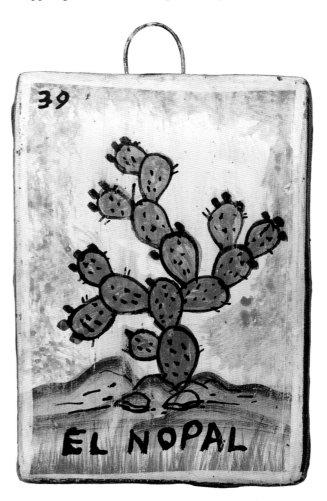

Painted earthenware "El Nopal" (prickly pear cactus) from Mexican *lotería* game.

TEQUILA COCINA

Javier's Salsa de Aguacate
CREAMY AVOCADO SAUCE

My friend Javier Aviles shared this recipe, reminding me that it's *not* guacamole, but a traditional avocado salsa from his hometown, Luvianos, Mexico. Green tomatillos give a pleasing tartness to this creamy avocado sauce. It's delicious drizzled over crispy *flautas* (p. 205), grilled seafood, steaks, or salads, and it is addictive with chips and margaritas. Spoon it over poblano *rajas* (p. 208), sprinkled with pomegranate seeds to celebrate the colors of Mexico's flag.

- 4 cloves garlic
- 1 pound tomatillos (about 18)
- 4–8 serranos, seeded and stemmed
- ½ teaspoon salt
- ¼–½ white onion, chopped
- 4 ripe avocados, peeled and loosely chopped
- Juice of 1–2 Mexican limes
- ½ or more cup cilantro, chopped
- Chopped green onions

Mince garlic in a blender. Add tomatillos, serranos, salt, and onion and blend, using short pulses. Set aside. Add avocados to blender, along with small batches of the tomatillo salsa and the lime juice. Do not overprocess. Place in a bowl and sprinkle with lots of finely chopped cilantro and green onions.

Salsa Rosita
PINK POMEGRANATE SALAD DRESSING

Fresh pomegranate seeds (use fresh raspberries in a pinch) produce a tart and tangy flavor and rosy pink color to this celebratory salad dressing, while flecks of cayenne, lime zest, and a splash of tequila give it Mexican flair. The slightly nutty yet delicate flavor of avocado oil makes this dressing especially elegant for any fruit or mixed greens salad.

For a fiesta salad platter, serve segments of ruby red grapefruit, tangerines, and avocado wedges on a bed of red-tipped lettuce. Sprinkle with pomegranate seeds (or raspberries or pink peppercorns) and pass the Salsa Rosita! Serve in autumn, when citrus and pomegranates are best, or during summer's raspberry season.

- 3 tablespoons fresh pomegranate seeds or 15 ripe raspberries
- 3 tablespoons raspberry vinegar
- 1 tablespoon freshly squeezed lime juice
- 3 tablespoons 100% agave tequila *blanco*
- 5 tablespoons minced red onion
- ¼ teaspoon crushed dried cayenne pepper
- Coarsely grated zest of 1 lime
- 1 tablespoon granulated white sugar
- Cantina Classic Pink Peppercorn Citrus Salt to taste (or commercial spicy Mexican seasoning salt)
- ¼ teaspoon freshly ground pink peppercorns
- ⅝ cup avocado or grapeseed oil

Combine pomegranate seeds (or raspberries), vinegar, lime juice, and tequila in a blender and purée until bright pink. Strain through a fine mesh strainer, using the back of a spoon to press out all of the juice.

Rinse and dry blender. Add onion, cayenne pepper, lime zest, sugar, salt, and peppercorns along with pink tequila mixture, and blend. With motor running, add oil in a steady stream to emulsify. Adjust flavorings, adding salt and more lime or sugar as needed. Pour into a jar and refrigerate—it will thicken. Keeps for several days. *Makes 1 generous cup.*

Note: Avocado oil is low in saturated fat, making it a healthy oil alternative.

Drunken Sugarplum Chutney

Redolent of sweet plums, tart cranberries, crystalized ginger, and spice and lavishly splashed with tequila, this chutney is my signature holiday gift. A small Ginger Curried Cheese Ball, on which to mound the chutney, makes the package even more special.

It is so versatile—use it to frost Queso Sabroso, a savory cheese ball; spread it on turkey sandwiches; or stuff some in rolled up boneless chicken breasts or pork tenderloin. I even love a spoonful of it in my morning oatmeal! Drunken Sugarplum Chutney is the secret ingredient to a cheerful and extraordinarily pretty pink cocktail of the same name (p. 168).

- 1¾ cups dried cranberries
- 1¾ cups dried cherries
- 2 cups dried pitted plums (prunes), loosely chopped
- 3 navel oranges, loosely chopped (with peel)
- 1¼ cups tequila *añejo*, plus ½ cup more
- 32-ounce bottle of cranberry juice
- 4 12-ounce packages fresh cranberries
- 2 ounces dried *flor de jamaica* flowers (p. 98)
- ½ pound chopped Australian candied (crystalized) ginger
- 2 tablespoons whole coriander seeds
- 5 3-inch cinnamon sticks
- 2 teaspoons whole allspice and 6 cloves, ground in a spice grinder
- 1 teaspoon salt
- 2 teaspoons crushed dried cayenne
- 2 cups sugar
- 1 cup amber agave syrup
- Whole fresh or dried red cayenne *al gusto*, optional
- 12 kumquats, halved, optional

Plump dried fruit and oranges in 1¼ cup tequila for at least 20 minutes. In a large, nonreactive pot, add plumped fruits, cranberry juice, and 2 of the packages of cranberries, along with the other ingredients.

Bring to a gentle boil. Lower heat and simmer until cranberries pop, stirring occasionally. Add remaining 2 packages of cranberries and simmer until chutney is thick, adjusting flavorings to your taste—which for me means several shots more of tequila! Pour into sterilized jars. Keep refrigerated. *Makes about 18 half-pint jars.*

Let's Salsa! Chunky Salsas Frescas

ANOTHER KIND OF TEQUILA COCKTAIL

MEXICAN STREET VENDORS sprinkle salt, chile powder, and fresh lime juice on slices of mango, pineapple, watermelon, jícama, cucumbers, and oranges to sell as hand-held snacks. Or they chop the fruits coarsely to serve from paper cones like a fresh fruit cocktail.

Borrowing from this tradition, but adding contemporary flair—and, of course, a good splash of tequila—I've created colorful, chunky medleys that I call *salsas frescas*. Refreshing, healthy, low in fat, these salsas are colorful and make versatile presentations.

Let's salsa! The salsas that follow are as lively as the Latin dance of the same name. Most of these recipes are for party portions, but can easily be halved.

SALSA STEPS

- Combine chopped vegetables, chiles, fruits, and spices in a mixing bowl. Toss gently with liquid ingredients to avoid bruising tender fruits and vegetables.
- Flavor salsas with Cantina Classic Spicy Seasoned Salts like Sal de Sangrita or Hibiscus Flower and Orange Zest, or use commercial spicy Mexican seasoned salts, to bring out flavors.

- Chill salsas for several hours or overnight, tossing occasionally, so that flavors mingle. Adjust seasonings before serving, adding more chile, lime, salt, and tequila as needed.
- Use slotted spoon to drain excess liquid before serving.
- Serve salsas in clear, long-stemmed margarita glasses to showcase colors and texture.

HOW TO SALSA

- By the bowlful! (Best breakfast ever!)
- By the bowlsful! Place a variety of salsas on the table to complement foods hot off the grill, for dunking with chips, or to embellish Tostadas Compuestas or quesadillas.
- Atop field greens as a salad (add grilled meats or seafood for a more substantial meal).
- Mounded upon cheese balls.

Drink Suggestions

Shots: Fiesta Tequila Frozen in Ice, Sangritas, Margarita Picosita

Glasses: margaritas or frozen fruit margaritas, spritzers, Chatazo, Pepino Picosito, Mexican Mojito

FIESTA PRESENTATIONS FOR SALSAS

Use the following for "containers" in which to serve colorful *salsa fresca* medleys. Mound them with Barco de Oro (Mango and Pineapple Salsa Tropicana), Corn Salsa Prontísimo, Fiesta Frijoles, or Pancho Villa's Nopalitos or with guacamole, refried beans, or Muy Bueno Bean Dip. For a cornucopia of color, pass a platter, choosing from any of the following:

Corn Husk Boats

Soak 8 dried corn husks (used to make tamales) in water for several hours; pat dry. Tear 2 husks into ½-inch strips for tying the ends of the corn husk boats. Place a whole small lime in the center of each moistened husk and wrap the husk around the lime, tying at both ends with the torn strips. Allow to dry; remove the lime, leaving a cavity for filling. *Makes 6 "boats."* May be made days in advance and stored in airtight containers.

Poblano Peppers

Roast and peel *poblano* peppers (or substitute Anaheim or New Mexico peppers), leaving stems intact (p. 208). Carefully make about a 2½-inch slit down the center

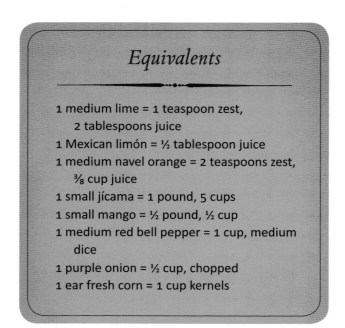

Equivalents

1 medium lime = 1 teaspoon zest,
2 tablespoons juice
1 Mexican limón = ½ tablespoon juice
1 medium navel orange = 2 teaspoons zest,
⅜ cup juice
1 small jícama = 1 pound, 5 cups
1 small mango = ½ pound, ½ cup
1 medium red bell pepper = 1 cup, medium dice
1 purple onion = ½ cup, chopped
1 ear fresh corn = 1 cup kernels

of each pepper and remove seeds; mound salsa within. Chill before serving. For added flavor for savory salsas, marinate *poblanos* in olive oil, vinegar, minced garlic, salt, and pepper for an hour before stuffing. You may wish to decrease the other chile peppers called for in the recipe.

Baby Pumpkins

Cut off the tops of miniature pumpkins and carefully hollow them out for filling.

Fruit Salsas

Pico de Gallo (Bite of the Rooster)

The chile-, salt-, and lime-seasoned fruit sold by Mexican street vendors inspired this chunky *salsa fresca*. As you pick up a bite-sized piece of fruit with your thumb and forefinger, your remaining fingers resemble a rooster's comb, and as you plop the chile-flavored morsel into your mouth, you get the "bite of the rooster," or the *pico de gallo*.

Cut fruit into larger bite-sized chunks to serve from a platter, accompanied by icy shots poured from a bottle of Fiesta Tequila Frozen in Ice, or chop ingredients into smaller pieces when using the salsa as a condiment for grilled seafood, poultry, and pork, or as a refreshing salad atop greens. Your favorite Cantina Classic Spicy Mexican Seasoned Salt will surely bring out the flavor of the fruit!

Marinade:
- 4 tablespoons Citrus- or Pineapple-Infused Tequila or tequila *blanco*
- 3 tablespoons freshly squeezed orange juice
- 4 tablespoons fresh lime juice
- 1 teaspoon crushed dried red chile
- ½ teaspoon of your favorite Cantina Classic Spicy Mexican Seasoned Salt or commercial brand

Chopped ingredients:

- 1 medium jícama, peeled and cut into bite-sized chunks
- 1 fresh pineapple, peeled and cut into bite-sized chunks
- 4 navel oranges, peeled and cut into bite-sized chunks (or part ruby red grapefruit)
- 3 or more serrano peppers, chopped
- 1 small red onion, chopped
- Pure ground chile powder to taste, optional
- Garnishes: pure chile powder, pomegranate seeds, or nasturtium blossoms

In a small bowl, whisk together ingredients for marinade and set aside. In a large glass bowl, toss chopped ingredients with marinade. Chill several hours, stirring occasionally. Drain (and drink!) excess liquid. Toss liberally with additional Cantina Classic Spicy Mexican Seasoned Salt and lime juice, if needed. Dust with chile powder before serving. *Makes approx. 8 cups.*

Note: Don't be confused. Pico de Gallo is also another name for the ubiquitous (uncooked) spicy, chunky table sauce—made with fresh chopped tomatoes, onions, chiles, and cilantro—also called *salsa picante.*

Barco de Oro
MANGO AND PINEAPPLE TROPICANA SALSA

Mexican fruit vendors have ingenious ways of enticing passersby to make a purchase. They can turn a mango into a flower! First, they cut an unpeeled mango in two slices from either side of the seed. Then, they discard the seed, making crisscross cuts in both slices without piercing the peel. When the mango is turned half inside out, it becomes a "flower," which the vendors sprinkle with red chile and lime. Take a bite from the mango, then take a sip of a shot of *blanco* or *reposado.*

This versatile fruit salsa celebrates tropical flavors—eat it by the bowlful on a summer day for breakfast or as a lively dessert. Complement grilled fish, pork tenderloin, chicken, or lamb chops with this refreshing medley, or mound it in avocado halves with grilled shrimp, lobster, or curried chicken salad. Add a big spoonful to a bowl of black beans or a warm quesadilla. For an enticing presentation, fill lots of Corn Husk Boats (p. 220) with this colorful salsa and arrange them on a big platter.

For the marinade:

- 3 tablespoons Cantina Classic Citrus-, Pineapple-, or Chile-Infused Tequila or tequila *reposado*
- Zest of 1 orange
- 4 tablespoons fresh lime juice
- 1 tablespoon peeled and grated ginger

For the mango/pineapple mixture:

- 3 medium mangoes (not too ripe), peeled, medium dice
- 2 cups fresh pineapple (not too ripe), medium dice
- 1½ cups red bell pepper, medium dice
- 1½ cups jícama, peeled and chopped into medium dice, sprinkled with fresh lime juice
- 3 or more fresh hot peppers, minced (preferably red-ripened Fresnos, serranos, or 1 habanero)
- 1 red onion, chopped
- ¼ cup cilantro, chopped
- 3 tablespoons fresh mint, finely chopped
- ½ teaspoon Cantina Classic salt (such as Spicy Mexican Seasoned Salt or Hibiscus Flower and Orange Zest)
- Fresh lime juice

In a small bowl, mix together ingredients for marinade; set aside. In a large glass bowl, combine chopped ingredients and toss gently with marinade and salt. Chill for several hours or overnight, turning occasionally. Drain excess juices (sip with a shot of tequila!). Toss with more seasoned salt and lime juice to taste before serving. *Makes approx. 7 cups.*

Note: Grill pineapple and peppers, or replace red bell peppers with vine-ripened red cherry tomatoes.

Variation: For a quick summer dessert, add a generous splash of Cantina Classic Zesty Ginger Syrup and serve salsa (omit onions if you wish) atop crispy fried flour tostadas sprinkled with cinnamon sugar.

¡Muy Bonita! PRETTY WATERMELON & CUCUMBER SALSA WITH ZESTY TEQUILA GRANITA

You can eat your salsa . . . and drink it, too! This is a party in a bowl: colorful, vibrant, and a bit wild. Show off the pretty colors of tequila-marinated watermelon balls and slices of crunchy, green pickling cucumbers from small, clear, wide-mouthed margarita, sorbet, or champagne glasses. Top with a rosy *granita* (an icy sorbet) and garnish with a wedge of lime and a mint sprig. Pass bowls of Cotija cheese for added texture and enjoy a sweet, salty, piquant, cold, and refreshing surprise with each bite. Serve as a salad, between courses, or as a light, summery dessert.

Once eaten, sip the juice remaining in the glass (perhaps with a bit more *granita*), accompanied by (or mixed with) an ice-cold shot of tequila *blanco*.

- 5 cups sweet, seedless watermelon balls (chill and reserve any watermelon juice released while making them)
- 5 cups (about 1½ pounds) pickling cucumbers, medium slice (to produce a decorative edge, tine the length of the cucumbers all around with a fork before cutting them)
- 2 tablespoons white sugar
- 1 teaspoon or more Cantina Classic Spicy Mexican Seasoning Salt (or a commercial brand)
- 1–2 red Fresno peppers, finely diced
- 1 serrano pepper, finely diced
- 2 teaspoons grated orange zest
- 2 teaspoons grated lime zest
- 1 large bunch green onions, sliced with some green tops
- 3 ounces chilled tequila *blanco* (use 100-proof for less dilution)
- 3 tablespoons fresh lime juice, preferably from Mexican (Key) limes
- 2 tablespoons fresh mint, finely chopped
- 2 tablespoons cilantro, loosely chopped
- ¾ cup Cotija cheese, loosely crumbled
- *Granita* (for recipe, see below)
- Mint or cilantro sprigs for garnish
- Lime wedges

Keep watermelon balls chilled as you prepare other ingredients. Place sliced cucumbers in a 9 × 13–inch glass dish. Sprinkle both sides of the cucumbers with the sugar, Spicy Mexican Seasoning Salt, hot peppers, citrus zests, and green onions, pressing well into the cucumbers. Drizzle with tequila and lime juice, as you toss in the watermelon balls, fresh mint, and cilantro. Add another light sprinkling of seasoned salt, if you wish. Chill, basting often, as lots of juices will release. After about half an hour, pour off enough of the liquid to make the *granita* (recipe follows), still leaving some liquid to baste the watermelon and cucumbers.

Granita

I can't offer an exact recipe for the *granita*, as it will depend upon the amount and sweetness of the reserved watermelon juice and the flavor of the liquid rendered from the marinated watermelon and cucumbers. Here's an approximation, but flavor to suit your own taste:

- ¾ cup reserved watermelon juice
- ¾ cup marinade drained from watermelon and cucumbers
- Splash of tequila (not too much or *granita* won't freeze)
- Splash of Cointreau
- Squeeze of lime
- Agave syrup
- Cantina Classic Spicy Mexican Seasoning Salt

Pour *granita* ingredients into to a small, shallow stainless steel pan. As it freezes (within about ½ hour), scrape across the top of the *granita* with a fork to break up ice crystals. Freeze and scrape again, until *granita* resembles consistency of shaved ice—approx. 1 hour.

Serve the colorful cucumber and watermelon medley in chilled glasses, spooning some of its juices into each glass. Top each with a big spoonful of the icy *granita*. Garnish with a sprig of fresh mint or cilantro and a wedge of lime, and pass a shaker of the seasoned salt, bowls of loosely crumbled Cotija cheese, and icy shots of tequila *blanco*! *Serves 10 or more.*

Note: Scoop out remaining watermelon after making balls and freeze for making Summertime Sandía Watermelon Cooler.

Savory Salsas

Pancho Villa's Nopalitos MARINATED CACTUS SALSA SPIKED WITH AGAVE SPIRITS

I can just imagine "La Adelita" (Villa's reputed paramour and good cook) and other *soldadas* (women soldiers) of his revolutionary army scraping spines from nopal cactus pads by the side of the *tren militar* (military train) to feed the troops.

Nopalitos and tequila or mezcal, Mexico's beloved national spirits, join forces in this cactus salsa. How many of your friends have eaten cactus? Surprise them! Serve Pancho Villa's Nopalitos with homemade tostada chips and shots of tequila and Sangrita . . . and toast to Pancho and Adelita!

Fortunately, today you don't have to be an Adelita. You can find jars of *nopalitos* or bags of them already cut into strips (with their pesky spines removed), ready for cooking. Many Latin American stores carry fresh nopal paddles, if you want to cut them yourself.

- 24 ounces *nopalitos*, packed in water, rinsed, and drained (about 2 cups) or equivalent freshly cooked (see Note)
- 1 pint red cherry tomatoes halved, salted, and drained in a colander
- ½ small red onion, chopped
- 4 or more pickled jalapeños *en escabeche* (in jars or cans), chopped (reserve brine)

Marinade:
- 3 cloves garlic, minced
- 1 teaspoon dried Mexican oregano, crumbled
- ½ teaspoon *tomillo* (thyme)
- 1 tablespoon brine from jalapeño *escabeche*
- 2 tablespoons mezcal *or* tequila *reposado*
- 2 tablespoons red wine vinegar
- 4 tablespoons olive oil
- Salt and pepper to taste
- Garnishes: small chunks of *queso fresco* or *queso* Cotija, red onion rings, cilantro sprigs, avocado slices, lots of chopped cilantro, fresh lime juice. Add chopped artichoke hearts and crumbled feta for a nontraditional touch.

If using bottled *nopalitos*, rinse them under cold running water; drain well. Mix together ingredients, except for garnishes. Chill before serving. Adjust flavorings, adding more jalapeños, lime juice, cilantro, and salt, if needed. Drain off excess liquid before serving. Garnish to please. *Makes 4 cups.*

Note: *Nopalitos* taste rather like cooked green beans crossed with okra (and have some of that same mucilaginous character). They lose color and texture when sold in jars. Served as a vegetable, nopales traditionally accompany *carne asada* (grilled beef), scrambled eggs, shrimp, and pork dishes, but are best known as a marinated salad. Packed with vitamins and minerals, *nopalitos* lower cholesterol and blood sugar. (May come in handy if you imbibe too much tequila.)

Cooking Cactus

To cook fresh nopales and retain green color and texture: Put 2 teaspoons of oil into a large cast-iron skillet. When hot, add a chopped onion and wilt. Add 3 cloves minced garlic and 2 chopped serranos, tossing to heat. Add 1 pound fresh nopales, cut into ¾-inch strips. Simmer for about 25–30 minutes; cactus will release *baba*, a mucilaginous liquid. Cook until juices have been extracted, loosely covering the pan toward the end of cooking, so nopales can steam. A 1-pound bag of fresh nopal strips will yield about 5 cups.

To grill nopales: Whole nopal cactus pads are delicious when rubbed with olive oil, salt, pepper, and lime juice and cooked on a hot grill or *comal* for about 15 minutes. Cool and cut into strips.

Fiesta Frijoles
A BLACK BEAN AND CORN SALSA PARTY

The sweet flavor of corn kernels combines with black beans doused in a spicy tequila marinade to make this festive and filling salsa. It tastes even better when made a day in advance, and it lends itself to many variations. Serve Fiesta Frijoles with homemade tostada chips (p. 204), or as an accompaniment for Queso Sabroso or Smoky Chipotle Torta. Mound in corn husk boats (p. 220), serve as a condiment for grilled meats, or eat by the bowlful.

Marinade:
- 1½ teaspoons *comino* (cumin) seeds, toasted
- 1 *chile de árbol*, seeded and stemmed
- 4 cloves garlic, minced
- 1 teaspoon dried Mexican oregano
- 3 tablespoons tequila *reposado* or mezcal
- 4 tablespoons red wine vinegar
- ½ teaspoon salt
- 5 tablespoons olive oil

Salsa ingredients:
- 3 cups cooked black beans, chilled and drained
- 3 or more serranos or jalapeños, chopped
- 1 small red onion, chopped
- 2 cups frozen organic corn kernels, thawed or fresh
- 1 pint red cherry tomatoes, quartered, lightly salted, and drained in a colander

Before serving:
- ½ cup fresh cilantro, chopped
- 6 green onions, chopped
- Salt to taste
- Juice of 1–2 fresh limes

Grind *comino* and *chile de árbol* in a spice grinder. Combine with other marinade ingredients in a small bowl, whisking in the olive oil last.

Preparing Vegetables for Salsas

TOMATOES: Sprinkle chopped tomatoes (cut small, cherry, or pear tomatoes in half) lightly with salt and drain in a colander to release excess liquid before adding to recipe. If recipe is held overnight, add chopped tomatoes a few hours prior to serving.

CORN: To cold-toss fresh corn kernels: blanch for 30 seconds in rapidly boiling water. Immediately refresh in a colander set in a bowl of ice water. When frozen organic corn is used, simply thaw and drain well before using; do not cook. To roast corn kernels: place in a hot, dry (no oil) cast-iron skillet or *comal* and cook until browned, turning only once (about 5 minutes).

CHILES: Roast green chiles and make *rajas* (p. 208).

In a large bowl, combine salsa ingredients, and toss with marinade. Chill for several hours or overnight, tossing occasionally. (If recipe is held overnight, add tomatoes a few hours before serving.) Toss with cilantro, green onions, salt, and lime before serving. *Makes approx. 7 cups.*

Note: Substitute speckled red and white Southwestern Anasazi beans or red kidney beans.

Variations: Small cubes of Pepper Jack cheese; Crumbled *queso fresco* or feta; cooked, chopped nopales (cactus strips); cubes or wedges of avocado; 3 or more chopped *chipotles en adobo*; splash of Chile-Infused Tequila.

Corn Salsa Prontísimo

When I take a big bowl of this salsa to potlucks, everyone asks for the recipe. It is colorful and sassy . . . and so easy to make! Serve with homemade tostada chips (p. 204), grilled meats, Queso Sabroso, or Smoky Chipotle Torta . . . or eat as a one-bowl meal.

- 4 cups frozen organic corn kernels, thawed, but not cooked, *or* fresh corn kernels (see Note)
- 32 ounces bottled chunky red salsa picante (I prefer "hot")
- 3 cloves garlic, minced
- ½ cup chopped red onion
- 2 or more chopped fresh serranos or jalapeños
- ¾–1 pint red cherry tomatoes, halved or quartered, salted and drained (see sidebar, p. 224)
- ½ teaspoon freshly ground *comino* (cumin)
- 2 tablespoons tequila *reposado*

- Salt to taste
- Fresh lime juice to taste
- Lots of freshly chopped cilantro
- 2 avocados, cubed and sprinkled with lime
- 1 bunch green onions, chopped with some tops

Combine ingredients—except cilantro, avocado, and green onions—in a bowl. Chill several hours or overnight, tossing occasionally. Before serving, gently mix in avocados and cilantro, adjusting seasoning to taste. Sprinkle with green onions. *Makes approx. 7 cups.*

Note: When using fresh corn cut off the cob, use the cold-toss method (see sidebar, p. 224). Look for locally made salsas—refrigerated roasted red tomato salsas taste particularly good in this recipe. Add small cubes of jalapeño Jack cheese, if you wish.

Colorfully painted earthenware market vendor.

Festive Frijoles

HAVE SOME TEQUILA WITH YOUR BEANS!

A POT OF *FRIJOLES* (pinto or black beans) provides filling and nutritious fare for buffets and parties. Let guests select from a variety of garnishes served in small bowls: grated/crumbled cheese, chopped tomatoes, green onions, chopped jalapeños or serranos, *chipotle chiles en adobo*, or chunks of avocado. I collect small wooden and ceramic bowls, which I fill with salt, dried oregano, and crushed dried red chile for sprinkling into individual bowls. Keep a bottle of Chile-Infused Tequila (p. 138) on hand for those who want an extra splash of flavor.

Frijoles Sabrosos (Delicious Beans)

For me, a hearty bowl of beans is a meal in itself, made even better with a quesadilla or a chunk of cornbread. The innate peppery nature of tequila adds character to *frijoles*, especially when they're cooked *en olla*, in an unleaded clay pot, which imparts earthiness, authenticity, and depth of flavor.

- 1 pound pinto beans, rinsed and sorted
- 1 quartered white onion
- 3 cloves garlic
- 1 teaspoon *comino* (cumin)
- 1 teaspoon dried Mexican oregano
- Salt to taste, added toward end of cooking

Place beans in a pot (preferably earthenware) and cover with 2 inches of water or broth. Bring to boil; immediately reduce heat and simmer for 1½–2 hours, adding salt the last 30 minutes of cooking (see sidebar for tips and additional flavorings).

Note: For *frijoles negros* (black beans) add, to the recipe above, 1 tablespoon olive oil, 2 bay leaves and three dried red chiles, omit *comino*, and add a few sprigs of epazote, the "bean herb," along with salt, toward the end of cooking. Black beans require longer cooking time than pintos, simmering until thick and inky. I love a bowl of black beans generously splashed with Sweet and Spicy Tomato Salsa.

Refritos (Refried Beans)

Mexicanos usually fry *frijoles* in hot lard. Called *refritos*, these beans have a creamy texture and earthy essence—pure comfort food. Most now prefer to fry beans in hot vegetable oil, though a bit of bacon fat sure adds flavor! *Refritos* are a must for Tostadas Compuestas. A first layer of *refritos* helps other ingredients adhere to the crispy tortilla.

For 4 cups of cooked beans in their broth: Heat 2 tablespoons oil or lard (or part bacon fat) in a cast-iron skillet. Add 1 small chopped white onion and cook until translucent. Add 2 cloves minced garlic (optional) and cook briefly. Slowly add beans with a small amount of reserved broth. Using a bean or potato masher, crush beans coarsely over low heat, adding more beans and enough liquid to produce a thick and creamy texture. You may add ½ cup grated cheese, stirring until it melts. Spread on tostadas or nachos, or serve as a side dish.

Hints for Cooking Frijoles

- I don't soak beans before cooking.
- Always add *hot* water to the pot, if needed, as beans simmer. Too much liquid dilutes flavor, so add a small amount.
- To prevent beans from toughening, add salt during the last 30 minutes of cooking.
- Add 2 or more dried red chiles—smoky, dried chipotles, anchos, *guajillos*, or New Mexico *chiles colorados*—to the beans as they cook. Remove stems and seeds and plop chiles in the pot.
- Add a generous splash of tequila or mezcal during the final 10–15 minutes of cooking.
- Cook *frijoles* a day in advance of serving to produce a thick and flavorful broth. The beans will absorb more flavor, too.

Muy Bueno Bean Dip

Like the ever-popular Middle Eastern hummus, this tasty bean dip is filling and packed with protein. It has a more assertive personality though! Dip chips in it or spread as a layer on tostadas or nachos.

To make: Drain cooked beans (pinto or black beans), reserving broth. Using a bean masher or food processor, purée beans, adding just enough broth to make a thickened paste. (Leave some beans whole for texture.) Add 2 bunches chopped green onions, minced garlic, and minced fresh jalapeños or *chipotle chiles en adobo* to taste. Sometimes I add a generous handful of *queso Cotija* or *queso añejo* or shredded Parmesan. Garnish with a dollop of Crema Mexicana (Mexican sour cream), chopped green onions, and sprigs of cilantro. Serve warm or at room temperature.

Here's another version, especially delicious when made with *frijoles negros* (black beans): fill a shallow serving dish with Muy Bueno Bean Dip. Garnish with a band of red Salsa Borracha or Chimichurri Rojo and crumbled *queso fresco*, *Cotija*, or Parmesan. Garnish with fresh epazote or cilantro sprigs. Spread on tostadas topped with Pancho Villa's Nopalitos, have a shot of mezcal *y ¡echar un grito para más!* (Shout for more!)

Frijoles Borrachos a la Charra
DRUNKEN BEANS COWGIRL-STYLE

Often called *frijoles charros* (cowboy beans), these beans are flavored with bacon and beer and a hearty tomato salsa splashed with tequila. A bowl of these beans is a meal in itself—they'll steal the show at a barbecue. Let guests add garnishes from small bowls filled with freshly chopped onion, cilantro, serranos, and dried oregano. Serve with hot flour or corn tortillas or cornbread.

RECIPE CONTINUED ON NEXT PAGE

For the frijoles:
- 1 pound pinto beans, picked over and rinsed
- 1½ teaspoons whole *comino*
- 1 teaspoon dried Mexican oregano, crumbled
- 2 cloves garlic
- 2 dried red chiles, optional (p. 200)
- ½–1 Mexican beer (12 ounces), such as Bohemia, room temperature
- ½ pound bacon, cut into ½-inch pieces
- 1 teaspoon salt

For the salsa:
- 2 tablespoons bacon fat or olive oil
- 1 white onion, chopped
- 3 cloves garlic, chopped
- 3 medium tomatoes, chopped
- 2–4 serrano chiles, chopped
- 1 teaspoon crumbled dried oregano
- Salt to taste
- ½ cup tequila *reposado* or mezcal

Frijoles

Place beans in an earthenware *olla* or other large pot. Add *comino*, oregano, garlic, dried red chile peppers, beer, and enough water to cover beans by about 2 inches. Bring to boil; reduce heat and simmer, covered, for about 1 hour.

Meanwhile, fry bacon until slightly crisp. Drain, reserving 2 tablespoons bacon fat. Add bacon to beans with 1 teaspoon salt. Simmer, uncovered, for about another half hour.

Tomato salsa

Sauté onion in reserved bacon fat until wilted; add garlic. Add tomatoes, serranos, oregano, and salt to taste. Simmer for 6–8 minutes. Set aside.

Add tomato salsa and tequila to beans and simmer for 15 minutes, just prior to serving. (Beans may be cooked the night before with the tomato salsa. Reheat, adding tequila.) Serve with bowls of condiments at the table. *Serves 8–10.*

Variations: Add 3 or more dried chipotle peppers while cooking beans to give them a smoky flavor. Use jalapeño-flavored bacon.

Negros y Piña a la Criztina

BLACK BEANS AND PINEAPPLE SPIKED WITH MEZCAL

I love these *frijoles negros*, a recipe inspired by my sister Criztina, who loved Mexico and made her home in Pátzcuaro, Michocán, for nearly twenty years. She was an incredible cook! Her meals offered a surprise with every bite and influenced my own style of cooking.

What molasses adds to Boston Baked Beans, fresh pineapple gives to these tropical-flavored black beans—a hint of unexpected sweetness. I've added plenty of spice and smoky mezcal, promising to surprise and delight guests.

- Recipe for a pot of black beans (p. 226)
- 1 Mexican dark beer
- 2–4 dried *guajillo, puya,* or *ancho chiles*
- 1 3-inch stick of *canela* (cinnamon)
- 1 teaspoon freshly ground allspice
- 3 fresh bay or allspice leaves
- ½ fresh pineapple, cut into chunks (about 3 cups)
- Salt to taste
- 2 or more ounces mezcal or tequila *reposado*
- Green onions
- Crema Mexicana or sour cream, optional
- Crisp, crumbled bacon, optional

Simmer a pot of black beans, preferably in a clay *olla* (pot), using 1 Mexican dark beer as some of the liquid, and adding chiles, *canela*, and allspice instead of epazote. Do not add too much liquid.

Add pineapple chunks, salt, and mezcal or *reposado* during the last 15 minutes of cooking. Simmer until beans are thick and flavorful. Serve sprinkled with green onions—and a dollop of Crema Mexicana and crispy fried bacon bits, if you wish. I promise, you will want another bowl, and one for breakfast, too. *Serves 8.*

Beyond the Tequila Sunrise

BRUNCH ANYTIME

I LIKE BRUNCH. It's a leisurely way to entertain friends with comfort food: savory egg dishes, simmering bowls of *frijoles*, fresh fruit medleys, and sweet-smelling baked goods hot out of the oven. In fact, I like brunch morning, noon, and night.

Whether it's the Eagles describing "Another Tequila Sunrise," Bonnie Raitt singing about "drinking salty margaritas with Fernando," Joe Ely crooning about Juárez Mary's "ruby lips wet with tequila," Lila Downs's passionate rendition of "La Tequilera" (originally sung by Mexico's beloved *ranchera* queen, Lucha Reyes), or the famous 1958 "Tequila" instrumental by the Champs that makes you want to dance on the table . . . tequila is a song you won't forget!

Festive Quick Fixes

A buffet-style brunch is an easy party option. Serve a festive fruit-filled punch (pp. 173–183) from a big glass *agua fresca* jar—it's pretty enough for a centerpiece and guests can serve themselves.

Make it easy on yourself! You don't have to make every dish from scratch. Buy some items, then dress them up for the fiesta with recipes from this book. If you don't have time to make the luscious Spanish Almond Cake, arrange a selection of *pan dulces* (sweet pastries) from a local Mexican bakery on a platter. Serve Rompope, homemade Mexican eggnog, or coffee drinks laced with tequila (pp. 189–191).

Bring home some *barbacoa* (steamed beef) or *carnitas*, often available by the pound on weekends from your favorite Mexican eatery. Serve the meats with warm tortillas and bowls of chopped onions, serranos, cilantro, and *salsa picante*, and guests can assemble their own tacos. Spice them up with Salsa Borracha or Javier's Salsa de Aguacate and accompany with simmering bowls of Frijoles Borrachos a la Charra.

Tostadas Compuestas also make fun brunch and buffet fare. A platter mounded with Salpicón, a chipotle-marinated shredded beef, lends itself to colorful garnishes. Chunky Salsas Frescas (pp. 219–225) to eat by the bowlful, the seafood cocktail Vuelve a la Vida, or gazpacho served from long-stemmed margarita glasses are also great brunch selections.

My favorite make-ahead egg casserole, Cazuela de Huevos con Rajas, is flavored with green chile *rajas* and drizzled with Sweet and Spicy Tomato Salsa spiced with cinnamon and cayenne that's sure to please. Serve with Spicy Bison Meatballs.

Drink Suggestions

Pitcher: María Sangrita, Pique, Bloody Mary, Torito, Rompope, Chatazo, Vampiro

Shots: Sangritas, Cinco de Mayo shooters, Donají shooters

Punch jar: Ponche de Guadalajara, Torito

Glass: fruit margaritas, Sabor a Mí drinks, Mermeladas, spritzers, Pique

Mugs: Coffee drinks, Mexican hot chocolate, Ponche de Granada

Cazuela de Huevos con Rajas

GREEN CHILE AND EGG CASSEROLE WITH
SWEET AND SPICY TOMATO SALSA

I fondly remember the kitchen of Mary Luckett, a family friend from El Paso. A bright red Vulcan range sat like an altar within a *nicho* made of hand-painted Mexican tiles. I think you'll like her casserole recipe—one I first tasted forty years ago—just as much as I do. I'll always thank Mary for opening her kitchen and heart to me and inspiring a love of cooking. Pico de Gallo, a jícama and orange salad, or field greens dressed with Salsa Rosita go well with this cazuela, as do Spicy Bison Meatballs as a sausage alternative.

The sweet and spicy salsa reminds me of my grandmother's piccalilli, a piquant tomato salsa that she flavored with New Mexico green chiles. It's delicious over black beans, grilled eggplant, sautéed squash, or hamburgers, or even with tostada chips.

For the casserole:
- Butter
- 8 fresh New Mexico (Hatch) or Anaheim green chile peppers *or 6 poblanos*, roasted, peeled, seeded, and cut into *rajas* (strips) (p. 208)
- 4 cloves garlic, minced
- ½ cup finely chopped red onion
- 2 bunches green onions, chopped with some green tops
- 2 jalapeños, seeded and chopped, optional
- ¼ pound sharp yellow cheddar cheese, grated
- ¼ pound Monterey Pepper Jack, grated
- 3 tablespoons Parmesan, shredded
- 5 eggs, separated
- ¾ tablespoons flour
- ⅓ cup plus 1 tablespoon half-and-half
- Salt and pepper to taste
- Pure ground red chile powder
- Garnishes: chopped green onions, avocado wedges drizzled with fresh lime juice, pure mild red chile powder

Sweet and Spicy Tomato Salsa:
- 3 tablespoons unsalted butter
- 8 green onions, chopped with some tops
- 3 cloves garlic, minced
- 16-ounce jar home-style chunky tomato salsa (I like it HOT!)
- 2 teaspoons dark brown sugar
- ¼ teaspoon ground cinnamon
- ¼ teaspoon cayenne
- 2–3 tablespoons tequila *reposado*
- Salt and pepper to taste

Preheat oven to 350 degrees. Toss chile *rajas*, garlic, and onion and place in a buttered 9½ × 9½-inch baking dish. Sprinkle with grated cheeses and Parmesan. With an electric mixer, beat egg yolks until blended. Add flour, half-and-half, salt, and pepper, and mix until incorporated.

With clean, dry beaters, beat egg whites until peaks form. Fold egg whites into yolk mixture with a spatula and spread evenly in baking dish, using a fork to swirl the chiles into the egg mixture. Sprinkle with chile powder.

Bake uncovered 25 minutes or until golden. Garnish with chopped green onions and avocado slices; sprinkle with chile powder. Pass the salsa at the table.

For the salsa: In a medium saucepan, melt butter. Add onions and garlic and cook, stirring for 3 minutes. Stir in chunky salsa, brown sugar, and spices and bring to boil. Reduce heat; add tequila and simmer for 5 minutes, stirring occasionally. Adjust seasonings, adding more spice, sugar, or tequila, and salt and pepper. Sprinkle with a pinch of cinnamon and cayenne and pour into a small pitcher to serve over *cazuela. Serves 8.*

Gazpacho

Spain's popular gazpacho is a chilled soup brimming with chopped tomatoes, peppers, cucumbers, and onions doused with olive oil and vinegar. I've come up with some other versions that are, of course, laced with tequila. Serve these summery gazpachos from icy cups rimmed with Cantina Classic Homemade Seasoned Salt at a buffet, with a condiment "bar" nearby with choices of optional garnishes. Presented in long-stemmed jumbo margarita glasses, gazpacho also makes a lovely first course or luncheon meal. Here's a trio of gazpachos with Mexican flair. Recipes may be halved.

Gazpacho Macho
GAZPACHO LACED WITH TEQUILA

There's a pronounced Mexican bravado to this Spanish favorite—it's like eating spicy salsa with a spoon. It's zesty and refreshing, and it's even better when you substitute homemade *sangrita* for the tomato juice. Serve it chilled with shots of ice-cold tequila and condiment bowls of avocado chunks, boiled or grilled shrimp, lime wedges, chopped cilantro, and tostada chips.

- 4 large, vine-ripened tomatoes (about 2 pounds), seeded and chopped, or equivalent cherry and pear tomatoes
- 1 yellow bell pepper, seeded and diced
- 1 red bell pepper, seeded and diced
- 4 cloves garlic, minced
- 2–4 serrano peppers, seeded and minced
- 2 unpeeled hothouse cucumbers
- 6 green onions, diced with tops
- 1 medium red onion, diced
- ½ teaspoon each: freshly ground allspice, black peppercorns, and coriander seeds
- 3 cups chilled tomato juice or Sangrita
- 3 or more tablespoons fresh lime juice
- 1 cup chilled 100% tequila *blanco* or *reposado*
- 5 tablespoons sherry vinegar
- Your favorite Cantina Classic Seasoned Salt (like Sal de Sangrita) or commercial brand to taste
- 4 tablespoons finely chopped fresh cilantro
- 3 tablespoons finely chopped fresh basil
- 4 tablespoons extra virgin olive oil

Chop and dice vegetables by hand and place in a large bowl. Add remaining ingredients, whisking in olive oil last. Chill at least 6 hours or overnight. Adjust flavors, adding more vinegar, lime juice, salt, or freshly chopped herbs, if needed . . . and of course, *más* tequila! *Makes about 10 cups.*

Note: If you prefer a smoother consistency, briefly purée gazpacho in blender or food processor, but reserve some of the diced vegetables to add for texture.

Gazpacho del Sol
GOLDEN GAZPACHO SPIKED WITH TEQUILA

The flavors of this summer soup linger like the memory of a tropical vacation. For a special first-course presentation, dip rims of chilled goblets into Cantina Classic Spicy Mexican Seasoned Salt, fill with golden gazpacho, and garnish with a slice of star fruit. Served as a chilled compote sprinkled with toasted coconut, alongside cinnamon tostadas (see Note), it makes a splendid summertime dessert.

- ½ ripe pineapple, peeled, cored, and diced (about 3 cups)
- ½ ripe cantaloupe or small honeydew melon, diced (about 3 cups)
- 1 large golden bell pepper, diced
- 2 Granny Smith apples, diced
- 1 large mango (or 2 nectarines), finely chopped
- 2 or more serranos, minced
- 1 tablespoon fresh ginger, minced
- 2 teaspoons lemon zest
- 4 or more tablespoons fresh lime juice
- 1 cup chilled 100% tequila *blanco* or Pineapple-Infused Tequila
- 2–3 cups chilled pineapple juice
- ½ teaspoon freshly ground white pepper
- Cantina Classic Spicy Seasoned Salt like Hibiscus Flower and Orange Zest, to taste
- Citrus Syrup or light agave syrup to taste, optional
- Garnishes: finely chopped jícama drizzled with fresh lime juice, mild chile powder, lime wedges, fresh mint, toasted coconut, slices of star fruit, cinnamon tostadas

Dice fruits and vegetables by hand and place in a large bowl. Stir in remaining ingredients, adding more pineapple juice as needed. Chill at least 6 hours, or overnight. Since fruit flavor varies, taste to adjust the balance of sweet and acidic—add more tequila, syrup, or lime juice as needed. *Makes about 10 cups.*

Note: For cinnamon tostada chips, follow recipe on page 204, using flour, instead of corn tortillas. Sprinkle with cinnamon sugar after frying.

¡Qué Fresa! Con un Beso de Tequila
STRAWBERRY GAZPACHO WITH A KISS OF TEQUILA

Sue Simms, friend and fabulous cook, created this refreshing recipe to serve on blistering days at her San Angelo ranch. Its rosy, vibrant splash of summertime colors makes it a lovely treat for lunch . . . or breakfast! Adding tequila *blanco* enhances the citrus and strawberry flavors—better yet, add some strawberry-infused tequila. Serve for brunch in chilled goblets garnished with fresh strawberries, accompanied by cinnamon tostadas for dessert, or as a delightful first course for grilled salmon.

- 1 quart fresh, ripe strawberries, hulled, quartered, and chopped
- 4 navel or blood oranges, peeled (all white pith removed) and chopped
- ½ cup celery, minced
- 1 large red bell pepper, finely chopped
- 6 red ripe Roma tomatoes, seeded and chopped
- 2 or more fresh red-ripened Fresnos or jalapeños, minced
- 1 cup chilled tequila *blanco* or Cantina Classic Strawberry-Infused Tequila
- 2 tablespoons fresh lime juice
- 2 tablespoons balsamic vinegar
- 2 teaspoons grated orange zest
- 2–3 cups freshly squeezed orange juice
- 2 tablespoons fresh mint, finely chopped
- Splash Cantina Classic Citrus Syrup or light agave syrup, optional
- Cantina Classic Pink Peppercorn Citrus Salt to taste
- Garnishes: whole fresh strawberries, cinnamon tostada chips, lime wedges, mint sprigs, edible flowers

Mix ingredients together and chill for at least 6 hours. Add more fresh orange juice and tequila if thinner texture is desired. Since fruit varies in flavor and ripeness, adjust ingredients for a balance of sweet and tart. Sprinkle with seasoned salt before serving. *Makes about 10 cups.*

Platos Fuertes

THE MAIN ATTRACTIONS

P ART OF THE FUN of party fare is its presentation. A bottle of tequila frozen in ice (p. 130) or a party punch brimming with surprises certainly animates conversation. Likewise, dishes accompanied by bowls of festive garnishes and condiments inspire creativity and encourage guests to participate in making their own meal.

I like to have fun at my parties, so I often serve food that can be made in advance, leaving me free to mingle with my guests. The following dishes have tequila drinks and fiestas in mind. Serve them as main courses, buffet style, or as small-plate appetizers.

Salpicón Norteño
SPICY SHREDDED BEEF IN CHIPOTLE MARINADE

This is a nostalgic recipe for me. While living in El Paso in the 1960s, we gaily crossed the border to Julio's Café Corona in Juárez just to eat *salpicón* and sip limey, hand-shaken, tequila-laden margaritas . . . and sing with the mariachis. The restaurant has since moved to El Paso, as tourists rarely venture across the Rio Grande anymore.

Salpicón is a fiesta in itself! Its name is derived from the Spanish word for "splash." Indeed, this chilled, spicy marinated beef dish is flecked with color: chopped tomatoes, red onions, cilantro, bite-sized cubes of avocado, cubes of creamy white cheese, and smoky strips of brick-red chipotle peppers. (You'll love it made with bison or venison roasts, too.) Easy on the host, it tastes better made a day ahead, then served at room temperature. Mound it on a platter, garnish festively, and let guests scoop it onto crispy tostadas or warm corn tortillas. It's always a party favorite!

RECIPE CONTINUED ON NEXT PAGE

Spiked Chipotle Sauce:
- 1 7-ounce can *chipotles en adobo* sauce
- 3 tablespoons tequila *reposado*
- 1 tablespoon red wine vinegar
- 2 cloves garlic, minced
- Pinch of salt

Mix ingredients together in a bowl, leaving whole chipotles intact. Set aside, stirring occasionally.

Beef:
- 2 pounds flank steak (or venison or bison roast; see Note)
- 3 cloves garlic, minced
- Salt and pepper
- 1 tablespoon olive oil
- 4 cups beef stock
- 3 bay leaves
- 1 white onion, peeled and quartered, each quarter studded with 2 cloves
- 2 carrots, quartered
- 1½ teaspoons whole *comino* seeds
- 1 teaspoon whole peppercorns
- ¼ teaspoon whole allspice berries
- 3 dried New Mexico red chiles
- 2 teaspoons crushed Mexican oregano
- 1 teaspoon salt

Marinade
- 3 cloves garlic, minced
- ½ teaspoon ground *comino*
- ¼ teaspoon ground black pepper
- 1 teaspoon dried Mexican oregano, crumbled
- 2 tablespoons tequila *reposado*
- 3 tablespoons lime juice
- 2 tablespoons red wine vinegar
- ½ teaspoon salt
- 3 tablespoons reserved Spiked Chipotle Sauce
- 2 or more whole spiked chipotles, chopped (from the Spiked Chipotle Sauce)
- 5 tablespoons olive oil

Chopped ingredients
- 1 large white onion, chopped
- ½ pound Monterey Jack cheese (or Pepper Jack), cut into ½-inch cubes
- 6 Roma tomatoes, chopped, salted and drained
- ¾ cup chopped cilantro
- Lots of freshly squeezed lime juice to taste
- Salt to taste
- 2–3 avocados, cut into small cubes and drizzled with fresh lime juice
- Garnishes: reserved spiked chopped chipotles, red onion rings, cilantro sprigs, yucca blossoms, tostada chips

Cooking the meat: Rinse flank steak and pat dry. Generously rub meat with garlic, salt, and pepper. Heat olive oil in a 3-quart Dutch oven. Sear meat for about 5–7 minutes on each side. Cover with stock, adding bay leaves, onion, carrots, spices, chiles, oregano, and salt. Bring to boil, then reduce heat. Simmer gently for approx. 1½–2 hours, turning once, until meat is tender. Allow to cool in stock for 20 minutes. Cut into 2-inch pieces (reserve broth for other uses) and shred, discarding any fat or membrane.

Preparing the marinade: Mix ingredients in a bowl, except for the olive oil. Drizzle it in last while whisking to incorporate. Adjust seasonings if necessary. Reserve extra chipotles/sauce.

Marinating the beef: Place shredded beef in a large marinating dish with chopped onion. Toss with the marinade; cover and chill for 6 hours or overnight, turning occasionally. A few hours before serving, add cheese, chopped tomatoes, and cilantro. Drizzle with fresh lime juice, salt, and toss gently. Keep chilled.

To serve: Remove *salpicón* from refrigerator 30 minutes before serving. Gently toss in avocado chunks. Mound *salpicón* in the center of a platter, adding remaining garnishes around and on top of meat in a decorative pattern. Serve tostadas and/or warm tortillas on the side. Serve any remaining spiked chipotles at the table.

Note: Make *salpicón* with boneless shoulder of venison or buffalo flank instead of flank steak. You will need to cook it longer, and add more olive oil when searing meat.

Pollo Borrachito
ROASTED CHICKEN IN DRUNKEN CHILE SAUCE

This roasted chicken is rubbed with Salsa Borracha, and its cavity is stuffed with oranges, onion, a tequila-spiked chile salsa, and fresh herbs, making it moist and succulent. Carve at the table (hot or cold) or shred from the bone to use in tacos, salads, or sandwiches. For a fiesta, mound shredded Pollo Borrachito on a platter surrounded by orange slices and cilantro sprigs and accompany with a bowl of Salsa Borracha for guests to scoop into warm tortillas or mound atop crispy tostadas.

The chicken:
- 1 whole chicken, 3–4 pounds
- ⅓ cup Salsa Borracha
- ½ teaspoon whole *comino* seeds
- 3–4 cloves garlic, cut into slivers
- Generous handful of fresh oregano, cilantro, Mexican marigold mint, marjoram, and/or thyme sprigs
- 1 orange, cut into wedges
- 1 white onion, cut into wedges
- 3 or more whole dried red *chiles colorados* or *guajillos*, optional
- Salt and freshly ground pepper to taste
- Paprika

Preheat oven to 450 degrees. Rinse chicken and pat dry. Rub Salsa Borracha generously inside cavity of chicken and under skin, then lightly all over. Insert *comino* seeds, garlic slivers, and some of the herb sprigs in various places under the skin of the chicken. Stuff remaining herb sprigs, orange, onion wedges, and whole chiles into the chicken's cavity. Sprinkle chicken liberally with salt, freshly ground pepper, and paprika.

Place on a foil-lined baking pan in the middle of the oven; reduce heat to 350-degrees. Bake for about 1 hour, basting every 15 minutes until chicken is tender. *Serves 4 as an entree, 8–10 shredded as an appetizer.*

Note: To prevent irritation from the chiles, wrap your hand in a plastic bag before rubbing chicken with salsa.

Albóndigas de Búfalo Borracho SPICY BISON
MEATBALLS WITH TEQUILA DIPPING SAUCES

The tequila in bison, or *búfalo* (buffalo), meatballs adds a kick to this dish. At your next fiesta, offer these tasty tidbits (a healthy red meat alternative) for dunking in one (or more) of your favorite tequila-spiked dipping sauces (see Note). Try them as "sliders," formed into mini-patties, instead of meatballs, and sandwiched between cornbread or sourdough biscuits. Or substitute for fatty sausage at breakfast or brunch.

- ⅓ cup dried cranberries or cherries
- 3 tablespoons tequila *reposado*
- ¼ teaspoon each whole allspice berries and black peppercorns
- ½ teaspoon whole *comino*
- 1–2 dried red *chiles de árbol*
- 1½ tablespoons olive oil
- ¾ cup chopped red onion
- 3 cloves garlic
- 1 pound ground bison
- ½ cup tostada chips, crushed medium-finely in a food processor or with a rolling pin
- 1 large egg, beaten
- ¼ teaspoon salt
- ⅛ teaspoon cinnamon
- 3 tablespoons combination of Cantina Garden fresh herbs (such as cilantro, mint, sage, rosemary, mint marigold)
- Oil for cooking

Plump cranberries (or cherries) in tequila and set aside. Grind whole spices and chiles in a spice grinder and set aside. Heat oil in heavy skillet and cook onions and garlic until translucent, but not browned. Allow to cool.

In a bowl, combine bison meat, cooked onion/garlic mixture, tostada chips, beaten egg, ground spices, salt, cinnamon, and fresh herbs. Drain the plumped cranberries (reserve liquid) and coarsely chop. Mix ingredients together, but do not overwork. With dampened hands, pat meat gently between palms to compress slightly, then roll into balls or small patties.

Heat 1 tablespoon olive oil in a cast-iron skillet. In 2 batches, cook meatballs on all sides, until lightly browned yet still slightly pink inside (about 8–9 minutes). Or heat them on a greased baking sheet in a 350-degree oven for about 15 minutes, turning once. *Makes 20 bite-sized meatballs or about 10 small patties.*

Note: These all make delectable dipping sauces: Smoky Chipotle Pesto, Chimichurri Rojo, Drunken Sugarplum Chutney, or Tequila-Spiked Jalapeño Jelly Glaze. Serve chunky salsas frescas as condiments and side attractions.

Chiles en Serapes TEQUILA-MARINATED BEEF WRAPPED AROUND ROASTED GREEN CHILES

Mexicans sometimes wrap woven cotton or wool *serapes* (blanket-like shawls) around their shoulders for warmth. In this recipe, tender tequila-marinated beef (or boneless chicken breasts) wraps around whole roasted Hatch or Anaheim green chiles or *poblanos* stuffed with grated cheese and chopped green onions. Quickly seared on both sides, the tender meat is enhanced by the flavor of the roasted chile and creamy melted cheese and makes a wonderful special entrée dish. Serve Chiles en Serapes with Frijoles Borrachos a La Charra, or your favorite beans and guacamole, or accompanied by Mango and Pineapple Tropicana Salsa mounded in a corn husk boat (p. 220).

Roast chiles, marinate meat, and grate cheese several hours in advance, so that only last-minute cooking is required. This recipe may be assembled several hours before serving and stored, covered, in the refrigerator until you're ready to grill.

- 3 boneless New York strip steaks (approx. ¾ pound each), well trimmed, butterflied, and split to make 6 servings (or chicken breasts; see Note)
- 4 cloves garlic, minced
- Salt and pepper to taste

For the rub:
- 1 teaspoon whole *comino*
- ¼ teaspoon black peppercorns
- 1–2 dried *chiles de árbol*, optional
- 2 tablespoons pure mild chile powder or paprika
- 1 tablespoon tequila *reposado*

For the marinade:
- 2 cloves garlic, minced
- 2 tablespoons tequila *reposado*
- 2 tablespoons red wine vinegar
- 1 tablespoon fresh lime juice
- ½ teaspoon dried oregano
- 4 green onions, chopped
- 2 tablespoons cilantro, finely chopped
- 3 tablespoons olive oil
- Salt and pepper to taste

For the chiles:
- 6 New Mexico or Anaheim peppers or *poblanos*, roasted and peeled, with stems left intact (p. 208)
- 1 cup grated *queso blanco*, Monterey or Pepper Jack, or Colby
- 6 green onions, chopped

Rub each piece of beef on both sides with the minced garlic and sprinkle with salt and pepper.

Grind the *comino*, peppercorns, and dried chile in a spice grinder. Mix with the chile powder and drizzle in tequila (add a bit more, if you like). Divide the rub evenly among the 6 pieces of steak, rubbing onto both sides with the back of a spoon.

Combine ingredients for the marinade, whisking in the olive oil last. Put meat in a glass dish (or resealable plastic bag), cover with the marinade, and chill for at least 4 hours, or overnight, turning occasionally.

Carefully make a slit in each roasted chile and remove some of the seeds. Stuff with about 2 tablespoons grated cheese and 1 chopped green onion. Fold a piece of steak over each chile (secure with a pick if necessary), leaving the stem and the tip of the chile exposed. Broil chiles under a preheated broiler 4 inches from the flame, sear on a hot griddle, or grill for about 3–4 minutes each side. Serve immediately. *Serves 6.*

Note: Try substituting 6 boneless, skinless chicken breasts—lightly pounded to ¼-inch thickness—for the steak. Wrap them (starting with the small end) around the chiles and bake seam side down and in a lightly oiled pan (cover loosely with foil) in a preheated 350-degree oven for about 18 minutes, browning them the last few minutes under the broiler.

Poblanos are generally larger than Anaheim peppers, and you may need only use ½ per serving, folding it tightly around the cheese filling.

Pozole Colorado Estilo Tapatío

JALISCO'S BELOVED PORK AND HOMINY STEW WITH RED CHILE

Like the Mexican flag, red, white, and green versions of this hearty hominy stew are found throughout Jalisco, colored and flavored with various chiles, herbs, and vegetables. Oscar Alvarez, head cook at Austin's renowned Fonda San Miguel restaurant for nearly thirty years, shared his recipe with me.

You'll probably be pleased that we left out the traditional pig's head and feet, and used chicken broth instead of boiling a big fat hen, and canned hominy, instead of cooking dried corn kernels with powdered lime.

Pozole is a feast in itself, filling and flavorful. It's always served at the table with little bowls of condiments: dried oregano, cilantro, crushed *chile pequín*, sliced radishes, chopped onions, and shredded cabbage or lettuce. And, of course, sipping tequila and listening to mariachi music is a must!

Pork:
- 2 tablespoons vegetable oil
- 1 pound pork butt or shoulder, fat removed, cut into bite-size pieces
- 1 medium white onion, chopped
- 3 cloves garlic, chopped

Chile sauce:
- 6–8 dried red chiles such as *guajillo*, *puya*, or New Mexico dried red chiles
- ¼ white onion, loosely chopped
- 2 cloves garlic
- Salt to taste

Pozole stew:
- 6 cups rich, homemade chicken broth
- 1 15-ounce can white hominy (pozole), drained
- Salt and pepper

Condiments:
- 4 limes, cut in quarters
- ½ cup white onion, chopped
- 3 tablespoons dried oregano
- ½ cup chopped cilantro
- 12 radishes, grated or thinly sliced
- ⅓ green cabbage, shredded
- 2 tablespoons ground *chile pequín* or *chile de árbol*

To cook the pork, heat oil in a soup pot; add pork, onion, and garlic. Cook for 20 minutes on medium-low heat, stirring often. Meanwhile, make chile sauce.

On a hot griddle, toast chiles on both sides for just a few seconds; do not burn or they will taste bitter. Remove stems, veins, and seeds. Soak in enough hot water to cover for 20 minutes, until softened. Grind in blender with onion, garlic, and enough of the soaking water to make a slightly thick sauce, seasoning with salt. Strain to remove bits of chile skin (only if necessary) and set aside.

Add broth, hominy, salt, pepper, and chile sauce mixture to pork. Bring to slow boil; reduce heat and simmer, partially covered, for another 30 minutes, or until meat is tender. Serve in warmed bowls with a selection of condiments.

Camarones a la Diabla CHILE-SEARED SHRIMP

These devilishly delicious shrimp, seared in a fiery red chile salsa, are easy to make and can be presented in many ways. Serve them right out of the hot skillet—pick shrimp up by the tail and dunk in the spicy sauce. Top black bean nachos with them for appetizers, accompany them with rice and beans for a main course, or ladle them over pasta, garnished with crumbled *queso fresco* and chopped cilantro.

For the best quesadilla, loosely chop the chile-seared shrimp and add as filling to a folded corn tortilla with grated Jack cheese; heat on a hot griddle until cheese melts. It's one of my favorite quick meals, especially when accompanied with a side of Nopalitos Borrachos and a shot of agave spirits.

Jalisco's popular bottled Salsa Valentina (see Note), readily available in Latin American markets, and a good splash of tequila (or mezcal, which imparts its characteristic smoky flavor), have shrimp dancing with the devil in the frying pan.

Salsa:
- 3 cloves garlic
- ¼ white onion (reserve the rest)
- ½ teaspoon dried Mexican oregano
- 1 teaspoon *comino*, freshly ground
- 2 *chiles de árbol*, ground, optional
- 8 or more ounces mild or hot Salsa Valentina, your choice
- 3 tablespoons mezcal or tequila *reposado*

Chile-seared shrimp:
- 1½ pounds medium shrimp, peeled, deveined, with tails intact
- Salt and pepper
- 3 tablespoons oil
- ¾ (remaining) white onion, sliced *media luna* (in half wedges)
- 4–6 cloves garlic, loosely chopped
- 3 bay leaves
- 1 teaspoon Mexican oregano
- 4 tablespoons ketchup
- 2 tablespoons mezcal or tequila *reposado*
- Garnishes: chopped cilantro, fresh lime juice

For salsa

In a blender, combine salsa ingredients and purée to a thickened sauce. Set aside.

For shrimp

Toss shrimp generously with salt and pepper. Heat oil in a large cast-iron skillet. Add onions and cook until translucent. Mix in garlic, but do not brown. Add shrimp, bay leaves, and oregano. Cook over medium-high heat for 3–4 minutes, shaking pan and tossing shrimp. Remove shrimp, onions, and garlic with a slotted spoon. Set aside, cover and keep warm.

If needed, add a bit more oil to the pan. When hot, add prepared salsa; simmer on medium heat for 7 minutes, stirring often. Add ketchup and mezcal or tequila toward the end of cooking.

Return shrimp to pan and cook a few minutes, until shrimp are smothered in the sauce. Sprinkle with fresh lime juice and cilantro.

Note: Salsa Valentina comes in two styles. The yellow label is milder than the extra-hot black label. Salsa Tamazula, a similar brand, may be substituted.

Camarones Cantineros

BARTENDER'S SHRIMP SAUTÉED WITH
SUMMER TOMATOES AND BASIL

It's summertime and 103 degrees in Texas. I wish I were on my father's fishing boat off the coast of Guaymas, in the state of Sonora, where we used to buy shrimp right off the boats in the middle of the Gulf of Mexico. Instead, I'll:

+ Play Linda Ronstadt's *Canciones de Mi Padre* (*Songs of My Father*) to hear her sing "La Barca de Guaymas" ("The Boat from Guaymas").
+ Take out my favorite cast-iron skillet and cook some shrimp.
+ Pour some tequila—some for the chef, some for the shrimp, and some to toast my father.
+ Make an ice-cold Sirena's Splash to sip with the shrimp.

In this easy summertime recipe, red, orange, and yellow cherry tomatoes from the farmer's market, fresh basil, and fragrant spices mix it up with the shrimp. Orange zest, capers, and tequila add bright flavors, too. Eat it by the bowlful or as an appetizer on small plates, hot or at room temperature. Make sure each serving has some "pot liquor" in which to dunk warm, crusty *bolillos* (Mexican rolls) or *crostini* made from the *bolillos*. Enjoy the shrimp over rice or pasta, too. Prep all ingredients before you begin this quick sauté.

- 1 pound shrimp, deveined, peeled, with stem intact (see Note)
- Cantina Classic Sal de Sangrita or salt, pepper, and cayenne (in a pinch)
- 1 pint fresh orange, yellow, and red cherry or pear tomatoes, quartered, lightly salted, and drained in a colander
- 4 tablespoons tequila *reposado*

- Juice and zest of 1 navel orange
- 2 tablespoons olive oil
- ¾ white onion, cut into *media lunas* (half wedges)
- 1 tablespoon dried marjoram, crumbled
- 3 bay leaves, preferably fresh
- 1 teaspoon thyme
- 4 cloves garlic, chopped finely
- 3 or more whole dried cayenne or *chiles de árbol*
- 3 tablespoons butter
- Big handful chiffonade of fresh basil and/or cilantro sprigs
- 1 bunch green onions, chopped
- 3 tablespoons capers

Sprinkle Sal de Sangrita generously on both sides of shrimp and set aside.

Drain tomatoes in a colander.

Combine tequila with orange juice and zest and set aside.

Heat olive oil in a large skillet over medium-high heat. Add onions; cook for 3 minutes, seasoning with the herbs. Add garlic and cayenne. Reduce heat and sauté for 2 minutes without burning.

Add butter to pan and turn up heat. Sear shrimp on both sides. Add tequila/orange mixture; toss with shrimp. Cook shrimp until they turn bright pink, taking care not to overcook them. (4–5 minutes cooking time total). Toss in tomatoes, fresh basil, green onions, and capers at the end. *Serves 4 (or more as appetizer).*

Note: Use fresh herbs (fresh lemon thyme sprigs are lovely) whenever possible instead of dried; allow 3–4 times more fresh herbs than dried. Try using Citrus- or Chile-Infused Tequila in this dish. Using unpeeled shrimp gives added flavor, but guests must peel them at the table and eat with their hands, and it's messy.

Pescado Margarita

GRILLED FISH WITH SASSY CITRUS TEQUILA VINAIGRETTE

Why marinate fish? It can get soggy, and you discard most of the marinade anyway. Instead, drizzle grilled, baked, or pan-seared fish with this tangy reduction vinaigrette at the table. Serve Pescado Margarita as a main course, or flake it for fish tacos or tostadas, along with shredded cabbage, red onions, and cilantro. Sometimes I also offer Javier's Salsa de Aguacate for drizzling on the seafood at the table.

Sassy Citrus Tequila Vinaigrette:
- ½ teaspoon orange zest
- ½ teaspoon lemon zest
- ½ cup fresh orange juice
- ¼ cup fresh lemon juice
- 3 tablespoons tequila *reposado*
- 2 tablespoons shallots, minced
- 1 teaspoon coriander seeds, freshly ground in a spice grinder
- ¼ or more teaspoon cayenne (or ½ teaspoon paprika)
- 2–3 tablespoons olive or grapeseed oil
- Salt and pepper
- Fresh lime juice to taste
- 1–2 teaspoons agave syrup, optional
- 1 green onion, chopped

Zest citrus and reserve. Squeeze fresh juice. In a small saucepan, combine citrus juices, tequila, shallots, ground coriander, and cayenne. Simmer until reduced by half, about 10 minutes. Cool for 5 minutes before adding zest. Pour into a small bowl. When cool, whisk in olive oil, season with salt and pepper and a squeeze of fresh lime juice, and sweeten with agave syrup, if needed. Sprinkle with green onions before serving. Pass a small plate of lime wedges at the table. *Makes about ½ cup.*

Note: Though coriander is the seed of the cilantro plant, it's citrusy and spicy, not pungent and strong like cilantro.

Variations: Use avocado oil instead of olive oil for a lighter flavor. Replace shallot with grated ginger, and substitute pineapple juice for the orange juice.

Tacos al Pastor and Carne Adobado
PORK IN RED CHILE ADOBADO SAUCE

Jalisco is a rich pork-producing state, and many of its inhabitants love to eat as much as they love to drink tequila! They frequent roadside eateries just to eat *carnitas*, succulent morsels of pork simmered in huge copper cauldrons of bubbling lard. Crispy on the outside, yet tender and moist inside, they taste surprisingly ungreasy. Strolling mariachis and tequila are often added accompaniments (as are tortillas, chopped onions, *salsita*, and cilantro.)

Jaliscans also stand hungrily in lines meandering around the block awaiting their fill of irresistible pork *taquitos*. Street vendors carve chile-marinated *al pastor* (shepherd's style pork) from vertical rotisseries called *trompos* because they resemble huge slowly spinning toy tops. Sometimes, a big chunk of skewered pineapple drips its juices over the meat as it roasts. With swift slashes from a sharp knife, tender slices fall onto corn tortillas, garnished with chopped onions, cilantro, homemade fiery *salsa taquera*, and a squeeze of fresh lime juice.

Other cooks simply marinate chunks (or slabs) of *puerco* (pork) in *adobo*, a brick-red chile marinade, cooking it *a la parrilla* (on a hot griddle or grill). Today, tacos made in this manner are often also called *tacos al pastor*, even though they are not made in the traditional *trompo* style.

Countless versions of *carne adobado* appear on restaurant menus, flavored with each cook's personal touch. Latin American markets here even sell already marinated cubed pork to take home to cook. Often, *achiote* paste (made from ground annatto seeds from Yucatán) is added to give the meat a bright red color. Some may add fresh pineapple to the recipe (see Variations), though I omit *achiote* and pineapple in this more traditional Jalisco recipe.

Jaliscans mound *carne adobado* upon crisp corn tostadas layered with refried beans, shredded cabbage, sliced radishes, crumbled *queso fresco*, chopped onions, and avocado wedges, topped with hot sauce.

These *tostadas tapatías* will be a hit at your table, too. The meat is also delicious in warm corn tortillas with the same condiments. Look for smaller, coaster-sized corn tortillas—because you will want to eat so many of them! (Layer two per serving, so tortilla won't fall apart with the warm, moist meat and sauce.)

Many cooks guard their recipes for *adobo*—not disclosing their blend of spices, chiles, and seasonings. What's my secret? Tequila, of course! It balances flavors of piquant chiles and pungent spices. I've never heard mention of Jalisco cooks adding tequila to their *adobos*. Perhaps it's their secret ingredient, too? Here's a recipe that's easily accessible for home cooks.

Pork:
- 2 pounds pork shoulder or butt, cut into bite-sized pieces

Adobo sauce:
- 6 *guajillo* chiles or New Mexico dried red chiles
- 4 *puya* chiles
- 3 ancho or *pasilla* chiles
- 3–4 dried *chiles de árbol* or cayenne or dried *chile pequín* to taste (optional, for added fire)
- 1½ cups boiling water

Adobo spice blend:
Grind in a spice grinder:
- 1 teaspoon *comino*
- 4 whole cloves
- ¼ teaspoon allspice berries
- 1 teaspoon whole coriander seeds
- ¼ teaspoon black peppercorns

Other ingredients for adobo sauce:
- 2 medium tomatoes
- 1 white onion, quartered
- 4 cloves whole peeled garlic
- 1 teaspoon Mexican oregano, crushed
- ¼ teaspoon best quality ground cinnamon
- 2 crumbled fresh bay leaves
- 1 cup orange juice with pulp
- ½ cup apple cider vinegar
- 4 tablespoons tequila *reposado*
- 1 teaspoon salt
- Brown sugar or *piloncillo* to taste, optional
- Vegetable oil
- 1 white onion, cut into *media lunas* (half wedges)
- Salt and pepper

Condiments:
- Bowls of chopped white onion and cilantro, quartered limes, *salsa taquera* (your favorite table hot sauce for tacos)

Rinse and dry chiles. Remove stems; make a slit down each chile to remove seeds, and pull out veins. Flatten chiles on a *comal* or griddle with a spatula and heat for about 5 seconds on each side to release flavor. Take caution not to burn them or they will taste bitter. Tear chiles into large pieces and place in a bowl with enough boiling water to cover them; soak for about 20 minutes, turning occasionally.

Roast tomatoes, onion, and garlic on the hot griddle until lightly charred on all sides.

In a blender, grind chiles and enough of their soaking water (reserve any extra) to make a thick purée. Add tomatoes, onion, garlic, ground spices, oregano, cinnamon, and bay leaves, along with the orange juice and vinegar and tequila. Blend ingredients, adding more reserved chile water, if needed. Adjust flavorings, adding more crushed *árbol* or *pequín* chiles and seasonings, if needed. (Adobo *sauce should yield approx. 3 cups.*)

Place pieces of pork in a resealable plastic bag with enough *adobo* to coat the pieces well, pressing it into the meat (allow about ½–¾ cup *adobo* per pound of meat; reserve any extra; see Note). Marinate 6–24 hours, turning occasionally.

To cook pork: I like to cook this in two batches, so meat cooks evenly. *Per batch:* Heat a few teaspoons of oil on a griddle or in a large, heavy skillet, preferably cast iron. Add ½ of the onion wedges and cook briefly. Pat excess marinade from pork. Sprinkle meat with salt and pepper and add to the pan. Cook until pork is tender (20 minutes or so), adding some reserved *adobo*, if needed. Keep warm until serving. I like chunkier pieces for *tostadas tapatías*, but if you prefer, transfer pork to a cutting block and loosely chop meat for tacos.

Note: For a milder sauce, use fewer *guajillos* and more *anchos*. Use leftover *adobo* for a marinade for chicken or shrimp, or rub into pork loin before roasting. Spread it on tostadas layered with refried beans and melted *queso blanco.*

Variations: Add a cup of fresh pineapple chunks to the marinated pork as it cooks or serve small chunks of fresh pineapple as another condiment. Use pineapple juice instead of orange juice in the *adobo.*

To grill: Marinate thin slabs of lean pork loin in *adobo* and cook on a hot grill until tender, then cut into bite-sized pieces for tacos. Accompany with chunks of grilled pineapple (grill unpeeled slices, peel, then cut into chunks).

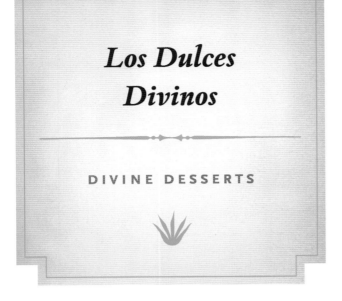

Los Dulces Divinos

DIVINE DESSERTS

*No hay mal
Que por bien no venga.*

—

*Every cloud
Has a silver lining.*

S OMETIMES A SNIFTER of fine *añejo*, an exotic tequila liqueur or a special tequila/coffee drink is dessert enough. Other times, you may long for something more. From an elegant citrus flan, to a spicy carrot cake with margarita frosting, to shot glasses filled with decadent dark chocolate *marquise* to spread on shortbread cookies, tequila shines as an unexpected ingredient.

Drink Suggestions

Snifters: *añejo* and *extra añejo*, Cantina Classic
   tequila liqueurs, Rompope (eggnog)
Shots: Kahlúa shooters or Rompope
Glasses: elegant after-dinner drinks and
   tequila nightcaps
Mugs: coffee drinks and Café del Diablo

Flan a La Tequilera

CITRUS FLAN FLAMBÉED WITH TEQUILA

This dessert is a lovely way to light up a fiesta. Turn off the lights and flambé this luscious golden flan custard at the table, delighting guests with a spectacle of blue flames ablaze in the dark. Velvety and rich, redolent of citrus and spice, it makes a splendid finale for a spicy Mexican meal. I serve it on a large platter surrounded with half-slices of oranges and lemons. Don't forget snifters of *añejo* or Ambrosia, a gingered-tequila liqueur.

- 1 cup granulated sugar for caramelizing
- 1 cup granulated sugar for flan
- 1 quart half-and-half
- Zest of 3 oranges, avoiding bitter white pith
- ¼ teaspoon salt
- ½ teaspoon mace
- 7 farm-fresh eggs
- 2 egg yolks
- 3 tablespoons tequila *añejo*
- 2 tablespoons Grand Marnier
- ½ teaspoon Mexican vanilla
- Freshly grated nutmeg
- 2 tablespoons tequila *añejo*
- Garnishes: orange and lemon slices,
   lemon-scented herbs, edible flowers

For caramelized sugar: In a small, heavy saucepan on low heat, slowly melt sugar until it dissolves. Raise heat slightly; stir gently as sugar caramelizes. When fluid and deep amber in color, pour into a 10-inch × 2-inch round (1½-quart) baking dish, swirling it around to evenly coat bottom of dish and halfway up sides. Work quickly and carefully with heavy mitts, as it is very hot! Set aside on a rack. (May also be poured into 12–14 individual ramekins.)

For flan: In a heavy pan, on medium heat, scald half-and-half with orange zest, salt, and mace. Remove from heat. Whisk eggs and yolks together in a large bowl along with the 1 cup sugar. Gradually add scalded half-and-half mixture to egg mixture, stirring gently. Add tequila, Grand Marnier, and vanilla. Strain into the caramelized dish or into ramekins (include some zest, if you wish).

Set flan dish in a *baño de María* (water bath)—a large pan with deep sides (I use a roasting pan). Pour enough hot water into the larger pan to come halfway up sides of flan dish. Bake in preheated 325-degree oven on center rack for about 1½ hours (45 minutes for ramekins). Should water begin to boil in the *baño*

de María while flan is cooking, lower oven temperature slightly to avoid air bubbles forming in the flan. It is ready when the center of the flan is gently set. Remove from oven, leaving in the water bath for about 15 minutes. Cool before covering and refrigerate overnight.

To unmold flan: Slide a knife around the rim of the flan. Set flan dish in a pan of hot water for 30 seconds to loosen it, then carefully invert onto a platter. Use a larger platter with a raised edge to prevent caramel from spilling (place the platter on top of the flan dish and quickly flip it over). Serve whole flan on a large platter and lightly sprinkle with nutmeg. Arrange a circle of thinly sliced oranges halves around the edge of the flan, overlapped with a circle of half lemon slices, edible flowers, or sprigs of lemon-scented herbs.

To flambé: In a very small, heavy saucepan, warm 2 tablespoons of tequila (do not boil!). Turn off lights and ignite tequila at the table, pouring it over the flan. *Serves 10 to 12.*

Note: Experiment using Cantina Classic tequila liqueurs instead of the tequila and Grand Marnier called for in the recipe.

Hoppin' Jalapeño

SPICY JALAPEÑO CARROT CAKE WITH
MARGARITA FROSTING

I've always been a prankster. In high school, I made chocolate cupcakes for the football team for Halloween. Randomly, I put orange jellybeans in the center of some and pickled jalapeños in others. These created a locker room frenzy, as hungry athletes scarfed them down after a game. Truly, a trick or treat! I'm sure those cupcakes inspired this whimsical recipe.

My Hoppin' Jalapeño Carrot Cake has been served at the Texas governor's mansion, weddings, and many happy celebrations. It's a surefire (no pun intended) crowd-pleasing carrot cake, hoppin' with flavors and flecked with fresh jalapeños, which offer a spicy surprise (you may find yourself adding another jalapeño each time you make it!). Classic margarita ingredients flavor the cream cheese frosting.

Both cake and frosting are best made a day ahead to enhance flavors. Frost cake just before serving. Decorate with orange and gold marigolds or calendulas (or sprinkle with their petals), lime and orange zest . . . or colorful whole jalapeños with stems. Oh, and this recipe makes delicious cupcakes, too!

Cake:
- ½ cup golden raisins
- 3 tablespoons tequila *añejo* (or fruit- or citrus-infused tequila, p. 141)
- 2 cups all-purpose flour
- 2 teaspoons baking powder
- 1 teaspoon baking soda
- ½ teaspoon salt
- 2 teaspoons cinnamon
- 1 tablespoon ground ginger
- 1 teaspoon freshly ground allspice
- 4 large eggs
- 1 cup safflower oil
- 1 cup granulated sugar
- 1 cup dark brown sugar
- 2 teaspoons coarsely grated lime zest
- 1 tablespoon coarsely grated orange zest
- 3 cups grated carrots, tightly packed
- 1 can (8 ounces) unsweetened crushed pineapple, drained
- ¾ cup sweetened coconut flakes
- 4 or more fresh jalapeños, seeded and finely chopped

Frosting:
- 8 ounces cream cheese, room temperature
- 5 tablespoons unsalted butter, room temperature
- 2 cups confectioner's sugar, sifted
- 1 tablespoon tequila *añejo*
- 1 tablespoon Grand Marnier
- 1 teaspoon lime zest
- 1 teaspoon orange zest

In a small bowl, plump raisins in tequila and set aside. Sift flour, baking powder, soda, and salt. Stir in spices and set aside. In a large bowl, beat eggs until pale yellow; add sugars and slowly mix in oil. On low speed, add dry ingredients just until blended. Fold in carrots, pineapple, plumped raisins, coconut, and jalapeños.

Pour into buttered/floured 12-cup bundt pan and bake for 55 minutes in a preheated 350-degree oven or until tester comes out clean. Cool 10 minutes before removing from pan; cool cake on rack.

Make cake a day in advance of frosting; store at room temperature, tightly covered. Once frosted, store in the refrigerator.

Frosting: In a bowl, blend cream cheese and butter until smooth. Slowly mix in sugar, tequila, orange liqueur, and lime and orange zests. Consistency will be thinner than most cream cheese frostings, so there may be some left over. (Thicken with more cream cheese if desired.) Cover and chill cake, but serve at room temperature. *Serves 12.*

Note: Add a big handful of chopped crystalized ginger to the cake. Use some red Fresno peppers instead of or in combination with the jalapeños.

Sometimes you just need a good bar. Here's one that you won't find on every corner. This "margarita" bar has the same flavorings as the famous cocktail. It sings of citrus—tart and limey, laced with tequila and a hint of Cointreau. It makes those popular overly sweet lemon bars seem mundane. Before serving, dust lightly with sifted powdered sugar and garnish festively with edible flowers *or* pass a small bowl of Cantina Classic Pink Peppercorn and Citrus Salt.

Fair warning: don't even *think* about tasting just a wee bite from the corner of the pan while it's still hot. You'll want to eat the entire pan! Friend and recipe tester Kristina Wolter scoops it, while warm, into small ramekins. She says the first bite hits you like the first sip of a freshly made margarita . . . with the added richness of a chess pie.

Shortbread crust:
- 1 cup flour
- 1 tablespoon fine-grind cornmeal (for some crunch), optional
- ¼ cup plus 1 tablespoon confectioner's sugar
- 1 tablespoon grated orange (or Minneola tangelo) zest
- ½ cup chilled unsalted butter, cut into small pieces
- ¼ teaspoon salt

Tequila-lime filling:
- 1 cup granulated sugar
- 3 tablespoons flour
- Pinch of salt
- 3 large eggs
- ⅓ cup freshly squeezed key lime juice
- 1 tablespoon grated Persian lime zest (or orange or lemon) without any bitter white pith
- 2 tablespoons tequila *reposado*
- 2 tablespoons Cointreau
- Garnishes: purple Johnny-jump-ups, pansies, mint or lemon verbena sprigs, raspberries, or blueberries

Preheat oven to 350, with rack in center. Butter an 8 × 8-inch pan (or line with parchment or foil).

Crust: In a food processor, pulse dry ingredients and zest for crust. Add butter and salt and briefly pulse until mixture resembles coarse crumbs. Press evenly onto the bottom of the pan and just slightly up the sides (sides should not be too thick). Bake for 18–20 minutes, until edges are lightly golden brown. Cool on a rack while you make the tequila lime filling.

Filling: Mix dry ingredients together in a bowl. Beat eggs in a bowl with an electric mixer until thick and golden; mix in dry ingredients. Scrape down the sides as you mix in the lime juice and zest, tequila, and Cointreau.

Lower oven temperature to 325 degrees. Pour filling over warm crust and bake for about 20 minutes or until filling has set in the center. Take caution not to overcook the crust or the filling.

Cool on rack. Cut into bars and sprinkle lightly with sifted powdered sugar, if you wish. They taste best served the day they are made and look lovely garnished with purple Johnny-jump-ups or other edible flowers. *Makes 16 bars.*

Tipsy Toronja Pie
RUBY GRAPEFRUIT CHIFFON PIE

Ruby grapefruit and tequila partner perfectly in many drinks (see Atotonilco's Chatazo cooler, or Jalisco's much-loved Paloma spritzer)—and also in dessert. Each bite of this chiffon pie melts in your mouth— an ethereal way to end an evening, especially after a spicy Mexican meal. Make this when Texas Rio Star grapefruit are in season, garnishing the pie with ruby grapefruit segments.

Crust:
- 1¼ cups crushed graham crackers
- 2 teaspoons grapefruit zest, coarsely grated (without white pith)
- 1 tablespoon granulated sugar
- 5 tablespoons butter, melted

Pie filling:
- 1 envelope unflavored gelatin
- 1½ cups fresh ruby red grapefruit juice, unstrained, with seeds removed
- ½ cup plus 2 tablespoons sugar
- 2 teaspoons grapefruit zest, grated without white pith
- Pinch of salt
- 3 eggs, separated
- 3 tablespoons premium tequila *blanco*
- 1 tablespoon fresh lime juice
- ½ pint whipping cream
- 1–2 tablespoons sugar
- Garnishes: ruby red grapefruit segments, curls of grapefruit peel, edible flowers, herb sprigs, citrus leaves

Crust: In a bowl, mix together crust ingredients. Press evenly with the back of a spoon into bottom and partially up sides of a 9½-inch glass pie pan. Chill for 15 minutes in the refrigerator. Bake in a preheated 350-degree oven for 8 minutes or until crust is lightly browned. Cool on a rack.

Pie: Soften gelatin in grapefruit juice. In a small, heavy saucepan, combine grapefruit mixture with ½ cup sugar, zest, and salt. Heat to near boiling, stirring constantly. Remove from heat. Lightly beat egg yolks in a bowl. Slowly spoon several tablespoons of the hot mixture into the yolks, before returning yolks to saucepan. Heat on low for one minute, stirring gently.

Remove from heat; add tequila and lime juice. Mixture should be tart and full-flavored but not too sour (add a bit more sugar, or agave syrup, if needed). Pour into a chilled stainless steel bowl and chill until mixture mounds on a spoon, approx. 1 hour.

In a chilled bowl, whip the cream until it forms soft mounds, adding remaining sugar, depending upon tartness of grapefruit mixture. Set aside.

In another bowl with clean beaters, beat egg whites with a pinch of salt until stiff peaks form. In a large bowl, fold whipped cream and egg whites into grapefruit mixture. Turn into crust. Refrigerate for at least 6 hours or overnight. Garnish and serve on chilled plates. *Serves 8–10.*

Note: Sometimes I substitute blood orange or tangerine juice/zest for the grapefruit, decreasing sugar slightly.

¿Cuál es la diferencia entre un hombre guapo y un feo?
¡Tres copitas!

—

What is the difference between a handsome man and one who is not?
Three shots!

Chocolate and tequila make a happy marriage. Imagine: a dollop of thick, dark, creamy chocolate *marquise* and a melt-in-your-mouth shortbread cookie. Accompany it with a sip of *añejo* . . . and it's a fine romance!

You'll find this dessert is a celebration in itself, a fun and interactive ending to a meal. Friends sit around the table, toasting one another with shots of *añejo*, as each guest decides whether to spread the decadent *marquise* on a cookie or eat it by the spoonful with a cookie on the side. Or will they sprinkle a few flakes of sea salt, pinched from a bowl passed around the table, on the chocolate to temper its richness? Animated conversation will ensue!

You'll need two shot glasses for each serving and a demitasse spoon or small spreader. Present each guest with one shot glass filled with *marquise* and another with your favorite tequila *añejo*. Accompany with two or three cookies per person on a dessert plate. Encourage guests to eat a small spoonful of the chocolate or spread it atop each cookie. A sip of *añejo*, a taste of dark chocolate, and the love story begins!

I was inspired to create this recipe when I tasted an unforgettable dessert at Fino, a restaurant in Austin, prepared by their pastry chef Erin Echternach. Her chocolate *marquise*—at once reminiscent of a sumptuous truffle and a velvety pâté—had an unexpected sprinkling of coarse sea salt, which added an exhilarating flavor. Erin served each guest a spoonful of this rich chocolate to spread upon a slice of Spanish pound cake with blood orange confit on the side.

Wanting to add Mexican flair, I envisioned the *marquise* with Mexican wedding cookies, those beloved pecan shortbread cookies served at marriages and festive occasions throughout Mexico and the Southwest. They're small and round and just firm enough to spread with chocolate—but don't press too hard: inside, they're as crumbly as a sand tart.

Erin's Decadent Chocolate Marquise:
- 6 ounces bittersweet chocolate (the best you can find, 60–70% cocoa)
- 4 ounces unsalted butter
- 1 tablespoon tequila *añejo*
- 4 egg yolks
- ⅔ cup powdered sugar
- Pinch of salt
- 3 tablespoons best quality Dutch processed cocoa powder
- 2 egg whites
- 1 teaspoon sugar
- ⅓ cup plus 2 teaspoons whipping cream
- Orange wedges

Melt chocolate and butter together over a double boiler. Mix in tequila. Set aside to cool to room temperature (approx. 10 minutes). Whisk in egg yolks, one at a time. Sift together powdered sugar, salt, and cocoa powder; whisk into chocolate/egg mixture. Beat egg whites and sugar until they form soft peaks; gently fold into chocolate mixture until well blended. Whip the cream to soft peaks; fold into chocolate mixture.

Spoon chocolate mixture into shot glasses (see Quick Tip). Place filled glasses on a cookie sheet, cover with plastic wrap, and chill for 3 or more hours before serving. (You can fill fewer shot glasses, freezing remaining *marquise* for up to a month, but you'll probably just eat it right out of the freezer.) *Makes about 1 quart or enough for 16 shot glasses (or freeze some for later use).*

Note: Erin pours the *marquise* into silicone muffin tins, freezes them and pops them out as needed to serve cold or at room temperature. She uses Valrhona Caraibe French chocolate, but you can experiment with imported bittersweet Mexican chocolate, too.

Try a dollop of *marquise* with Spanish Almond Cake, instead of cookies, with a spoonful of Drunken Sugarplum Chutney on the side of the cake.

Quick Tip: Here's a quick way to make a pastry bag for piping *marquise* into the shot glasses and preventing messiness. Place *marquise* ingredients in a quart-size ziplock bag. After sealing, snip off ¼ inch diagonally from a corner of the bag. Squeeze to pipe *marquise* into the shot glasses.

David Cabrera, pastry chef at Austin's popular Fonda San Miguel restaurant, shared his recipe for traditional Mexican wedding cookies. You can't eat just one! When serving these cookies topped with *marquise*, don't sprinkle them with powdered sugar. Otherwise, dust them lightly, and enjoy each bite with a snifter of *añejo*.

- 8 ounces unsalted butter
- ½ cup powdered sugar (and more for dusting cookies)
- ½ teaspoon Mexican vanilla
- Zest of 1 orange
- ¼ teaspoon ground cinnamon
- 2 cups all-purpose flour, sifted
- ¼ teaspoon salt
- 1¼ cups finely chopped pecans

In a large mixing bowl, cream butter and sugar with an electric mixer at low speed until light and fluffy. Beat in vanilla, orange zest, and cinnamon until combined. Slowly mix in flour, salt, and pecans until a firm dough forms. Shape dough into 1-inch balls. Place 1 inch apart on ungreased baking sheets. Bake in a preheated 325-degree oven for about 20 minutes, until edges start to brown. Remove and cool on wire racks. Dust lightly with sifted powdered sugar while still slightly warm. *Makes about 3 dozen cookies.*

Note: Substitute zest of 2 lemons and nutmeg for the orange and cinnamon.

Painted tin *milagro* saying, "Your heart always entwined with mine."

Pastel de Almendras SPANISH ALMOND CAKE LACED WITH TEQUILA AÑEJO

Inspired by a Spanish recipe that used brandy, this orange and almond dessert resembles a moist pound cake. It's fragrant and delicious hot out of the oven with coffee at a Sunday brunch or served at the end of a meal, topped with Mexican whipped cream and a dollop of Cliff's Tequila-Orange Marmalade. For a winter treat, serve this cake with a snifter of luscious Rompope eggnog.

- 1 cup plus 2 tablespoons whole almonds, lightly toasted (p. 185)
- 1 cup all-purpose flour
- 1½ teaspoons baking powder
- ¼ teaspoon salt
- ½ pound unsalted butter, room temperature
- 1 cup sugar, preferably vanilla-scented
- 4 eggs
- ¼ teaspoon pure almond extract
- 3 tablespoons tequila *añejo*
- 2 teaspoons orange zest
- 1 teaspoon lemon zest
- ¼ teaspoon freshly grated nutmeg
- Butter/flour for baking pan
- Garnishes: dusting of confectioner's sugar and freshly grated nutmeg, Mexican Whipped Cream

Preheat oven to 325 degrees. Finely grind almonds; reserve 2 tablespoons. Combine 1 cup ground almonds with flour, baking powder, and salt. Set aside. Cream butter and sugar with an electric mixer. Add eggs, one at a time, mixing well. Blend in almond extract, tequila, citrus zests, and nutmeg. Mix in the almond/flour mixture until incorporated.

Spread batter into a buttered and floured 9½-inch × 2-inch pan (or springform pan). Sprinkle with remaining 2 tablespoons of ground almonds. Bake on middle rack until tester comes out clean (approx. 40–45 minutes). Cool 10 minutes. Remove from pan, inverting onto a platter. Dust lightly with confectioner's sugar and nutmeg and top with Mexican whipped cream. *Serves 8–10.*

Cliff's Tequila-Orange Marmalade

I cherished the jars of orange marmalade that my dear friend and bon vivant, Cliff Alsup, used to bring me. Here's his recipe: "Discard thick ends from 12 navel oranges and 3 lemons, then slice them as thin as possible. Measure cut fruit, and for each 4 cups (packed with juice), add 1 cup water and 2 cups tequila *reposado*. Let stand overnight. In the morning, bring to boil and cook until fruit is tender, which may take as long as 2 hours. Measure cooked fruit, and for each cup of fruit, add 1 cup sugar. Cook until sugar is dissolved; boil rapidly until it gels. Pour into hot sterilized jars and seal." Delicious on toast or muffins, with vanilla ice cream (by the spoonful), or to flavor and sweeten tequila cocktails.

Cheesecake Glazed with Tequila-Scented Orange Marmalade with Fresh Flowers

Here's an easy dessert to impress guests. When you don't have time to make Cliff's Tequila-Orange Marmalade, simply place contents of an 18-ounce jar of best quality orange marmalade into a small saucepan. Add a big splash of tequila *añejo*, a smaller splash of Cointreau, grated zest of an orange, and a pinch of nutmeg. Heat briefly until ingredients are incorporated and fragrant. Cool to room temperature, and it will thicken.

Spread evenly on top of your favorite chilled homemade or purchased cheesecake (or mini cheesecakes made in muffin tins). Chill cheesecake for several hours, as glaze sets. Prior to serving, press colorful edible flowers (see Cantina Garden, p. 111), or thin slices of orange halves into the glaze and expect a lot of compliments.

Variation: Frost a cheesecake with Drunken Sugarplum Chutney and serve with crisp apple and pear slices for dessert.

Tequila for Whatever Ails You

Para amor y dolor,
tómate unos tequilas.
Si no se te quita,
se olvida.

—

For heartbreak and pain,
drink a few tequilas.
If they don't go away,
You'll forget it anyway.

A Shot a Day Keeps the Doctor Away

JUST LIKE TEQUILA, Lázaro Pérez is a part of Jalisco's colorful history. He ran a *botica* (pharmacy) of grand repute in Guadalajara and was also a historian, astronomer, meteorologist, and biochemist. In 1887, he wrote *Estudio sobre el maguey llamado mezcal en el estado de Jalisco*, a comprehensive study on the maguey. Pérez promoted imbibing tequila in moderation to prevent the immoral consequences of inebriation.

Pérez extolled tequila's virtues, citing its benefit as a general tonic, diuretic, digestif, and poultice for inflammatory aches and pains, as well as an antiseptic for wounds. He believed that tequila eases hunger, quenches thirst, stimulates the appetite, gives vigor and longevity to the aged, calms respiratory distress, and diminishes the depression of poverty. He also claimed that tequila enlivens the intelligence, prevents boredom, and procures pleasant illusions! (No wonder I like it!)

Señor Pérez suggested that the weak or the aged may prefer to dilute their tequila with water and sugar or drink it as a tea, sweetened and flavored with anise or cinnamon.

Many Mexicans believe in tequila's attributes as an aphrodisiac, an aftershave, and an antiseptic, as well as a blood purifier and a cure for venereal disease. Mexican women have told me that they rub it on the gums of their teething babes and sip tequila during labor to ease the pain and to "gain strength."

Today many Mexicans, especially those living in rural areas, drink tequila as a panacea for anything that ails them—and as a preventive measure as well. Remember Don Aurelio (p. 129) and his words of wisdom? Tequila, he said, makes it possible *"para comer y dormir con gusto"* (to eat and sleep with pleasure). Like this famous mezcalero, many of his compatriots imbibe tequila not just for inebriation, but for what they believe to be its restorative and curative purposes, treasuring both the invigorating and the soothing spirit of the agave.

My prescription? Tequila need not be slugged down in numerous shots, although some seem to think so. Instead, sip slowly in reverence of its virtues. Remember, moderation is always the best medicine!

Tequila en el jarro
Para el catarro.

—

Tequila in a jar
For the catarrh.

FOR COUGH

My friend Javier Aviles made this tasty *té de limón* (lime tea) for me when I was flu-stricken. It helped me feel better (or not feel the pain), soothed my cough, and put me to sleep. This recipe is for two servings: one for the patient, one for the nurse.

- 3 cups water
- 1 3-inch piece of cinnamon
- 2 fresh citrus leaves, optional
- Peel of ½ lime, cut into thick strips
- 4 teaspoons honey (or agave syrup)
- 1 juicy lime, cut in half
- 4 ounces tequila *reposado*
- Ground cayenne to taste

Bring water to boil in a small saucepan, along with the cinnamon, citrus leaves, and lime peel; reduce heat. Simmer on medium heat for about 10 minutes until it turns a rich golden color. Meanwhile, place in each mug 2 teaspoons of honey, juice of half a lime, 2 ounces tequila, and cayenne to taste. Pour in enough of the cinnamon/citrus tea to fill each mug, stirring well to dissolve the honey. ¡Salud! To your health! *Makes 2 servings.*

Note: When fresh citrus leaves are not available, use more lime peel and add more fresh lime juice to the mug.

> *Para un catarro, un jarro,*
> *y si no se te quita, la botellita.*
>
> ———
>
> *For a cough, a cup.*
> *The whole bottle, if that's not enough.*

A Love Potion

Some say a few shots of tequila are all the love potion one needs . . . but just in case, here's another elixir.

Damiana Love Tonic

Tequila and damiana, a pungent and aromatic herb, are two well-regarded aphrodisiacs, which I've combined in a spirited love potion. Imbibe before bedtime. At the least, it may inspire sweet dreams.

- 1½ ounces dried Damiana leaves (available in herbal and health food stores)
- Peel of 1 orange, cut in a continual spiral
- 1 pint tequila *blanco* or *reposado*
- ½–¾ cup Cantina Classic Citrus Syrup

In a glass bottle, infuse damiana and orange peel in tequila for a week, shaking daily. Strain through paper coffee filters; discard damiana leaves. Sweeten to taste, adding one tablespoon of syrup at a time (I like it slightly bitter). Store in a cool, dark place. Some sediment may settle. *Makes a pint.*

Hangover Helpers

In Mexico, salt, lime, and plenty of chiles (or another shot of tequila) seem to be the ubiquitous prescription for the ill effects of a hangover, which Mexicans call by the picturesque names *la cruda* (raw) or *sancochado* (half-baked). When I once asked an elderly Mexican man what to do to relieve a hangover, he chuckled, "Si traes una cruda, ponte otra borrachera." (If you have a hangover, get drunk again.)

Trading one pain for another seems to be the best Mexican remedy for too much alcohol. *Un clavo saca otro clavo* (one nail drives out the other), whether the replacement pain comes from *another* drinking bout, a bite into a searing serrano, or eating any morsel doused in fiery *salsa picante*. Sweating, screaming, and swearing are requisite accompaniments.

400 Rabbits Still Making Mischief

The 400 rabbits, collectively known as "Centzon Totochtin," were the offspring of Mayahuel, the goddess of the maguey. She fed them with pulque abundantly flowing from her four hundred breasts. Her favorite son, Ometochtli, known as "Two Rabbits," reigned over the hundreds of raucous *conejos*, the four hundred ways in which to drink pulque, and the four hundred consequences of intoxication. Each of these carousing rabbits (perhaps the first party animals?) represented a different form of inebriation.

Apparently, four hundred was the magical number of infinite possibilities (or the number of rabbits seen hopping through one's head when in a state of drunkenness) in Aztec mythology. In his chronicles of pre-Hispanic life, Franciscan Fray Bernardino de Sahagún (1499–1590) cited the four hundred consequences of intoxication in *The Diverse Manners of Drunks*. Although de Sahagún wrote in the sixteenth century, the manners of drunks do not seem to have changed much today. Let's blame it on those reveling rabbits!

Some recommend a cup of hot tea, especially *yerbanís* (Mexican mint marigold), *estafiate* (artemisia), or *hierba buena* (mint). Others suggest freshly squeezed orange juice spiced with chiles, or a tall glass of sparkling mineral water sprinkled liberally with salt and lots of fresh lime juice. Fresh papaya, doused with lime juice and dusted with salt and chile powder, is another purported cure, especially for easing gastric distress.

Mexicans use the humorous names *Levanta Muertos* (Raise the Dead) and *Vuelve a la Vida* (Return to Life) to describe perky consumable remedies purported to cure the hangover. Any variety of tongue-searing *salsas picosas* (or drinks or dishes peppered with them) may be called by those names, too.

Two of the most traditional hangover remedies are *menudo*, a spicy tripe and chile soup, and *Vuelve a la Vida*, which is also the name for a *picante* seafood cocktail. Ceviche (fresh fish or shellfish marinated in lime juice) and other seafood concoctions are also sometimes called *Vuelve a la Vida*.

Para mal de cruda
Aquí está la cura.

—

For a bad hangover
Here is the cure.

Many North Americans may rather suffer the ill-fated consequences of a hangover than even consider swallowing spoonfuls of a chile-flavored soup made from calf's feet and the lining of a cow's stomach, known as *panzita* (tripe). But cantinas, restaurants, and late-night street vendors throughout Mexico serve *menudo* (especially during the weekends) for those who have imbibed more than they wished. They line up for steaming bowls of the fiery, rich broth with tender chunks of honeycomb tripe.

Bowls of chopped onions, cilantro, oregano, and wedges of lime, as well as a fiery salsa made from *chile de árbol* or *pequín*, always accompany *menudo* at the table. Pozole (hominy) is an optional addition. *Menudo* has become a weekend specialty in restaurants north of the border as well, better in some places than in others. Making it at home assures quality ingredients and freshness.

- 2 calf's feet, well washed, split in half lengthwise, then crosswise, optional
- 2 onions, quartered
- 2 bay leaves
- 6 quarts water
- 5 pounds honeycomb tripe with fat shaved off, cut into ¾-inch pieces; soaked and thoroughly rinsed several times
- 8–10 dried ancho chiles
- ¼ pound dried *guajillo* chiles
- 6–8 cloves garlic, minced
- 1 teaspoon marjoram
- 2 teaspoons Mexican oregano
- 1 teaspoon thyme
- 1 teaspoon *comino*
- 5 leaves epazote, optional
- 2 cans (15 ounces) hominy, rinsed, optional
- Salt to taste
- Garnishes: small bowls filled with chopped white onion, chopped serranos or whole *chiles pequines*, chopped cilantro, dried oregano, lime wedges, and hot sauce

Place calf's feet, onions, and bay leaves in a large stockpot; add water. Bring to a boil, then simmer uncovered on medium heat for 1½ hours, occasionally skimming the foam. Strain and reserve the stock.

Return strained stock to the pot, along with the cooked calf's feet and tripe, and bring briefly to boil. Reduce heat immediately and simmer for 3 hours or longer, or until tripe is almost tender. (Do not let it boil for long or the tripe will toughen.) Then, separate the meat from the bone of the calf's foot, discarding the gristle, skin, and bone. Or, the meat may be eaten later from the bone from the soup bowl.

While tripe is cooking, remove stem and seeds from the dried chiles and soak in hot water to cover for 15 minutes. In a blender, grind chiles with the garlic, herbs, and *comino* and enough of the soaking water to form a thickened sauce; set aside.

Add chile sauce to tripe soup and bring to a boil, along with the spices and the salt. Reduce heat and simmer the last 30 minutes or until the tripe is tender. Add epazote and hominy during the last 15 minutes, with additional salt to taste. Serve piping hot with the garnishes and a basket of hot tortillas. *Serves whoever will eat it!*

Note: Tripe must be very fresh (crystal white) and well washed. Calf's feet are now readily available (often frozen) in Latin American grocery stores; pig's feet may be substituted. Frozen pozole (instead of canned) is now often found in Latin American markets.

Menudo para el crudo.

———

Menudo for a hangover.

Vuelve a la Vida
SPICY SEAFOOD COCKTAIL

~~~~~~~~~~~~~~~~~~~~~~~~~~~

In *palapas* (thatch-roofed restaurants) on the beach in Mexico, waiters serve this invigorating medley of *mariscos* (seafood) in tall soda fountain glasses with spoons. I serve it in long-stemmed, wide-mouthed margarita glasses lined with a lettuce leaf, colorfully combining fresh pink shrimp with chunks of avocado, freshly chopped onion, tomatoes, and cilantro in a spicy cocktail sauce. Layer this seafood cocktail on crispy, fried tostadas, too, for a healthy *botana* (appetizer).

Cooks in Yucatán and Campeche drizzle smoky chipotle salsa over the top. Sometimes I drizzle it with Chile Pepper–Infused tequila, a fitting *Levanta Muertos* indeed. If you accompany it with a sparkling tequila spritzer, Michelada, or Sirena's Splash, how could you help but come back to life?

- 1½ pounds fresh small shrimp, boiled/seasoned (do not overcook!), peeled, and deveined, and/ or other seafood
- 6 Roma tomatoes, chopped
- 1 small white onion, chopped
- 2 or more serranos, chopped
- 10 ounces home-style spicy seafood cocktail sauce (ketchup-based)
- Salsa Valentina, to your taste
- ½ cup fresh lime juice
- ¼ cup tequila *blanco*
- 2 tablespoons olive oil
- 1 teaspoon dried Mexican oregano, crumbled
- Salt and freshly ground pepper to taste
- ½ cup fresh cilantro, chopped
- 2 avocados, cubed or cut into wedges
- fresh lime wedges
- Garnishes: fresh cilantro, lime wedges, thin strips of canned chipotle peppers (optional), or your favorite bottled hot sauce to taste

Mix together ingredients except for avocado. Chill for several hours, tossing occasionally. Adjust seasonings and gently toss in the avocado cubes or use wedges as garnish. Sprinkle with juice from fresh lime wedges. *Serves 6–8.*

Note: Fresh oysters, clams, bay scallops, crabmeat, and/or squid may be used for part of the shrimp. Add ½ cup pimento-stuffed green olives.

A day without tequila is a day you will remember.

ROBERT DEL GRANDE, CHEF/OWNER, CAFE ANNIE, HOUSTON

Toro Bravo Bullshot

~~~~~~~~~~~~~~~~~~~~~~~~~~~

Fellow tequila enthusiast Mark Mattingly and I have sampled tequilas together for more than thirty years. What's his secret for the morning after? A good dose of homemade beef bouillon spiked with chipotle-flavored tequila, a surefire way to wake you up!

- 2 ounces Chile Pepper–Infused Tequila (preferably made with chipotles)
- 5 ounces best beef bouillon
- Dash of Worcestershire sauce
- Freshly cracked pepper
- Lime wedge

Fill a glass beaker with ice. Add peppered tequila and remaining ingredients, and stir until chilled. Strain into a highball glass with ice and a squeeze of fresh lime juice. *Serves 1.*

Note: For a change, substitute 3 ounces of clam juice and 2 ounces of tomato juice for the bouillon.

Gracias

A los mezcaleros y los tequileros,
A los cantineros y los cocineros,
A los mariachis y los artesanos
Y para mis memorias inolvidables
Les doy mil gracias.

—

To the agave field-workers and distillers
To the bartenders and the cooks
To the mariachis and the folk artists
And for my unforgettable memories
I give my heartfelt thanks.

I RAISE *UN CABALLITO* de tequila y otro de mez-cal in honor of many who have shown the way. I thank generous souls from both sides of the border, too numerous to mention, yet greatly appreciated, who offered knowledge and gracious hospitality.

Muchísimas gracias to my parents, Patricia and the late Stuart Hutson, who encouraged my travels, holding their breath each time I embarked alone on another agave adventure; to my brother "El Rey," my sister Cynthia, my beloved personal assistant Lula Garcia, Tita y Sancho, and many *amigos queridos* for support during this project . . . and also to Robert Denton and Marilyn Smith, who included me in many forays into tequila (and mezcal) country long before others dared tread there, and who also provided photographs of some Mexican locations.

Cheers! to the University of Texas Press, which gave me this opportunity to share my love for Mexico and her agave spirits. To Bill Bishel, who first said "Yes!" and also created the map of Mexico found in this book. *Un abrazo fuerte* for my sponsoring editor, E. Casey Kittrell, for patience, humor, great ideas, and quips in perfect Spanish, and another one for manuscript editor Lynne Chapman, for bringing together *all* of the many details of this book with great care, kindness, and constant attention to detail. *Gran respeto* for copy editor Sally Furgeson, who had her hands full with a manuscript with many elements, including two languages. Gracias to production editor Regina Fuentes for her diligence in the production of this book and for sharing with me her love of Mexico's customs and songs. And thank you to proofreader Melissa Tullos for her keen eye and to indexer Kay Banning.

Author with mariachis in Chapala, Jalisco.

I raise a bottle of the best tequila to book designer Lindsay Starr, who'll have readers shouting "¡Viva Tequila!" as soon as they see the cover. Her creative design made each of the three distinct sections in this volume a separate book in itself, yet she tied them all together in a cohesive and celebratory style. Perusing this book is like strolling through my home, a fiesta indeed! Thanks, also, to Ellen McKie, Design and Production Manager, for her enthusiasm. A toast of gratitude to the director of the Press, Dave Hamrick; to Nancy Bryan, Assistant Marketing Director; and to others involved in marketing and promotion: Brady Dyer, Bailey Morrison, Christopher Farmer, and publicist Colleen Devine. Gracias to everyone else on staff, including the guys in the warehouse, who always play great music as they ship books, and to Brenda Jo Hoggatt for her ever-present smile . . . and for keeping orders filled.

Muchísimas gracias to Ann Clark and Jim Peyton, fellow cookbook authors, who read the original manuscript, offering great encouragement and enthusiasm, and some of their own great ideas . . . and to Bruce White for his constant thoughtfulness and support in the promotion of this book.

Much gratitude to John Pozdro, for tireless hours and creativity spent in bringing the folk art to life (and for many other photos in this book) . . . to Woody Welch, who certainly captured my spirit in his author photo of me as I raised a shot by my back door near the mosaic "stairway to tequila heaven" . . . to photographer/designer Kevin Greenblat for using that photo in *Austin Expressions* . . . to Bill Records, for his photograph of me singing with Austin's Mariachi Estrella . . . and to Karen Dickey—an accordion and a *canción* in heaven. *Le doy gracias* to Julie Marshall, illustrator of my first tequila book, for her watercolor rendition of my home cantina, found again in this edition.

Gracias to Melody Lambert for her spirited agave icon used throughout the book, and to creative souls Karina Prado and Renee Mims for artistic inspiration. Gracias to Victor Guerra, for his poetic translation of many of the *dichos* in the book.

A toast to Karen Dante, manager of King Liquor in Austin, for her endless curiosity, for seeking answers to my questions, and for keeping my glass and my cantina always filled with new tequilas and mezcals . . . and to tequila tracker Bob Wolter, in appreciation of our long conversations about our favorite agave spirits and for generosity of time and spirit, and to his wife, food blogger Kristina (girlgonegrits), for testing recipes and for her festive drink recipes. *Muchísimas gracias* to Tom Gilliland, Miguel Ravago, and the bartenders and staff of Fonda San Miguel who cheered me on, and to Jaime Holditch—for bartending lessons.

And I lift my glass . . . *un tequilito al cielo*, to my sister Criztina Peabody, who loved Mexico as much as I do and made it her home for many years. She greatly inspired my style of cooking and my love of art and all things beautiful. I often read to her parts of this book as I was writing it. I wish she'd had the chance to hold it in her hands.

To Moondance and Mayahuel, and the Magical Maguey, my gratitude.

And to you readers, too!

LUCINDA HUTSON
October 2012

RESOURCES

www.tastetequila.com (very professional "hip to sip" site with tequila reviews, great recipes, bars, news, and videos; its innovative new mobile app, Tequila Matchmaker.com, offers a NOM database and tequila ratings, and will match you with tequilas that fit your taste while also showing you where to find them)

www.tequilainterchangeproject.org (nonprofit organization that advocates for and educates about the preservation of sustainable, traditional, and quality practices in the tequila industry)

www.tequilarack.com (sophisticated site from renowned tequila educator and blogger that includes tequila talk, news, tasting notes, videos, and a portfolio of exclusive handcrafted micro-distilled 100% agave *reposados* and Don Cuco mezcal)

www.pocotequila.com (one of the first sites that I used and that I still love to visit—true *mexicano* design and lots of good tequila information)

www.tequilawhisperer.com (quirky and informative; Michael "Lippy" Lipman, an illustrator, rock 'n' roll buff, and tequila aficionado, has a weekly archived video series reviewing brands and featuring great live interviews with dynamos in the tequila/mezcal industry)

www.tequilaaficionado.com (tequila and mezcal ratings and reviews, informative blogs, travel information)

www.tequilatracker.com (blog site that explores the people and stories behind the brands; well researched and informative)

www.fortequilalovers.com (website by tequila lovers, for tequila lovers, and featuring "Agave Activists" from around the world; packed with useful information)

www.thetequilaguy.com (tequila headlines, extended list of reviews, and information on brands and bottles)

www.tequileros.org (National Chamber for the Tequila Industry—more industry-oriented, with good tasting notes; you'll see the big producers and brands, with photos of bottles)

www.tequilaconnection.com (excellent resource site with everything you need to know about tequila)

www.examiner.com/tequila-in-national/ryan-kelley (Tequila Examiner: informative site for keeping up with tequila news, recipes, and stories)

www.muchoagave.blogspot.com (exudes a passion for all things agave; videos and reviews)

www.experiencetequila.com (great site and company for anyone wanting a small group–guided tour of tequila country; the whole concept of "Experience Tequila" is to absorb and interact with the culture, people, and history of the region)

www.cwrangel.wordpress.com/tag/tequila (very informative, well-researched Danish tequila lover's site showing tequila's popularity abroad)

www.facebook.com/agaveidiots and www.agaveidiots.com (global social network for tequila and mezcal connoisseurs and newcomers alike; tasting notes and events, reviews, agave awareness, restaurant/bar news, cocktail highlights)

www.tequilaneat.com ("no salt, no lime, no ice"—good links, blog, and general info, including a downloadable spread sheet of tasting notes)

www.agave52.com (large tequila events/tastings preserving culture, art, history, and traditions for tequila lovers in California)

www.wahakamezcal.com ("About Mezcal" illustrates mezcal production on this hip and contemporary site)

www.acamextequila.com.mx (Academia Mexicana del Tequila has this folksy site with curious facts and a good glossary; strives to protect tequila's image)

www.tequilavinomezcal.com (Academia Mexicana del Catadores, or Academy of Tasters, offers news and information related to Mexico's national drink on this *mexicano* site for aficionados)

BIBLIOGRAPHY

Baker, Charles Jr. *The Gentleman's Companion*. New York: Crown Publishers, 1946.

Barrios, Virginia B. *A Guide to Tequila, Mezcal, and Pulque*. Mexico, D.F.: Minutiae Mexicana, S.A., 1988.

Bruman, Henry J. *Alcohol in Ancient Mexico*. Salt Lake City: The University of Utah Press, 2000.

Chadwick, Ian. "In Search of the Blue Agave." www.ianchadwick.com.

Colen, Bruce David. "Tequila." *Town and Country*, June 1988.

Copper, Brad. "The Man Who Invented the Margarita." *Texas Monthly*, October 1974.

Corman, Marion, and Felipe P. Alba. *The Tequila Book*. Chicago: Contemporary Books, Inc., 1978.

Corn, Elaine. "Margarita Man." *Chile Pepper Magazine*, September/October 1992.

Curtis, Gregory. "The Truth About Tequila." *Texas Monthly*, September 1975.

Cutler, Lance. *The Tequila Lover's Guide to Mexico and Mezcal*. Vineburg, California: Wine Patrol Press, 2000.

Emmons, Bob. *The Book of Tequila*. Chicago: Open Court Publishing Company, 1997.

Farga, Amando, and José Inés Loreda. *Historia de la comida en México*. Mexico, D.F.: Litográfica México, S.A., 1980.

Gonçalves de Lima, Oswaldo. *El maguey y el pulque en los códices mexicanos*. Mexico, D.F.: Fondo de Cultura Económica, 1986.

Guerrero, Raúl. *El pulque*. Mexico, D.F.: Editorial Joaquín Mortiz, S.A., 1985.

Kretchmer, Laurence. *Mesa Grill Guide to Tequila*. New York: Black Dog & Leventhal Publishers, Inc., 1998.

Kuri-Aldana, Mario, and Vicente Mendoza Martínez. *Cancionero popular mexicano, volúmenes 1 y 2*. Mexico, D.F.: Consejo Nacional para la Cultura y las Artes, 1992.

Mason, Charles T., and Patricia B. Mason. *A Handbook of Mexican Roadside Flora*. Tucson, Arizona: University of Arizona, Press, 1987.

"Mezcal arte tradicional." *Artes de México*, Número 98 (Julio 2010).

Novo, Salvador. *Cocina mexicana, o historia gastronómica de la Ciudad de México*. Mexico, D.F.: Editorial Porrúa, S.A., 1976.

Ostrosky, Jennie, and Felipe Alcántar. *El maguey*. Mexico, D.F.: Consejo Nacional para la Cultura y las Artes, 1993.

Pacult, F. Paul. "Tequila Rising." *Connoisseur*, October 1991.

Parsons, Jeffrey R., and Mary H. Parsons. *Maguey Utilization in Highland Central Mexico*. Ann Arbor: Museum of Anthropology (Anthropological Papers), University of Michigan, 1990.

Pérez, Lázaro. "Estudio sobre el maguey llamado mezcal en el estado de Jalisco." Programa de Estudios Jaliscienses Instituto del Tequila, A.C. Guadalajara, Jalisco, 1990.

Pla, Rosa, and Jesús Tapia. *El agave azul de las mieles al tequila*. Mexico, D.F.: Instituto Francés de América Latina, 1990.

Ruy Sánchez, Alberto, and Margarita de Orellana. *tequila: A Traditional Art of Mexico*. Mexico, D.F.: Artes de México, 2004.

Serra Castaños, Román, et al. *Norma Oficial Mexicana—Tequila*. Mexico, D.F.: March 31, 1978.

Swain, Roger. "Agaves in the Southwest." *Horticulture*, November 1987.

Thompson, Helen. "Barroom Brawl." *Texas Monthly*, July 1991.

Tunnell, Curtis, and Enrique Madrid. "Making and Taking Sotol in Chihuahua and Texas." Third Symposium on Resources in the Chihuahuan Desert Region, United States, and Mexico, published by the Chihuahuan Desert Research Institute, Alpine, Texas, November 1990.

Valenzuela, Ana G., and Gary Paul Nabhan. *¡Tequila! A Natural and Cultural History*. Tucson: University of Arizona Press, 2003.

Vizcarra, Miguel Claudio Jiménez. *Origin and Development of the Agro-Industry of Mezcal Spirits Called Tequila*. Guadalajara: Benemérita Sociedad de Geografía y Estadística del Estado de Jalisco, 2008.

Weston, Edward. *The Daybooks of Edward Weston*. New York: An Aperture Book, 1973.

Zamora, Rogelio Luna. *La historia del tequila, de sus regiones y sus hombres*. Mexico, D.F.: Consejo Nacional para la Cultura y las Artes, 1991.

ABOUT THE ART

BY NOW, YOU'VE ALREADY visited the tequila cantina in my backyard, at least in these pages. Perhaps you can also imagine my brightly painted purple cottage, surrounded by a whimsical garden that would fit right in to a Mexican *barrio*. If you entered my home, you'd walk into a veritable folk art museum filled with souvenirs from my treks through pulque, mezcal, and tequila *tierra*. Many of the artists who created these pieces are *amigos* I've met along the way, making the collection even more meaningful to me.

To illustrate this book, I've taken these *tesoros* (treasures) off my shelves, bringing them to life for you in photographs. For me, each illustration evokes a memory of Mexico, a colorful reminder of the people and country that have so inspired my life.

A heartfelt and most gracious thanks to John Pozdro, who captured the spirit of each piece of folk art with his enchanting photographs. In a few cases, I've taken artistic license, slightly altering the original piece with some added whimsy, such as putting miniature carved bottles of tequila into the hands of mermaids.

During decades of visits to the land of the agave, I have photographed the documentary/location shots found in *¡Viva Tequila!* A few shots were taken by traveling companions. When I styled the other photos in the book, I used folk art, dishes, glasses, and other props from my personal collection.

Mexico has added great richness to my life. In return, my goal is to help preserve some of the disappearing expressions of her culture and traditions. In doing so, I also offer you a glimpse into the soul of the country that stole my heart many years ago.

PHOTO CREDITS

196. Photo by John Pozdro.
197. Photo by John Pozdro.
198. Photo by John Pozdro.
202. Photo by John Pozdro.
204. Photo by John Pozdro.
206. Photo by John Pozdro.
207. Photo by John Pozdro.
208. Photo by John Pozdro.
209. Photo by Lucinda Hutson.
212. Photo by John Pozdro.
214. Photo by John Pozdro.
216. Photo by John Pozdro.
219. Photo by John Pozdro.
223. Photo by John Pozdro.
226. Photos by John Pozdro.
229. Photo by John Pozdro.
231. Photo by John Pozdro.
233. Photo by John Pozdro.
235. Photo by John Pozdro.
236. Photo by John Pozdro.
238. Photo by John Pozdro.
239. Photo by John Pozdro.
241. Photo by John Pozdro.
243. Photo by John Pozdro.
245. Photo by John Pozdro.
247. Photo by John Pozdro.
250. Photo by John Pozdro.
253. Photo by John Pozdro.
254. Photo by John Pozdro.
257. Photo by Robert Denton.
258. Photo by John Pozdro.

CANTINA INDEX

Note: *Italic* page numbers refer to illustrations.

COMIDA INDEX

Note: *Italic* page numbers refer to illustrations.

GENERAL INDEX

Note: *Italic* page numbers refer to illustrations.